D1429428

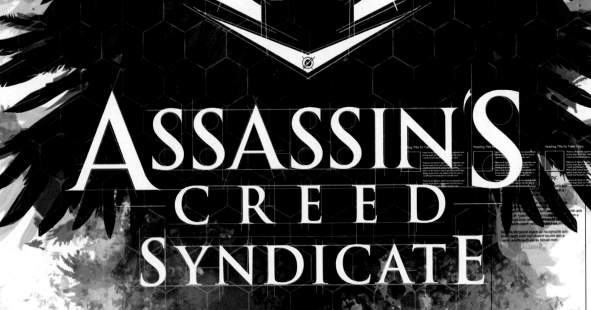

FOREWORD

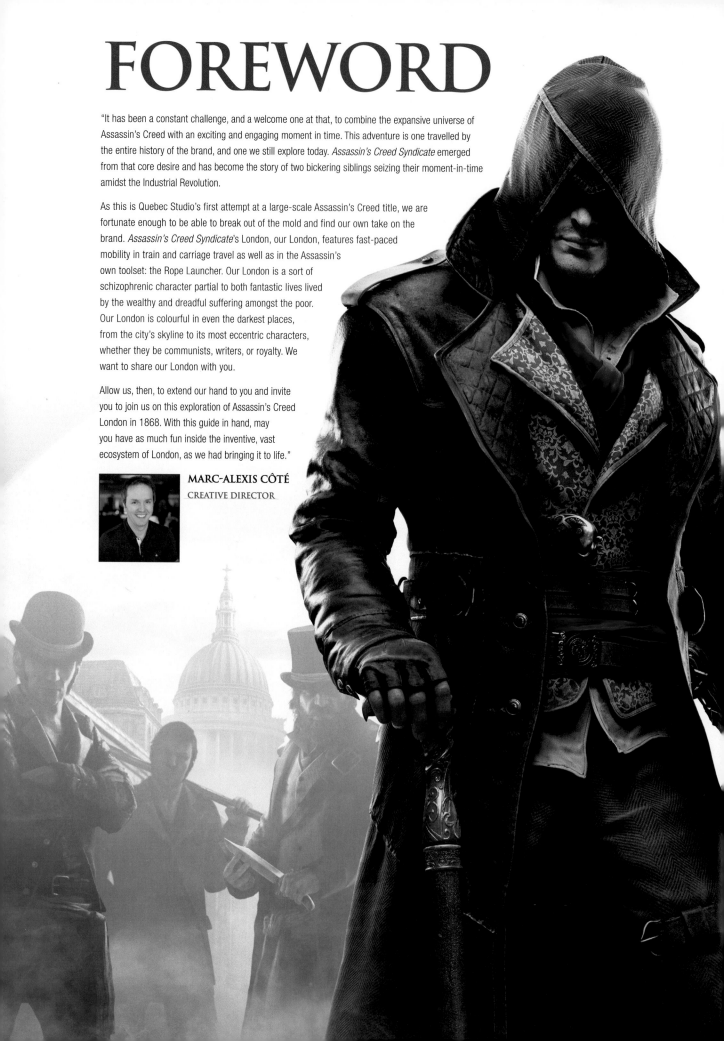

"It has been a constant challenge, and a welcome one at that, to combine the expansive universe of Assassin's Creed with an exciting and engaging moment in time. This adventure is one travelled by the entire history of the brand, and one we still explore today. *Assassin's Creed Syndicate* emerged from that core desire and has become the story of two bickering siblings seizing their moment-in-time amidst the Industrial Revolution.

As this is Quebec Studio's first attempt at a large-scale Assassin's Creed title, we are fortunate enough to be able to break out of the mold and find our own take on the brand. *Assassin's Creed Syndicate*'s London, our London, features fast-paced mobility in train and carriage travel as well as in the Assassin's own toolset: the Rope Launcher. Our London is a sort of schizophrenic character partial to both fantastic lives lived by the wealthy and dreadful suffering amongst the poor. Our London is colourful in even the darkest places, from the city's skyline to its most eccentric characters, whether they be communists, writers, or royalty. We want to share our London with you.

Allow us, then, to extend our hand to you and invite you to join us on this exploration of Assassin's Creed London in 1868. With this guide in hand, may you have as much fun inside the inventive, vast ecosystem of London, as we had bringing it to life."

MARC-ALEXIS CÔTÉ
CREATIVE DIRECTOR

TABLE OF CONTENTS

THE ESSENTIALS

INTRODUCTION

London, 1868. The Industrial Revolution is in full swing. It is a time of incredible innovation and progress. Manufacturing has been revolutionized, with more goods being created, faster and better than ever before. Medicine has been transformed—saving countless lives—and scientific experimentation flourishes. It is also a time of rampant economic growth and the ascendance of capitalism. But this progress comes at a price, paid entirely by the working class. Crime, poverty, and exploitation are the hallmarks of their existence. And this is exactly how Crawford Starrick, Grandmaster of the British Rite, has organized things. Wealth, knowledge, and power are to be accumulated by the Order to ensure the maintenance of an EMPIRE—one that now extends across the globe. Should things continue according to plan, all the world will be united beneath the Templar banner. If it costs some their happiness and freedom along the way, well, so be it. Progress requires sacrifice.

DEFAULT CONTROLS SUMMARY

PLAYSTATION 4

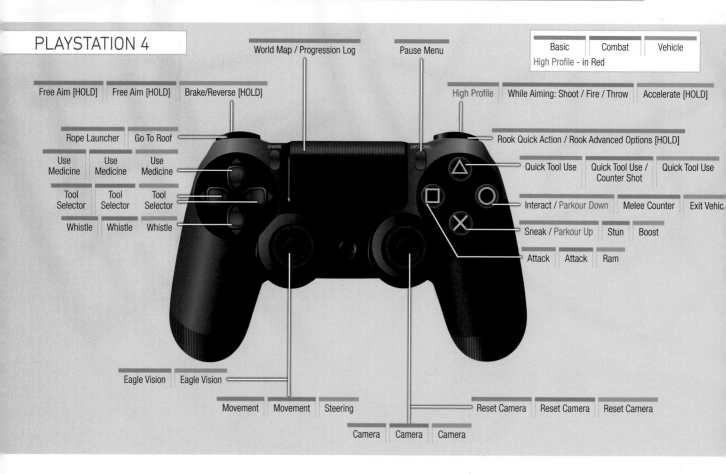

Basic	Combat	Vehicle

High Profile - in Red

World Map / Progression Log

Pause Menu

Free Aim [HOLD]   Free Aim [HOLD]   Brake/Reverse [HOLD]

High Profile   While Aiming: Shoot / Fire / Throw   Accelerate [HOLD]

Rope Launcher   Go To Roof

Rook Quick Action / Rook Advanced Options [HOLD]

Use Medicine   Use Medicine   Use Medicine

Quick Tool Use   Quick Tool Use / Counter Shot   Quick Tool Use

Tool Selector   Tool Selector   Tool Selector

Interact / Parkour Down   Melee Counter   Exit Vehic

Whistle   Whistle   Whistle

Sneak / Parkour Up   Stun   Boost

Attack   Attack   Ram

Eagle Vision   Eagle Vision

Movement   Movement   Steering

Reset Camera   Reset Camera   Reset Camera

Camera   Camera   Camera

XBOX ONE

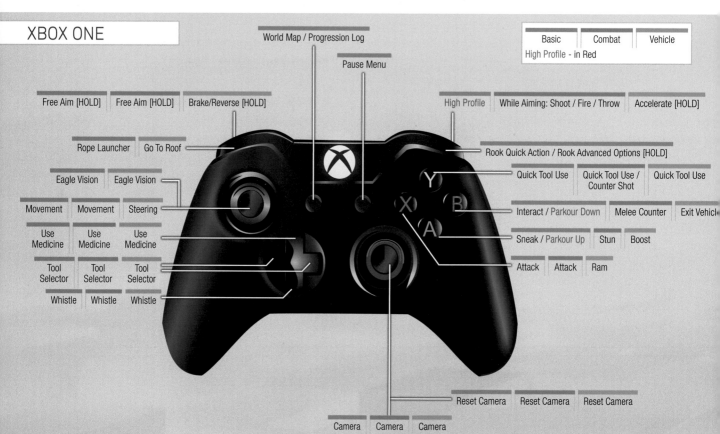

Basic	Combat	Vehicle

High Profile - in Red

World Map / Progression Log

Pause Menu

Free Aim [HOLD]   Free Aim [HOLD]   Brake/Reverse [HOLD]

High Profile   While Aiming: Shoot / Fire / Throw   Accelerate [HOLD]

Rope Launcher   Go To Roof

Rook Quick Action / Rook Advanced Options [HOLD]

Eagle Vision   Eagle Vision

Quick Tool Use   Quick Tool Use / Counter Shot   Quick Tool Use

Movement   Movement   Steering

Interact / Parkour Down   Melee Counter   Exit Vehicl

Use Medicine   Use Medicine   Use Medicine

Sneak / Parkour Up   Stun   Boost

Tool Selector   Tool Selector   Tool Selector

Attack   Attack   Ram

Whistle   Whistle   Whistle

Reset Camera   Reset Camera   Reset Camera

Camera   Camera   Camera

GAMEPLAY
MOVEMENT

WALKING

Use **Left Stick** to walk. Note that you can only blend in in with the crowd when idle or walking, not when in Stealth Mode.

FREE RUNNING

To Free Run, hold **R2** / **RT** and navigate using **Left Stick**. While Free Running is the fastest way to get around, it also draws the most attention.

STEALTH MODE

Toggle Stealth Mode with ⊗ / Ⓐ. Your footsteps become much more quiet and you crouch, making it harder for enemies to detect you. Your movement speed is drastically slowed, and free running immediately causes you to leave Stealth Mode. While in Stealth Mode you automatically snap to corner covers.

PASS OVER

Hold **R2** / **RT** when running toward low objects to pass over them without breaking momentum.

PASS UNDER

Hold **R2** / **RT** when running towards a low gap to slide through it without breaking momentum.

DESCEND

To Descend while free running, hold **R2**+◎ / **RT**+Ⓑ.

LEAP OF FAITH

Perform a Leap of Faith from a high point by holding **R2**+◎ / **RT**+Ⓑ and using **Left Stick** to aim toward a haystack below.

FAST SLIDE

Slide down steep slopes more rapidly by holding **R2**+◎ / **RT**+Ⓑ.

SWIMMING

Swim in any direction using **Left Stick**. Swim faster by holding **R2** / **RT**.

LIFTS

Quickly ascend to the rooftops by navigating into a lift object while holding **R2**+⊗ / **RT**+Ⓐ. Not only is this a great way to escape, the falling counterweight can kill enemies below.

CLIMBING

Climbing is essential for an assassin, as high ground always grants you the advantage in surveillance and combat.

CLIMB UP

Hold **R2**+⊗ / **RT**+Ⓐ when free running toward a vertical surface to start climbing up.

CLIMB DOWN

Hold **R2**+◎ / **RT**+Ⓑ while climbing to climb down quickly.

CLIMB ACROSS

Use **Left Stick** to climb in any direction across a vertical surface.

DROP

Hold ◎ / Ⓑ to drop straight down while climbing or hanging.

WINDOW ENTRY

When climbing adjacent to a window, press **L1** / **LB** to enter it.

WALL EJECT

While climbing, hold **R2** / **RT** and press ⊗ / Ⓐ without touching **Left Stick** to perform a 180° wall eject. You can use this to move upward between two facades, or reach objects directly behind you. You can also perform a small variation of the wall eject with **R2**+◎ / **RT**+Ⓑ.

VEHICLES AND DRIVING

Carriages line the streets in London. Different styles of carriages have varying levels of Speed, Handling, and Damage Resistance. Keep in mind that this is London, so driving should be done on the left side of the street.

DRIVING

Although the carriages have different stats, they all are controlled with the same basic controls:

❖ Press ◎ / Ⓑ to enter or hijack a vehicle. If there are two people in the vehicle, and the passenger is not a civilian, they may try to shove you out. To avoid this issue, jump to the top of the vehicle and assassinate both the driver and passenger.

❖ To Accelerate, press and hold **R2** / **RT**; to slow down and stop or reverse, use **L2** / **LT**.

❖ Use **Left Stick** to control the direction of the carriage.

❖ Press ⊗ / Ⓐ to give your carriage a temporary speed boost. This action is infinitely repeatable, but the effect does not stack.

❖ Ram other carriages by pressing ◎ / ⊗ and pushing **Left Stick** in the direction you would like to ram. If you are in a smaller vehicle you may want to try to outmaneuver the enemy carriages instead of ramming them as chances are your vehicle will get destroyed very quickly.

❖ To climb onto the roof, press **L1** / **LB**. The Carriage continues to be led down the road by the horse until you switch back into the driver's seat by pressing ◎ / Ⓑ, or jump off to the ground or onto another carriage.

VEHICLES

Each Carriage has different stats. Larger carriages are faster and have more durability, but lack handling. Smaller carriages are able to maneuver through tight gaps and around corners. However, they are not as durable or fast as the bigger carriages.

SIZE	PICTURE	NAME	ACCELERATION	HANDLING	RESISTANCE
Small		Hansom	5	5	1
Medium		Landau	4	4	2
Medium		Growler	4	5	3
Large		Cargo	3	3	3
Large		Fire Truck	4	1	5
Large		Omnibus	2	2	4
Large		Police	4	2	4

GAME STRUCTURE AND PROGRESSION

THE ESSENTIALS

WALKTHROUGH

SIDE QUESTS

COLLECTIBLES

REFERENCE & ANALYSIS

EXTRAS

CONTROLS

GAMEPLAY

PROGRESSION

ON SCREEN DISPLAY

STEALTH

KEY ABILITIES

COMBAT

ASSOCIATES

Progressing in *Assassin's Creed Syndicate* isn't just limited to the story. There are a wide array of different activities that advance your levels as well as change the world around you.

VIEWPOINTS AND MAPS

Press **Touchpad / Back Button** to access the Map.

The Map is an excellent tool to plan activities and explore your surroundings. To unfog the map, reach a Viewpoint and synchronize. While in the map, the different icons show you the available activities in London. Use **Left Stick** to select an icon and view detailed information and the available interactions.

Cycle through the icon filters with **L1 / LT** and **R1 / RT** and cycle through sub-filters using **DPAD LEFT** and **DPAD RIGHT**.

STORY MEMORIES

Story Memories take you through the lives of twin Assassins Jacob and Evie Frye as they build a gang of Rooks to take down the Blighters, overthrow the Templars, and save the people of London.

Story memories appear as a Gold Icon on your map.

CONQUEST ACTIVITIES

In each borough, there are four Conquest Activities that must be completed in order to unlock the final Gang War activity to conquer that borough. Some Conquest Activities are only unlocked after speaking to Associates, so remember to seek them out via their Icons on the map.

The first four Conquest Activities in the Borough can be completed in any order.

	CHILD LIBERATION Children are being worked under squalid conditions in factories all across London. Infiltrate the factories to free them and bring the factory owners to justice.
	TEMPLAR HUNT Track down Templars of note and assassinate them in signature style to send a message.
	BOUNTY HUNT Take a Templar captive then shove them into a carriage and deliver them (alive if possible) to Abberline at the drop off point.
	GANG STRONGHOLD Infiltrate a Blighter Gang Stronghold and clean it out so that the Rooks can move in.
	GANG WAR Once all Conquest Activities are complete, confront the remaining Blighters in an all-out gang war. Kill their leader to claim the Borough for the Rooks.

INCOME ACTIVITIES

Income Activities are a way to gain money and resources to buy new Gang Upgrades and Craft Gear Upgrades. The type of Income Activities vary from Borough to Borough. Some Income Activities are only Unlocked after speaking to Associates.

	FIGHT CLUB Fight Club gives you hand to hand combat in a closed arena. Fight your way through the rounds of ever increasing difficulty to claim the highest rewards.
	STREET RACING Battle it out on the streets of London, racing carriages against rivals for money.
	CARGO HIJACK Raid the Blighter vehicle convoys for money and resources.
	CARGO ESCORT Escort a vehicle convoy to a safe location, fighting off Blighters along the way.
	TRAIN ROBBERY Board the enemy train and then leap from carriage to carriage, stealing valuable cargo and fighting Blighters.
	BOAT RAIDS Board the Blighter boats, steal the manifest from the boat master, and mark valuable cargo for the Rooks.
	SMUGGLER'S BOAT Sabotage boats full of Blighter cargo to disrupt their operations.

 ## MICHAEL REUGE'S VAULT

Music boxes are hidden throughout London. Be observant and follow the clues in the Secrets of London section of the Progression Log that lead to each box. They can be used in a secret vault located underneath a dig site in the City of London borough.

Collecting all of the music boxes grants access to the Precursor armor.

 ## CROWD EVENTS

These short events can happen anywhere, at any time, around the city. You will be asked to chase and tackle thieves, chase and kill criminals, or protect and help civilians. Completing these tasks grants you cash rewards.

COLLECTIBLES

Collectibles are different items found throughout the city, which grant the player small amounts of XP and, in some cases, schematics as well. For a full walkthrough of the locations and amounts of all the Collectibles consult the Collectible section.

HELIX CREDITS

Players can purchase various items, which grant various bonuses, with Helix Credits. This in-game currency can be earned through finding Collectibles, such as Beer Bottles, Historical Poster Ads, Letters from the Front, and Helix Glitches. Helix Credits can also be earned by finding collectibles which will appear randomly in the world at various times. You can even share these locations with your friends! If you just want your Helix Credits right now, you can also purchase them with real-world currency.

EARNING HELIX CREDITS

COLLECTIBLE	# COLLECTED	CREDITS
Helix Glitches	50	50
	100	50
	All (180)	100
Letters from the Front	All (100)	100
Beer Bottles	All (20)	100
Historical Poster Ads	All (50)	125

HELIX CREDIT REWARDS

ITEM NAME	EFFECT
Medium Pounds Pack	Add £10,000 to the player's wallet
Large Pounds Pack	Add £100,000 to the player's wallet
Common Crafting Resources Pack	Give 1500 Leather, 1500 Metal, and 1500 Glass to the player
Rare Crafting Resources Pack	Give 750 Jewels, 750 Silk, and 750 Chemicals to the player
Crafting Resources Complete Pack	Give 2000 Leather, 2000 Metal, 2000 Glass, 1250 Jewels, 1250 Silk, and 1250 Chemicals to the player
Unique Crafting Resources Pack	Give every unique crafting resource
Short XP Boost	Increase XP received by 75% for 2 hours
Long XP Boost	Increase XP received by 75% for 12 hours
Tools Crafting Plans	Unlock every crafting plan required to upgrade the player Tools
Gear Crafting Plans	Unlock every crafting plan required to create gear for the player
Treasure Hunt Map	Display every treasure hunt location on the map
Helix Glitch Map	Display every Helix Glitch on the map

ON SCREEN DISPLAY

The On screen display or HUD (Heads Up Display) provides the player with all the information they need to survive on the harsh streets of London.

1 Mini-Map: The Mini-Map is found at the bottom left of the screen. It displays a top view of the surrounding environment, as well as the compass direction at which the player is looking with the small triangle being north. Different icons and feedback are displayed as you discover them through exploration and the use of Eagle Vision. To unfog the Mini-Map, reach a Viewpoint and synchronize. The Mini-Map changes colors during combat situations with yellow showing enemies who are alerted, and red representing open conflict.

2 Health Bar: At the bottom left corner of the Mini-Map is the Health Bar. It can be upgraded in the Skills menu.

3 Experience Bar: This meter shows the current amount of experience gained towards the next Skill Point. Once the meter is full, it grants a Skill Point and resets.

4 Level: Underneath the Mini-Map is a number showing your current Level. This makes for a good quick reference before attempting or entering high level activities.

5 Equipment Indicator: This shows the current equipped tool and its remaining ammunition. Pressing **DPAD LEFT / DPAD RIGHT** opens the equipment selector. It is located above the Puppeteer.

6 Puppeteer: At the bottom right, the Puppeteer shows the available interaction for each button. The instructions update to match the Assassin's current available actions.

MARKED ENEMIES

To Mark an enemy, Activate Eagle Vision and move the camera so that the enemy is in the center of the screen for a short time. Once you mark an enemy, their level and faction is displayed above their head, even when not in Eagle Vision.

GPS

When driving a vehicle, the GPS appears as a line on both the Mini-Map and on the road, showing the fastest route to your destination. It is only visible if you have set a marker on the map, or if your current objective requires you to travel to a destination.

STEALTH

The key to being a good assassin is maintaining stealth. Staying stealthy isn't as easy as it sounds, as there are a ton of factors that play into your ability to remain unseen. Stealth Mode can be toggled on or off by pressing ⊗ / Ⓐ.

STEALTH RING

The Stealth Ring appears if you are in stealth mode and anonymous. It shows the direction of nearby enemies and if they are above or below you.

THREAT RING

The Threat Ring becomes visible when enemies detect you. Each enemy is represented by an arrow on the Threat Ring and the color of the arrow shows the alertness level of the enemy, from white, to yellow, to red.

DETECTION

If you are in the line of sight of an alerted foe, they spot you. Enemies, such as Templars and Blighters, always notice you, even if they weren't in an alert state. A detection icon appears above an enemy's head to let you know that they can see you. The longer you are in sight, the more it begins to fill, moving from gray, to yellow, to red, signaling their level of aggression. While the grey gauge fills, they pose no threat. When it fills with yellow, enemies are more suspicious and physically investigate the target. Once the gauge is filled with red, the enemy comes after you, looking for a fight. Protectors, such as police and royal guards, only acquire you as a target if you perform an illegal action.

In Restricted Areas (displayed on the Mini-Map as red), enemies spot you much more quickly. The closer the enemy is, the faster the detection meter builds. Avoid contact with the enemy by breaking the line of sight before the detection meter fills all the way with red. In Restricted Areas, the gauge starts already filled with yellow, so you don't have a lot of leeway before the enemies move to attack. Use stealth mode to evade enemy detection. When their gauge is fully red, they attack.

LAST KNOWN POSITION

Once the Detection icon fills completely with yellow, enemies investigate your last known position. If you move, and interrupt their line of sight, you leave behind a last known position ghost, and enemies move to investigate it. However, if you are already in conflict with an enemy, breaking line of sight may not solve your problem. The enemies search more aggressively, and aren't always fooled by your last known position.

ENEMY AWARENESS

When you near an enemy, they cycle through a few levels of awareness, shifting from unaware, to suspicious, and then to combat.

SUSPICIOUS STATE

As described under Detection, enemies become aware of you when you are in their line of sight. The longer you remain, the more aggressive they become. Enemies are not the only ones who can become suspicious of you. Protectors, such as police and royal guards, become suspicious when they see you perform any violent actions, such as shoving through civilians or wielding a weapon.

CONFLICT

If enemies are in conflict with you, the Mini-Map turns red until the conflict is resolved. Enemies chasing you have red icons over their heads.

PROTECTOR INVESTIGATIONS

When Protectors (for example, the London Police), represented by blue icons on your Mini-Map, perceive something suspicious without knowing the source, they investigate. While this is true of all enemies, Protectors are only interested in you if you seem suspicious. When Protectors investigate a dead body, they blame suspicious people close to their investigation area. Use this knowledge to create a diversion or throw a dead body near some enemies, disappear, and let the Protectors do the rest.

THE ESSENTIALS
WALKTHROUGH
SIDE QUESTS
COLLECTIBLES
REFERENCE & MAPS
INDEX
CONTROLS
GAMEPLAY
MOVE & CON
ON SCREEN DISPLAY
STEALTH
KEY ABILITIES
COMBAT
ASSOCIATES

VANISHING

Being able to vanish is one of the most important skills in the game. Vanishing helps you avoid higher level enemies, as well as unnecessary fights in the streets.

BREAKING THE LINE OF SIGHT

To escape from conflict and vanish, you must break line of sight with all of your opponents. To do this, escape using alleys, enter a window, use the Rope Launcher to quickly reach a rooftop, or even use a smoke bomb. Once the Line of Sight is broken, the Last Known Position silhouette appears. That means it's time to hide.

HIDING FROM ENEMIES

Once the Line of Sight is broken, enemies begin searching for you. Make sure you remain hidden until the search is over. You can keep moving to stay out of their line of sight, take cover behind a wall or behind a hiding door, etc., blend into the crowd, or even ascend to the rooftops. When the search is over, the Mini-Map returns to its usual color, and you have vanished successfully.

AFTER CONFLICT

When you've successfully vanished, enemies return to their previous routine. However, they remember you and are suspicious of you in the future, which allows them to detect you more quickly.

KEY ABILITIES

EAGLE VISION

Eagle Vision is an Assassin's sixth sense. It allows you to spot enemies, allies, and hidden objects. Eagle Vision can be improved in the skill menu by purchasing the Eagle Vision II and III skills.

Press **L3 / Left Stick in** to toggle Eagle Vision on or off. It remains on until you deactivate it or perform certain actions such as pressing **R2 / RT**.

While using Eagle Vision, different elements are highlighted in the world and on your Mini-Map:

❖ Memory Objectives are highlighted in Gold.
❖ Hiding places and useful objects (Explosives, Alarm Bells, etc.) are highlighted in white.
❖ Enemies are highlighted and appear on the Mini-Map as red.
❖ Police are highlighted and appear on the Mini-Map as blue.
❖ Allies are highlighted and appear on the Mini-Map as green.

ASSASSINATIONS

Assassinations kill enemies in a single strike. Different types of assassinations offer advantages and disadvantages. For example, while an Air Assassination may be quick, it is easily noticed by the enemies. For example, it takes the assassin a moment to get up, after performing an Air Assassination. This could potentially allow other enemies to get close.

A target can only be assassinated when they are highlighted in red and the assassination button is shown in the Puppeteer.

LOW PROFILE ASSASSINATION

While anonymous, press ⊙ / ✕ to assassinate an enemy from up close. Low profile assassinations are silent and create no commotion as long as you remain unseen while assassinating your target. The dead body, however, does attract some attention.

HIGH PROFILE ASSASSINATION

You can assassinate while in High Profile mode (while running holding **R2 / RT**), but doing so creates noise and causes a commotion around your target.

12

AIR ASSASSINATION

When positioned above a target, press ⚪ / ✕ to assassinate them from above. This causes you to leap off of your perch, landing on top of the target. This creates a lot of commotion, as well as penalizing you with a slow recovery from the attack.

DOUBLE ASSASSINATIONS

Double Assassinations are unlocked in the Skill Menu. When two enemies are close to one another and both are highlighted red, you can perform a Double Assassination. Double Assassinations are available for Low Profile, High Profile, and Air Assassinations.

LEDGE AND COVER ASSASSINATIONS

When hanging from a ledge, a window, or while hidden, press ⚪ / ✕ to assassinate the target. This pulls them out of the window or over the ledge, leaving them on the ground below.

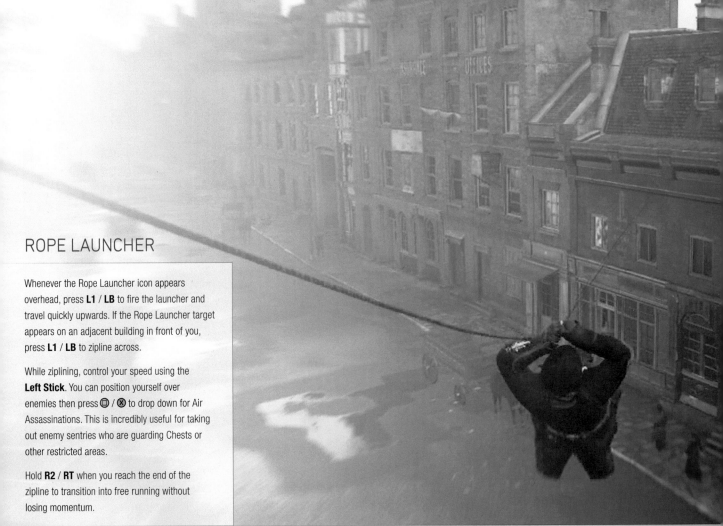

ROPE LAUNCHER

Whenever the Rope Launcher icon appears overhead, press **L1** / **LB** to fire the launcher and travel quickly upwards. If the Rope Launcher target appears on an adjacent building in front of you, press **L1** / **LB** to zipline across.

While ziplining, control your speed using the **Left Stick**. You can position yourself over enemies then press ⚪ / ✕ to drop down for Air Assassinations. This is incredibly useful for taking out enemy sentries who are guarding Chests or other restricted areas.

Hold **R2** / **RT** when you reach the end of the zipline to transition into free running without losing momentum.

COMBAT

For most Assassins open combat is the last resort. However, sometimes combat is the best or only course of action!

ATTACKING

Press ⬜ / ✕ to attack, and then continually press ⬜ / ✕ to perform combos.

COUNTER ATTACKS

When you see an enemy's health bar light up, press ◯ / Ⓑ to counter incoming melee attacks.

COUNTER SHOT

Press △ / Ⓨ to shoot enemies before they shoot you! Counter Shots can be performed when the △ / Ⓨ appears above the player. If you have no ammunition, a dodge is performed instead.

BREAK DEFENSE

Press ✕ / Ⓐ to break the defense of an enemy in a blocking or counter stance, making them vulnerable to melee attacks.

STUN

Press ✕ / Ⓐ to stun an enemy and daze them for several seconds.

QUICK SHOT

Press Ⓐ / Ⓨ with a throwing knife or gun equipped to perform a quick shot. Quick Shots can be used during combat or as a way to initiate combat. If you are planning to open combat with a quick shot, it is a much better option to aim your weapon for a critical hit instead.

COMBOING

Practicing combos makes you much better at fighting multiple enemies. The key to maintaining your combo meter is managing enemy attacks and using the right type of counter.

TOOL COMBO

During combat, press Ⓐ / Ⓨ to use a tool (such as throwing knives or a pistol) in combat without breaking your combo. This is useful for quickly lowering an enemy's health, or attacking multiple enemies at once.

THE ESSENTIALS

WALKTHROUGH

SIDE QUESTS

COLLECTIBLES

REFERENCE & ANALYSIS

INDEX

THE DRIVER

CONTROLS

PROGRESSION

ON-SCREEN DISPLAY

STEALTH

KEY ABILITIES

COMBAT

ASSOCIATES

COMBO BREAKER

Failing to counter an enemy's first attack may open you up to being hit by a combo. Press Ⓞ / Ⓑ at the right time to deflect each attack in the combo. The enemy's health bar flashes at each opportunity.

UNSTOPPABLE COMBOS

Some unique enemies can perform unstoppable combos. Press Ⓞ / Ⓑ at the right time to deflect each attack in the combo. If you succeed in deflecting every attack, you strike them back.

TARGET SWITCHING BONUS

Attacking a different target in a combo results in a 25% increase in damage for the first attack on that target. Because of this, switching between targets is often a good strategy to not only prevent them from attacking, but also get them all to the near death state where you can perform a multi-kill.

MULTI-KILL

Once an enemy is near death, marked by a flashing health bar and struggling to stand, press Ⓞ / ✕ to finish them. If there are multiple enemies near death in close proximity, you automatically perform a multi-kill, granting you bonus XP.

ASSOCIATES

Associates are your friends in London. Completing different Conquest and Income Activities grants influence to the related Associate, leveling them to unlock different crafting plans for items and tool upgrades as well as some Rare Materials.

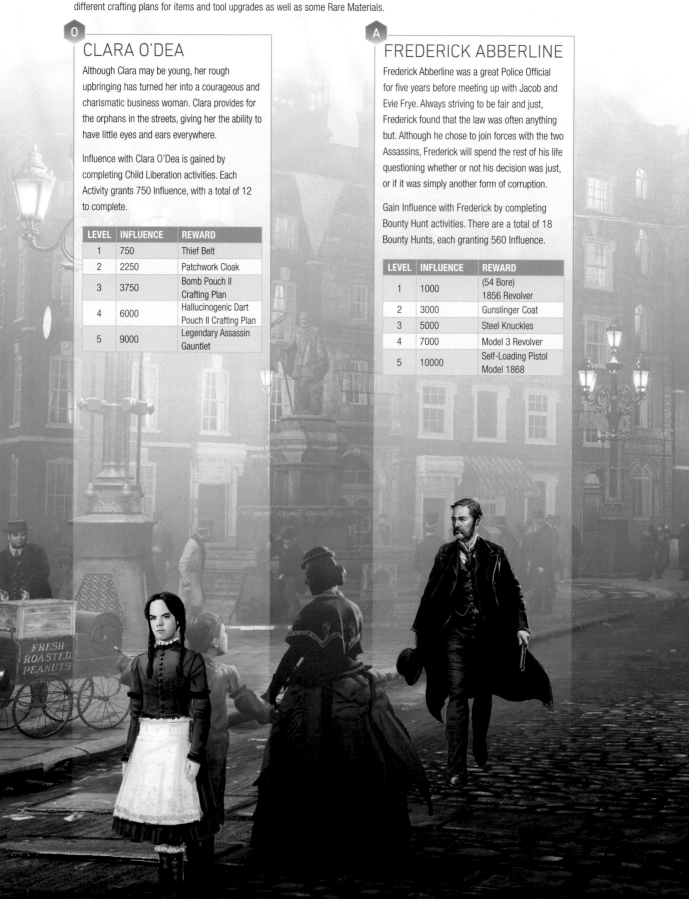

CLARA O'DEA

Although Clara may be young, her rough upbringing has turned her into a courageous and charismatic business woman. Clara provides for the orphans in the streets, giving her the ability to have little eyes and ears everywhere.

Influence with Clara O'Dea is gained by completing Child Liberation activities. Each Activity grants 750 Influence, with a total of 12 to complete.

LEVEL	INFLUENCE	REWARD
1	750	Thief Belt
2	2250	Patchwork Cloak
3	3750	Bomb Pouch II Crafting Plan
4	6000	Hallucinogenic Dart Pouch II Crafting Plan
5	9000	Legendary Assassin Gauntlet

FREDERICK ABBERLINE

Frederick Abberline was a great Police Official for five years before meeting up with Jacob and Evie Frye. Always striving to be fair and just, Frederick found that the law was often anything but. Although he chose to join forces with the two Assassins, Frederick will spend the rest of his life questioning whether or not his decision was just, or if it was simply another form of corruption.

Gain Influence with Frederick by completing Bounty Hunt activities. There are a total of 18 Bounty Hunts, each granting 560 Influence.

LEVEL	INFLUENCE	REWARD
1	1000	(54 Bore) 1856 Revolver
2	3000	Gunslinger Coat
3	5000	Steel Knuckles
4	7000	Model 3 Revolver
5	10000	Self-Loading Pistol Model 1868

THE ESSENTIALS

WALKTHROUGH

SIDE QUESTS

COLLECTIBLES

REFERENCE & ANALYSIS

INDEX

PROGRESSION

ON SCREEN DISPLAY

STEALTH

KEY ABILITIES

COMBAT

ASSOCIATES

NED WYNERT

Ned Wynert may not be who many think he is. Born Henrietta Marty Wynn, he was raised in American "polite society" and was expected to play the part under strict social constraints. Out of these constraints, Ned Wynert was born. Sneaking out of the house and assuming his identity as Ned Wynert, he found his home among petty thieves and darker influences, making a stronghold for himself in Southwark. The only thing stopping Ned from taking over the rest of London is the Blighters.

Influence with Ned Wynert is achieved by 20 Carriage and Train Raids. The Carriage Raids grant 500 Influence and the Train Raids grant 250.

LEVEL	INFLUENCE	REWARD
1	1000	Fire Opal
2	3000	Golden Obsidian
3	6000	Black Diamond
4	10000	Serrated Death Kukri
5	15000	The Mars Firearm

ROBERT TOPPING

Accidently wandering down an alley and getting lost, Robert Topping sought refuge in a small crate for the night. Upon waking up, he found himself with his new family in the circus where he learned a vast amount of skills, or so the story goes. Eventually Robert returned to London under the employment of his uncle and now he is the bookie for underground prize-fighting and street racing rings.

Influence with Robert Topping is gained from Street Racing and Fight Club Income Activities. There are 12 Races to complete, adding 250 influence each, and seven Fight Clubs, granting 1000 influence each.

LEVEL	INFLUENCE	REWARD
1	1000	Exotic Cane-Sword
2	3000	Jade Dragon Cane-Sword
3	5000	Light and Dark Cane-Sword
4	7000	Flame Dragon Cane-Sword
5	10000	World's Greatest Cane-Sword

HENRY GREEN

Although we know him as Henry Green, his actual name is Jayadeep Mir. Henry is the name he chose to mask his identity while on his mission in London. Unlike most Assassins, Henry strays away from violence, focusing on books and learning about everything, and everyone, around him.

Influence with Henry Green is achieved by completing Gang Strongholds and Templar Hunts. Each of the 12 Gang Strongholds grants 750 Influence, while the 18 Templar Hunts grant 350 Influence each.

LEVEL	INFLUENCE	REWARD
1	1000	Ruby Kukri
2	3000	Master Ruby Kukri
3	6000	Throwing Knives Pouch II Crafting Plan
4	10000	Master Assassin's Kukri
5	15000	Legendary Assassin Kukri

WALKTHROUGH

A SPANNER IN THE WORKS

MISSION OVERVIEW

Memory Type: Templar Conspiracy

Suggested Level: 1

ASSASSIN
Jacob Frye

REWARDS
£: 1000

XP: 2000

Belts: Initiate Belt

CHALLENGES
There are no Challenges in this first Memory.

This Sequence serves as a refresher course for returning *Assassin's Creed* fans and assists new players on these fundamental moves:

❖ Free Run

❖ Air Assassinate

❖ Attack, Stun, Counter, and Knock Out

❖ Climb

❖ Free Run Up and Free Run Down

❖ Loot, Carry, and Throw

❖ Eagle Vision

❖ Stealth

❖ Throw Knives

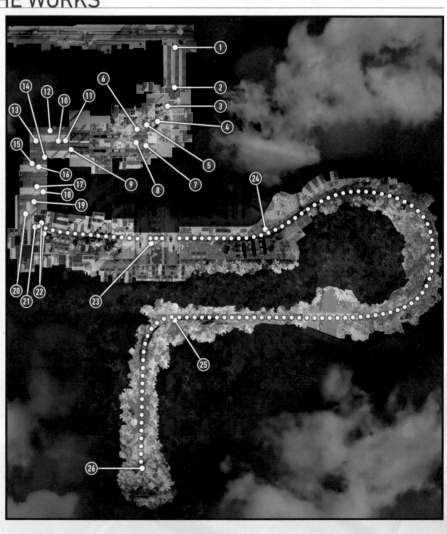

OBJECTIVE: LOCATE AND ASSASSINATE RUPERT FERRIS

THE ESSENTIALS
WALKTHROUGH
SIDE QUESTS
COLLECTIBLES
REFERENCE & APPENDIX
INDEX

SEQUENCE ONE
SEQUENCE TWO
SEQUENCE THREE
SEQUENCE FOUR
SEQUENCE FIVE
SEQUENCE SIX
SEQUENCE SEVEN
SEQUENCE EIGHT
SEQUENCE NINE

CURRENT OBJECTIVE: REACH FERRIS

LOCATION: FERRIS IRONWORKS, CROYDON—1868

> **MAP VIEW AVAILABILITY**
>
> The overhead map menu is an extremely useful tool when coordinating an assassination…unfortunately, it's also a feature that is not available until you reach London.

Playing as Assassin Jacob Frye, you begin this memory standing in the smoldering Ferris Ironworks building while standing on the edge of a second-story walkway **(1)**. The environmental challenges in this room are there to help familiarize you with Free Running (Hold **R2 / RT**). It allows you to climb and leap across what are seemingly humanly impossible jumps. Basically, it's the button that makes you a parkour superstar. Run through the middle of the ironworks building, through the hopeless child laborers—or try leaping furnaces and running on railings—to reach the exit marked with a small, green hexagon.

CURRENT OBJECTIVE: SABOTAGE THE MACHINES

FREE RUN TRAINING

You reach the other end of the building only to discover the door is locked. To get out of a building that has been built to keep energetic children from escaping, one must think on their feet. An "accidental" environmental hazard comes to mind. Turn back the way you came and run up along the ramp on the right. Leap to the metal beam and then leap to the hanging metal panel. Jump from the metal grate to the pipe, and then to the next catwalk. Approach the steam pipe wheel and press ◎ / ⑧ to sabotage the machine.

Stopping the furnaces from pumping out their steam creates quite a workplace hazard. There are two more wheels to turn to completely throw a wrench in Ferris's operation.

Turn to the left and run across the metal panel. Jump to the hanging girder. Make sure that you are not holding the Free Run Up button while crossing the girder or you'll latch onto and climb up the suspension chain. This tries to stop you from developing a habit of holding the Free Run Up button all the time, especially when it's not needed.

Leap to the ledge on the second level and turn left to run up another ramp; leapfrog off a pipe to grasp onto a railing. Pull up and head left to turn the second steam wheel. This puts a halt to another machine.

Behind the second wheel is a long wooden plank bridging a large gap between walkways. Run along this board and turn right to reach the last steam wheel. Turn the wheel to complete the job. One of Ferris's Thugs enters through the previously locked door to inspect the emergency.

CURRENT OBJECTIVE: ASSASSINATE THE THUG

AIR ASSASSINATE

Out of a short cinematic you find yourself standing at the edge of a ledge looking straight down on the Thug who just entered the ironworks. The enemy is highlighted with a brightly glowing red outline and this only happens when the enemy is directly below you and within attacking distance. Use Eagle Vision **(L3)** to quickly identify enemies and the immediate threat. This particular Thug is a person of higher interest (like a leader) and is glowing yellow. A lesser threat (such as a common enemy) glows red.

Now turn off Eagle Vision **(L3)**. Notice the target glows even brighter in normal view, which is considerably darker than the mystical world of Eagle Vision. This target lock is very important. So make sure you see a target lock and not just a red glowing enemy. If you attempt an air assault without it, you'll miss your attack, land in his or her view, and more often than not, blow your cover. This comes at a high price this early in the game—you may possibly get the snot beat out you for a mistake like that.

Press ⬤ / ✖ to execute the Air Assassination. It's an instant kill (retractable wrist-knife to the throat) that warrants no attention unless you are within eyeshot of another enemy. After the kill, you walk into the courtyard **(2)** in a very short cinematic. Here you face a few more challengers and more basic training.

CURRENT OBJECTIVE: KILL THE THUGS

ATTACK

The first Thug pulls a knife and draws back. This is an opening. Attack the vulnerable enemy with ⬤ / ✖. Keep pressing the attack button repeatedly to achieve combos. Continue an attack until the enemy blocks or until they are on the ground, dead.

COUNTER

The second Thug is designed to teach you about the Counter attack. The Counter ⬤ / Ⓑ starts with a dodge and if you continue to press the Counter button you come back at the enemy with a Counter attack. Soon after, if the enemy is not dead, follow up with more Attacks or use Stun moves if the enemy has just blocked your last hit.

Expect plenty of battle variety. Different enemy types have varying attack patterns and degrees of aggressiveness. You will have mastered combat only when you have become familiar with each enemy's attack pattern and have learned how to effectively react to each move. Defeating the enemy in close combat gets easier as you level up. Spending Skill Points to purchase Skills allows you to become stronger and gain amazing abilities.

BREAK DEFENSE

The last enemy in the yard is designed to teach you how to break a defense. No matter how hard or how many times you hit an enemy that is defending (arms up over their face) you cannot land a hit. You must start your attack with a defense breaking move; press ✖ / Ⓐ to break the enemy's defense. As soon as you break through the block, follow up with attacks. Repeat as necessary. After defeating the three Thugs, open the very large doors **(3)** to the south.

THE ESSENTIAL

WALKTHROUGH

SEQUENCE ONE

SEQUENCE TWO
SEQUENCE THREE
SEQUENCE FOUR
SEQUENCE FIVE
SEQUENCE SIX
SEQUENCE SEVEN
SEQUENCE EIGHT
SEQUENCE NINE

LOCATION: RAIL YARD

FREE RUN UP

The doors open to a smoggy-afternoon-in-London landscape. There's a man giving a speech from a ledge in front of you and a large crane (4) in front of him. Reaching the top of that crane is your current goal. This is Free Run Up training. Press and hold the ✗ / Ⓐ button while holding **R2** / **RT** to Free Run Up climbable surfaces such as the scaffolding in this area. Simply press these buttons while pushing forward on the Left Control Stick for directional movement.

Watch as you climb effortlessly to the top of the scaffold. If you reach a stopping point when you're scaling walls, a roadblock that prevents direct upward movement, then look for areas to the left or right that you can latch onto to proceed upwards. Move right or left to continue around. Large blank areas on a surface or barriers stop your upward progression. There's just nothing to grab onto.

FREE RUN DOWN

Once you have reached the end of the crane (marked with a green hexagon in a halo beam) look for the scaffold platform (5) with an extended wooden plank below you. Press forward, hold **R2** / **RT** + ◎ / Ⓑ for Free Run Down to leap from the end of the crane and catch and swing from the wooden plank below. You land very close to the Thug, so rush him and attack him before he realizes you are a danger. If your stealth ring remains white while he is looking at you, then you can still pull off a one-hit execution. You caught him off-guard.

LOOT, CARRY, AND THROW

When the "Loot [HOLD]" message appears while standing over the body of a defeated or unconscious enemy, press and _hold_ the ◎ / Ⓑ button. If the enemy has something on his or her body that can be removed, then this loot message appears and you can steal items and money. Do this with every kill if possible. There is an obtainable Skill that allows you to loot automatically during a stealthy kill. If you need to hide a body from other enemies, you can carry a body and throw it. Simply stand over the victim and tap the ◎ / Ⓑ button. Press ▢ / ✗ to toss the body down.

SNEAK

You can remain anonymous while standing upright only if you move slowly and use crowds and objects for partial cover. However, sneaking allows you to get closer to the enemy by crouching over and stealthily reaching cover closer to the enemy. Press the ✗ / Ⓐ button to crouch down and enter Sneak mode. You can increase your stealth stat (making you quieter) by purchasing particular Skills. See our Essentials section for more information on stealth, detection icons, enemy behavior, last know position, blending, and using cover.

EAGLE VISION

Stand still or walk slowly and press **L3** to engage Eagle Vision. Eagle Vision cannot be used while running. Look to your left to spot two enemies **(7)** in the area. Observe the nearby Thugs until they glow red in this view. The numbers above their heads indicate their level. When the number pops up above their head you can also be assured that they will be marked permanently on the radar. Once on radar, enemy movements can be studied. This is another valuable tool that can also be upgraded using Skill Points. Advanced Eagle Vision options allow you to mark enemies through walls, floors, and rooftops and can also reveal the direction the enemy is facing on radar.

EAGLE VISION COLOR KEY

Different people appear highlighted with different colors in Eagle Vision. This is also reflected on the radar. Red is a common enemy, Yellow is a person of more interest (such as a leader), Green is an ally, and Blue indicates that person is a police officer.

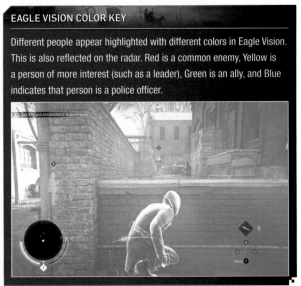

STEALTH RING

Climb up to the top of the building **(7)** on your left while remaining out of the enemies' view. Walk along the rooftop and drop down to the connecting pipe suspended over the two enemies' patrol route. Notice the Stealth Ring surrounding Jacob. Whenever you are in danger of attracting potential aggressors' attention, or while engaged in combat, a circular Stealth Ring surrounds your body. The Stealth Ring displays the positions of actual or aspiring combatants. The direction icons (they look like digital audio level graphs) on the Stealth Ring reveal the locations of every assailant that you need to assassinate or avoid. Notice that if an enemy is below you that the direction icons appear below the Stealth Ring. If the enemy is above you the icons appear above the Stealth Ring. Likewise, if you are on the same plane as the enemy, the direction icons appear above and below the Stealth Ring.

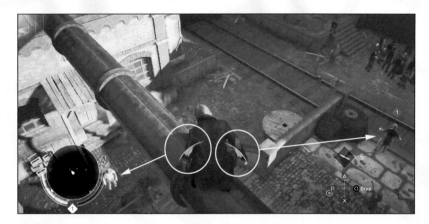

To defeat these enemies **(8)**, wait to Air Assassinate one Thug while the other is turned away. Execute one Thug, get to cover quickly, and then sneak up behind the next and finish him.

CURRENT OBJECTIVE: REACH THE STEEL FORGE ENTRANCE

Your next task is to reach the entrance to the steel forge **(9)** marked with a green hexagon. There are multiple Thugs that patrol the grounds and you should use this opportunity to practice combat, stealth attacks, and crowd blending. Take full advantage of the rooftops. High ground is the best location for scouting and marking enemies with Eagle Vision. Move about the area and attempt to stealthily remove each enemy, loot them, and move on to the next until you reach the large door to the steel forge.

STEALTH

Turn the wheel to open the doors to the steel forge. Just through the doors is an enemy **(A)** with his back to you. In front of him is the immense steel forge. This structure is large and offers a host of different route options to stealthily reduce the enemy. Make the nearest Thug your first victim by sneaking up behind him and silently executing him (Attack) or throw a knife directly at his head. Knife headshots kill lower level enemies with one hit. Higher level enemies can withstand a knife attack to the head. To compensate for this weakness, there are knife damage upgrades available through Crafting Upgrades.

Stealth makes you harder to detect and allows you to move faster. If you choose to take out enemies from a distance then use the throwing knife. From behind cover press and hold **L2 / LT** to aim and then press **R2 / RT** to throw the knife (or whatever throwing object you have selected). The knife focus-locks in on the victim and then auto-tracks the target as he or she moves. The enemy is highlighted using the same highlight style used to signify an Air Assassination lock-on.

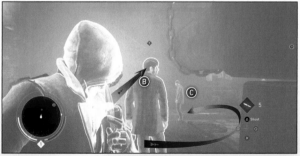

The enemy's torso acquires the knife's reticle in auto-lock. To get a headshot during a target lock-on scenario you will always need to adjust your aim upwards. If the target does not die when the knife hits, then you've missed the sweet spot and have to throw multiple knives to do the same job. It's best to only throw the knife when the target is somewhat still. If the enemy is patrolling, wait until they stop to have a look around. Sometimes it's best to miss a knife throw completely, causing the target to look to the sound of the knife striking a nearby object. This makes them stop moving and look around, creating a better headshot opportunity.

THE ESSENTIALS
WALKTHROUGH
SKIP QUESTS
COLLECTIBLES
REFERENCE & TRAINING
INDEX

SEQUENCE ONE
SEQUENCE TWO
SEQUENCE THREE
SEQUENCE FOUR
SEQUENCE FIVE
SEQUENCE SIX
SEQUENCE SEVEN
SEQUENCE EIGHT
SEQUENCE NINE

HEADSHOT PERK

Perk notices track the number of particular attacks or outstanding actions you've made. In this case, a Headshot Perk notice appears. Once you achieve 50 Headshots the Perk is active. The Headshot Perk increases Critical Hit damage. Tracking your Perks is easy. Simply enter the Options menu and select the Progression Log option. Scroll down through the next set of options until you find Perk. The complete Perk list is located there.

It's not an objective but you should try to defeat all the enemies in the area to gain combat experience and to acquire items from the bodies left behind. Use Eagle Vision as soon as possible. Mark the enemies in the area. The first section of the Steel Forge is divided into two equal size sides. The side you enter has three enemies almost in a straight line from the entrance to the back wall. All three can be killed with a thrown knife, or they can be silently executed (by sneaking up behind them and sticking a knife in their side using the Attack option). The first two Thugs **(A & B)** face the back wall. The third **(C)** faces the left but can easily be snuck up on from the right side of the room. Avoid being spotted by the Thugs on the right side of the room divide while doing this. If you don't want to risk being seen, simply throw a knife in the third Thug's head.

COVER ASSASSINATE

After killing the Thug located in the back right corner, look right and beyond the room-divide and mark the nearest Thug **(D)** on the radar using Eagle Vision. Sneak up behind the workbench to the left of the rightmost opening in the dividing wall. While covered, whistle toward the enemy by pressing D-Pad Down. Sound waves emanate from his head if he's in range and hears you. You have his attention. He approaches your hiding location. Stay crouched and pressed up against the workbench. When the enemy glows with a highlighted red outline (when he enters your attack range), press the Attack button to silently execute the enemy. If you wait too long, the enemy spots you and your cover is blown.

After killing the fourth Thug, head right while remaining on the left side of the divide. Scale the center of the dividing wall to perch on top of a high opening **(10)**. From here you can spot two patrolling Thugs **(E & F)**. They often stop near each other. Throw knives in their heads.

HIGH PIPE HOLE

High on the center dividing wall is a large hole **(11)** in the wall with a large pipe passing through it. This network of connecting pipes can be used (once you climb up to them) to travel between both sides of the building. You can also use this high vantage point to knife throw at the enemies below.

The remaining Thug is on the second level in the back right corner **(12)**. Loot the dead bodies of Thug **(E)** and **(F)**. Cross the floor staying close to the right side in case the guard on the upper walkway looks your way (you can duck under the walkway to avoid detection). Climb up the wall in the back corner and come up behind the Thug **(G)** that patrols from the room to the left to the window to the right. Assassinate him while he faces the window in the corner.

25

Enter the next room through the second level doorway—near your last kill. This new room **(13)** contains no enemies so just work your way across to reach the stairway on

the opposite side. Follow the green hexagon to a light beam in a doorway **(14)**. This is a location marker. Pass through it and follow the dark hallway to reach the next area.

A cinematic reveals Rupert Ferris working in a distant office. This event is triggered when you enter the room with the second doorway marker **(15)**. Crouch into Sneak

mode and cover behind the wood paneled rail on the right side of the stairwell entrance to your right.

Whistle to get the attention of the nearest Thug **(H)** at the bottom of the stairs. Wait for him to enter your striking radius as he ascends the stairs. Silently take him out and loot him as the second ground level Thug **(I)** walks away.

Sneak up to the rail overlooking the large ironworks chamber. With Eagle Vision you can mark two Thugs below. One is the second Thug you saw earlier **(I)** and the third **(J)** is closer to the far exit. Throw Knives at their heads from this second level walkway. If you are out of knives, leave them alone.

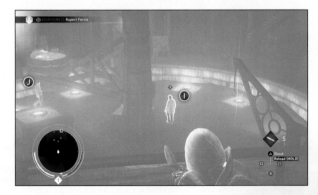

Follow the walkway around a corner until you come across a very wide support girder over the right side of the walkway railing. Climb this girder **(16)** to the top framework. Use Eagle Vision to spot the next target.

From your high perch in the room you can see the Assassination icon (Rupert's location in the next chamber over) and two more Thugs. You can take the Thug **(K)** on the right out with a throwing knife. Follow the left catwalk to another beam that leads to that walkway with the exit on the left. Through this doorway is the next Thug **(L)**. Fortunately, he stands with his back to you as you enter **(17)**.

Sneak up behind the Thug and terminate him. When you exit the small room he was in you find yourself in a large chamber that looks very similar to the last. With Eagle Vision you can spot a cluster of three Thugs on a second level walkway on the right side of the room. Remain crouched behind the railing while remaining patient as more enemies enter your sights. You should spot four patrolling Thugs on the lower floor. Just to the left of the cluster of second level enemies you can see the Assassination icon. This marks Ferris's office beyond these walls.

This room is a great example of the choices you face throughout the game. There are two very distinct approaches to solving most of these Challenges: killing everyone or just moving creatively out of watchful eyes to get to your main target more quickly. We'll cover the less verbose path but help you achieve the mission Challenges whenever applicable.

With that said, turn to the left side of the room—pivot left on the walkway and leap off the railing **(18)** to the winch contraption on the wall and again off the top of a suspended light fixture and next to the top of a large pipe. From this pipe you can either throw a knife at the Thug **(M)** below or continue to the next pipe and use either the last pipe or the edge of the little office rooftop to Air Assassinate this target.

After killing this Thug return to high ground. Get to the corner office rooftop and use a plank to leap and reach the ledge around the large furnace. Stop on the furnace ledge and look around. You see the cluster of three Thugs on the ledge to the right and Thugs left alive on the ground floor. Here you can see three Entry Points indicated by Entry Point icons, all of which are located as far away from each other as possible. The most direct route to Ferris is through the middle top Entry Point. Use the next plank to leap to the side of the wall across the gap. This wall has a large banner painted on it: Starrick & Co. The middle Entry Point **(19)** is accessible from this rooftop.

Rupert Ferris stands directly below your feet (provided you have passed through the Entry Point). Below the doorway is a large drop. Don't go down. Go over. Jump to the pipe across from the entryway. Turn your body completely around while perched on the pipe. Look down and you see Rupert Ferris standing just feet away with an Air Assassination red lock-on highlight around him.

Take Rupert out without a struggle by performing an Air Assassination. Next, the memory and environment surrounding you fades to white and reveals the Animus white room. This is the transitional train station that connects your world with the world of virtual memories. Rupert is a bit upset you pulled him out of that memory and vocally expresses it while Jacob kneels at his dying side.

CURRENT OBJECTIVE: ESCAPE ON THE TRAIN

When the memory kicks back in you find yourself beside Rupert's dead body. So you need to flee the scene. You must escape the ironworks to complete the memory. Pivot around in the room until you face the green Reach icon. Pass through the doorway **(20)** nearest the Reach icon. Pass through another room and you'll spot the target marker in the next room marked "Private."

Climb the stairs in the next room to reach a brightly lit loft. An open door is to the left of the stairs. Your vision beyond the exterior balcony is overexposed by the intense sunlight. Run through the *Reach* icon at the doorway and leap off the end of the balcony (Free Run Down) **(21)** to drop down onto a train that's seconds away from leaving the station.

LOCATION: MOVING TRAIN

Remain on the car you drop down on and defeat the two Thugs that jump on from the platforms **(21)** beside the train. Your cover is blown so you have to result to hand-to-hand combat. Defeat the first two Thugs and, when the train passes under the first tunnel, two more Thugs jump aboard from a side platform **(23)**. Rush to attack them as they climb up between the train cars to catch them in a vulnerable state.

When fighting a large group of enemies it's good to switch focus to the next closest enemy once the original enemy enters a blocking stance. The second enemy's attacks are more likely to land when your current enemy is blocking. So instead of Stunning a blocker, move onto the next target and come back to the blocker later. You can also take a quick break between Attack combos to throw a knife at him to break the block and do some serious damage in the process.

Another enemy jumps aboard from the platform **(24)** and a couple more follow after that. But once you leave town, no more jump aboard. Once you defeat all of the Thugs, a cinematic begins. Thugs in a horse-drawn wagon activate the railroad switch **(25)** and send you and the train on course for a broken bridge. Jacob just barely escapes the train wreck using some quick thinking, quick feet, and superstar-quality parkour moves.

THE ESSENTIALS
WALKTHROUGH
SIDE QUESTS
COLLECTIBLES
REFERENCE & ANALYSIS
INDEX

SEQUENCE ONE
SEQUENCE TWO
SEQUENCE THREE
SEQUENCE FOUR
SEQUENCE FIVE
SEQUENCE SIX
SEQUENCE SEVEN
SEQUENCE EIGHT
SEQUENCE NINE

CURRENT OBJECTIVE: REACH SAFETY

LOCATION: TRAIN WRECK SITE

When control returns to you we find Jacob gripping the edge of the rails above a 30-foot drop **(26)**. Press down on the Left Control Stick to drop from grip point to grip point. Alternatively you could also press the ⊙ / Ⓑ button to Drop from point to point. When you reach the bottom of the track section you discover the drop is too big for a Left Control Stick drop. So you must use the Drop button to release your grip from the rails.

Slide down to the top of the bent sheet metal and jump from the end to clear a gap and reach the top of a demolished train car.

Continue working your way clockwise and downward through the winding path of destruction. Use Free Run Down at the next big drop and then leap into the Reach target marker. This concludes the first Sequence. You made it through alive. Good job. A mission completion display window appears upon completion of all memories. Here you can rate the memory and check out your rewards.

A SIMPLE PLAN

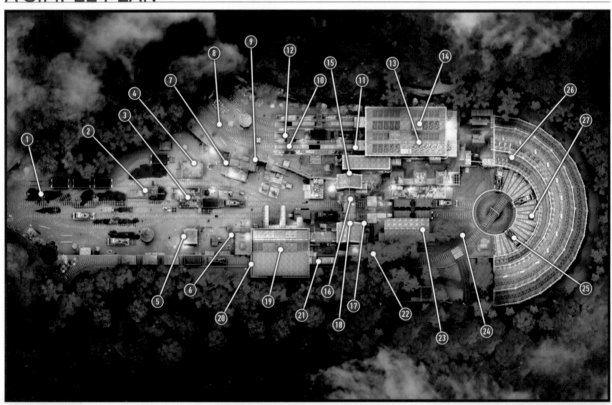

MISSION OVERVIEW

Memory Type: Templar Conspiracy

Suggested Level: 1

ASSASSIN	**CHALLENGES**
Evie Frye	Air Assassinate Brewster
	Kill 5 Enemies with Hanging Barrels

REWARDS

£: 1000 + 75 (Full Synch Bonus)

XP: 2000 + 100 (Full Synch Bonus)

Cape: Thrifty Cloak

LESSONS

❖ Cover Assassination   ❖ Leap of Faith

❖ Knife Throw (Moving Target)   ❖ Smoke Bombs

❖ Quick Throw   ❖ Slide Under

OBJECTIVE: ASSASSINATE DAVID BREWSTER AND RECOVER HIS PIECE OF EDEN

THE ESSENTIALS
WALKTHROUGH
SIDE QUESTS
COLLECTIBLES
REFERENCE & ANALYSIS
INDEX

SEQUENCE ONE
SEQUENCE TWO
SEQUENCE THREE
SEQUENCE FOUR
SEQUENCE FIVE
SEQUENCE SIX
SEQUENCE SEVEN
SEQUENCE EIGHT
SEQUENCE NINE

CURRENT OBJECTIVE: DETACH LOCOMOTIVE
LOCATION: STARRICK AND CO., CORYDON, MOVING TRAIN

MAP VIEW AVAILABILITY

The overhead map feature is not available until you reach London. You're getting closer.

Now we switch focus to Jacob's twin sister and fellow assassin, Evie Frye. You begin this memory as a stowaway on a train headed for the Starrick and Co. Trainyard. You shoved yourself in a corner and now you are taking cover behind crates.

COVER ASSASSINATION

Your first task is to eliminate the immediate threat, which is the Thug who's booting passengers without tickets off the train. Although you had an opportunity to perform the Cover Assassination in the previous sequence, the game really wants to drive it home with this next segment.

Remain crouched and press D-Pad Down to whistle at the Thug in the doorway. The pulsating sound waves around his head indicate that he did, in fact, hear you. He turns and walks toward you. When the Thug is highlighted red, press the Assassinate button to silently take him out while behind cover. If there were nearby enemies here and they did not look directly at you, you would remain undetected at the end of this move. Evie slips back behind cover automatically as she throws the body behind her. This is a very useful move. Loot the body for knives to add to your collection.

KNIFE THROW: MOVING TARGET

Continue onto the next train car by leaping the gap or by carefully walking across the coupler between cars. You spot another Thug on the next car while peering through the exit.

He's standing behind pallets with his back to you. The game suggests you throw a knife at this enemy. Accurately throwing knives on a moving train is not the easiest thing to do. The trick is to aim ahead of the target and let the slipping pull your target into your crosshairs. Or, simply put, aim carefully.

QUICK THROW

Quick Throw is another useful knife-throwing technique. All it requires is a weak target selection (yellow highlight around the enemy), and, of course, a throwing knife in your inventory. Press the Quick Throw button ▲ / Ⓨ to throw the knife—without manually aiming. Typically, you will not achieve a headshot with a Quick Throw and a lot of times one knife doesn't kill the target when it's a torso shot. Be ready to follow up with more knife throwing or rush the victim and finish him off with close combat.

You can find a Chest inside the next car, but the door is on the far side. You can obtain Throwing Knives and some money inside (see our Chests tip on the next page).

Run across the train until you reach the flatbed car with two Thugs with their backs to you. Air Assassinate the closest enemy and then sneak up behind the second Thug and silently take him out. If they are both out of reach, try throwing a smoke bomb between them and take them both out while remaining anonymous.

Cross over five more cars working your way toward the engine. Two Thugs are six cars up. They often jump to the rooftop of the passenger car and

remain facing the engine with their backs to you. Run and quickly pull yourself up to the rooftop. Since they are so close to each other, choose to kill the enemy that is closer to you first. That way there's a chance the second enemy won't see you as you silently take out his buddy. Strike the second as quickly as you can out of the assassination animation.

A Thug is relaxing inside a car two railcars ahead, nodding off and leaning on the wall. Sneak into this car, hugging the right wall. Cover behind the wall and whistle for him to trap him into a Cover Assassination. Or, you can just skip over the rooftop of this car and continue with the objective: detaching the locomotive. However, there is a Chest in this car that is worth investigating.

CHESTS

Chests contain crafting items and money. There are Chests scattered and hidden all over London and each one that you kick open counts toward a goal. There are 345 Chests and 26 Big Chests. However, the Chests found in this sequence do not count toward those totals. Once in London you can track your collections in the Progress Tracker found in the Progression Log.

A Detach marker can be seen as you approach the locomotive. Jump to the engine and enter the marker. Then turn back towards the coupler between the locomotive and the first car. Press ⊚ / Ⓑ to start detaching the coupler. Evie prepares to punch. Press ▢ / Ⓧ repeatedly to break the coupler. When successful, the cars are left in the distance and a cinematic takes you into the trainyard.

CURRENT OBJECTIVE: REACH VANTAGE POINT

LOCATION: STARRICK AND CO. TRAINYARD

When you disembark in the railyard, Evie automatically takes cover behind a group of coal barrels **(1)** as four Thugs and a Brute walk by. The group is exiting the railyard completely. If you need knives, follow the last Thug and silently execute him. Loot him and quickly return to your hiding place behind the coal barrels.

Use Eagle Vision to spot the three enemies ahead. There's a Brute **(B)** to the far left and a Thug **(A)** and a Brute **(C)** on the right side of the locomotive. If you have a knife you may choose to throw it at the Thug's head **(A)**. If you don't have a knife then study the Brutes' patrol routes so that you have time to silently execute the Thug and duck behind the locomotive before either Brute spots you. Killing the Thug with a knife causes the left Brute **(B)** to investigate his body. This puts him in whistle range and you can Cover Assassinate him from behind the barrels. This leaves the last Brute **(C)** as a single, easy kill. Sneak up behind him when his back is to you.

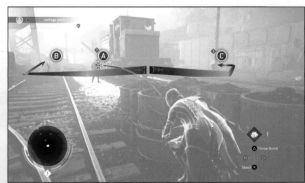

Follow the rails past the locomotive and, while in Eagle Vision, you can mark a Brute to the left of a tower sitting in the middle of the railyard. You can also spot a Thug in the distance on the right. Avoid both of these enemies by sneaking directly to the lift at the top of the stairs. Press **R2 + ⊗** or hold **RT + Ⓐ** while running towards the lift to activate it. Evie jumps up on the lift, grasps the rope with tension and cuts below her hand. This quickly snaps her to the top of the tower **(2)** like a rubber band.

Once on top of the tower, climb to the end of the extended arm and enter the *Reach* marker. In a cinematic we see Lucy Thorne threatening scientist, David Brewster—your target. She expects results from his invention sooner than expected. Such is life. After the conversation, a passerby is kidnapped and sent to Brewster's lab for interrogation and possibly something more sinister.

THE ESSENTIAL
WALKTHROUGH
SIDE QUESTS
COLLECTIBLES
REFERENCE & ANALYSIS
INDEX

SEQUENCE ONE
SEQUENCE TWO
SEQUENCE THREE
SEQUENCE FOUR
SEQUENCE FIVE
SEQUENCE SIX
SEQUENCE SEVEN
SEQUENCE EIGHT
SEQUENCE NINE

CURRENT OBJECTIVE: REACH LABORATORY

LEAP OF FAITH

CHALLENGE: KILL 5 ENEMIES WITH HANGING BARRELS

Mark a few enemies below using Eagle Vision from your beautifully high position at the top of the tower. Notice how objects of interest glow white, for instance the haystack below **(3)**. To perform a Leap of Faith directly into the haystack, push forward on the Left Control Stick and Hold **R2 + ◎ / RT + Ⓑ**. The sounding thud of your body hitting the hay does not alert the enemy no matter how close to the hay they are. Haystacks become instantaneous cover but you cannot remain inside them when you have been spotted.

After their conversation ends, the furthest Thug **(E)** walks away and stops with his back to you. When this happens, whistle to attract the attention of the next Thug **(D)**. When the Thug approaches the haystack, press the Assassinate button to stab him and pull him in with you. This is executed all in one smooth motion. The enemy has to be close enough that he is highlighted target red before a successful haystack attack. Don't wait too long to grab the enemy. If he inspects the area long enough he discovers you and blows your cover.

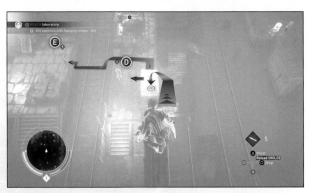

Now exit the haystack and sneak over to the Thug **(E)** on the next train platform **(4)** to the left. His back remains to you as long as you make no noise. Silently execute him and loot his corpse.

KILLING 2 THUGS WITH BARRELS

Activate Eagle Vision and mark the enemies **(F & G)** on the far right side of the trainyard. One of the Challenges in this memory is to kill five enemies with hanging barrels. To secure two of these specialized kills, head back across the previous platform, passing the haystack and continue to the backside of the Croydon Station building **(5)**. Climb to the rooftop and look over the far edge and down on the three Thugs below. The closest Thug **(F)** should be dealt with after you drop the barrels **(6)** on the other two **(G)** near the next building. Notice the barrels highlight yellow. While holding a throwing knife, take aim at the hanging barrels above their heads. The reticle turns red when you are assured a target lock on the barrels. Throw the knife and watch the barrels fall, killing the two unfortunate Thugs below.

Before the remaining Thug **(F)** gets too curious about the fate of his comrades, run off the edge of the rooftop and along the pulley arm just below the rooftop. This allows you to get close enough above the Thug to obtain an Air Assassination lock-on. If you waited too long to attack this Thug then use the haystack below to perform a whistling haystack attack. Loot all three of these victims to maintain a robust knife collection.

There are four more enemies on the opposite side of the railyard. Keep in mind that killing everyone is not a prerequisite, but there are two more Thugs standing under hanging barrels **(10)** that will all but complete the Challenge for you. So sneak back to the other side again and climb the castle-looking wall **(7)**, avoiding the Thug **(H)** on the ground.

Walk along the wall, but only move when the Thug on the left **(I)** starts walking further left **(8)**. With his back to you, sneak quickly to catch him before he turns around. Eliminate him and then double back toward the castle wall. Take cover behind the far left corner **(9)** of the wall. Get a good view of the two Thugs below the hanging barrels **(J)**. Throw a knife at the barrels before one of the guards walks away. If you've killed all four with barrels then you only need one more to satisfy the Challenge.

Now walk along the top edge of the castle wall and follow it to the right corner. Walk out onto the extended metal platform (that looks like a drawbridge) and from the edge you can perform an Air Assassination on the Thug **(H)** below.

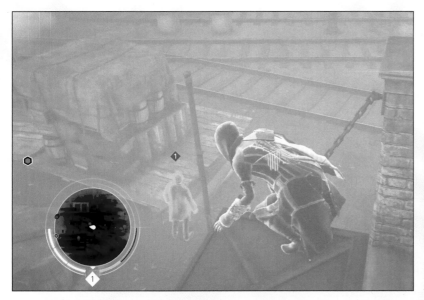

Return to the last hanging-barrel-kill-zone and you spot a Brute guarding the station entrance **(11)**. Your next objective is inside that building. He's facing your direction. The easiest way past this guy is to travel through the tunnel **(12)** that runs under the train cars on the left.

The tunnel splits into alternate tunnels to the left and right and if you continue forward you come across a sleeping Thug. He's leaning up against the right tunnel wall. Sneak up to him, hugging the right wall, and execute him. At the end of his tunnel and to the left you can find a chest to top off your knives and smoke bombs. Follow the southernmost tunnel to the ascending stairs. Sneak slowly. Just as you crest the floor you can see a Brute partially hidden behind potential cover to your left **(13)**.

Once the Brute is looking the other direction, exit the stairs slowly and hide behind the crates. Whistle for the Brute and perform a Cover Assassination on him when he comes to investigate.

THE ESSENTIALS
WALKTHROUGH
SIDE QUESTS
COLLECTIBLES
REFERENCE & ANALYSIS
INDEX

SEQUENCE ONE
SEQUENCE TWO
SEQUENCE THREE
SEQUENCE FOUR
SEQUENCE FIVE
SEQUENCE SIX
SEQUENCE SEVEN
SEQUENCE EIGHT
SEQUENCE NINE

CURRENT OBJECTIVE: SPEAK WITH CAPTIVE

After Cover Assassinating the Brute, head left up the stairs to the second level. When you reach the top of the stairs, pivot around and look for the Thug leaning up against some crates on the second floor. Must have been a tough day. That's not the first sleepy one you've seen. Work your way around the left hallway and come up right beside this Thug and execute him silently.

Climb the crates the Thug was leaning up against and jump up to the third floor railing. Drop down onto the walkway and follow the hallway left into the open door on the left, where you find the captive with two guards.

SMOKE BOMBS

Enter the marker on the right side of the room and press D-Pad Right to switch from Knives to Smoke Bombs. Since you do not yet have the skill to assassinate two close enemies at once (yet) the next best thing is to fill the room with smoke so you can assassinate them both without being discovered. To throw the Smoke Bomb, press and hold **R2** / **RT** button and aim with the Right Control Stick. Enemies have difficulty seeing you through the smoke so their defense is down. Take these two Thugs out and then inspect their captive, Robert Topping.

Press the ⊚ / Ⓑ button when prompted. Robert reveals the location of the secret lab and asks you to untie him. Evie tells this carny to get himself out of the bind since he managed to get himself into it…but he mysteriously vanishes the moment you turn your back. Robert Topping later becomes an associate in London.

CURRENT OBJECTIVE: LOCATE KEY

Exit the room through the opposite door. Turn left in the hallway and find the ladder to a loft. Climb the ladder to the loft and exit **(14)** the building through the open skylight. Once you are out on the rooftop, you can spot the green blip marking the location of the next objective: Locate the key.

Walk along the peak of the rooftop heading to the right toward the green blip. When you reach the gable, pivot to the left to see a lower flat rooftop and then another building beside that one. In Eagle Vision, enemies in view around that building begin to mark. Drop down off your rooftop, cross the flattop building and clamber to the peak of the next building's rooftop **(15)**.

THE ESSENTIALS

WALKTHROUGH

SIDE QUESTS

COLLECTIBLES

GEAR & WEAPONS

INDEX

Activate Eagle Vision and mark the enemies below. There's a Brute **(K)** below you. On the ground level is a Thug **(L)** walking towards some hanging barrels. There's another Thug **(M)** on the same walkway **(16)** as the Brute. This Thug patrols the interior of the next building and this walkway. The last Thug **(N)** you can mark crouches on the edge of a platform jutting off the right side of the walkway.

Begin this slaughter by throwing a knife at the hanging barrels **(17)** when the Thug **(L)** walks under them. This has the potential of being your final barrel kill, thus completing the Challenge. If not, there are a few more opportunities to make up for any misses. Next, when the patrolling Thug **(M)** disappears into the next building, perform an Air Assassination on the Brute **(K)** below you. Quickly sneak up to the crouched Thug **(N)** on the right and assassinate him from behind. Lastly, crouch and cover beside the open door of the next building and whistle for the patrolling Thug **(M)**. When he comes to investigate, Cover Assassinate him.

After defeating the enemies in the area, hop up to the top of the rooftop **(18)** that the patrolling guard was under (there is a Chest worth opening on the first floor of this building if you want to divert your course). Leap across the winches to reach the next building to the right. Get to the opposite side of the rooftop peak and enter through an open skylight **(19)**.

Walk along the rafters while looking downward with Eagle Vision activated. You are looking for an enemy that is highlighted yellow and marked with a Steal icon. This key holder **(P)** and a Brute **(O)** walk toward the doorway below. To mark them you may need to walk across the beams heading to the right from the skylight platform and look around the platform obstructions. Later you will be able to spot enemies through walls and floors (but not just yet).

Drop from the rafters down to the second level where you can find a chest full of goodies in the right corner. Approach the chest and kick it open using the ◎ / ⑧ button. Inside are money, knives and smoke bombs.

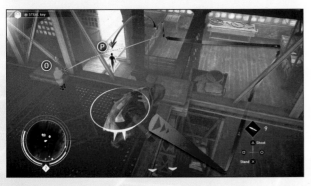

Stand up next to the railing overlooking the Brute **(O)** and throw a knife into his head or let him keep walking behind the train if you don't have a knife. Make sure the Thug that is difficult to see directly under your platform has walked away to the left. Then, hop up on the rail and perform an Air Assassination on the key holder **(P)** and then quickly loot his body for the key. Exit the building through the large open door **(20)** to avoid being detected by other enemies inside.

PLAYING NICE

It is not necessary to assassinate the key holder to get the key. If you want to avoid more bloodshed, sneak up behind him, hold ◎ / ⑧, and take the key without his ever knowing.

CURRENT OBJECTIVE:
LOCATE SECRET LAB ENTRANCE

Climb up the door **(20)** and the side of the building to reach the rooftop again. Once on top you see the green blip of the next objective in the distance, some 150 meters away. Run past the skylight **(19)** and stop at the far end of the rooftop. Below is a parked train **(21)**. Jump down into the train car and hop toward the front of the locomotive.

Standing on the train's large smokestack, look to the line of trees ahead **(22)**. You can leap to the nearest branch and continue through the trees by hopping through the V-split at the top of their trunks.

From the last tree, jump to the rooftop of the shelter **(23)** and then continue jumping through the next couple of trees and finally to a metal water pipe **(24)** where you can perform an Air Assassination on a Brute below **(Q)**.

Climb up on the nearest train **(25)** and have a look around. You could enter the train station through the guarded entrance, but alternatively the open window **(26)** above is an option, as is the short tunnel **(27)** in front of the train. We will guide you using the tunnel route; it's a shorter distance to your destination.

Once in the short tunnel, walk to the end and climb the right wall and only latch onto the opening above. Do not pull yourself up into the room above yet. Activate Eagle Vision and find the two guards nearby. There's a Brute **(R)** that patrols from the left wall to where the Thug **(S)** stands at the right wall.

When neither guard is looking, pull up into the room and take immediate cover behind the shelf on the right. From here you can throw a knife at the Thug's **(S)** head. Next you can either whistle for the Brute as he inspects that body and then Cover Assassinate him or you can just throw a knife at his head.

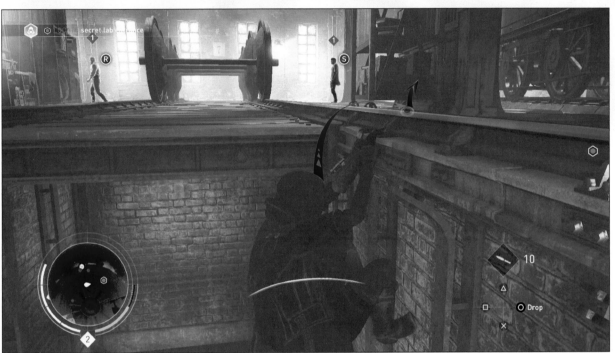

Enter the rafters above using any route you desire as long as you keep your cover. The Brute guarding the door can see through some of the grated walls near him so don't get too close. You can jump to the platform above him and either Air Assassinate him or throw a knife at his head. With that done, use the key to unlock the door he was guarding.

39

CURRENT OBJECTIVE: LOCATE SIR DAVID BREWSTER

ACQUIRE DOUBLE ASSASSINATION SKILL

The next room is nothing more than a very large elevator shaft. Enter the lift and press the Activate button on the lift lever to reach the lower level. This completes the current objective. Now you must locate Sir David Brewster. A message appears at the top of the screen: You Have Earned 3 Skill Points. Next, a Skill Upgrade tutorial screen appears. It goes on to explain that you gain XP from Memories, Skilled Assassinations, and London Activities. Each 1,000 XP earned gives both Jacob and Evie a single Skill Point to spend on new Skills. So the twins share Skill Points. Keep that in mind when you are upgrading one—the other is waiting.

The Skills menu opens. Purchase the Double Assassination skill. We also suggest you purchase Loot Takedown and Eagle Vision II now.

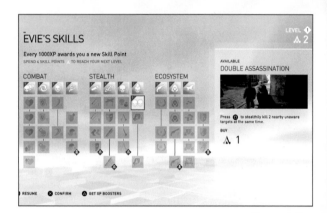

When the elevator reaches the bottom floor you quickly realize why you purchased Double Assassination. Through the next passageway stand two unaware Thugs with their backs to you. They stand side-by-side and as you sneak up to them you now acquire a double lock-on—both enemies glow with a red highlighted outline. When this lock-on is achieved, press the ◯ / ✕ button once and watch as Evie skillfully executes both Thugs.

Sneak into the right tunnel and find the Thug carrying on a conversation with someone through a ramped exit. Execute him from behind.

Head up the ramp and find two more Thugs standing side-by-side with their backs to you. Sneak up and Double Assassinate them. Head left along the walkway and jump to a pipe in the next room. Follow the pipe around to the end and leap to a thick bar and swing to the floor in the next room.

Follow the hallway to another set of pipe-jumping challenges until you reach a well-lit window on the left that triggers a cinematic of the Piece of Eden machine in Brewster's secret lab.

THE ESSENTIALS
WALKTHROUGH
SIDE QUESTS
COLLECTIBLES
SEQUENCE & ANALYSIS
INDEX

CURRENT OBJECTIVE: ASSASSINATE SIR DAVID BREWSTER

AIR ASSASSINATE BREWSTER

Follow the hallway to the end where you find two entrances into the lab along the right wall. These are two high windows in the laboratory so when you enter you are near the ceiling; safe from watching eyes. We recommend entering the farthest window. Start by jumping to the nearest pipe.

Use Eagle Vision to mark the Brute **(T)** patrolling the ground level. There are two Thugs **(U & V)** that you may not be able to mark because of pipe obstructions. They patrol the distant second level walkway. You spot them when you get closer. Jump a couple of pipes and then jump to the top of the light fixture when the two Thugs leave the room. Now from the light fixture, Air Assassinate the Brute **(T)** below. Climb up the large circuit machines to reach the second level walkway.

SEQUENCE ONE
SEQUENCE TWO
SEQUENCE THREE
SEQUENCE FOUR
SEQUENCE FIVE
SEQUENCE SIX
SEQUENCE SEVEN
SEQUENCE EIGHT
SEQUENCE NINE

Sneak into the lab and notice both the Thug and the Brute nearby both have their backs to you. First eliminate the Thug on the left and then sneak up behind and kill the Brute who's looking over the railing.

Round the corner and climb the supply shelf. Jump from the top of the shelf to a couple of beams to avoid the patrolling Thug below. From the third rafter, pivot left in the corner and jump to the next rafter and then drop down to the high catwalk.

Cross the catwalk and jump to the nearest light truss. Follow the truss to the left so you are aligned with Brewster's patrol pattern below. As soon as you acquire an Air Assassination lock-on, perform the attack and finish off the scientist.

In the Animus room, Evie and Sir David Brewster have a surprisingly civil conversation where Evie commits to carrying on the scientist's experiment. He warns that Miss Thorne has already found another Piece of Eden more powerful than the last.

CURRENT OBJECTIVE: ESCAPE THE SECRET LAB

When you return to the lab, the Piece of Eden machine becomes unstable (no doubt from all the power they pushed to it). Now Evie must escape the lab with her life.

The first of many Reach markers appears in the next room. Rush up the stairs and veer left to pass through the first checkmark.

Run forward and take the first possible right to find the next Reach marker near another hallway. This leads to a dead-end where you must climb up to reach a second level hallway.

Run toward the next marker, veering through the archway on the left. The ceiling falls in just as you pass under the archway and dumps you into a pool of murky water. Continue forward by swimming a short distance and then crawl up the side of flooring to reach the next marker.

SLIDE UNDER MOVE

Out of the water you are immediately faced with a new obstacle. This is overcome with a new move: the Slide Under. Continue moving forward and press **R2** / **RT** to slide under the debris in the doorway. Evie executes the move like she's sliding into home plate.

CURRENT OBJECTIVE: ESCAPE DEBRIS

Squeeze through the narrow passage (simply press forward) and you reach a very low tunnel through the wreckage. This leads to an area where Evie must scuffle under a grate. From under the grate is a drop and then another Slide Under obstacle.

You come out in the elevator shaft (the same one where you earned your Double Assassinate Skill Points), but now the lift is destroyed. Begin climbing the far wall to reach the top and to complete this sequence. You are about to enter London. This is where a barge-full of options and memories open up for you, and Evie and Jacob are reunited....

THE ESSENTIALS
WALKTHROUGH
SIDE QUESTS
COLLECTIBLES
REFERENCE & ANALYSIS
INDEX

SEQUENCE ONE
SEQUENCE TWO
SEQUENCE THREE
SEQUENCE FOUR
SEQUENCE FIVE
SEQUENCE SIX
SEQUENCE SEVEN
SEQUENCE EIGHT
SEQUENCE NINE

SOMEWHERE THAT'S GREEN

MISSION OVERVIEW

Memory Type: Templar Conspiracy	**REWARDS**	**LESSONS**
Suggested Level: 1	**£:** 410 + 75 (Full Synch Bonus)	❖ Skills ❖ Viewpoint Synchronization
	XP: 250 + 100 (Full Synch Bonus)	❖ Collectibles ❖ Carriage Driving
ASSASSIN **CHALLENGES**	**Kukri:** Ivory Kukri	❖ Mult-Kill Finishers ❖ Switch Characters
Jacob Frye Arrive before Evie		

LOCATION: TRAIN STATION OUTSIDE LONDON

After Jacob assassinates Rupert Ferris and Evie takes out David Brewster, the sibling assassins rendezvous at a nearby train station to share their accomplishments. While quite proud of their achievements, George Westhouse—their punctual comrade—focuses on the mission failures: the lab explosion and the train derailment. Jacob asks George if the Templars in London are the next target. George suggests patience, as the Templars are well rooted in London and have been for the past 100 years. George recommends letting the Council guide their next move. The twins follow their hearts and together agree to take on London alone. They hop on the next train for London.

LOCATION: (CURRENT DAY) ABSTERGO HISTORICAL RESEARCH OFFICE

Shaun and Rebecca infiltrate the Abstergo Historical Research facility and ambush a Templar, Isabelle Ardant, after her videoconference with Alvaro Gramatica. Shaun and Rebecca overhear them talking about their plans to search for the artifact (a Piece of Eden). The agents themselves are ambushed but escape using a smoke bomb and a nearby window. Bishop orders the synchronization of Jacob and Evie's memories to help find something that puts them ahead of the enemy's search for the Piece of Eden.

LOCATION: WHITECHAPEL, LONDON

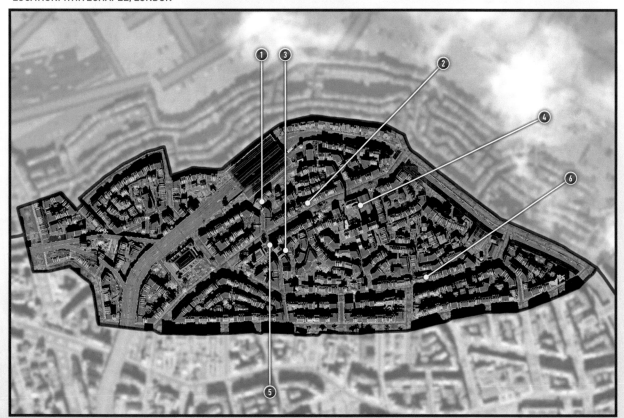

MAP VIEW AVAILABILITY

The overhead map feature is now available, press the touch pad button to access the world map. For more information on map features and using the map, see the Essentials section of this guide.

Evie and Jacob arrive in London in the East End district of Whitechapel. Jacob's heart begins to pump faster as he takes in the bustling city. Evie, on task as usual, gets right to the mission: finding Henry Green (the Assassin watching over London) and formulating a plan of attack against the Templars.

A little boy bumps into Jacob **(1)**, pickpockets him, and runs off. Jacob, visibly upset, takes off after the little street urchin with Evie close behind.

Turn left at the top of the stairs and continue to follow the yellow blip if you do not actually see the boy. At the end of the muddy street is a route choice. You can either slide under the hole in the pile of junk or run around the junk using the stairs to the left. We suggest running around the junk.

CURRENT OBJECTIVE: CHASE THE THIEF

The little thief is marked by an orange blip on the screen and Mini-Map. Begin the chase by running into the narrow alley across the street from the Whitechapel Station. This opens to a cul-de-sac where you can see the boy running up some stairs in the distance. Stay close to the target.

If you slide under then you have to immediately turn to the right, scale a gate and run down the stairs. You risk grabbling onto wall objects that could slow you down. If you take the stairs, turn right and round the corner. Continue up the next set of stairs to reach another paved street **(2)**.

If you don't see the thief when you reach the brick road and can see his yellow blip moving in front of the storefronts across the street, don't be tempted to follow the dot, instead run into the narrow alleyway directly across the street.

ILLUSTRATIONS

Notice the glowing paper stuck on the left wall at the entrance of the alleyway. This is a collectible Memory Item. There are varying amounts of collectible types in each district. This is one of five Illustrations hidden in Whitechapel. Take it now and continue after the boy by running to the right as you exit the alley.

COLLECTING HISTORICAL POSTER ADS

There are 50 hidden illustrations and each district has their own collection tracker. See Progress Tracker/Miscellaneous to study your collection progress. See the Collectibles section in this guide for help finding all the hidden items.

CURRENT OBJECTIVE: LOCATE THE KID

After taking a right out of the alley, you can sprint forward through the next alley where you see the kid **(3)** waiting for you or you can make a quick detour to the left and kick open your first collectible Chest.

CHESTS

There are 345 hidden Chests and each district tracks their own Chests. This Chest you found is a small Chest. It contains money and crafting items. There are also 24 Big Chests. See Progress Tracker/Miscellaneous to see your collection progress. See Collectibles in our guide for help finding all the hidden items.

If you haven't figured it out already, there's no way you were going to tackle that kid. You just can't stop him. Continue toward the little thief in the clearing at the end of

the alleyway. The little boy has lead you into an ambush and also into another fighting lesson…

CURRENT OBJECTIVE: KILL THE THUGS

MULTI-KILL FINISHERS

The little pickpocket takes off into the distance as two Thugs **(3)** approach you with knives in their hands and killing in their eyes. You can perform a couple of Quickshots with Ⓐ / Ⓨ to weaken them very quickly. These two Thugs have a really low pain threshold and become critical with just a few attacks. When both enemies are swaying and lingering toward death you are prompted to press the Ⓞ / Ⓧ button to "Finish" them. When two enemies are in a critical state and in close proximity together, an automatic finishing move is performed and afterward, two bodies lie on ground. You can execute up to four near-death enemies in a group. The more victims in the Multi-Kill Finisher the more XP you earn per kill.

SKILLS

After defeating the two Thugs in the ambush, Evie appears through a nearby alley. Before you follow her, now would be a great time to pause the game to enter the Main Menu. From there, select Skills. Remember when Evie got Skill Points during the last sequence? Well, that means Jacob has some Skill Points to spend now too, because Skill Points are distributed (or duplicated) equally to both twins. So if Evie earns two Skill Points, then so does Jacob. You currently have four Skill Points to spend on Skills. Evie will have three since you spent one already in the last Sequence.

We strongly suggest you give Jacob the Double Assassination that you gave Evie and Loot Takedown is extremely convenient. Eagle Vision II and Health Boost I would be our next two recommendations. You reach Level 2 after purchasing four Skills.

SKILL POINTS AND SKILL PURCHASING

For more information on Skill Points, Skills, and a Skill purchasing strategy, see our Skills and Leveling section of this guide.

CURRENT OBJECTIVE: FOLLOW EVIE

When you meet up with Evie at the alleyway she quickly picks up the pace and turns her walk into a trot and from a trot into a full speed run. She's acting like your little sister again and wants to race you to the next destination **(4)**.

THE ESSENTIALS
WALKTHROUGH
SIDE QUESTS
COLLECTIBLES
REFERENCE & ANALYSIS
INDEX

SEQUENCE ONE
SEQUENCE TWO
SEQUENCE THREE
SEQUENCE FOUR
SEQUENCE FIVE
SEQUENCE SIX
SEQUENCE SEVEN
SEQUENCE EIGHT
SEQUENCE NINE

CURRENT OBJECTIVE: REACH THE FACTORY

CHALLENGE: ARRIVE BEFORE EVIE

Chase after Evie through the alleyway, avoiding crowds the best you can. In the clearing veer left with her and try to pass her in the park. She'll veer left again around a pylon; you should run between them and head straight for the green marker which you can now see at the top of the factory ahead.

Scale the factory building and enter the green marker **(4)** on the rooftop before Evie and you successfully pass the Challenge. While on the rooftop the twins meet Henry Green, the young Assassin trying to keep the peace in London.

Henry immediately recognizes the Frye twins from a description that had been given to him. He introduces himself and expresses his condolences for the passing of their father. Jacob asks Henry about Crawford Starrick. Henry, under the impression that the Council sent the twins to help him with the Templars in London explains that London must be freed and that Starrick sits at the helm of the most sophisticated Templar infrastructure ever built.

Jacob gets the idea to rally the civilian gangs to their side and goes as far as quickly naming the faction, The Rooks. Jacob asks Evie if she has a better idea and she suggests finding the Piece of Eden (and at this moment this becomes Evie's quest, while Jacob rolls with his mob rules strategy).

Henry exclaims that he will show you the lay of the land and points to the large factory chimney....

CURRENT OBJECTIVE: SYNCHRONIZE WITH THE VANTAGE POINT

Climb the large chimney beside the assassins. To reach the top you have to grab onto the next closest indented brick or sliver of ledge. Ultimately you end up climbing up in a clockwise corkscrew motion (always moving to the right on your way up).

VIEWPOINT SYNCHRONIZATION

Once on top, walk across the plank to the end and press the ◎ / ® button to synchronize. When you arrive in a district, the entire map is fogged red so no details can be seen. Conquest Activities must be completed to clear this fog. To mark the map with points of interest (and items if you have purchased treasure maps) you must synchronize from a high Viewpoint. There are a few Viewpoints in each district that must be reached, such as the chimney you're standing on now. These areas are marked with a 🦅.

After synchronization, Henry describes the chaos in Whitechapel is a result of Starrick's influence. Evie promises to help restore London and Henry invites the twins to his shop to discuss the plan.

CURRENT OBJECTIVE: FOLLOW HENRY GREEN

Henry performs a Leap of Faith off the end of the chimney. Climb out to end of the chimney plank and do the same, landing in the haystack below. Walk beside Henry (blue blip on the Mini-Map) and listen to him as he talks about Rexford Kaylock, one of Starrick's gang leaders particularly interested in Henry's arcane research into one of the precursor artifacts (Pieces of Eden). After the conversation, Henry begins to run. Keep up with him.

When you reach the next corner **(5)** you literally run into Charles Dickens spilling his latest work all over the sidewalk. Evie helps him gather his papers. The author scuttles off into the pub. Henry says he knows everything in this city and to keep that connection in your back pocket.

Kaylock's gang sees the commotion with Charles Dickens and spots Henry. He hands each twin a revolver and points you to his carriage. He wants you to throw them off his trail and instructs you to meet him at the curio shop.

CURRENT OBJECTIVE: DESTROY THE THUGS' CARRIAGE

CARRIAGE DRIVING

Typically you press ◎ / Ⓑ to enter a carriage to drive or to hijack it from another driver, but you regain control of Jacob while he is behind the reins. Press the **R2** button to accelerate. Press ⊗ / Ⓐ to whip the horse for a speed boost. Whip it as much as you please, you won't kill it or wear the horse out. Steer with the Left Control Stick and when a carriage is beside you (and you've gained some speed) press ▢ / ⊗ to ram and damage another carriage.

There are two enemy-driven carriages after you. They appear as red blips on the Mini-Map. To complete the Challenge you need to use speed and the ram feature until both are destroyed. When you can flip the enemy carriage over you have taken them out. When you have lost the enemy and have become anonymous (no enemies have seen you), the objective updates.

CURRENT OBJECTIVE: REACH HENRY GREEN'S SHOP

After you destroy the carriages a route marker appears on the Mini-Map and a thin guideline appears on the actual road ahead of you. These markers aid you in finding your way around town. You can select points of interest on the map to create these route markers to help you quickly navigate to your destination.

LONDON DRIFT PERK

Whenever you drive a carriage at high speed, take the opportunity to perform a London Drift in every cornering situation where it makes sense. With speed and while cornering, press and hold the brake button **L2** to perform a drift. This is actually very helpful for rounding corners at high speed. After 10 big drifts, this perk unlocks increased control of the vehicle while boosting.

Enter Henry's Curio Shop and step into the marker to complete the objective. Henry lays out a few portraits on the desk in front of you. He explains that the people in the pictures are helpful contacts across the city. After the twins argue a bit about strategy, Henry pushes a sketch of Sgt. Abberline's face towards the twins. Henry goes on to explain that they need the police to turn a blind eye to

your activities and that Abberline is a master of disguise. Then you will need urchins. "Children make for excellent spies," he says. He shows a picture of Clara O'Dea. Finally, he pushes a picture of one of Starrick's gang bosses, Rexford Kaylock, toward the twins and implies this should be your next Templar target.

This completes the first Memory in Sequence 3 and unlocks the Whitechapel Conquest Activities (Templar Hunts, Gang Strongholds, Child Liberation, and Bounty Hunt). Walk to the next memory down the street or jump in a carriage and drive toward the hexagon with the "A" on the map.

THE LONDON MAP

Press the Touch Pad button to access the London Map. An icon legend is available by pressing the **L3** button. Conquest Activities are marked on the map. Once you complete those activities the red fog of war is lifted from that borough indicating that the Templars are no longer in control of that area. Once you have completed all the Conquest Activities (Templar Hunt, Gang Stronghold, Child Liberation, and Bounty Hunt) the Templar Crime Boss challenge is unlocked. Defeat the crime boss to conquer the borough.

SEQUENCE MEMORIES VS. CONQUEST ACTIVITIES

Press the Touch Pad button to access the London Map. Notice the four mission icons on the map in Whitechapel. Typically the hexagonal icons represent Sequence Memories while the irregular pentagon symbolizes Conquest Activities. To introduce you to the Conquest Activities, the first two Memories are a Bounty Hunt and a Child Liberation. Confused? Don't stress it. This is the last instance of this shell trick. Currently you have two available "Memories": *Abberline, We Presume* and *To Catch an Urchin*. When all four are beat, the red fog is removed from Whitechapel.

SWITCH CHARACTERS

When you exit Henry's shop you are presented with the option to switch characters. Press the **Options** or **Menu Button** to open the Main Menu, then press **R3** to Switch between Evie or Jacob. You don't need to switch right now, but just know that you can do so whenever you are anonymous and not in a current memory or activity. Evie favors the stealth approach while Jacob is more confrontational. Evie and Jacob share money, XP (Skill Points), and rewards, but have separate gear and skills.

If you have not played as Evie since Sequence 2, then switch characters now and spend her three remaining Skill Points. We suggest purchasing the following Skills: Health Boost 1, Loot Takedown, and Eagle Vision II. Evie reaches Level 2 after purchasing her fourth Skill.

GEAR UPGRADE

We suggest you take this time to spend some money on some better gear. Purchase and equip the Noble Cane-Sword and equip the Thrifty Cloak.

BOUNTY HUNT: ABBERLINE, WE PRESUME

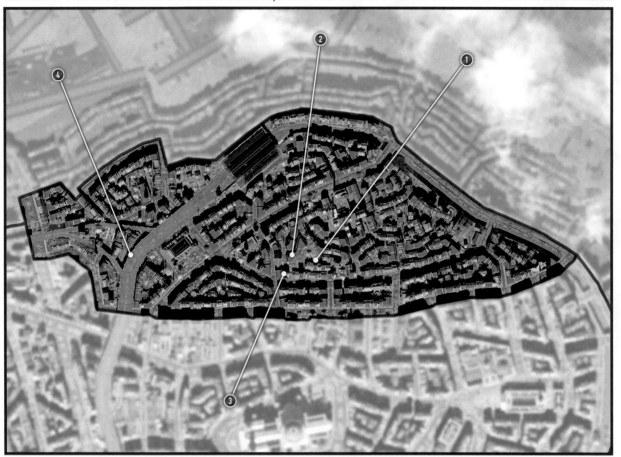

MISSION OVERVIEW

Memory Type: Bounty Hunt	
Suggested Level: 2	

REWARDS	**LESSONS**	
£: 132 + 75 (Full Synch Bonus)	❖ Tackle	❖ Restrain
XP: 200 + 100 (Full Synch Bonus)	❖ Kidnapping	❖ Shove In

ASSASSIN	**CHALLENGES**
Jacob or Evie Frye	Bring back the target alive

LESSONS: ❖ Escorting Captives, ❖ Shove In (into Carriage)

OBJECTIVE: REACH HIGH GROUND

LOCATION: WHITECHAPEL BACK ALLEY

Which Frye twin you are controlling determines which twin you meet up with in the Whitechapel back alley **(1)**. Once the twins are together again, press ✕ / Ⓐ to accept this Memory. When the memory starts, neither Jacob nor Evie can find the police officer they were to meet at this location. Suddenly a hunched-over old lady approaches the twins and offers her assistance. Jacob snatches the bonnet off her head to reveal the master of disguise, the bumbling Sergeant Frederick Abberline.

Abberline lays out the rules of their "partnership." He tells the Frye twins that he will provide the names of criminal gang members and that they will bring them to him…quietly.

KIDNAPPING

While undetected behind an enemy, press ◎ / Ⓑ to Kidnap them. Move slowly with the **Left Control Stick** near enemies to shrink your detection radius. Moving faster with **R2** makes you easier for enemies to detect. Press ◎ / Ⓑ to shove a kidnapped captive into an enclosed carriage.

When control returns to you, Abberline (re-disguised) tells you to stay within the bounds of the law, for his sake. This means you should not kill the target (don't worry about the other enemies, they'll get what's coming to them). So this means you need to work stealthily. You could rush in and risk getting beaten to death or chasing the target all over town, or you can choose to do it quietly and much more quickly. We usually take this approach.

Abberline adds, "…attempt to make them talk, then bring them to my carriage." He makes it sound like he's waiting nearby, but he is far away from the crime scene. You have the option to throw the victim into a nearby carriage and there are usually plenty of options around every corner. Look for the most inconspicuous route to a nearby carriage. This means you do not have to risk walking a kidnapped victim through a guarded exit. Then you must deliver the "package" to Abberline's carriage—usually a few blocks away—to remain inconspicuous.

You must reach high ground. Follow the green blip to the rooftops. Climb up to the top of the nearby stair ledge and then jump and cling to the side of the building to the left. Get to the rooftop by grabbing onto grip points and continue to the right across the rooftops to find Dalton and his thugs.

Activate Eagle Vision while walking along the rooftops and as you approach the courtyard **(2)** full of enemies. Look through the rooftop and you start seeing highlighted shapes. These enemies have no way of seeing you through walls and rooftops. This is your advantage and the power of Eagle Vision II (Upgrade to that Skill now if you have not already).

SURVEYING AND BASIC ATTACK STRATEGY

Always approach an area of enemy activity from the highest point in the area. Activate Eagle Vision. There are often Watchers with rifles on rooftops scouting the area for threats, ones that look a lot like you. Always look high and in many directions before you move closer to the scene of most activity. Next, look all around you including under your feet. Once you have all the enemies marked on your map, the next step is to study their movements. Find an area where you can start taking out single targets one at a time. If there's no opening create one with a knife headshot. This is the process. Stick to it and you will ace every challenge presented, even those beyond your skill level. If you can get one hit kills on everybody, it doesn't matter how high their level is; you will come out victorious.

Take in your surroundings from the edge of a rooftop overlooking Homer Dalton and his henchmen. There are four Thugs that could cause a problem, and possibly a fifth depending on your exit strategy. One Thug patrols through the middle of the courtyard **(A)**. He's got to go. Another two **(B & C)** stand still with their backs to you. Throw a knife at the heads of the patrolling Thug **(A)** and static Thug **(B)**. That's all the Blighter killing you need to do.

KIDNAP

Leap of Faith into the haystack no matter who's facing you (it's always instant cover) and wait for Homer Dalton **(D)** who is highlighted yellow on the map and in Eagle Vision to walk with his back to you. Sneak out of the hay and come up behind him to quietly tackle him using ⓞ / Ⓑ.

TACKLE

Once he pulls himself to his feet, press the same button to kidnap him. Do this quickly or he will run off and into view of his henchmen if you let him. Make sure you do not hold the Kidnap button or you end up knocking the victim out. Then you'd have to carry him to the carriage and will have no moving cover as you would have had if you walked with the kidnapped victim to the carriage. Plus, knocking him out counts the same as if the kidnapped victim was dead and you'll lose the Challenge in this mission.

CHALLENGE: BRING BACK THE TARGET ALIVE
ESCORTING CAPTIVES

When you have Homer Dalton's arm behind his back (kidnapped) notice the faster you walk him in the desired direction the larger the detection radius becomes. If an enemy or police officer enters that radius you are discovered and your victim escapes. The slower you walk the smaller the detection radius becomes. So walk slowly when you need to walk past a nearby enemy. Look to the short alleyway behind Thug **(C)** to find a nearby carriage, marked as a yellow blip on the Mini-Map. If you aren't looking there you'll see a beam of light emanating from the middle of the carriage.

RESTRAIN

As you walk with a captive they tend to want to leave your company for some reason. You'll feel them struggling (vibration in the controller) and you receive a Restrain prompt on screen. Press the Restrain button Ⓧ / Ⓐ to wrestle with the victim a bit and get some more compliant walking out of him.

SHOVE IN

When you reach the carriage **(3)**, direct the kidnapped victim toward the passenger door. You'll receive a Shove In prompt. Press ⓞ / Ⓑ to shove Dalton into the carriage. Again, make sure you do not hold this button too long or you knock the victim out. The victim takes a position on the floor staying low and inconspicuous, but sometimes yells as you drive away anyway.

Now get in the driver's seat and follow the marked route to Sergeant Abberline. Drive swiftly but avoid running into unnecessary trouble such as ramming into Blighters driving carriages.

Typically you won't have trouble when you escape with a kidnapped target but there are times that you are chased and have to ram the enemy off the road and then become anonymous before Abberline will accept the kidnapped victim. Follow the road marker to Abberline's carriage parked under the railroad tracks. This location is marked with the green blip **(4)** on the map as well as on screen.

Park the carriage in Abberline's detection radius and stay put or jump out. Abberline will take it from there. If the mission doesn't end then you need to become anonymous. If this is the case, you can actually leave the kidnapped victim and carriage in Abberline's detection radius and go climb some buildings or blend into a crowd to become anonymous. The second you do, the mission is completed. Notice the red fog has been lifted from the borough around the Bounty Hunt location.

ASSOCIATES AND LOYALTY

Find Associates like Abberline throughout London and aid them to increase their loyalty to the Rooks. Loyalty unlocks unique and valuable rewards. In other words, do missions for the Associates and they gift you weapons.

CHILD LIBERATION: TO CATCH AN URCHIN

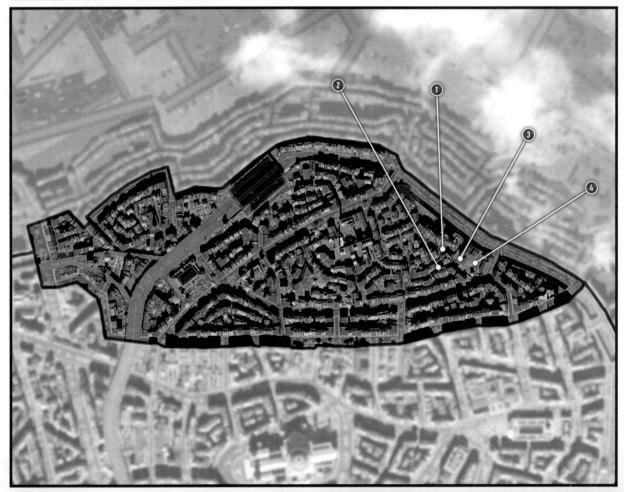

MISSION OVERVIEW

Memory Type: Child Liberation	**REWARDS**	**LESSONS**
Suggested Level: 2	**£:** 132 + 75 (Full Synch Bonus)	❖ Helix Glitch ❖ Explosive Crates
	XP: 200 + 100 (Full Synch Bonus)	❖ Alarm Bells ❖ Crowd Events
ASSASSIN Jacob or Evie Frye	**CHALLENGES** Do not trigger the alarm	

CURRENT OBJECTIVE: TACKLE THE THIEF
LOCATION: STREETS OF WHITECHAPEL

Approach the "O" hexagon icon **(1)** on the map in Whitechapel to meet up with whichever twin you are not controlling at the moment. Once there, Jacob and Evie walk together through the busy street when out of nowhere the same little pickpocket you chased earlier bumps into Jacob again.

Jacob recognizes the boy and chases after the little thief. Follow the yellow blip displayed on the Mini-Map and on screen. He only runs a very short distance until you stumble onto a group of children playing in an alley corner.

The children stop playing to stare down the intruders. Clara O'Dea steps forward, stands up straight, and dons a serious expression. She seems more mature than most children her age. Clara greets the two of you and welcomes you to Babylon Alley. She explains that it is here that the children make it their business to know the streets and provide kids the opportunity to control their own destinies.

Evie expresses that Henry Green thought they might be able to help one another. Clara agrees but adds that, in exchange for her services, they save the children suffering in several local factories—factories powered almost entirely by child labor. In return, Clara offers intelligence.

CURRENT OBJECTIVE: REACH THE WAREHOUSE

When control returns to you **(2)** head for the factory **(3)** only a few buildings away from where you start. Activate Eagle Vision as you approach so you don't get noticed before you even enter the attack planning stage. Hop up to the top of the brick wall and then clamber to the rooftop of the factory.

CURRENT OBJECTIVE: KILL THE FOREMAN
CURRENT OBJECTIVE: FREE ALL 9 CHILDREN
CHALLENGE: DO NOT TRIGGER THE ALARM
LOCATION: RADCLYFFE MILL

Once on the rooftop, look all around using Eagle Vision to mark all the enemies and children inside the building. The child laborers appear as green blips on the Mini-Map and green silhouettes on screen. The Foreman appears as a red blip and a yellow silhouette. You also see white glowing objects: Chests and an alarm bell. If the enemy spots you and you cannot stop them in time, they ring the alarm bell; you can continue the mission but you will not pass the Challenge.

Many of these factories have the same layout. Once you find good attack strategies for the floor plan, then these practiced stratagems work well for all similar factories. For the current factory layout, we suggest attacking from the flat rooftop at the southeast corner **(4)**, where you can find an open third-story doorway.

Enter the open doorway while sneaking and dispatch the first Blighter Thug just inside with his back to you. He is the only enemy on this level so you don't need to worry about being spotted. Make sure to raid the Chest next to the doorway inside.

HELIX GLITCH

Hop up on the railing in the middle of the third level floor and jump through the floating Helix Glitch over the multi-story gap. Land on the railing on the other side of the hole. There are 11 more Helix Glitches to find in Whitechapel. See the Collectibles section for information on acquiring all the Helix Glitches in London.

From the opposite side of the room near the stairs that lead down, turn and face the middle opening lined with the railing. Remain here until you see the Foreman walk into view and then stop. Throw a knife at his head when he stands still.

Get off the rail and take the stairs down to the next lower level. Take cover behind the tall stack of crates at the bottom of the stairs. Whistle to attract the attention of the female Watcher patrolling the far side of the room. Perform a Cover Assassination on her. That's two floors cleared.

Now jump up on the side of the rail closest to the stairs that lead down. Look down the opening to the ground level. You can spot the alarm bell and a guard that stands to the left of it. If he rings that bell you lose the Challenge. Throw a knife at his head if you have one, otherwise leave him for later.

Remain near the crates and pivot to face the open doorway on the floor below in the northeast corner. You can spot a patrolling Thug. Throw a knife at his head. Follow the walkway around to reach the Child Laborers in the corner where the Watcher began her patrol.

Scope out this floor and the one below with Eagle Vision. Locate the next children in the opposite corner on the lower floor. There is a Thug standing with his back to them. Walk up to the closest ledge on your side and, if you are out of knives, toss a Smoke Bomb on his floor. Quickly jump over and assassinate him (this keeps your cover as long as you find cover when the fog clears).

THE ESSENTIALS
WALKTHROUGH
SIDE QUESTS
COLLECTIBLES
APPENDICES
INDEX

SEQUENCE ONE
SEQUENCE TWO
SEQUENCE THREE
SEQUENCE FOUR
SEQUENCE FIVE
SEQUENCE SIX
SEQUENCE SEVEN
SEQUENCE EIGHT
SEQUENCE NINE

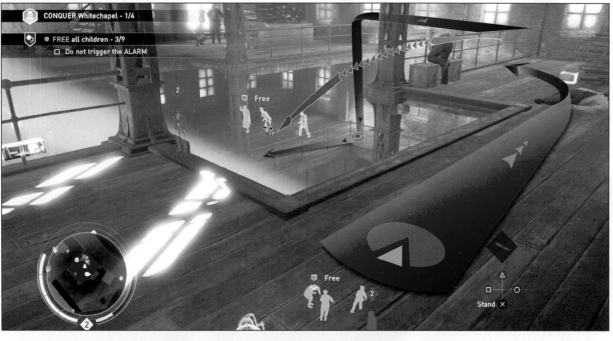

EXPLOSIVE CRATES

Find the explosive crates near the ledge. Pick one up and you can aim and throw these just like a Smoke Bomb, only these explode and kill nearby enemies. You can also shoot the explosive with a firearm to ignite it, or ignite crates without picking them up. Simply hold the ◎ / Ⓑ button longer. But make sure to quickly get away from it. You only have a few seconds before it explodes.

CUT OFF THAT ALARM!

If you can get to an Alarm Bell unnoticed, then approach it, press the ◎ / Ⓑ to cut the rope and sabotage it.

After clearing all but the ground level, you can dispatch any survivors below with a pistol. Get into position along the opening in the floors from the second level and pull the trigger. One shot to the head for each. They won't be able to ring that bell now. Free the remaining children to complete the memory.

AVAILABLE MEMORIES

The next two available memories are the Gang Stronghold (Spitalfields) and Templar Hunt: Harold Drake. Choose whichever you wish to play next.

CROWD EVENTS

While running around in the streets, you soon come across Crowd Events. These are often such things as Thugs harassing a civilian (scare them off or kill them) or thieves running off with peoples' money (tackle them). These are Perks. Help out the civilians when you can to unlock features. For more information, see the Perks section of this guide.

GANG STRONGHOLD: SPITALFIELDS

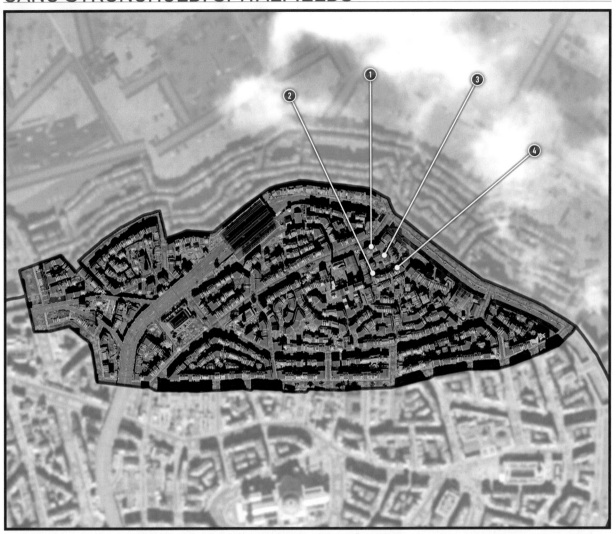

MISSION OVERVIEW

Memory Type: Gang Stronghold **Suggested Level:** 2	**ASSASSIN** Jacob or Evie Frye	**REWARDS** **£:** 264 + 75 (Full Synch Bonus)	**LESSONS** ❖ Freeing Captives
	CHALLENGES Free and protect captured Clinkers	**XP:** 250 + 100 (Full Synch Bonus) **Kukri:** Ruby Kukri	

OBJECTIVE: ELIMINATE ALL BLIGHTERS

CHALLENGE: FREE AND PROTECT CAPTURED CLINKERS

LOCATION: NORTHEAST WHITECHAPEL

Spitalfields acts as the headquarters to Kaylock's division of London's most notorious gang, the Blighters. You must defeat all 10 enemies in the area and free the two captured Clinkers (green-dressed gang members that become Rooks).

Approach the castle icon on the map to locate the Gang Stronghold. When you get close to the location, activate Eagle Vision and begin scanning the area **(1)** to find the nearest threat and then to start marking enemies. The first thing you see when approaching this area from the northwest corner is two policeman and some kind of enemy in-between the buildings.

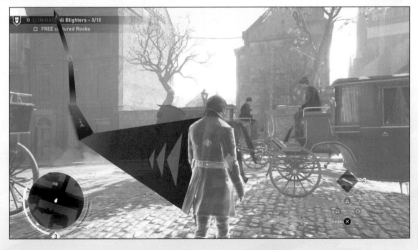

ARCHETYPES

Below is an explanation of every enemy archetype. You encounter most of these on every high-level intrusion.

Soldiers (Thug): The most common enemy. Uses melee and simple attack combos.

Brutes: Powerful, but predictable, melee fighters.

Watchers: Whistle when they see you, use ranged weapons, strong and try to remain at shooting distance from you.

Enforcers: Throw Flash Bombs to blind you and position themselves strategically, depending on the enemy group size.

Lookouts: Quick, but have low combat skills. When alerted, they run to fetch reinforcements.

THE ESSENTIALS
WALKTHROUGH
SIDE QUESTS
COLLECTIBLES
REFERENCE & ANALYSIS
INDEX

SEQUENCE ONE
SEQUENCE TWO
SEQUENCE THREE
SEQUENCE FOUR
SEQUENCE FIVE
SEQUENCE SIX
SEQUENCE SEVEN
SEQUENCE EIGHT
SEQUENCE NINE

Continue with Eagle Vision activated and scale the building on the corner to get to the rooftop to assess the situation. Locate your first Lookout **(A)**. While marked and in Eagle Vision, when prompted press the **R3** button to identify the Lookout. You need to stay anonymous until this guy is dead or he calls in reinforcements.

Also notice the captured Clinker is appearing as a white highlight right now. He's on his knees and guarded by a Soldier **(B)** in a central courtyard.

Jump onto the next rooftop (nearest the captive Clinker) and head to the right (west) side of the rooftop and Air Assassinate the Watcher **(C)** below when she walks under the eaves of your rooftop.

Once on the ground, either climb back up to the top of the roof again or cover around the corner of the same house and look in the alley behind the house. Another Soldier **(D)** can be spotted. He has a short patrol pattern back there. Cover Assassinate him, attracting him using a whistle or get back on the roof and Air Assassinate him from above.

If you dispatch this Soldier **(D)** too close to the opening to the east then you spot a Soldier **(E)** near a haystack. He sees the dead body and investigates if this is done in his view. Either take cover behind the last corner and whistle for him or climb to the rooftop and Air Assassinate him **(E)** while he stands over the body **(D)**. If he did not see the body, then enter the haystack from behind and take him out from inside the hay.

Notice the Watcher **(F)** through the building near the haystack. This Watcher is actually patrolling a balcony between buildings. There's no connection through the open building so get to the rooftops and Air Assassinate her when she stops at the end of the short balcony.

59

FREEING THE FIRST CAPTIVE CLINKER

Return to the original rooftop near Watcher **(C)** and Soldier **(D)**. Now head to the edge of the rooftop facing the courtyard with the captive Rook **(3)**. Perform an Air Assassination on the Watcher **(B)** from the edge of the rooftop. Afterward, face the Rook in green clothes on his knees and press ◎ / Ⓑ to free him. You do not need to recruit him—getting him involved could blow your cover.

Head into the building to the west of the freed Rook **(3)**. Stop at the left side of the stairs leading to the second level and then whistle for the Watcher **(G)** up there. When she descends the stairs and enters your kill zone, Cover Assassinate her.

Exit the way you entered and get to the rooftop. Walk to the far end to spot the Soldier **(H)** and the Watcher **(A)** on the ground below.

ASSASSINATING THE WATCHER

You can drop down on the rope between buildings and get a Double Kill Air Assassination from when the Watcher **(A)** approaches the Soldier **(H)**. You could also wait until the Watcher is in the nearby alleyway and Air Assassinate them separately. You just can't let that Watcher call for reinforcements.

That leaves two enemies to kill to reach the goal. These two **(I & J)** stand next to each other to the west. They are watching over the last captured Rook **(4)**. Run to the rooftop and then to the other side.

You achieve a Double Kill lock-on on the two Soldiers below. Take them both out from the edge of your rooftop and then free the last captive Clinker kneeling behind them. That's how you complete a Gang Stronghold. The newly recruited Rooks get together and burn the Blighter's flag at their headquarters. Gang Strongholds are Associate

Activities and help for those from here on out can be found in the section titled Associate and Income Activities.

REX KAYLOCK STRIKES

After completing the Gang Stronghold challenge, Rex Kaylock appears with a small force of his Blighter gang (four Soldiers). He talks some smack then takes off using a Rope Launcher and leaves his Soldiers to do the fighting for him. Quickly Recruit some Rooks by walking up to them and pressing the **R1** button. In this situation they fight with you if you recruit them or not; they won't just stand there and get pummeled. Help or follow Kaylock to the rooftop.

THE 19TH CENTURY
WALKTHROUGH
SIDE QUESTS
COLLECTIBLES
TROPHIES AND AWARDS
INDEX
SECRETS

SEQUENCE ONE
SEQUENCE TWO
SEQUENCE THREE
SEQUENCE FOUR
MULTI OBJECTIVE
SEQUENCE SIX
SEQUENCE SEVEN
SEQUENCE EIGHT
SEQUENCE NINE

TEMPLAR HUNT: HAROLD DRAKE

MISSION OVERVIEW

Memory Type: Templar Hunt	ASSASSIN	CHALLENGES	REWARDS	LESSONS
Suggested Level: 2	Jacob or Evie Frye	Kill target with a crate of dynamite	**£:** 132 + 75 (Full Synch Bonus) **XP:** 200 + 100 (Full Synch Bonus)	❖ Dynamite Crate Assassination

OBJECTIVE: LOCATE HAROLD DRAKE

LOCATION: SOUTHWEST WHITECHAPEL MARKET

Take a carriage ride or run on rooftops to the Gang War **(1)** icon on the west side of Whitechapel. What you find is a large covered marketplace with a good amount of security around the target. Activate Eagle Vision as you approach and it does not take long until the yellow blip appears, marking your target: Harold Drake.

A Templar Hunt's objective is to kill the target and escape, so with these challenges we find the best way to do the least amount of killing, hit the target, and then jet away. This is going to be much quicker than previous strategies.

OBJECTIVE: KILL HAROLD DRAKE

Get to the northwest corner of the market's rooftop. Locate the target. Find the balcony below the roofline of the main building. Jump down to this balcony (there are balconies on both sides of the building so make sure you are on the one closest to Harold Drake **(A)**.

Remain near the corner of the balcony and the wall you just leaped off of and then pivot to the left and look through the concrete rails. These are openings into the building. And there is a clear view to the crate of dynamite at Harold Drake's feet. Shoot the crate with one bullet and then take off running toward the nearest exit from Blighter Territory, which is the red zone on the Mini-Map.

Run back up the side of the building and return the way you came, toward the tracks. At the end of the rooftop is a long rope that connects to the bridge. Run along this and then directly across the tracks to get out of the zone, become anonymous, and complete the Challenge.

GANG WAR

After beating the four Associate Activities in each borough (Templar Hunt, Bounty Hunt, Child Liberation, and Gang Stronghold) the Gang War in that borough unlocks. In this case it's the crowned-brass-knuckle icon back in the southeast where the Gang Stronghold was located.

GANG WAR AVAILABLE

GANG WAR: REXFORD KAYLOCK

MISSION OVERVIEW

Memory Type: Gang War Suggested Level: 2	ASSASSIN Jacob or Evie Frye	CHALLENGES None	REWARDS £: 164 XP: 200 Cane-Sword: Adept Cane-Sword	LESSONS ❖ Fighting a Protector

OBJECTIVE:
CONFRONT REXFORD KAYLOCK

LOCATION: NORTHEAST WHITECHAPEL STRONGHOLD

Collect items and open Chests that stand between the Templar Hunt location and the Gang War Stronghold. When you arrive **(1)** you find Henry Green waiting for you. He says all that stands between you and Whitechapel is the villain controlling the borough. He hands the twins Ivory Kukri and tells you to gather your allies.

LOCATION: WHITECHAPEL TRAIN STATION

You exit a carriage after a mediator settles Kaylock's terms. You find your stop is at the Whitechapel Train Station. This is a war over Kaylock's train hideout. Next thing you know you and seven Rooks line up and face down seven Blighters in formation across the yard **(2)**. The best way to get this party started is by lobbing a smoke bomb right between warring gangs.

OBJECTIVE: ELIMINATE 10 BLIGHTERS

Run into the cloud and start performing Attack Combos on the nearest enemies. If one blocks, move to the next closest target. You won't encounter many blocks in a cloud of smoke; most everyone you attack dies at the end of one good combo.

Lay down a second smoke bomb as the first cloud dissipates. This allows you to finish off the remaining Blighters without so much as a bruise.

OBJECTIVE: KILL REXFORD KAYLOCK

LOCATION: MOVING TRAIN

After you defeat the tenth Blighter, you see Kaylock atop his train hideout as it begins to move away from the station.

Run after it, leaping to the passenger platform in the train station **(3)**. Match the train's speed and immediately latch onto the side of the train and scramble up to the top.

You must confront the Soldiers before you can get to Kaylock who's a few cars ahead. Attack one enemy at a time. They are weak and go off the edge of the train after a simple combo.

There's a Brute to fight just before you get to Kaylock. As soon as the Brute jumps onto your car, lay into him with a combo. He breaks the first attack so be prepared to Counter, then Stun, and then Attack once again to finish him off. Now for Kaylock's turn.

KAYLOCK BATTLE

Start by accepting Kaylock's invitation for first blood; he left himself wide open for attack. Lay into him with a complete combo and then Counter his retaliation attack. Next, break his defense that follows. Then lay into another long combo attack. By the end of this second combo, you end up kicking Kaylock off the train for a quick victory. Nice Job.

The Rooks now run Whitechapel and you have gained a Train Hideout. The broken grappling hook gun is recovered after the battle. Rooks rejoice in the streets, celebrating their victory. This Sequence ends and Sequence 4 continues on the train with some new faces.

TRAIN HIDEOUT

GANG UPGRADES

THE ESSENTIALS
WALKTHROUGH
SIDE QUESTS
COLLECTIBLES
REFERENCE & ANALYSIS
INDEX

SEQUENCE ONE
SEQUENCE TWO
SEQUENCE THREE
SEQUENCE FOUR
SEQUENCE FIVE
SEQUENCE SIX
SEQUENCE SEVEN
SEQUENCE EIGHT
SEQUENCE NINE

CURRENT OBJECTIVE: SPEAK WITH AGNES

You find yourself in the train hideout that you just won in your first Gang War. A lady sits on a bench in the train's study. This is Agnes Macbean. She is a Scottish woman who quickly becomes your best friend after you hire her to be your assistant.

Henry enters the car with an armful of books. He's pleased with your new hideout. Jacob is overly focused on the broken grappling hook. Henry offers help getting it fixed.

Speak to your assistant, Agnes on the train. She appears as a green blip on the Mini-Map. She asks you to check the safe in the same car. The safe is highlighted with glowing white light.

CURRENT OBJECTIVE: COLLECT INCOME FROM THE SAFE

Walk up to the safe and Collect Income using the ◎ / Ⓑ button. The safe accumulates money and sometimes crafting items over time. Check it regularly. You are warned with a screen prompt when the safe is full.

CURRENT OBJECTIVE: INTERACT WITH THE GANG UPGRADES MAP

Either switch cars and interact with the Gang Upgrades map on the wall of another car or just enter the Main Menu and access Gang Upgrades.

TASK: BUY THE MEDICINE MARKET UPGRADE
Purchase the only upgrade available: Medicine Market. This allows you to buy medicine in shops. Use medicine during combat to quickly recover health. Press D-pad Up to administer medicine. Check the Twins' Skills. You should have purchased all of the second tier Skills by now and both be Level 3.

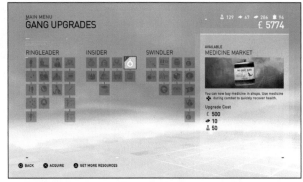

POLICE BRIBES

While you are in the Gang Upgrades, we suggest purchasing Police Bribes if you can afford it now. This forces the Police to turn a blind eye to some of your illegal actions in London.

FREEDOM OF THE PRESS

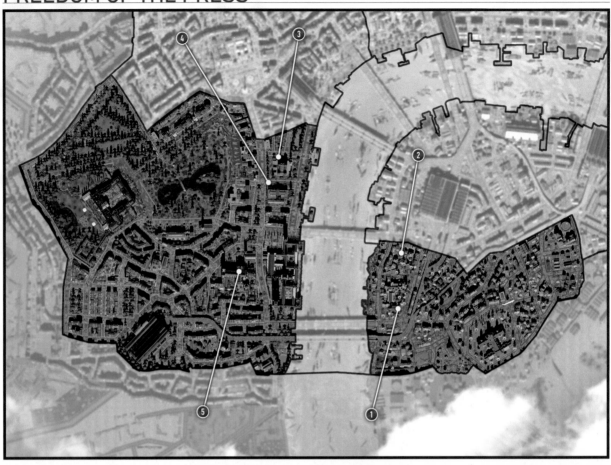

MISSION OVERVIEW

Memory Type: Templar Conspiracy	**CHALLENGES**	**REWARDS**	**LESSONS**
Suggested Level: 2	Air Assassinate a guard from a zipline	**£:** 1500 + 75 (Full Synch Bonus)	❖ Zipline Assassination
	Install the fuses without going below	**XP:** 4000 + 100 (Full Synch Bonus)	
ASSASSIN	30m in altitude	**Outfit:** Outdoorsman Outfit	
Evie Frye			

LOCATION: TRAIN HIDEOUT

Take the train or a carriage to reach Lambeth, the borough in the southeast corner of London. Before starting this memory we suggest Synchronizing with the nearby Viewpoint **(1)**. Take a Leap of Faith into the hay below and head to Alexander Graham Bell's house **(2)** following the "B" icon on the map to begin the *Freedom Of The Press* memory.

LOCATION: LAMBETH; ALEXANDER GRAHAM BELL'S HOUSE

Henry, Jacob, and Evie find Alexander Graham Bell in his study intercepting Starrick's Morris Code transmissions, but he's frustrated, as all they are talking about is Soothing Syrup. Introductions are made and Jacob asks if he can fix the broken Rope Gun. As he fixes the contraption, he mentions that it would be great for fitting his fuses on top of Big Ben. Alex has been installing a new telegraph line for the Free Press Association to combat Starrick's Telegraph Company.

Evie volunteers to help Bell with his fuses—thus claiming the first use out of the Rope Launcher, now "gunless" and attached to the Assassin's gauntlet.

OBJECTIVE: DRIVE BELL'S CARRIAGE

Alex waits in an open carriage outside his house. Follow the green blip on the Mini-Map to find Alex. Enter the carriage and drive Alex to Big Ben

OBJECTIVE: REACH BIG BEN

While following the route marker to Big Ben, Alex talks about his inventions and during the ride, Evie helps him name one of his biggest. Stop in the marker near Big Ben **(3)** in Westminster.

ROPE LAUNCHER

A **L1** prompt now appears on climbable objects and structures indicating various rope attach points. Many large objects offer various attach points and you can find them by moving your camera view and/or your position. Press **L1** to attach the rope to an object. From a ledge, press **L1** to zipline across large gaps (press forward on the Left Control Stick to move). Control your speed using the Left Control Stick and use the **R2** to perform an Air Assassination when over an enemy.

Tutorial
Rope Launcher

CURRENT OBJECTIVE: INSTALL 3 FUSES

CHALLENGE: INSTALL THE FUSES WITHOUT GOING BELOW 30M IN ALTITUDE

Exit the carriage and hop over the metal gate around Big Ben. Look up from the base of the large clock tower and move around until you acquire the **L1** Rope Launcher prompt. This gets you all the way up to the bell tower platform above the clock. Climb up the windows to reach the bell where the first fuse box is found.

THE ESSENTIALS
WALKTHROUGH
SIDE QUESTS
COLLECTIBLES
REFERENCE & ANALYSIS
INDEX

SEQUENCE ONE
SEQUENCE TWO
SEQUENCE THREE
SEQUENCE FOUR
SEQUENCE FIVE
SEQUENCE SIX
SEQUENCE SEVEN
SEQUENCE EIGHT
SEQUENCE NINE

Walk up to the fuse box and press ◎ / Ⓑ to install the first fuse. Climb to the top of Big Ben to synchronize with the area and then climb back down to the bell tower platform. Climb onto the outer ledge facing south. To complete the altitude Challenge you need to attach the Rope Launcher to very high targets. Acquire the Rope Launch lock-on to one of the top tiers above the green blip on the next tower **(4)**.

Once on the tower, drop down to the lower platform where you can interact with the second fuse box. Walk to the southern edge of the tower platform and try to acquire a Rope Launcher lock-on to the top of the tall spire. Between the second fuse tower and this spire is a hidden Helix Glitch, which you zipline through if you acquire the high lock-on.

From the tip of the spire, acquire a Rope Launch lock-on on the next building to the south. Get a high lock-on and sail to this building now.

Now walk out onto the south edge of this tower and stand on a small gable. Notice you cannot acquire a Rope Launcher lock-on while hanging onto an object; you must have your feet on a platform or the ground to use the Rope Launcher. Now acquire a high lock-on on the tip of the tower below you to the south.

From the tip of the south tower, drop down to a lower ledge and then try to acquire a Rope Launcher lock-on to the large corner tower **(5)** where the final fuse box is located. You'll be able to achieve a lock-on just below the highest big windows. Rope Launch and then climb the tower to reach the rooftop platform.

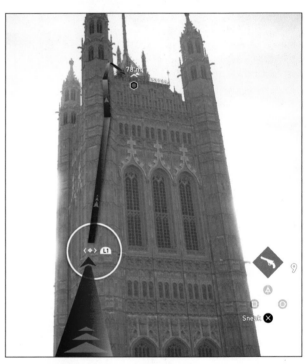

Install the final fuse using the route suggested and you pass the 30m altitude Challenge. Return the way you came to find Bell. You no longer have to remain above 30 meters.

WALKTHROUGH

THE ESSENTIAL

SIDE QUESTS

SKILLS & GEAR

REFERENCE & WALK...

MORE

SEQUENCE ONE

SEQUENCE TWO

SEQUENCE THREE

SEQUENCE FOUR

SEQUENCE FIVE

SEQUENCE SIX

SEQUENCE SEVEN

SEQUENCE EIGHT

SEQUENCE NINE

CURRENT OBJECTIVE: SPEAK TO BELL

Zipline back to Big Ben and then head to the street level to speak to Alexander Graham Bell who is waiting for you in the carriage **(3)**. He thanks you for your help now that he can continue the new line. Before he leaves he demonstrates a smoke bomb upgrade he's been toying with. This will give you a smoke bomb radius upgrade but first you need some metal components for crafting the bomb upgrade.

CURRENT OBJECTIVE: LOOT 200 METAL COMPONENTS

CHALLENGE: AIR ASSASSINATE A GUARD FROM A ZIPLINE

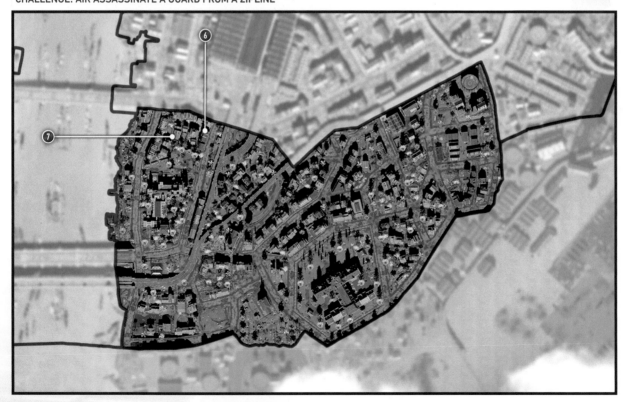

Take a nearby carriage to the general location of the two metal component crate locations **(6 & 7)**. This is near Bell's home. At location **(6)**, get to the rooftops and mark enemies with Eagle Vision.

You spot four enemies and a Chest below. A Watcher **(A)** stands in one place with a keen eye on the crate. A Soldier **(B)** and a Brute **(C)** have a long patrol route moving from the Chest to the next house to the west. The fourth enemy is a Soldier **(D)** who also stands still while watching the Chest just below the rooftop in the picture.

When the Patrolling Soldier **(B)** and Brute **(C)** stop near the Chest along their patrol route, throw knives at their heads until both are dead. If someone spots you, run back along the rooftop over the peak to get out of their view and then return when anonymous again.

Use the Rope Launcher to attach to one of the wooden ledges above the Chest jutting from the side of the building. Zipline across the rope and stop when above the Soldier **(D)** who is now inspecting the bodies of the fallen near the Chest. Don't worry about the Watcher **(A)** seeing you when you drop down and Air Assassinate the Soldier; the Watcher is slow and tries to shoot you. By that time you have rushed and killed her with a couple good combo attacks. You could also use a Smoke Bomb before you attack to make an easier battle. Loot the bodies and then open the Chest to collect 100 metal components.

Turn west and head for the yellow blip marking the location of the second Chest **(7)**. If you need knives, buy them from the street vendor (Shop) near the second Chest location. Activate Eagle Vision as you approach the Chest area. Find the Watcher **(E)** on the rooftop, identified by the crosshairs icon over this enemy's head. Climb up to the rooftop on the opposite end of the Watcher and then come up behind her in her patrol route and quietly assassinate her.

Get to the end of the rooftop facing the courtyard with the enemy Blighters and the Chest. There's one more Watcher **(H)**, two Soldiers **(F)** and **(I)** and a Brute **(G)**. The Brute and the Watcher move on a short patrol back and forth across the brick path below. Walk up to the edge of the rooftop and throw knives at the heads of the Brute **(G)** and the Soldier **(I)** when they stand near each other.

Now use the Rope Launcher to anchor to the rooftop above the Chest across the courtyard. Perform an Air Assassination on the Soldier **(F)** and then run up behind the Watcher **(H)** while her back is turned. Open the Chest.

THE ESSENTIALS
WALKTHROUGH
SIDE QUESTS
COLLECTIBLES
REFERENCE & ANALYSIS
INDEX

SEQUENCE ONE
SEQUENCE TWO
SEQUENCE THREE
SEQUENCE FOUR
SEQUENCE FIVE
SEQUENCE SIX
SEQUENCE SEVEN
SEQUENCE EIGHT
SEQUENCE NINE

CRAFTING

Crafting becomes available after collecting 200 metal components for Alexander Graham Bell. You craft new gear and tool upgrades in the inventory and crafting menus. Find unique resources and crafting plans in hidden Chests. Income activities (especially robbing cargo from trains, carts, and boats) provide large amounts of crafting resources.

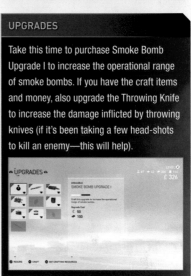

UPGRADES

Take this time to purchase Smoke Bomb Upgrade I to increase the operational range of smoke bombs. If you have the craft items and money, also upgrade the Throwing Knife to increase the damage inflicted by throwing knives (if it's been taking a few head-shots to kill an enemy—this will help).

CURRENT OBJECTIVE: REACH BELL'S WORKSHOP

Bell's workshop **(2)** is about 40 meters away from the second Chest. Follow the green blip on screen or on the Mini-Map to return there now. Inside, Evie finds Bell showing Jacob the first messages received via the mended lines you helped him repair. He reminds the two of you to call on him whenever you need him again as the twins hustle out of the workshop.

A QUICK AND RELIABLE REMEDY

LOCATION: TRAIN HIDEOUT

You begin this Sequence in the train hideout. Evie is already back to work and Henry is beside her. Their attention is brought to some commotion from the other side of the train car. A mysterious fellow in black is talking to Agnes. Ned Wynert introduces himself and offers assistance on anything relating to the finest transit system in the world.

Evie and Jacob discuss plans, and they both have their own agendas. Evie wants to continue to hunt for Pieces of Eden while Jacob wants more assassination targets. Henry appeases both of them by reassuring Evie that finding the precursor artifact will give them insight into what the Templars intend and then directs Jacob's attention to the Assassination Wall....

THE ESSENTIALS

WALKTHROUGH

THE CLIENT

COLLECTIBLES

REFERENCE & ANALYSIS

TOUR

SEQUENCE ONE

SEQUENCE TWO

SEQUENCE THREE

SEQUENCE FOUR

SEQUENCE FIVE

SEQUENCE SIX

SEQUENCE SEVEN

SEQUENCE EIGHT

SEQUENCE NINE

ASSASSINATION WALL

The Assassination Wall is now available in the train hideout. Use the Assassination Wall to track the next Templar target. Press the ◎ / Ⓑ button while Sequence 4 is selected on the wall to enter a window where you can confirm your choice to begin Sequence 4: A Quick and Reliable Remedy. Press ◎ / Ⓑ to confirm. Four icons appear on the London map: A Spoonful of Syrup, another Alexander Graham Bell mission (Cable News), a mission accessed from the train hideout (The Crate Escape), and a Ned Wynert Associate Activity at the Southwark train station.

STORY WALKTHROUGH ONLY

This walkthrough only covers those memories that advance the story. All other activities can be found in Associate Activities or London Stories. The mission order is arranged by the suggested level recommendation, from low to high.

THE CRATE ESCAPE

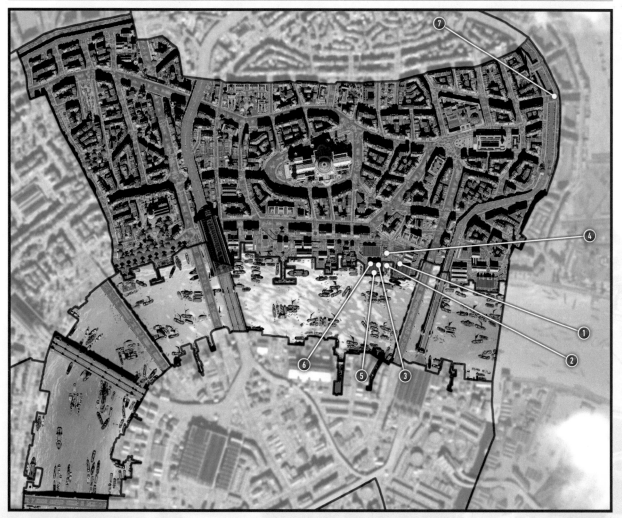

MISSION OVERVIEW

Memory Type: Templar Conspiracy
Suggested Level: 3

ASSASSIN	CHALLENGES
Evie Frye	None

REWARDS
£: 500
XP: 500
Cape: Hunter's Mantle

LESSONS
❖ Shooting from Carriage

73

UPGRADE YOUR FIREARM

We strongly recommend that you upgrade your firearm before starting this mission to give Evie an extra edge in the coming battles.

LOCATION: TRAIN HIDEOUT

The Crate Escape memory icon is located on the desk in the last car on the Train Hideout.

In the opening cinematic, Jacob teases Evie about her artifact hunt commenting that she sounds just like their late father. She responds, "If only." She thinks more highly of her father's quest than Jacob. Evie points to a picture of Lucy Thorne on the desk. Thorne is expecting a shipment tonight. Evie is certain that she is receiving the Piece of Eden Sir David Brewster mentioned.

CURRENT OBJECTIVE: SEARCH THE TEMPLAR CHEST

LOCATION: CITY OF LONDON, NEAR THE THAMES WATERFRONT

The mission begins on location (you do not need to travel to the site). Evie stands on the rooftop **(1)** of a large warehouse overlooking Lucy Thorne as she receives the shipment personally. She follows a Brute inside to fill out some of Starrick's paperwork. The Chest, believed to contain a Piece of Eden, is inside the cart under heavy guard, but out of Lucy's sight.

HELIX GLITCH

From the edge of the original rooftop, shoot the Rope Launcher at the top of the boat mast **(2)**. There's a Helix Glitch floating just in front of the boat. So once you are on the mast, shoot a rope to the rooftop of the building across the street and just zipline far enough to acquire the Helix Glitch and then return to the top of the boat mast.

Before you move from your perch, scan the area all around you with Eagle Vision active. You mark a Soldier directly below you and a couple of cops patrolling the street below (they stay some distance away from the cart). Further ahead near the cart with the Chest you can mark four enemies until you can get closer. Jacob mentioned taking out the snipers, but don't count on him. You won't be able to spot those until you get nearer to the cart.

Eliminate everyone to get to the Chest safely. Begin by dropping down to a small wooden plank sticking out of the west side of the building you are on.

Perform an Air Assassination on the Soldier below. Rope Launch back to the same rooftop corner afterward.

Zipline west to the edge **(3)** of the next rooftop, above the hanging barrels. When the Brute **(C)** walks away from the Soldier **(A)** that stands her ground at the boat yard entrance, drop down from the edge of the rooftop and Air Assassinate the Soldier. Duck back around the corner of the building to avoid the Brute's sight. Rope Launch back to the rooftop of the same building.

From the northeast edge of the rooftop, search for all the enemies using Eagle Vision. You find two Watchers **(B & E)** on high balconies to the west. Eliminate these two first from the group around the cart. Look across the street to see two Soldiers **(H & I)** at the mouth of an alley and a Brute **(G)** leaning on a door in the alley (behind some crates). These are optional kill opportunities. You just need to inspect the crate on the cart anonymously, so just clearing the snipers and the few around the cart is the bare minimum you have to do.

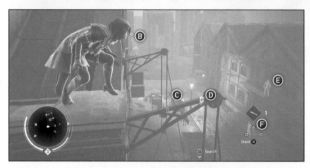

Optionally, you could take out the enemies, two Soldiers **(H & I)** around a barrel fire in an enclosed yard, on the outer region next. Zipline from your rooftop corner to the corner of the building **(4)** near them so that the line passes right over them. Zip down the line and Air Assassinate one Soldier and then quickly quiet the second before your cover is blown.

By now the Brute **(C)** has returned on his patrol route to the area of the hanging barrels where you dispatched the second Soldier **(A)**. Get back to the rooftop **(4)** and zipline to the corner of the previous building **(3)** and perform an Air Assassination on the Brute while he remains around the boatyard entrance. Eliminate him and duck around the corner inside the boatyard once more.

OUT OF THROWING KNIVES?

Search on the map for the nearby street vendor (Shop). There is one just behind the building **(3)**. Purchase knives from this vendor **(5)** if you are low. You may need them for the next few assassinations before you get to the Chest in the cart.

Get back up onto the rooftop and walk to the northern edge **(6)** so that you are standing over the Watcher **(B)** on the balcony below. Throw a knife at the head of the Watcher **(E)** on the balcony across the street. Now look down and position yourself for an Air Assassination on the Watcher **(B)** below you.

From the Watcher's **(B)** ledge below you can study the movements of the Soldiers across the street. One Soldier **(D)** remains standing around a barrel fire facing away from the patrolling Soldier **(F)**. Zipline above this patrolling Soldier and Air Assassinate him **(F)**. From his porch, hide behind the stair rail and whistle for the Soldier **(D)** warming near the barrel fire. Cover Assassinate this thug when she climbs the stairs.

You could enter the cart now and avoid killing the three remaining Blighters **(G, H & I)** in the alley. If you want to kill them all, get on the rooftop above them and perform a double Air Assassination on the two Soldiers standing at the alley's entrance **(H & I)**. The Brute **(G)** does not see you as he leans against a wall behind a stack of crates. Take him out from behind the crates by whistling and Cover Assassinating him.

Now enter the cart in the middle of the street and open the crate. Inside the crate is a book. In a cinematic, Lucy Thorne and the Brute come running out of the building witnessing Evie and Jacob stealing her cargo. Jacob takes the reins and Evie remains in the back of the cart to protect the Chest.

WALKTHROUGH

THE ESSENTIALS
SIDE QUESTS
COLLECTIBLES
REFERENCE & ANALYSIS
INDEX

SEQUENCE ONE
SEQUENCE TWO
SEQUENCE THREE
SEQUENCE FOUR
SEQUENCE FIVE
SEQUENCE SIX
SEQUENCE SEVEN
SEQUENCE EIGHT
SEQUENCE NINE

CURRENT OBJECTIVE: DEFEND THE TEMPLAR CHEST

Your job is to shoot all pursuing Blighters and dispatch any that make it into the cart with you, while being chased by multiple horse-and-carriage pursuers.

Watch the Stealth Ring around your body. It points to the direction of the nearest enemy. As soon as you see an enemy, begin shooting. The trick is to use the Quickshot since aiming the gun and hitting your target is nearly impossible while being thrown around in the back of the speeding carriage. So press the ▲ / Ⓨ button to shoot. You don't even have to aim. Jacob helps shoot enemies occasionally and he also throws you more ammo when you run out of bullets, so get trigger-happy. Keep an eye out for the prompt above your head to duck bullets. When it appears, mash the button to avoid being shot.

CURRENT OBJECTIVE: JUMP ON THE TRAIN

The battle continues at a very intense pace all the way up to the point when Jacob reaches the destination (7). Regardless of how many enemies are still living or attacking, stop everything and jump out of the cart and hop up onto the bridge railing to enter the Reach marker. You have 10 seconds to get from the cart to the marker or you are desynchronized. Evie and Jacob leap to the roof of their train and wave goodbye to the Blighters.

A SPOONFUL OF SYRUP

MISSION OVERVIEW

Memory Type: Templar Conspiracy **Suggested Level:** 3	**ASSASSIN** Jacob Frye	**CHALLENGES** Steal the plan undetected	**REWARDS** **£:** 410 + 75 (Full Synch Bonus) **XP:** 250 + 100 (Full Synch Bonus) **Brass Knuckles:** Crow's Strength

CURRENT OBJECTIVE: TACKLE THE MERCHANT

LOCATION: LAMBETH

CONQUEST ACTIVITIES

Now is a good time to start Conquest Activities to not only clear the Blighters from the territory, but also to earn more Skill Points, Money, and Crafting Items. At this point it is nice to have a larger Knife Pouch and in Gang Upgrades, Rook Training I and Allies in Arms. These come in very handy when you are trying to complete the Challenges the first time you play a Memory.

PURCHASE SMOKE BOMBS

To complete the Challenge in this Memory it is extremely helpful to have a couple of Smoke Bombs in your pouch before you start. Find a nearby street vendor and purchase Smoke Bombs before starting this Memory.

Approach the snake oil merchant on the dock near The Thames in Lambeth by following the man-in-a-hat hexagonal icon **(1)**. This is a mission for Jacob only. He investigates a new drug that is ravaging London and must uncover its creator. At the docks, Jacob intervenes in an altercation between the wife of a syrup customer—who is now zombified—and the merchant that sold him the poison. The merchant pulls a knife and Jacob slaps it away with lightning reflexes. The merchant, quickly realizing he is out of his league takes off running.

The merchant heads north along the shoreline. He's represented as a yellow dot on the Mini-Map. Follow him closely as he sprints past a dock on the right and veers right into a tunnel **(2)** at the far end of the dock.

A short distance into the tunnel you find the merchant behind a locked gate of impassible bars **(3)**. The tunnel forks to the left here. Run through the open tunnel on the left to try to catch up to the merchant at another junction.

In the left passageway you leap over a junction to the continuing tunnel. Jump over short bars, slide under the next grate, and in the clearing you must leap and grasp onto a suspended chain, and then swing to two beams and another chain to reach the continuing tunnel. Only press the **R2** button while doing this so you don't climb to the top of the chains. If you were quick enough, you see the snake oil salesman run through this tunnel just ahead of you. Follow him to the left.

Climb the stairs at the end of the tunnel to reach the park outside **(4)**. The merchant should be just a little ways ahead of you. Make a beeline for him and tackle him **(5)** using the ◎ / Ⓑ button.

After the merchant gets to his feet, he spills the beans on the whereabouts of his supplier. He says they make a run each day between the gasometers and

the asylum. Bring up the large London Map and set a marker on the green "Locate" blip **(7)** to the northeast.

CURRENT OBJECTIVE: LOCATE THE DISTRIBUTOR

CHALLENGE: STEAL THE PLAN UNDETECTED

Hijack a carriage from the street **(6)** just outside the park and drive north and take a right at the intersection. Pass under two bridges and slow down just beyond the second bridge **(7)** and activate Eagle Vision while looking to the houses on the right side of the street. You spot the leader (glowing yellow) amongst a gang of Blighters. Roll up close enough that he begins to move to his carriage in the street but not close enough to be spotted.

CURRENT OBJECTIVE: STEAL DISTRIBUTOR'S INFORMATION

CHALLENGE: STEAL THE PLAN UNDETECTED

This particular task does not follow the rules of what it normally means to be "detected" in the rest of the game. So to complete this particular Challenge you cannot kill the distributor; you must sneak up behind him and hold the ◎ / Ⓑ while the Steal meter fills to take the info without him knowing. Anonymously killing him without anyone noticing does not count. There is not enough time to do this at the first location **(8)**, so you must wait for him to enter his carriage and head to the second location **(9)**.

WALKTHROUGH

SEQUENCE ONE
SEQUENCE TWO
SEQUENCE THREE
SEQUENCE FOUR
SEQUENCE FIVE
SEQUENCE SIX
SEQUENCE SEVEN
SEQUENCE EIGHT
SEQUENCE NINE

Follow him to the second location and get out of your carriage at a safe distance. The distributor exits the carriage and walks through the alleyway between buildings. A guard at the front entrance follows him. They both stop at the far end of the alley (10) for a few moments.

Instead of trying to kill all the Blighters in the alley and sneaking up behind him when he's alone, it's easier to just sabotage his ride. As soon as he enters the alley, kill his driver (9). Try using a hallucinogenic dart or a throwing knife. Drive his carriage southwest to the previous corner or just far enough that he can't find it. Exit the carriage and go to a hiding spot near the alley and wait for the distributor to return.

When the distributor returns he finds a dead body (his driver) instead of his carriage. When he inspects the body, throw a smoke bomb at him, rush to him, stay behind him, and then press and hold the Steal button until the gauge fills. Once you have the information the Challenge is complete and you can actually kill the distributor now or just leave.

CURRENT OBJECTIVE: LOCATE DISTRIBUTION BOSS

You must locate the distribution boss after stealing the information. A green blip appears on the map at a very large fight club (12) to the north. Take a carriage ride to the southwest corner of this building to find a couple of Rooks (11) under the rail bridge. Recruit them. If they have the Allies in Arms upgrade, then they are going to be extremely useful, as they will out-arm any of the Blighters inside the fight club.

Activate Eagle Vision and approach the west entrance to the fight club. Hide behind the crates and pallets (13) to the left of the entrance. Look at the Brute on patrol around this entryway and acquire the "Fight" icon that tracks around the Brute. Press **R1** to command the Rooks to fight the Brute. If they are holding guns (Allies in Arms upgrade) then they immediately open fire on the enemy. Since you physically did not attack the enemy, you remain anonymous.

CURRENT OBJECTIVE: KIDNAP DISTRIBUTION BOSS
CHALLENGE: REMAIN UNDETECTED

Continue scanning the inside of the building with Eagle Vision to spot the distribution boss. Now the objective changes. You must kidnap the boss and the Challenge is to do this undetected. There are several ways to go about this. You could infiltrate the building from high entryways and use the rafters like a spider attacking prey one at a time (Air Assassinate and then quickly Rope Launch back to the high rafters to find the next target). Or you could push through the crowd in the upright position to use the crowd as cover and then come up behind the target to kidnap him. This is the most risky strategy; as you may be spotted and fail the Challenge.

We cover the quickest route to results. Continuing with the Rook strategy, head to the north side of the fight club exterior. Hug the north wall, look into the building, and mark enemies. Send your Rooks after the guard near the lower north entrance **(14)**.

Next, face the wall to see the second level inside. There's a Brute on a catwalk who's one of the more difficult enemies to take out unnoticed from inside. Sic your Rooks on this enemy. This often scares the distribution boss into a full run. Rope Launch to the rooftop of the fight club so you can keep an eye on him.

Watch as the boss runs out of the south exit **(15)**. Use the Rope Launcher to quickly catch up to him. Reduce your distance to him so you do not fail the memory.

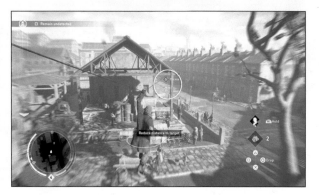

The distribution boss does not get too far down the road heading east until he decides he feels safer near the fight club and begins to double back. Leap off a rooftop and kidnap him on the sidewalk **(16)**. Cops often patrol this route so walk him into a nearby alley or gated area to interrogate him.

CURRENT OBJECTIVE:
INTERROGATE DISTRIBUTION BOSS

Once in a secure area, release your hold on the boss and allow him time to spill the beans. This completes the Memory.

UNNATURAL SELECTION

MISSION OVERVIEW

Memory Type: Templar Conspiracy	ASSASSIN	CHALLENGES	REWARDS	LESSONS
Suggested Level: 3	Jacob Frye	Kill everyone in the building with the gas.	£: 410 + 75 (Full Synch Bonus)	❖ Knock Out
			XP: 250 + 100 (Full Synch Bonus)	
			Belt: Dark Leather Belt	

CURRENT OBJECTIVE: OPEN THE DISTILLERY'S DOOR

LOCATION: STARRICK BREWING COMPANY, SOUTHWARK

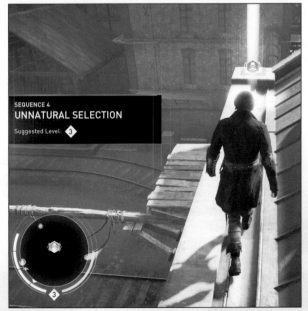

Get to the corner **(1)** of the rooftop across the street from the Starrick Brewing Company in Southwark to begin this mission. From your perch you spot an old gentleman peeking into the cloudy windows of Starrick's large brick building. He then tries to enter through the large front doors but finds them locked. Before the patrolling Blighters spot him he ducks into a booth beside the doorway.

Activate Eagle Vision from the ledge where you start the memory. Notice the mixture of many level three and level four Blighters below. A group of three Blighters patrol starting from the far right and they pass through the courtyard in front of the main doors to the brewery. One Soldier stands guard at the door facing the street. There are hanging barrels above his head. There's also another group of two Blighters that patrol from the left and approach the guard at the door.

As they are getting into position underneath the barrels, move left along the ledge until you reach a column that holds some hanging barrels on your building. This allows you to get in knife-throwing range of the barrels above the door across the street. Once all three Blighters stand beneath the barrels, let a knife fly and take out all three enemies at once.

You do not need to be stealthy if you do not feel like it. You could rush down there and defeat everyone, but this is a much safer approach if you think you may be outnumbered. Next, drop the barrels attached to your building on the Soldier that has a short patrol route underneath them.

You can continue to use the two haystacks below to single out and Cover Assassinate every one of the patrolling guards below or you could just take out the remaining Soldier in the entrance courtyard when no one else is looking. When the patrolling Soldiers are far off, shoot the rope at the brewery so that you pass over the top of the remaining Soldier in the courtyard. Air Assassinate him and then run for the door and press ◎ / ⑬ to break the lock. In a cinematic, the old gentleman hiding in the small booth joins you; and it's a good thing he does…

CURRENT OBJECTIVE: FOLLOW YOUR ALLY

LOCATION: STARRICK BREWING COMPANY INTERIOR

Once inside, activate Eagle Vision as you follow the old man through the ground floor of the brewery. Notice and mark the many different enemies on the floors above. Follow the man closely. He knows when to move to avoid the Blighter's wandering eyes above.

He stops at a table with plans on it for a bit. Be patient; he'll move again. He discovered Devil's Snare (Opium) is being added into the syrup. That doesn't sound healthy. He finally stops at a large valve on the side of the central boiler. He turns the wheel and sabotages the machine. Poisonous gas issues from the valve area. The man tells you to find a way out quickly and runs for cover in the next room.

CURRENT OBJECTIVE: SABOTAGE THE PRESSURE VALVES

CHALLENGE: KILL EVERYONE IN THE BUILDING WITH THE GAS

KNOCK OUT

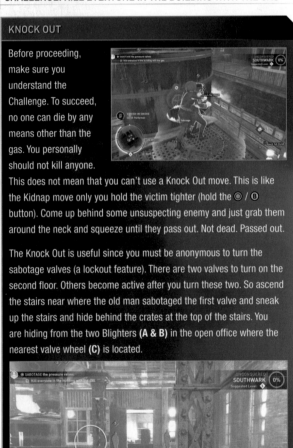

Before proceeding, make sure you understand the Challenge. To succeed, no one can die by any means other than the gas. You personally should not kill anyone.

This does not mean that you can't use a Knock Out move. This is like the Kidnap move only you hold the victim tighter (hold the ◎ / ⑧ button). Come up behind some unsuspecting enemy and just grab them around the neck and squeeze until they pass out. Not dead. Passed out.

The Knock Out is useful since you must be anonymous to turn the sabotage valves (a lockout feature). There are two valves to turn on the second floor. Others become active after you turn these two. So ascend the stairs near where the old man sabotaged the first valve and sneak up the stairs and hide behind the crates at the top of the stairs. You are hiding from the two Blighters **(A & B)** in the open office where the nearest valve wheel **(C)** is located.

SABOTAGE 1

Save this wheel for second. Instead of heading into that room now, sneak into the open stairwell/room on the left. Stay to the left as much as possible so you can sneak up behind the Soldier on the right side of the room with her side to you. Sidle up and knock her out with the chokehold.

Notice the stairs in this room (there's also a booth if you need to hide at some point). Exit the room through the next door (beside the booth) and sneak along the walkway and veer right around a stack of barrels to find the first sabotage valve wheel **(D)**. Turn it and then continue further along the walkway.

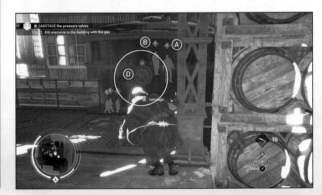

SABOTAGE 2

Notice the large pipe hanging just below the ledge. Hop over the rail and follow the pipe to the opposite walkway. Clamber over the rail and take cover beside the office doorway. Now you are on the opposite side of the Soldier's **(A)** and Brute's **(B)** office where valve **(C)** is located.

Study the Brute's and Soldier's patrol pattern around the room. Move into the room sticking to the left side of the desk in the middle as the Brute walks around the far side of the desk to join the Soldier **(A)** near the sabotage wheel.

Stay on the opposite side of the desk from the Brute **(B)**. When he moves back to the left side of the room where you are, move around the far end of the desk and Knock Out the Soldier **(A)** at the wheel with his back to you. Turn the sabotage wheel and then sneak up behind the Brute and knock him out.

SABOTAGE 3

After turning the first two wheels, two more activate two floors above you. Mark the enemies above while in Eagle Vision if you have not already. The next two sabotage valves

are directly above the previous ones on the same central machine. Reenter the stairwell/room where you killed the Soldier near the booth. Climb the stairs to the next floor. Use Eagle Vision to find the Chest around the other side of the wall at the top of the stairs. Enter this balcony and take the items from the Chest.

Double back through the stairwell/room and exit the other door to find another staircase. Climb these stairs to the fourth floor where the sabotage valves are located. You can cover behind some crates at the top of the stairs and study enemy patrol routes while in Eagle Vision. When the coast is clear just zip into the little cubby on the left and turn the next valve **(E)**.

SABOTAGE 4

If you go further past the third valve you find that side of the floor is heavily patrolled. Turn back towards the stairs but instead of going down, jump up on the inside rail facing the barrel stack on the rooftop of the office across the gap. Jump to the edge of that rooftop when the coast is clear and then get to the top of the barrel shelf.

From the top of the barrel shelf, turn toward the center of the room and jump to the top of the boiler and then walk over above the last Sabotage valve **(F)** and drop down to the platform. Turn the wheel quickly before you are spotted.

THE ESSENTIALS
WALKTHROUGH
SIDE QUESTS
COLLECTIBLES
TROPHIES & AWARDS
MAPS

SEQUENCE ONE
SEQUENCE TWO
SEQUENCE THREE
SEQUENCE FOUR
SEQUENCE FIVE
SEQUENCE SIX
SEQUENCE SEVEN
SEQUENCE EIGHT
SEQUENCE NINE

CURRENT OBJECTIVE: SABOTAGE THE MACHINE

With all the pressure valves closed off you must now throw the main switch, which is on the top floor. The quickest way up there without being seen is to head back the way you came to the top of the barrel shelf and then use the stairs behind the shelf to reach the top floor.

Sneak up slowly and spot the two patrolling Soldiers **(G & H)**. They enter the open office at the end of the walkway and pass through before continuing through the room and passing by the floor lever **(J)**. Follow behind them and enter the office when the Soldier inside **(I)** has his back to you. Knock him out and then exit the office through the next door. Pull the lever **(J)** to sabotage the machine.

CURRENT OBJECTIVE: ESCAPE THE AREA

When you pull the lever you must then escape the room or be trapped inside with all the Blighters you're about to gas. Run up the ramp just beyond the lever and start leaping from pipe to pipe to rafter to escape window. There are multiple escape windows. Just get to the closest one you can as quickly as you can. Jump to the window and a cinematic leads you out of the mission. Congrats on the passing that Challenge!

In the ending cinematic you learn you have been assisting none other that Charles Darwin, the father of evolutionary theory. He shares with you his discovery while inside the brewery. He says every batch of syrup has been sent to Lambeth Asylum. He runs off and adds that he'll meet you at the asylum to continue the investigation.

ON THE ORIGIN OF SYRUP

MISSION OVERVIEW

Memory Type: Templar Conspiracy **Suggested Level:** 3	**ASSASSIN** Jacob Frye	**REWARDS** **£:** 410 **XP:** 250 **Schematic:** Reinforced Gauntlet Schematic	**LESSONS** ❖ Go To Carriage Roof

LOCATION: LAMBETH ASYLUM

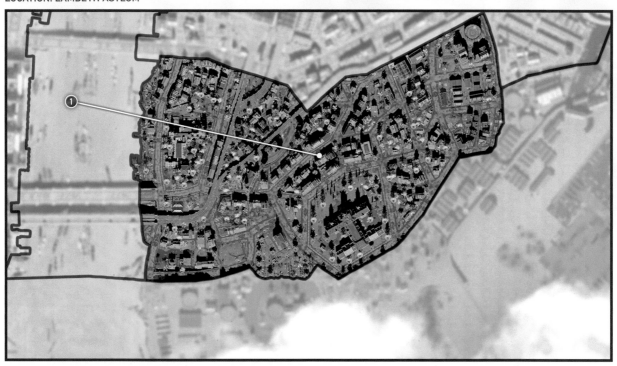

Do any necessary side missions or upgrading to get those crafting items and gang upgrades you have your eye on. Check to make sure you've spent all your Skill Points for more Skills. Now follow the Assassin icon in Lambeth to find Charles Darwin **(1)** arguing with Richard Owen in front of the asylum.

They loudly debate evolutionary theory—a favorite of Darwin's conversation starters. Darwin insists that Richard confess to having slammed his theory in an "anonymous" article. Richard escapes in a carriage and Darwin entices you to chase him down, feeding your flame by telling you that Richard Owen works at the asylum and he'd know something about the syrup. Off you go!

CURRENT OBJECTIVE: HIJACK MR. OWEN'S CARRIAGE

You find yourself on the sidewalk facing Richard Owen's fleeing carriage. Run forward and hijack the first cart you reach and whip the horse to move. Avoid hitting cops or Blighters' carriages. You don't need the added distraction right now.

Drive up beside Richard's carriage using boost to get you there quickly. Press the **L1** Go To Roof button when prompted. After you get to the rooftop and face Richard, press forward and **R1** to leap to his rooftop. Once there, face the driver and press ◎ / Ⓑ to hijack the carriage.

CURRENT OBJECTIVE: DAMAGE THE CARRIAGE TO SCARE OWEN

Now that the driver has been removed from the equation, you must use speed and the carriage Ram move **LS** + ◎ / Ⓧ to damage the carriage and to empty the Damage gauge at the top of the screen. Ram left and right into other carriages, explosive barrels, destructible objects, and brick walls.

CURRENT OBJECTIVE: BECOME ANONYMOUS

When 90% damage is done, Richard asks you to stop the carriage. Stop the vehicle after leaving a red zone on your Mini-Map. Become anonymous then stop. Owen confesses, "Dr. John Elliotson! He formulated the elixir! He is the man you want! Not me!"

CABLE NEWS

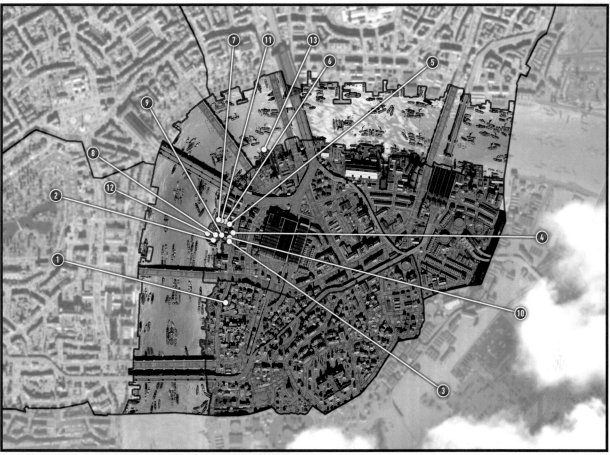

THE ESSENTIALS
WALKTHROUGH
SIDE QUESTS
COLLECTIBLES
REFERENCE & ANALYSIS
INDEX

SEQUENCE ONE
SEQUENCE TWO
SEQUENCE THREE
SEQUENCE FOUR
SEQUENCE FIVE
SEQUENCE SIX
SEQUENCE SEVEN
SEQUENCE EIGHT
SEQUENCE NINE

MISSION OVERVIEW

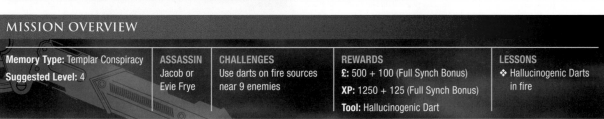

| **Memory Type:** Templar Conspiracy **Suggested Level:** 4 | ASSASSIN Jacob or Evie Frye | CHALLENGES Use darts on fire sources near 9 enemies | REWARDS **£:** 500 + 100 (Full Synch Bonus) **XP:** 1250 + 125 (Full Synch Bonus) **Tool:** Hallucinogenic Dart | LESSONS ❖ Hallucinogenic Darts in fire |

LOCATION: ALEXANDER GRAHAM BELL'S WORKSHOP, LAMBETH

Follow the B icon on the map (1) in Lambeth to talk to Alexander Graham Bell who is in his workshop working on a new tool to aid your cause. He intercepts a wire containing the recipe for a powerful hallucinogenic serum. Bell designs it into a dart mechanism that can be attached to your gauntlets. He hints that it adopts the form of a gas when introduced to heat.

CURRENT OBJECTIVE: LOCATE THE MISSING CREW

HALLUCINOGENIC DARTS

Hallucinogenic Darts can be fired at enemies to cause them to attack their allies. A person shot with the serum does not survive. They are either killed by allies or eventually die from the effects of the serum. You currently can only hold two darts at a time, but this can be increased through upgrades. More darts are usually found in Chests, looted bodies, or can be purchased from shops.

Upon exiting Bell's workshop you spot two Blighters messing with a civilian down the street near a parked carriage and an alley with a Chest. Sneak up behind them and dispatch them both to help the citizen and then loot the Chest. Take the carriage to the

green blip (2) to locate the missing crew at the docks in The Thames area.

89

When you roll up on the docks and warehouse area marked on the map you find a group of Rooks on a nearby corner **(A)**. We suggest leaving them out of this battle if you wish to complete the Challenge. Exit the carriage and dispatch the Blighter Soldier **(B)** on the sidewalk in front of the warehouse.

Rope Launch to the top of the warehouse **(3)** and walk along the rooftop using Eagle Vision to spot the green blip through the building's rooftop. The missing crew is located here and a new objective is given once you have seen them within 50 meters.

CURRENT OBJECTIVE: LOCATE THE MISSING CREW

CHALLENGE: USE DARTS ON FIRE SOURCES NEAR 9 ENEMIES

From the large warehouse rooftop, move northward following the outer edge of the Restricted Area (red area on the Mini-Map). Continue to the northwest corner **(4)** of the next rooftop and then face west down to the shelter with four patrolling Blighters. There are three level three Soldiers and a level four Brute. A single Soldier **(C)** stands next to a barrel fire on the sidewalk. Two Soldiers **(E)** patrol inside the shelter and the Brute **(D)** patrols the street area.

HALLUCINOGENIC DARTS IN FIRE

To satisfy the Challenge you are going to have to get creative because you cannot find nine enemies already standing next to fire barrels. So you must lure Blighters to the fire barrels. Select the Hallucinogenic Darts and take aim at the fire barrel. Notice how a white area of effect ring surrounds the barrel. This represents the effective range of the gas once you shoot a dart at the fire barrel. Currently only the Soldier **(C)** is in that area of effect. So go ahead and shoot the barrel to release the gas cloud that affects the Soldier **(C)**.

Stay in position and watch what transpires. The affected Soldier goes nutty and the Brute **(D)** approaches and starts attacking him. The moment the Brute enters the blast zone, hit the barrel again with another dart. You would have used the same amount of darts if you had just shot the two enemies.

In this scenario you could have just darted both Blighters and gotten the same results, but that would not count toward the Challenge. Next, the four enemies in the area fight to the death. Usually none of them survive, as the dart eventually kills the affected victim. In this location, many area Blighters come to investigate the commotion. None of them reach the range of the fire barrel so just hide on the other side of the roof until they return to their normal positions in distant areas.

You are now out of darts. You can only carry two at a time right now. So finding a nearby crate is always your next objective after firing two darts. This is part of the Challenge strategy. Return to your corner **(4)** on the rooftop and drop down to open the Chest inside the shelter the Blighter Soldiers were patrolling.

Get to the rooftop of the next warehouse to the north in the Restricted Zone and perch on the northwest corner **(5)** of this building like you did the last. Look into the nearby open shelter **(6)**. Using Eagle Vision, you can spot four level three Blighters. One Soldier **(F)** has a patrol route that puts him in range of the fire barrel sitting in the middle of the sheltered area. Have your darts ready, aim at the barrel to see the blast range and wait for the patrolling Soldier to enter it. When he does, shoot the barrel.

The Soldier goes nuts and the three Blighters nearby all descend on him at once and begin attacking him. As soon as one of the unaffected enemies enters the barrel gas radius, shoot the fire barrel with a dart again. You will probably only get two barrel kills here, but that leaves you with only five more to go. Easily finish off the lone survivor with a knife to the head.

From your rooftop corner, look to your right with Eagle Vision and you can spot a Large Chest behind a wall on the next sidewalk. Get off the roof and open that Chest to collect more darts.

Continue counter clockwise around the outer edge of the Restricted Zone by hopping back up onto the last shelter and cresting the second rooftop peak while heading west toward the edge **(7)**. You spot a crane platform where you can see two Blighters **(G & H)** already in range of a fire barrel behind the crane. Quickly shoot a dart at the barrel and strike two more off the Challenge list.

Stay on the rooftop and watch the battle that occurs between these two crazy Blighters and the two Soldiers that come running from under the shelter you are on to attack their infected allies. You most likely will not witness another Blighter entering that fire barrel's effect radius. Continue to the south edge of the shelter rooftop and use the Rope Launcher to reach the next shelter to the south. The Blighters underneath this next shelter may spot you, but you quickly become anonymous as you continue to the south edge of this rooftop **(8)**.

You should have one dart remaining. If you do not have one then you need to go raid a Chest and return to this spot **(8)** on the south edge of the shelter rooftop near the hostages. Quickly find the group south of the shelter on the dock. There are three crewmembers taken hostage and kneeling on the ground in front of three Blighters and a fire barrel. Quickly shoot a dart at the fire barrel as the Brute **(J)** and the Soldier **(I)** are standing in its area of effect.

Watch as the two infected allies attack each other and the armed Soldier **(K)**, who is not infected, begins shooting at them. Throw a knife at the survivor then get down there and free the crew **(2)**. Loot the nearby Chest and find another to the south around the barges. Use Eagle Vision to find the Chests. There are a lot of Chests in this area and you should take the time to open them all; besides needing more darts, the crafting items they contain will come in handy.

CURRENT OBJECTIVE: LOCATE THE CABLE LINES

OBJECTIVE 2: LOOT THE 3 CABLE LINES FROM CRATES

Return to the original warehouse rooftop **(2)** and get to the west edge. Look down and you can get a better view of the Blighters under the shelter **(8)** you were on top of just a few moments ago. Use the Rope Launcher to zipline to the narrow top edge of the wooden post between your warehouse and the shelter. From a perch on top of this pole you can quickly shoot the fire barrel under the shelter, infect the three Blighters, and finish the Challenge. Watch them tear each other apart.

There are three cable lines to locate. They appear as yellow blips on the world map and Mini-Map. The first two are located under the north shelter **(11)** and on the east side of the Restricted Zone, on the north side of the first warehouse **(10)**.

The third cable line crate **(12)** appears and is marked on the map after opening the other two crates. This one is located near the water on the west side of the Restricted Zone and behind the large crane. Defeat the enemies there if you have not done so already and loot the third crate.

CURRENT OBJECTIVE: REACH THE CARGO SHIP

After looting the crate, a barge is seen cruising by in The Thames and a Blighter onboard warns the others that there's trouble on the docks, meaning you. After the cinematic, run north along the dock and you quickly recognize there is a path of floating objects, old pier posts, boats, and structures that form a makeshift path for you to use to keep up with the barge. A flawless run allows you to board the barge before it reaches it's destination but there's no reward or advantage to getting on the barge before it reaches it's destination. So, just keep up with it and don't get too far behind.

You should not have to enter the water whatsoever. Start by leaping across logs and pier posts to reach the first barge where you Slide Under some crates to make it to the next barge where you can Rope Launch to the top of the mast and then zipline to the rail bridge.

You could also continue under the bridge using the continuing floating logs and such. Zipline seems faster. Cross over the bridge and do a Leap of Faith into a haystack on a barge below.

On the next barge, Rope Launch to the top of the mast and then to the next road bridge. Cross over the bridge and drop down to the small row boats. Cross the row boats to the final barge and just stay there and activate Eagle Vision.

When you arrive at the location where the Blighter barge docks **(13)**, use Eagle Vision to spot the many level three Blighters on the barge and on the dock. You also see a few Rooks nearby. Give them a little time to settle in—you'll see why. Head to the docks to your right and open the Chest. By the time you get there, a gang of Rooks attacks the barge of Blighters.

Head to the dock and help the Rooks defeat all the Blighters and then enter the green blip on the barge to complete the Reach objective.

CURRENT OBJECTIVE: LOOT THE CRATE

Open the last crate on the bow of the Blighter's barge (now orange on the Mini-Map). Open the crate to discover poison inside.

Back at Alexander Graham Bell's, the twins receive the bad news that Starrick's poison syrup has found its way onto the open market. Take this time to play some Conquest Activities to earn more skills and to be able to afford upgrades and crafts.

THE ESSENTIALS
WALKTHROUGH
SIDE QUESTS
COLLECTIBLES
ACHIEVEMENTS/TROPHIES
INFO

PLAYING IT BY EAR

MISSION OVERVIEW

Memory Type: Templar Conspiracy	**ASSASSIN**	**CHALLENGES**	**REWARDS**
Suggested Level: 4	Evie Frye	Discover all 7 of Kenway's memorabilia collection	**£:** 700 + 100 (Full Synch Bonus)
		Complete the piano puzzle without hitting a false note	**XP:** 500 + 125 (Full Synch Bonus)
			Outfit: Defender's Garb

LOCATION: TRAIN HIDEOUT

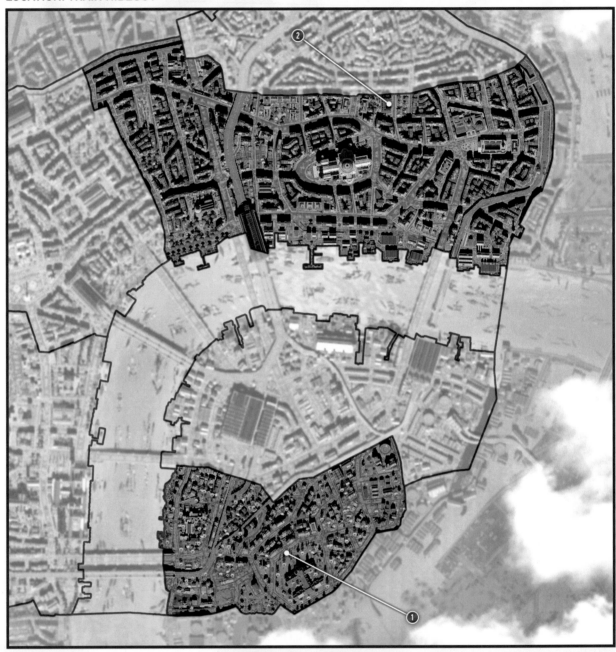

Locate the train hideout on the world map and select it. Choose to Fast Travel to the train. Once on the train you notice that Agnes has a mission for you, Stalk The Stalker. That will have to wait for now. Enter the next cabin to find Henry Green waiting to speak to Evie. Evie's search for the Piece of Eden continues as she examines the notebook recovered from Miss Thorne's chest.

CURRENT OBJECTIVE: FIND THE JACKDRAW SCULPTURE

LOCATION: CITY OF LONDON

Enter the carriage **(1)** and allow Henry to get on before you take off. Follow the route marker to the green blip **(2)** in northern London a few city blocks away. Speed and drift in every corner opportunity to execute a few more London Drifts (Perk). Walk into the green zone indicated on the Mini-Map around the large mansion **(2)**. Lucy Thorne is seen entering Kenway's mansion. Evie accepts the added challenge of entering without Lucy knowing.

CURRENT OBJECTIVE: FIND KENWAY'S SECRET

LOCATION: KENWAY'S MANOR, CITY OF LONDON

Approach the manor with Eagle Vision activated to spot and mark the level four and five enemies around and inside. You also can spot the secret inside the southeast section of the mansion. The first objective is met when you spot the yellow glowing grand piano on the first floor. This updates the objective: *Examine the room for clues.*

THE ESSENTIALS
WALKTHROUGH
SIDE QUESTS
COLLECTIBLES
REFERENCE & MAPS
INDEX

SEQUENCE ONE
SEQUENCE TWO
SEQUENCE THREE
SEQUENCE FOUR
SEQUENCE FIVE
SEQUENCE SIX
SEQUENCE SEVEN
SEQUENCE EIGHT
SEQUENCE NINE

CURRENT OBJECTIVE: EXAMINE THE ROOM FOR CLUES

CHALLENGE: DISCOVER ALL 7 OF KENWAY'S MEMORABILIA COLLECTION

COMPLETE THE CHALLENGE BEFORE ENTERING THE PIANO ROOM

When you enter the piano room the Challenge opportunity ends. You must physically unlock the door (the piano is highlighted yellow while in Eagle Vision) so you can't accidentally enter. If you haven't found all seven memorabilia before entering, you fail the Challenge.

Look at the mansion on the World Map and you discover that there are six Entry Points into the mansion, the majority of them along the northern half of the building.

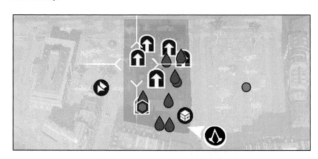

You can easily get to the rooftop of the house without entering the gated yard by walking up to the gates on the southeast side of the building (the gate is only a few feet away from the side of the mansion). Walk along the southern edge of the rooftop and Air Assassinate one of the patrolling Soldiers below and then Cover Assassinate the second.

Remain on the south side of the mansion exterior and look up to the last row of windows on the southwest corner of the building. You find an open window (Entry Point) on the second story. Enter this window to breach the interior.

As soon as you enter the window, run forward and to the right to dispatch a Soldier (if he has patrolled into the room when you enter). You have the element of surprise so you can easily make quick work of him before the Soldier in the next room becomes a witness.

After dispatching the first Soldier, sneak quickly to the left side of the open doorway at the end of the dining room table. Cover and whistle for the Soldier in the next room and Cover Assassinate him.

CLUE 1: MAP

You can find the first clue in the room adjacent to the dinning room Entry Point. Look for and examine the Map on the table near the window. There is also a booth to hide in beside the table if needed.

Exit the map room and head left in the hallway. Notice the locked door on the left at the end of the hallway (glows white while in Eagle Vision). This simply leads back into the dining room. So cover beside the open right door, whistle for the guard in the anteroom, and Cover Assassinate him when he inspects the noise.

Enter the anteroom and hide in the booth in the back right corner. Whistle for the closest Soldier in the next hallway. Cover Assassinate him when he inspects the sounds behind the curtains.

Cover beside the hallway doorway near the booth in the anteroom and whistle for the female Soldier in a room beside the hallway (you can spot her using Eagle Vision). Cover Assassinate her when she inspects the sounds. Remain in your hiding spot and whistle again for the next nearest Soldier in the same room. Show him the same fate.

CLUE 2: PLUME HAT

Before you enter the next hallway, head back to the table with the floral arrangement in the anteroom and examine the plume hat on the table beside the flowers. That's two.

CLUE 3: PAPERWEIGHT

In the next hallway, enter the first room on the left. Move to the left side of the room to the table between the windows where you can find a small paperweight. Examine the glass cube to discover the third clue. Exit this room and head back into the anteroom. Head down the stairs to the first floor.

CLUE 4: HANGING SWORDS

Examine the swords hanging on the wall under the stairs near the booth. This is your fourth clue.

CLUE 5: HANGING PISTOLS

Head to the other side of the room and find the hanging pistols on the wall under the stairs. Examine them. These are the fifth clue.

CLUE 6: MODEL SHIP (NORTH)

In the anteroom, turn and head north and then enter the north hallway. Turn right in the hallway and head to the table near the end. Examine the model ship; this is your sixth clue. There is a locked door in the north hall. Unlock this door and enter to find a Chest at the foot of a bed.

CLUE 7: MODEL SHIP (SOUTH)

In the anteroom, turn and head south and then enter the south hallway. Turn left in the hallway and head to the table at the end. Examine the model ship; this is your last clue.

PIANO ROOM PUZZLE

CHALLENGE: DISCOVER ALL 7 OF KENWAY'S MEMORABILIA COLLECTION

Once you have discovered all seven clues, head into the south hallway on the first floor, unlock the locked door and enter the piano room. You meet up with Henry inside. Search for more clues before you examine the grand piano. Using Eagle Vision, examine the writing on the wall above the fireplace. Music notes appear on a staff, they are: D, A, D, E, F, D.

Approach and examine the piano in the room. A keyboard appears. The notes appear above the keys. Controller buttons also appear on the keys. Press the corresponding controller button to play the correct key. When you hit a bad note the sound of two notes play. Do not start over if this happens; simply play the correct note next. However, you fail the Challenge if you hit an incorrect note. The correct note order is: D, A, D, E, F, D (or follow our numbered keys in the picture).

CURRENT OBJECTIVE:
EXAMINE KENWAY'S TREASURE

A large trap door in the floor opens once the melody is played correctly. Henry leads the way into the hidden cellar below the music room.

Open the Chest on the right side of the cellar and then examine the strange engraved disk on the table in the back of the room, marked with a green blip.

Evie picks up a piece of paper with some writing on it. She uses Eagle Vision to reveal the Assassins' symbol and tells Henry it's a history of the London assassins…bolt holes, vaults, and a hidden key. Just as they find what they were looking for, Lucy Thorne is heard on the floor above in the music room. She quickly notices the opening in the floor. Henry rushes to the lever in the cellar to close the floor from below.

CURRENT OBJECTIVE: OPEN THE SECRET HATCH

To escape the cellar, move to the left (east) side of the room and examine the ship wheel. A ◉ / ⊗ button prompt appears on screen. Quickly mash this button to turn the wheel, which opens a hidden passageway in the same wall.

CURRENT OBJECTIVE:
ESCAPE THE KENWAY MANSION

Follow the open tunnel to the end where you can find a ladder leading to an alley outside. You could also Rope Launch to a building above and zip out quickly. This completes the memory.

OVERDOSE

MISSION OVERVIEW

Memory Type: Templar Conspiracy **Suggested Level:** 4	**ASSASSIN** Jacob Frye	**CHALLENGES** Halt the electroconvulsive therapy session Do not fire a single bullet	**REWARDS** **£:** 1230 + 100 (Full Synch Bonus) **XP:** 1000 + 125 (Full Synch Bonus) **Firearm:** Model 1 Revolver

LOCATION: OUTSIDE LAMBETH ASYLUM, LAMBETH

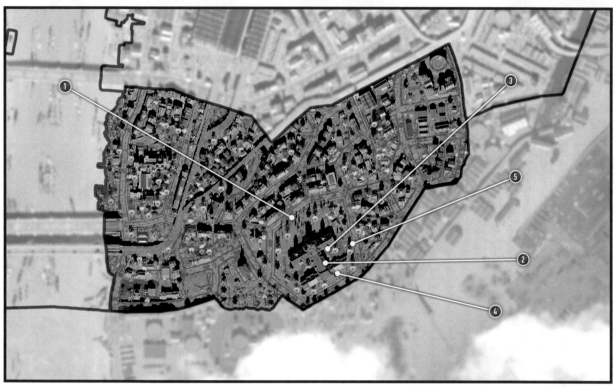

Jacob meets Charles Darwin outside of Lambeth Asylum. As the weather grows worse, Jacob relays what he has learned about John Elliotson and Starrick's Soothing Syrup. Jacob proceeds into the asylum alone to keep Darwin out of harm's way.

CHARLES DARWIN STORIES

Completing this memory opens the Charles Darwin Stories.

TIME ANOMALY

Completing this memory unlocks the Time Anomaly.

CURRENT OBJECTIVE: REACH THE VANTAGE POINT

You begin this memory facing the North side of the asylum where the main entrance is located and locked. There are six entry points into the building. You are looking for the one that gets you closest to the eagle icon (Vantage Point).

The entry point that gets you to the vantage point the quickest with the least amount of confrontation is on the east side of the building. We suggest walking close to the asylum with Eagle Vision activated so you can start marking orderlies inside along the way.

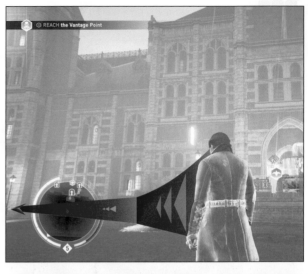

Once you have reached the east side of the building you see an entry point (open window) along the right wall above a locked door and another entry point on the back wall behind a tree on the second floor. Scale the back wall and enter the open window **(2)** behind the small tree.

Once in the building, turn left and enter the first room on the right. The Vantage Point is an observation window with a view into the mezzanine where an audience of young doctors, rich men, and nurses watch as Dr. Elliotson performs a trepanation on a live subject.

The tool in the doctor's hand jolts back, the audience gasps, and blood quirts from the patient's head. The patient shakes and goes still. The doctor explains that too much pressure can sometimes result in unexpected outcomes. He moves to a speaking tube and asks for a cadaver to be sent up.

In the cinematic you are introduced to the different gameplay elements in this memory. First you see the Young Doctor in the morgue who receives the call for a cadaver. Finding him presents you with a unique kill opportunity… not his death, but a way to uniquely kill Dr. Elliotson.

In the same cinematic you see a scene concerning the first Challenge: a couple of orderlies preparing to perform electroconvulsive therapy on a patient.

Lastly you see a nurse being fired and her key being taken away. This is your infiltration opportunity.

THE ESSENTIALS

WALKTHROUGH

YOUR OBJECTIVE

CHALLENGES

WEAPONS & SUPPLIES

SHOPS

SEQUENCE ONE

SEQUENCE TWO

SEQUENCE THREE

SEQUENCE FOUR

SEQUENCE FIVE

SEQUENCE SIX

SEQUENCE SEVEN

SEQUENCE EIGHT

SEQUENCE NINE

CURRENT OBJECTIVE: ASSASSINATE DR. ELLIOTSON
ALTERNATE OBJECTIVE: SPEAK TO THE NURSE
ALTERNATIVE OBJECTIVE: HIDE THE CORPSE

CHALLENGE 1: HALT THE ELECTROCONVULSIVE THERAPY SESSION
CHALLENGE 2: DO NOT FIRE A SINGLE BULLET

As soon as control returns to you, remain in the position near the observation window and activate Eagle Vision. Look all around the area, mostly to your right and down to the floor. From this position you can mark a lot of orderlies and the three primary players in this memory. Look at eye level to the right, near a glowing ladder, to spot the Nurse **(A)**. She has a key icon hovering around her. Press **R3** to identify her. You learn that the ability to unlock all doors in the asylum is the advantage to helping this lady. You must find her now and speak to her.

Look down at your feet and find the Young Doctor **(B)** with the purple skull icon hovering around. I know what you're thinking: where do I get one of those, right? Beats having a key floating around, any day. Press **R3** to identify the Young Doctor. You learn that you can take the place of the cadaver the doctor ordered to the medical theater. This allows you the opportunity to uniquely kill the doc. After identifying the Young Doctor and in the same general location below you can see, mark, and identify the cadaver **(C)**.

How you go about beating these Challenges is entirely up to you. There are multiple ways in and out of rooms and plenty of entry points in and out of the asylum; the strategic options are endless. We take you through the quickest route we found while slaying few souls.

SPEAK TO THE NURSE

Head back out into the previous hallway and exit the building through the same Entry Point **(2)** used to get inside.

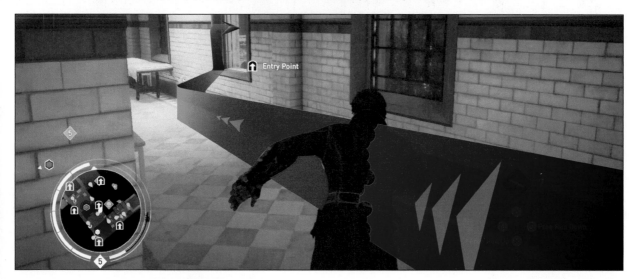

Once outside, look to your left. Find the Entry Point **(3)** window over the large locked door at the top of the stairs. Enter the asylum through that window.

Once inside you cannot come back through that route (you enter an entryway with nothing to grab onto or Rope Launch out of). Drop down from the interior balcony to the floor. Turn and face the locked wooden doors. Find the Nurse in the right corner beside the door. Also notice two exits in this entryway, also to your right. The nearest orderly **(D)** is in the next room looking down at something on a desk. Do not alert him. Identify the Nurse and talk to her.

ALTERNATE OBJECTIVE: STEAL THE MASTER KEY

The Nurse wants to speak to Mrs. Nightingale. She says one of the brutes stole her key and she can't get out. You tell her to stay there and you'll take care of it. Sneak up to the edge of the doorway near the Nurse and use Eagle Vision to spot the brute **(F)** with the key two rooms away.

Sneak up behind the orderly **(D)** in the next room leaning on the desk. Silently execute him from behind and then sneak quickly into the hallway behind you and silently take out the orderly **(E)** in the next doorway with his back to you. He sometimes turns around so catch him when he's not looking.

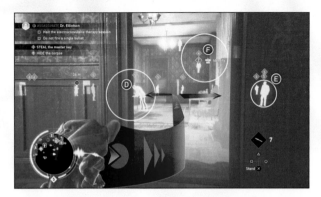

Move into the anteroom while hugging the right wall and stopping to cover behind the roll-top desk. Sit here and study the movements of the remaining orderlies in the area. The two **(G & H)** near the fireplace stay put and talk a while but one of them occasionally leaves and returns patrolling a path that comes as close as the other side of the screen behind the roll-top desk. The key bearer **(F)** patrols a little of the upstairs balcony and the goes up and down the stairs between the floors.

Lastly, an orderly **(I)** patrols the entire upper floor balcony. You start your attack when he's not looking. So whistle for the patrolling orderly **(H)** when he is near, or whistle for the key holder when he is at the bottom of the stairs, whichever comes first. If one sees you, cover assassinate the other. Usually only that one orderly comes running. This ends up being an easy and quick kill. If this happens to you, duck into the previous room to become anonymous before you proceed.

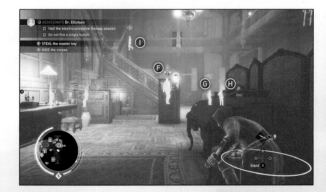

MASTER KEY ACQUIRED

CHALLENGE 1: HALT THE ELECTROCONVULSIVE
THERAPY SESSION

You gain the key the moment you kill the key bearer (if the auto loot Skill has been purchased). Head back to the Nurse in the previous room and unlock the front door so she can leave the asylum. Now you have the master key to all the locked doors and have just unlocked your quick exit for the end of the memory.

Exit the asylum again through the double doors you just opened. Move directly across the courtyard in a southerly direction. You'll see an Entry Point icon **(4)** floating through the asylum's southeast wing. Use the Rope Launcher to get to the rooftop so you can scale down the other side of the building to the open window.

You find yourself in a scrub room in the patient ward with a bloody locked door on your left and an open floor vent on the right wall. Activate Eagle Vision and watch as the nearby patrolling orderly **(J)** walks past this vent. Slide Under the vent and assassinate the orderly from behind.

Turn around to the open hallway and use Eagle Vision to spot the orderly **(K)** just outside the door to the right. He is preoccupied and his face is buried in some cabinetry. Silently take him out and be ready to run to the east end of the hallway to stop the shock therapy event happening on the lower floor.

Dart into the room with the large balcony overlooking the electroconvulsive machine and two orderlies **(L & M)** wrestling a patient down on a gurney. Run up the balcony rail and perform a Double Air Assassination on the two orderlies before they shock the guy.

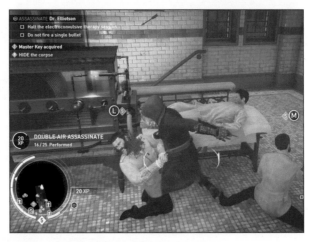

Quickly turn around in the same room and cover behind the island covered with bottles of Soothing Syrup and books.

Cover Assassinate the orderly **(N)** that patrols into the room shortly after you enter.

ALTERNATIVE OBJECTIVE: HIDE THE CORPSE

While in the shock therapy room, turn once again and face the electroconvulsive machine. There's a stairwell to the floor below behind that machine and a gurney. Head downstairs to the morgue now.

Stop and cover at the left corner on the landing midway down to the morgue level. Around the corner and down the stairs is an orderly **(O)**. Whistle at him then Cover Assassinate him when he reaches your kill zone.

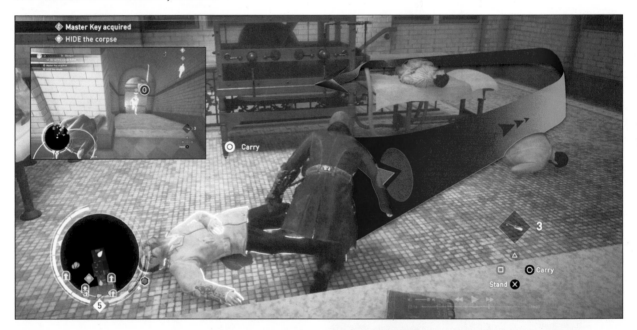

When you reach the morgue hallway, turn right and you see two exits along the left wall. All these rooms down here are interconnected so follow the patrolling orderly **(P)** around the hallway wall and silently dispatch him from behind.

Enter the back left corner room and approach the cadaver on the gurney. The Young Doctor is behind a screen and does not see you. Pick up the cadaver with ◎ / Ⓑ and carry him into the next room (follow the Hide Body icon) and throw him into the booth. Drop him inside the booth in the glowing marker to complete the task.

ALTERNATIVE OBJECTIVE: LIE ON THE STRETCHER

Return to the room where you found the cadaver and lie down on the same gurney. In a cinematic Jacob covers his body with a sheet and the Young Doctor begins pushing him into the anatomical theater.

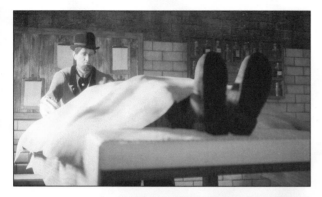

You are rolled right in front of Dr. Elliotson in the theater. While he rambles on to the audience a prompt appears on screen, ⬜ / ✗. This is the command to kill the doctor. Don't wait too much longer after he notices that you (as a cadaver) should not be wearing boots. If you execute him using the prompt then its an instant cinematic kill, otherwise you must fight him in front of a frantic audience.

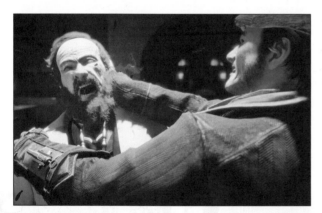

CURRENT OBJECTIVE: ESCAPE THE ASYLUM

Now with the doctor's dead body at your feet, you must escape the asylum to complete the memory. Use the master key from the Nurse to unlock the east door inside the anatomical theater. Wait for the orderly to pass by (use Eagle Vision to spot him) and then come up behind him in the open hallway and assassinate him.

Turn left in the hallway (heading north) and turn right into the next hallway. You quickly recognize where you are when you see the glowing ladder a couple of open rooms away. Head through the next room, toward the ladder, and turn right to escape the asylum through the door you opened for the Nurse.

Head east (left) out of the doorway to run to the street **(5)**, get out of the Restricted Zone, and complete the mission. You did not have to fire a shot during the entire memory so both Challenges have been met. Good work.

THE PERILS OF BUSINESS

LOCATION: CRAWFORD STARRICK'S OFFICE

Crawford Starrick sits in his luxurious office while Philip Twopenny reads the morning headline aloud, "Ellitson Expired And Simple Syrup Production Has Ceased."

Starrick calmly drinks his tea and explains that everyone in London is indebted to him for their livelihood. He thinks of Jacob Frye as an insignificant blemish who calls himself an assassin.

Starrick remains calm and pretends not to be distracted by these events when Lucy Thorne enters the office. Lucy says she is reaching the end of her research and Jacob will not be a problem much longer, and that his sister shall be gutted soon enough.

LOCATION: ASSASSIN SAFE HOUSE (PRESENT TIME)

Inside the assassins' safehouse in London, Rebecca tends to Shaun's wounds from their last encounter with the Templars. Bishop is communicating with

them through a drone sitting on a nearby table. Shaun reports that Berg's presence confirms that The Piece of Eden is in London. Bishop reports that the initiate's data synch suggests this artifact is actually the Shroud. Shaun's concerns are that he and Rebecca cannot go up against Sigma Team alone. Bishop orders them to keep a low profile while the initiate continues to synch the data.

ASSASSINATION WALL

Location: Train Hideout

Press ◎ / Ⓑ to access the Assassination Wall in the train hideout. The Sequence 5 overview appears onscreen. Your previous adventures are recapped in a window on the left. In this Sequence, Jacob looks to loosen the Master Templar's hold on London's transportation. Meanwhile, the race for the Shroud of Eden continues, and Evie hopes to gain the upper hand over her nemesis, Lucy Thorne. Press ✕ / Ⓐ to begin Sequence 5.

TAKE A STORY BREAK AND EARN STUFF

This game is best enjoyed with the many upgrades it offers. This also means out strong-arming the enemy and being fully weaponized. Do not ignore the available side activities or the upgrades that come from completing them. Your level should be no lower than the sequence number you are playing. In addition, to open Sequence 8 you need to have reached a certain notoriety, which comes with territory conquest.

THE ESSENTIALS
WALKTHROUGH
SIDE QUESTS
COLLECTIBLES
REFERENCE & ANALYSIS
INDEX

SEQUENCE ONE
SEQUENCE TWO
SEQUENCE THREE
SEQUENCE FOUR
SEQUENCE FIVE
SEQUENCE SIX
SEQUENCE SEVEN
SEQUENCE EIGHT

Four new Memories are marked on the London Map. While on the train, check the safe for cash and check to see if you can spend more Skill Points. You should at least be at level 5 by now. Take this time to check your inventory and see that you are using all the best gear available. Purchase more Gang Upgrades and do some Crafting if you can. You should have the Throwing Knife Upgrade II. This increases their attack strength and you can achieve one hit headshot kills once again. Smoke Bomb Upgrade II is recommended at this time as well.

AGNES'S (TRAIN) MEMORIES

The memories available through your train maid, Agnes, are covered in the Associate Activities section of this guide.

A ROOM WITH A VIEW

MISSION OVERVIEW

Memory Type: Templar Conspiracy	ASSASSIN	CHALLENGES	REWARDS
Suggested Level: 5	Evie Frye	Counter all of Lucy's strikes	£: 900 + 125 (Full Synch Bonus)
		Perform a Leap of Faith in a haystack while on a zipline	XP: 500 + 150 (Full Synch Bonus)
			Outfit: Lady Melyne's Gown

COME PREPARED TO FIGHT!

There is a different kind of fight at the end of this memory. Make sure that you are completely full on all items you can carry for this mission, especially medicine, knives, bullets, and smoke bombs. Check to see if you can upgrade any of these through Crafting.

LOCATION: MONUMENT, LONDON

Enter the marker on top of the store **(1)** facing the Great Fire Monument **(4)**. It appears there is a launch ceremony going on below. Jacob reconfirms that the hints Evie found in the Kenway house lead to this monument and then he continues to tease his little sister about her new friend, Henry Green. He makes a crack about not letting personal feelings compromise the mission and runs off leaving Evie to her quest. She's very pleased he left.

CURRENT OBJECTIVE: EXAMINE THE BASE OF THE MONUMENT

Walk to the edge of the rooftop where you begin the memory and face the large monument. Activate Eagle Vision. Look down and mark all the policemen (glowing blue) down below working crowd control. There's a civilian on the makeshift stage at the base of the monument introducing this Great Fire memorial. Scan a wider area and you see many green allies about. If you have been upgrading Rooks, they come in very handy for this mission.

Don't fight the police—they're really tough and lightning quick with that Billy-club-skull-cracking move they do. The strategy is to cause an incident that gives the crowd the upper hand in the fight to reach the stage for a closer look at the monument. An uncontrollable mob scenario is one that the police won't be able to control.

Rope Launch to the west wing **(2)** of the building and drop down to the top of the Tea Importer sign. Perch here and focus on the cop closest to you. This cop and a few others are keeping the crowd from rushing the stage. The item you are trying to examine is under the stage and accessible via a pathway through the front. The plan is to herd the crowd up to the front of the stage and use them for cover.

Since cops shake off low levels of hallucinogenics, select your throwing knives and throw it at the closest policeman's head **(C)**. Throw a few knives if they aren't upgraded enough (the Level 2 Knife Upgrade is recommended). When the cop goes down, the caring citizens crowd the stage, Remain in your position until the other cops **(A, B, D & E)** react to their fallen comrade.

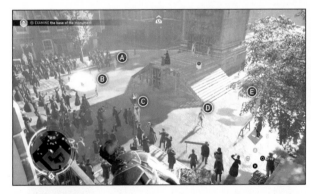

The first cop on the scene is usually **(D)**. Throw knives at the head of the first cop that inspects and then starts looking around. Given time, you will be spotted where you are perched. If you have enough knives to finish off another cop then do so, but if you don't, quickly Rope Launch to the rooftop directly above. You'll likely incur a yellow caution stealth ring. If it's red, hang it up and disappear far away. If orange, you can simply hide behind a gable or chimney until it turns white again or completely dissipates. If you receive a red stealth ring and you escape to the rooftops the cops quickly exit secret rooftop hatches and are all over you within seconds—so don't get a red stealth ring.

When all is calm and you are anonymous again, stand at the corner ledge just below the roofline. Work at acquiring a Rope Launch lock-on to the building to the north so that you can zipline directly over the policeman **(B)** or drop into the haystack near him.

After eliminating the cop **(B)** from the air, or from a whistling haystack assassination, quickly stand up straight and walk calmly through the crowd. Make a beeline for the large opening under the front side of the stage, just left of the Union Jack.

If you are not anonymous you cannot examine the emblem on the back wall under the stage. Crouch down to help lose the caution level. If it's orange, throw a smoke grenade at your feet. Once you are anonymous, examine the plaque. Evie places

the smallest of the disks she found in the Kenway mansion in the middle of the plaque. A cinematic shows another circular emblem rotate at the top of the monument. She takes the now larger disk and places it in her jacket.

CURRENT OBJECTIVE:
REACH THE TOP OF THE MONUMENT

Turn and face the crowd from under the stage. Activate Eagle Vision and relocate the remaining cops and roaming Blighters. Walk out from under the stage with the same tactic you used to get under it and then veer right, passing the haystack for the nearest building **(3)**. Quickly zipline to the rooftop.

From the corner of the building northwest of the monument **(4)**, turn and face the monument and try to get a Rope Launching lock-on as high on the monument as possible and zipline up.

Climb to the top of the monument **(4)** following the green Reach icon. Evie inserts the first disk into the ornament at the top of the spire. The emblem moves and reveals an engraving of the St. Paul's Cathedral dome. Evie leans out to face her next destination, which can be seen in the distance.

53 m

L1

CURRENT OBJECTIVE: FIND THE SECRET OF ST. PAUL'S CATHEDRAL
CHALLENGE: PERFORM A LEAP OF FAITH INTO A HAYSTACK WHILE ON A ZIPLINE

Get to the front of the monument (the northwest side) and use Eagle Vision to better identify the haystack below. Move your view directly above the haystack and get a Rope Launch lock-on on the corner of the building **(3)**. Also notice the Helix Glitch floating in the same area. Done correctly you will collect the Glitch, zipline, and drop into the haystack in one pass. Press ◎ / Ⓑ to drop from the zipline when above the haystack. You will not release from the zipline unless you are directly over the haystack. So if it's not working for you, reposition yourself on the line and try again.

Get back to the rooftops to get out of the area quickly. Move west toward the green blip **(6)** at St. Paul's Cathedral. Hijack a carriage to get there quickly. It's highly recommended that you have as much medicine and bullets as you can carry before proceeding, so stop at the street merchant shop **(5)** on the south side of the cathedral. Purchase medicine, bullets, smoke bombs, and knives in that order of importance (if you are on a limited budget).

Rope Launch to the rooftop of the cathedral by standing at the base of the wall near the merchant. Follow the green blip to a gear puzzle on the backside of a statue on the south side of the cathedral **(6)**.

CURRENT OBJECTIVE: SOLVE THE ST. PAUL'S PUZZLE

Approach the puzzle and press ◎ / Ⓑ to insert the two disks and to enter the puzzle interface.

There are six gears that can be rotated. Each gear has a number of symbols on them. These symbols have to match up to the connecting gear to solve the puzzle. We like to start with the bottom gear first. Select the different gears using **LS** and rotate the gears clockwise or counterclockwise using **R2** and **L2** / **RT** and **LT**. Use our picture to discover the correct combination. Align the correct symbols and the gears begin to move and open a window on the tall cathedral spire **(7)** in the distance.

CURRENT OBJECTIVE: REACH THE VAULT

Head to the open window at the top of the tallest cathedral tower. Once on the balcony below the open window, move to the opposite side and unlock the Chest. When you are ready, clamber up the side to enter the open window marked with the glowing destination marker.

CURRENT OBJECTIVE: EXAMINE THE ARTIFACT

Inside the small vault, examine the artifact on the dais. In a cinematic, Evie tries on the artifact and places it around her neck. A familiar voice is heard behind her, slightly startling Evie.

Lucy Thorne commands, "I'll take that." Evie responds, "You want the Shroud to cement your own power—but what if you cannot control it?" Lucy thinks it holds the power of eternal life. Evie questions Lucy's theory and the fight begins.

CURRENT OBJECTIVE: ASSASSINATE LUCY THORNE
CHALLENGE: COUNTER ALL OF LUCY'S STRIKES

The countering Challenge comes into effect during the last stage of the fight. You cannot finish this battle without blocking a good number of Lucy's attacks in the final round. We suggested you buy medicine before the battle for survival (not so much for beating the Challenge) and the bullets are used for getting you to that last stage more quickly.

LUCY THORNE FIGHT ROUND 1
Attack Lucy quickly at the beginning of the fight; don't let her strike first. If you wait too long, counter her attack by dodging it and start attacking.

Each time a combo string ends, do not attempt to throw in an extra combo. Instead, always prepare to counter Lucy's quick retaliation move. Her early attack is a single knife slash. Counter it, and then lay into her with the longest attack combo possible.

If your firearm (preferably the 38 caliber or better) is not selected, do so during your combo attack. At the end of your first combo begin shooting her using the Quickshot button ⊕ / ⓨ. Get in as many shots as you can; the amount of bullets shot entirely depends on the firearm you have. With a decent weapon you can drain half of her health, triggering the second stage of the fight.

LUCY THORNE FIGHT ROUND 2

Round 2 can last as long as you can maintain your health or until you do enough damage to Lucy at the end of her attack sequence. This stage starts with Lucy pausing to taunt you. At this point you cannot attack; you can only counter her attacks.

If you allow it to run its course then she has a ten hit combo. If you block the first five appropriately then you end her combo. This is where the Challenge comes into play. If you successfully block all of her attacks you complete the Challenge (Counter all of Lucy's strikes). On the flipside, if you fail to block one of her attacks but finish her off anyways, you cannot complete the Challenge. She continues to repeat this combo attack until you beat her, so you have multiple chances to complete the Challenge.

FINISH HER

As soon as Lucy exits her combo sequence (had you successfully blocked them all or not) pull out your pistol and Quickshoot her repeatedly until she tosses a smoke bomb and tries to take you out with a knife in a cinematic. This happens when 75% of her health is depleted. The women struggle over a knife and Lucy lunges for the artifact around Evie's neck while also aiming for the window. Lucy flies out the window while still holding onto the necklace that remains intact around Evie's neck.

Evie breaks the necklace free to keep the window shards from fatally wounding her. Lucy falls out of view. When Evie looks for her remains, Lucy and the shroud are gone. Pull the lever on the wall to open a sealed window. This is your exit out of the vault.

FRIENDLY COMPETITION

MISSION OVERVIEW

Memory Type: Templar Conspiracy **Suggested Level:** 5	**ASSASSIN** Jacob Frye	**CHALLENGES** Save Ms. Attaway's omnibus driver from his pursuer	**REWARDS** **£:** 660 + 125 (Full Synch Bonus) **XP:** 350 + 150 (Full Synch Bonus) **Kukri:** Bold Eagle Kukri

LOCATION: WEST LONDON

This is Jacob Frye's memory. He offers to help Miss Attaway destroy Starrick's omnibus company, starting with blowing up several of his omnibuses. The memory start location **(1)** is easy to spot; find Miss Pearl Attaway standing near a burning bus on the sidewalk in west London.

At first Miss Attaway thinks Jacob has come to assassinate her and he quickly explains that he'd like to partner up with her to take out the Millner Omnibus Company, which Starrick recently purchased. Pearl has been receiving threats on her life and Malcolm Millner has all but waged war on her since Starrick bought out his company. They have common enemies and similar short term goals.

113

CURRENT OBJECTIVE:
LOCATE ONE OF MILLNER'S EMPLOYEES

You begin this memory in the driver's seat of a large Attaway Transport Omnibus with Pearl in a passenger seat behind you. Follow the green blip marking one of Millner's employees driving another carriage to the south (2). Follow the route marked on the Mini-Map and on screen. Listen to the conversation between the two new acquaintances along the way.

CURRENT OBJECTIVE: KILL MILLNER'S EMPLOYEE
CHALLENGE: SAVE MS. ATTAWAY'S
OMNIBUS DRIVER FROM HIS PURSUER

When you cross over The Thames and reach the first intersection (2) in Southwark you spot a Blighter racing a carriage towards you from the right. This is your target. The location of the Attaway omnibus driver he's set on killing is not clear, nor does it matter because you can finish this objective with just a few bullets. Select your firearm and perform multiple Quickshots with ⃝ / ⓨ within close range until the Blighter in the driver's seat falls dead out of the vehicle. You can also threaten the driver or ram his vehicle until it is destroyed.

CURRENT OBJECTIVE: LOOT MILLNER'S EMPLOYEE

Jump out of the omnibus and defeat any Blighters that were in the area that respond to the violence. Loot the body of the driver to obtain the *Omnibus Route Schedule*. The schedule also has a note giving you a clue to follow next. This completes the Challenge of saving the driver from his pursuer.

CURRENT OBJECTIVE: DRIVE PEARL'S OMNIBUS
AND REACH MILLNER'S STORAGE YARD

Return to Pearl on her omnibus and drive to the storage yard following the green blip (3) on the Mini-Map.

Once you arrive, a cinematic shows Malcolm Millner screaming at his employees at the storage yard. Pearl wants you to serve him some of his own medicine. Jacob mentions he will call for the help of his gang to get this job done.

CURRENT OBJECTIVE: FIND A WAY TO
DESTROY THE OMNIBUSES

Head south from where you left Pearl and recruit the three Rooks near the sidewalk around the storage yard. Recruit them and have them hold their position. Continue to the top of the building behind them. Activate Eagle Vision and locate all the Blighters in the yard.

There are many ways to take out the seven Blighters around the yard. An easy way is to shoot a dart at the barrel fire **(A)** and infect two of the Blighters standing near it. Let them start the chaos. As Blighters are attacking Blighters, send in your gang to attack. While in Eagle Vision you can tag individual enemies that are in range for a Rook attack. Do this and sit back and watch how the fight unfolds. Perform Air Assassinations on anyone that survives. As you can see from our picture, we upgrade our Rook Soldiers to a high level early in the game to give them the advantage in battle.

CURRENT OBJECTIVE: PUSH THE CART OF EXPLOSIVES

When you scan the area using Eagle Vision, the cart of explosives **(B)** glows yellow. This changes the objective to pushing the cart. So jump down off the rooftop and get to the cart of explosives.

Mash the ⊗ / Ⓐ button continuously to push the cart forward into a parking place between two of Millner's large omnibuses. When it reaches the correct position, Jacob automatically lets go.

CURRENT OBJECTIVE: IGNITE THE CART FULL OF EXPLOSIVES

Now stay where you are, look to your left (east) and study your escape route. Ignite the fuse and run east toward the pile of wood stacked against the brick wall and then run up and over the wall and keep running east. Or, you can also escape by Rope Launching to the rail bridge above. You have 10 seconds to clear the red zone on the Mini-Map. This completes the memory.

In the ending cinematic, Jacob relishes in the glory of the Millner omnibuses going up in flames while sharing the moment with his new partner. Before Pearl leaves she mentions to Jacob that he is "hired." Jacob gives her a funny look and his words trail off as she rides away. Jacob tries to tell her that he actually doesn't work that way. But it falls on deaf ears.

BREAKING NEWS

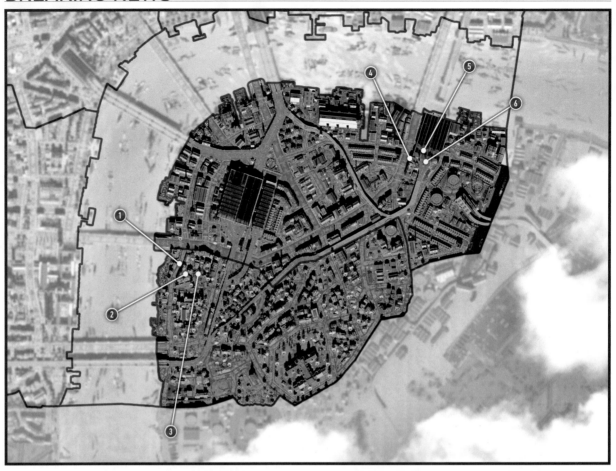

MISSION OVERVIEW

Memory Type: Templar Conspiracy	**ASSASSIN**	**CHALLENGES**	**REWARDS**
Suggested Level: 5	Jacob Frye	Electrocute thugs with voltaic bombs	**£:** 800 + 125 (Full Synch Bonus)
			XP: 1250 + 150 (Full Synch Bonus)
			Voltaic Bombs: Voltaic Bombs x 5

LOCATION: ALEXANDER GRAHAM BELL'S WORKSHOP, LAMBETH

Evie and Jacob visit Bell in his laboratory to continue their conflict with Starrick and his control of the press. Bell is experimenting with some copper and zinc used to create voltaic bombs. He tells the twins he's been working on a bomb that is meant to stun an assailant. The formula is not quite right so he needs to test them with your help. He also wants to destroy Starrick's transmitters once the bombs have been tested.

CURRENT OBJECTIVE: REACH THE ROOFTOP

In this memory you are Jacob Frye. You stand facing the back window in Bell's workshop when Bell left through the front door. Exit through the front door. Rope Launch to the top of Bell's rooftop. Turn and head north and enter the Reach maker on a wooden post connecting this building to the next.

CURRENT OBJECTIVE: WAIT FOR BELL'S SIGNAL

CHALLENGE: ELECTROCUTE THE THUGS WITH VOLTAIC BOMBS

BOMB ATTACK 1

In the opening cinematic, Bell mentioned that you guys were going to play a bit of a linguistics game with the Thugs. You need to clearly hear what Bell is saying as he speaks to a couple of Blighter Soldiers below. If you cannot hear him clearly, turn up the sound and if that doesn't do it, you can also try turning down the sound effects and music in the game so that the speech is louder.

You have four Voltaic Bombs in your inventory. Select one and aim at the Blighters below. Do not throw the bomb until you get the "fruit" reference in Bell's conversation. Bell is wearing rubber soles in his shoes, like the ones he handed Evie and you in his workshop. This means the electricity will not flow through the shoes and shock him. So technically you could include Bell in the bomb's effect radius and he won't get hurt. When Bell steps back and says, "*PEAR*-shaped," throw the bomb at the Blighters.

BOMB ATTACK 2

The first bomb is a failure. As Bell mentioned earlier, the formula has not been perfected. This first one turns out to be more of a stink bomb and the Blighters react as such. Bell and the Blighters move further into the alleyway (heading south). You notice many rooftop Chests in this area that are generated for this memory only. Each one only contains Voltaic Bombs. You can only hold four at a time so if you don't need any, don't bother opening any of these Chests. At Bell's second stop, stand on the edge of the rooftop and be ready to drop a bomb on the Blighters when you hear the words "donkey's *APPLES*." The bomb's blast has a much different and more promising look. Electricity shoots across the ground, shocking and damaging the thugs.

BOMB ATTACK 3

Bell and the two Thugs move a couple of more yards down the alleyway. Position yourself again and be ready to drop a third Voltaic Bomb on them when you hear a fruit word. This time Bell pushes one of the Thugs to count to three to see how far he makes it. Bell eventually ends a sentence with "…purple as a *PLUM*." Release the third bomb attack on the Blighters below.

CURRENT OBJECTIVE: ELIMINATE THE THUGS

After this last bomb attack you are quickly alerted to protect Bell by defeating the two thugs. Step out on the edge of a rooftop, the suspended rope, zipline, plank, or balcony and perform a Double Air Assassination on the two Soldiers.

CURRENT OBJECTIVE: FOLLOW BELL

Make sure you raid one of those many Chests around to fill your Voltaic Bomb pouch. Follow Bell as he walks from the back alley **(2)** behind the workshop to his waiting carriage **(3)** in a nearby driveway.

CURRENT OBJECTIVE: REACH THE TELEGRAPH STATION

Enter the driver's seat of Bell's carriage and drive him to the telegraph station some 700 meters away. Follow the route marker to the destination **(4)**.

CURRENT OBJECTIVE: ELIMINATE THE TWO THUGS

CHALLENGE: ELECTROCUTE THUGS WITH VOLTAIC BOMBS

LOCATION: STARRICK TELEGRAPH COMPANY, SOUTHWARK

Exit the carriage and recruit some nearby Rooks. Head to the large tunnel running through the Starrick Telegraph Company **(4)**. Get into bomb-throwing distance from the two Blighter Soldiers standing guard at the entrance to the telegraph company. Throw the Voltaic Bomb to shock the two Thugs. One bomb is not strong enough to kill, but it is all you need to complete the Challenge. So instead of wasting more bombs, rush in and finish them off with some assassin attacks.

CURRENT OBJECTIVE: DEFEND BELL

Bell catches up to you when the violence ends. He enters the room **(5)** the Thugs were guarding. Inside, Bell starts tampering with Starrick's transmitter. Stand next to him and face the door you just entered and wait for two of Starrick's Enforcers to enter to try to stop Bell. Throw a Voltaic Bomb at their feet (away from your Rooks) and order the Rooks to fight. Both Enforcers arrive one after the other. After defeating the second one, Bell finishes his work and leaves the building. He heads across the street (inside the tunnel) and enters the northern side **(6)** of the telegraph company.

Loot the bodies of the fallen to hopefully collect more Voltaic Bombs. Bell finds another transmitter to tamper with behind the lobby desk. Look for a group of three Blighters (a Soldier, a Brute, and an Enforcer) to appear from the hallway to the northeast. They are on their way to attack Bell. A Smoke Bomb and some assassin moves makes short work of this group.

Follow Bell as he runs east to the next large desk enclosure. Loot the Chest behind Bell as he tampers with the last transmitter. Watch for a group of Blighters to attack from the east. Use Voltaic Bombs, Smoke Bombs, and your Rooks to finish them off.

After defeating the third squad of Blighters you end up back in Bell's workshop in a closing cinematic. Alexander thanks the twins for helping continue the cause. Before the twins leave, Bell invites them to visit if they have time. This opens Bell's Associate Activity missions.

THE ESSENTIALS
WALKTHROUGH
SIDE QUESTS
COLLECTIBLES
REFERENCE & ANALYSIS
INDEX

SEQUENCE ONE
SEQUENCE TWO
SEQUENCE THREE
SEQUENCE FOUR
SEQUENCE FIVE
SEQUENCE SIX
SEQUENCE SEVEN
SEQUENCE EIGHT
SEQUENCE NINE

THE LADY WITH THE LAMP

MISSION OVERVIEW

Memory Type: Templar Conspiracy	**ASSASSIN**	**CHALLENGES**	**REWARDS**
Suggested Level: 5	Evie Frye	Do not kill the Peddler	£: 500 + 125 (Full Synch Bonus)
		Hijack the pharmacist's cart in less than 1 minute	XP: 300 + 150 (Full Synch Bonus)
			Schematic: Medicine Efficacy II

LOCATION: LAMBETH ASYLUM

Enter the memory marker at the door at the southeast wing of the Lambeth Asylum **(1)**. It is here that Evie finds Clara who is feeling under the weather. Clara tells Evie that the children under her care at the asylum are falling ill and that the usual tonics aren't working. Then Clara collapses in Evie's arms. Florence Nightingale hears Evie's cries for help and assists. Nightingale explains that ever since Elliotson was murdered, the district's been overrun with counterfeit tonic. Evie agrees to help get Miss Nightingale the supplies and medicine she needs to help Clara and the children there.

CURRENT OBJECTIVE: LOCATE THE PEDDLER

Time is of the essence in this mission. You must get the supplies and medicine and deliver them to Florence Nightingale in eight minutes. You start the mission outside the asylum entryway and a horse and carriage are nearby. Race this vehicle following the route marker on the Mini-Map and the green blip onscreen to the peddler's location **(2)**.

You should have no problem reaching the peddler in west Lambeth with seven minutes remaining on the clock—which appears at the top of the screen, constantly reminding you of your deadline.

Activate Eagle Vision and look south through a wooden fence to spot the yellow glowing silhouette of the peddler. The Challenge is not to kill him, but to steal the potion he holds.

CURRENT OBJECTIVE: STEAL THE PEDDLER'S POTION

CHALLENGE: DO NOT KILL THE PEDDLER

The biggest challenge at this location is the patrolling cop near the peddler. If you have purchased the Gang Upgrades "Police Bribes" then you have an easier time with this. Simply jump over the fence and sneak up behind the peddler without touching him and press and hold ◎ / Ⓑ while the steal gauge fills completely. If you do not have Police Bribes then you might want to wait until the cop's back is turned to steal from the peddler.

CURRENT OBJECTIVE: LOCATE THE PHARMACIST

Hop back over the fence, get back in your vehicle, and don't stop whipping the horse until you reach the pharmacist's location **(3)** in northeast Lambeth. You should reach the pharmacist's location marker with around five and a half minutes left on the clock.

CURRENT OBJECTIVE: DEFEND THE PHARMACIST

Activate Eagle Vision to find the pharmacist (a glowing yellow silhouette) behind the buildings near the location marker. There are three Blighters about to attack him while a fourth Blighter patrols near the sidewalk where you arrive. There's no time to think, just rush in and take them by surprise—a smoke bomb helps. Slaughter the four Blighters.

CURRENT OBJECTIVE: SPEAK TO THE PHARMACIST

If a Blighter blocks then quickly move onto the next closest Thug so they won't be tempted to attack the pharmacist. Talk to the pharmacist once you finish them off.

He thanks you and tells you the supplies he carries are for Miss Nightingale and that they are on the cart ready to go. Evie glances at the cart of supplies as a Blighter hijacks it and rides off.

CURRENT OBJECTIVE: HIJACK THE PHARMACIST'S CART

CHALLENGE: HIJACK THE PHARMACIST'S CART IN LESS THAN ONE MINUTE

You gain control of Evie while she's in a full run heading south down the street chasing after the stolen supply cart. Jump into the nearest carriage parked on the side of the road and whip the horse non-stop while following the route marker on the road. You should have about four and a half minutes left on the clock and the good news is that the stolen cart is headed toward the asylum. With speed and a little luck, you should actually reach the stolen cart just as it is passing the asylum.

Drive up alongside the stolen cart, matching its speed the best you can. Press **L1** to jump from the driver's seat to the roof. Leap over to the stolen cart using **R2 / RT** only. Face the driver and press ◎ / ⓑ to hijack the vehicle. If this only took you a minute from when you left the pharmacist then you have completed the final Challenge.

CURRENT OBJECTIVE: RETURN TO FLORENCE NIGHTINGALE

With around four minutes on the clock and the stolen supply cart in your possession (and hopefully you are near the Asylum), you must now return to Miss Nightingale. The first marker to appear is at the entrance to the Asylum grounds **(4)**. But the drive is not over; you must deliver it around back **(5)** near where the mission began.

When you enter the marker in the back and have returned in time, Nightingale assures you that now with the right medicine, Clara will survive and that she will petition for medicine regulations that should benefit all of London.

RESEARCH AND DEVELOPMENT

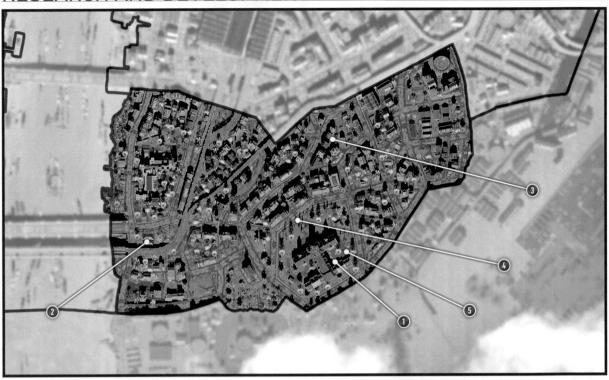

MISSION OVERVIEW

Memory Type: Templar Conspiracy	ASSASSIN	CHALLENGES	REWARDS
Suggested Level: 5	Jacob Frye	Do not kill a single policeman from the convoy	**£:** 660 + 125 (Full Synch Bonus)
		Detach the reinforcement wagons	**XP:** 350 + 150 (Full Synch Bonus)
			Cane-Sword: Sir Lemay's Cane

LOCATION: MOVING CARRIAGE, SOUTHWARK

Follow the moving assassin icon in Southwark to locate Pearl Attaway's carriage, which is in constant motion. You do not need to hijack the carriage, simply run up next to it and press ⊗ / Ⓐ to start the memory. Inside the carriage, Pearl seems distraught and tells Jacob that she told him to make an appointment but gives him the details of the next job regardless. This mission pertains to internal combustion engines (a new invention back then). She wants you to steal them before they're shipped to Millner by train.

CURRENT OBJECTIVE: LOCATE NED WYNERT

Ned Wynert has been taken into custody and is being moved from Southwark **(1)** to the City of London **(2)**, crossing the large bridge across The Thames along the way.

Get a carriage and follow the caravan consisting of three police carriages. Activate Eagle Vision to locate the one with Ned inside. Ned glows yellow. The objective is updated once you have located Ned (who is in the lead police carriage).

CURRENT OBJECTIVE: FREE NED WYNERT

CHALLENGE: DO NOT KILL A SINGLE POLICEMAN FROM THE CONVOY

To free Ned without killing any policemen all you need is a few Smoke Bombs. Stop the convoy by pulling your cart in their path. You need the cops on Ned's cart to exit and come after you. Throw a Smoke Bomb at the front of the convoy and the police and their horses become frantic. The convoy breaks up and the lead carriage with Ned in it takes off, pulling away from the convoy with or without the police onboard. The cart stops one or two city blocks away.

If the cart with Ned becomes unoccupied and the cops are not far behind, hijack it and take it someplace more secure. You cannot free Ned from the back until you have become anonymous. So if you are on foot, Rope Launch to the rooftops, duck around a corner, or enter an alley until you become anonymous. Losing the cops' attention takes more time than losing the Blighter's attention, so be patient, and keep moving and hiding. Once you are anonymous, return to the cart and free Ned.

Ned is grateful and curious why Jacob took time to save him. He kindly helps Ned out of the wagon and invites him to assist with the current job.

CURRENT OBJECTIVE: SEARCH THE CRATES

CHALLENGE: DETACH THE TWO REINFORCEMENT WAGONS

The mission picks up with Ned and Jacob on a train leaving the City of London train station **(3)**. There are three green blips onscreen and on the Mini-Map. These represent the locations of the three crates you must search. These crates travel on a train moving in the same direction as yours but on parallel tracks.

CRATE 1 AND DETACH WAGON 1

Head forward on the train, jumping up to the rooftop of the next car. From there you can see Millner's train running beside you. Run toward the front of your train so you can jump to the last car of the adjacent train. If you are quick enough from the start (when you gain control of Jacob) you can catch the second car on the adjacent train and acquire an Air Attack lock-on on the Blighter near the first crate. Air Assassinate this Soldier or jump to the car and eliminate him.

Walk up to the back edge of the second car and face the caboose. Detach the last car from the train to satisfy the first of the two Challenge duties.

Now search the crate on your car (it glows yellow when Eagle Vision is activated). Jacob finds the crate empty.

CRATE 2

Leap to the next car forward and sneak to the top of the coal barrels. Walk forward until you acquire the Double Air Assassination lock-on for both Blighters standing side-by-side with their backs to you. Air Assassinate these two and leap to the next train car.

From the top of the next train car you can see three Blighters and another crate to search that are two cars up the line. Use throwing knives from a distance to eliminate the enemy or shoot a couple with hallucinogenic darts and let them fight amongst themselves.

Jump to that car and eliminate the survivors and search the crate. Jacob discovers this one is empty as well.

CRATE 3

Leap to the next armored car (another reinforcement wagon) and walk to the far edge to acquire a Double Air Assassination lock-on on the two Blighters in the next car, which also holds the last crate.

Search the crate which has the engine you're looking for. Turn back towards the last car you were on and detach it to complete the Challenge.

CURRENT OBJECTIVE: DETACH THE CARGO WAGON

Now that you've found what you are looking for, head east to the front of the car and face the car with the patrolling Watcher. Walk up to the Detach marker between cars and before detaching it, make sure you remain on the car with the final crate. Detach the cars ahead from the car you are on. This keeps Millner's train moving along the tracks with its remaining Blighters and leaves you with the car containing the engine. The train with Ned on it on the parallel track is quickly approaching.

CURRENT OBJECTIVE: DEFEND NED

The train that Ned is riding on quickly catches up to the Blighter's train (since the engine was detached). Defending Ned is no longer a challenge since you have detached the two Blighter reinforcement wagons; there are no Blighters to protect him from. Simply jump trains and approach Ned to complete the mission. In the ending cinematic, Ned questions Jacob's decision to just *give* the engines away to his new partner. Jacob coldly reassures Ned not to worry; he will get paid for his involvement regardless.

SURVIVAL OF THE FITTEST

THE ESSENTIALS
WALKTHROUGH
SIDE QUESTS
COLLECTIBLES
REFERENCE & APPENDIX
INDEX

SEQUENCE TWO
SEQUENCE TWO
SEQUENCE THREE
SEQUENCE FOUR
SEQUENCE FIVE
SEQUENCE SIX
SEQUENCE SEVEN
SEQUENCE EIGHT
SEQUENCE NINE

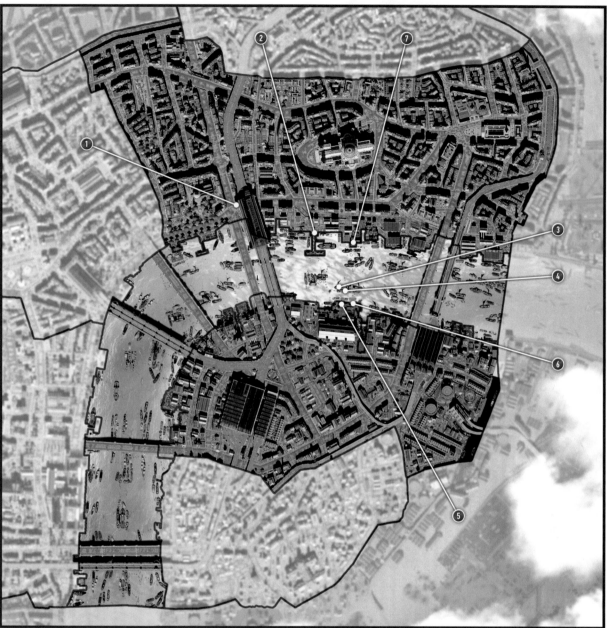

MISSION OVERVIEW

Memory Type: Templar Conspiracy	ASSASSIN	CHALLENGES	REWARDS
Suggested Level: 5	Jacob Frye	Do not touch the River Thames	**£:** 660 + 125 (Full Synch Bonus)
		Sabotage 2 contrabands at once	**XP:** 350 + 150 (Full Synch Bonus)
			Schematic: Black Leather Gauntlet Schematic

LOCATION:

CITY OF LONDON TRAIN STATION

Catch up to Pearl's moving carriage near the Train Station **(1)**. Enter the carriage and Jacob and Pearl share glasses of wine, celebrating the capture of Millner's combustion engines. Millner fled to the Thames to secure his ferry full of contraband. Pearl says she wants Millner dead. Jacob complies.

CURRENT OBJECTIVE: REACH MILLNER'S CONTRABAND

LOCATION: THE THAMES WATERFRONT, SOUTH LONDON

Pearl's carriage lets you out on the north shore of The Thames **(2)**. Your Challenge is to reach Millner's barge with the contraband **(3)** without touching The Thames. Do not swim at any point to reach the destination. You could start your trek across The Thames from the end of the pier where Pearl let you off, but you may want to find another less perilous path since Blighters and coppers patrol this pier.

Simply jump from rowboat, to pier post, to floating object and from one moving ship to the next to reach Millner's barge. If you find yourself in a position where there is nowhere to go but to go swimming, back track a bit and find a better route.

CURRENT OBJECTIVE: SABOTAGE THE CONTRABAND

CHALLENGE: SABOTAGE TWO CONTRABANDS AT ONCE
LOCATION: DOCKED BARGES NEAR THE THAMES'S SOUTHERN SHORELINE

You receive your new objective to sabotage the contraband once in the restricted zone around the group of docked barges **(3)**. With Eagle Vision you can spot the many Blighters aboard and the three glowing red contraband pallets.

Use the many shipping containers for cover while you whistle to create Cover Assassination opportunities or throw knives and darts to make quick work of the Blighters crowding around the contraband.

Do not destroy the contraband until you've defeated all the Blighters on the cluster of barges. When that is done, notice that the three contraband pallets are on separate barges. However, two of them are much closer together. First destroy the contraband that is alone and furthest east. Use Eagle Vision to quickly find the nearest crate of dynamite, which glows white.

Pick up and place a crate of dynamite next to the single pallet of contraband. Ignite the crate and walk away. The contraband explodes.

BLOWING UP TWO CONTRABANDS AT ONCE

Approach the remaining two contrabands that are stored very closely together. A plank **(4)** that connects the two barges separates the two pallets of contraband. It takes a little ingenuity to destroy both at the same time. You need to line up an odd number of dynamite crates across the plank between the two contraband **(A, B, C, D, E)**. Carefully place the crates of dynamite as equally spaced as possible from each other and the contraband. Make sure to place an equal amount of space between the last crate and the contraband on each barge. Use our picture for placement reference.

Position yourself away from the blast and where you have a clear view of the dynamite in the middle. Shoot the middle crate **(C)** with a pistol and watch the chain reaction blow both targets at once. If you do not have bullets, then you'll have to physically ignite the middle crate and quickly clear out. If you want a smaller explosion, you could also place only **(A** and **E)**, and use a Quickshot at **(E)** to complete the Challenge.

CURRENT OBJECTIVE: ASSASSINATE MALCOLM MILLNER
LOCATION: SHIPPING YARD BULKHEAD, SOUTHWARK'S NORTH SHORE

Now Malcolm Millner is marked on the Mini-Map. If you turn toward the south shoreline with Eagle Vision active you see Millner **(5)** glowing yellow and walking near a shipping crane.

You begin to spot the Blighters around your target as you approach the south shore with Eagle Vision active. The first two complications are the two armed Watchers **(F & G)** on the bulkhead. Since Millner moves to the southeast area of the shipyard, you need not even bother with the Watcher to the west **(G)**.

Jump in the water and swim to the eastern edge **(6)** of the bulkhead. Or, use the path of floating objects to run to this edge when the Watcher isn't watching. Exit the water by clinging to the edge of the bulkhead and shimmy toward the patrolling Watcher **(F)**. Reach out and pull her into the water when she walks in front of you. This is a Cover Assassination position; she highlights red as she enters your attack radius.

From that east corner **(6)** look due south around the corner to the side of the shipyard. Here you can spot a large group of Blighters **(H)**. This direction is calling you. This is where your target spends most of his time at the end of his initial patrol. Leap onto the ladder on the side of the bulkhead to the south. Latch onto the sidewalk's edge and just wall-walk until you are directly behind the two closest Blighter Soldiers **(H & J)**.

When your primary target **(I)** comes close to the area again, head to a high point to perform an Air Assassination. If he sees you he's no match for your skills and is dead with just a short combo. This assassination pulls you into the Animus white room. Millner knew he had it coming; Starrick was furious at him for losing the engines. Before he dies he mentions Starrick and Miss Attaway are family. Interesting news.

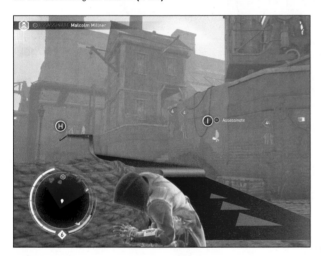

CURRENT OBJECTIVE: LOCATE PEARL ATTAWAY

These two don't move. They keep their backs to you. A Brute **(K)** patrols from the right to the left while your target **(I)** walks in and out of this area from the west. Now when the Brute returns he turns his back in this same area, so quickly attack him from behind.

If you rushed Malcolm just before the assassination and other Soldiers were watching (or even if you were engaged in battle with a couple of them), after killing Malcolm Millner all the enemies continue the battle where they left off. Kill them or throw smoke

and run back the way you came and start crossing The Thames again to reach the opposite (north) side. Yeah, the original side.

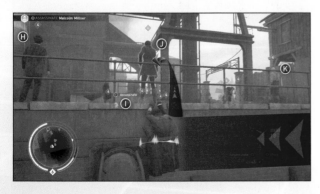

Jump across floating crates, barges coming and going, and pier posts; the path becomes clear when you just start running across.

When you near the south shore of the City of London you see Pearl Attaway entering the warehouse **(7)**. You see a couple of Soldiers in the alley to its right but don't worry about them; you won't be going that way.

CURRENT OBJECTIVE: REACH PEARL ATTAWAY

LOCATION: SOUTH LONDON WAREHOUSE INTERIOR

As soon as you get to the front of the warehouse, head to the left corner (west) and assassinate the Templar leaning on the wall, then Rope Launch to the roof and enter the open window on the third floor. Enter the window and follow the zigzagging path through the rooms until you begin overhearing a conversation between Starrick and Attaway. It's almost as if they were husband and wife, the way these two are going at each other. Jacob slides up to a boarded window to be close enough to hear and get a good view. Amidst the arguing, Pearl spills the beans about Jacob. She also includes that she will personally deliver the stolen engines when they arrive at the Waterloo Train Station. Now you know where she will be next.

CURRENT OBJECTIVE: ESCAPE THE AREA

After the conversation a couple of Blighters try to break the boarded door down—the only thing standing between you and them. So you need to go back the way you came and escape upstairs out that same window. There just happens to be a Chest sitting outside the edge of the restricted area. With Eagle Vision activated and you can easily see this Chest on a boat to your extreme left. Zipline down to the winch post on the dock, hop aboard the boat and, by the time you kick the Chest open, the mission ends…because you have left the restricted zone.

END OF THE LINE

MISSION OVERVIEW

Memory Type: Templar Conspiracy **Suggested Level:** 5	**ASSASSIN** Jacob Frye	**CHALLENGES** Free the station chief Use the secret passage	**REWARDS** **£:** 1980 + 125 (Full Synch Bonus) **XP:** 2500 + 150 (Full Synch Bonus) **Belt:** Crossroad Belt

LOCATION: A NORTHWEST SOUTHWARK ALLEY

Follow the Templar conspiracy icon on the map to a female Rook **(1)** leaning against a wall in a northwest Southwark alley. Start the memory here. She tells you that the stolen engines have just pulled into Waterloo. They're going to unload the train once Starrick's men arrive. Jacob's plan is to make the train leave early.

CURRENT OBJECTIVE: REACH THE VANTAGE POINT

LOCATION: WATERLOO TRAIN STATION

When control returns to you, you can spot a large eagle icon representing the vantage point objective hovering near the top of the Waterloo Train Station. There is an Entry Point through an open skylight. Rope Launch to the rooftop and enter the train station through this open skylight **(1)**. Drop down to the metal framework. The Vantage Point is located on the rafters just north of the window entrance.

Once in the Vantage Point, Jacob spots a Train Conductor below. This is a Stealth Opportunity (which means there's a Challenge involved so you should do it). A cinematic focuses on a man being held against his will elsewhere in the station. Then we see none other than Pearl Attaway sitting comfortably behind a big desk in a plush, armored train car. However, in the cinematic she has an unfortunate label: Assassinate. Looks like she'll be getting her comeuppance in this memory. Finally we are shown the Security Chief who offers a Unique Kill Opportunity.

CURRENT OBJECTIVE: ASSASSINATE PEARL ATTAWAY

CHALLENGE: FREE THE STATION CHIEF

CHALLENGE STEP: SPEAK TO THE CONDUCTOR

CHALLENGE: USE THE SECRET PASSAGE

LOCATION: WATERLOO TRAIN STATION INTERIOR

When you look down from the vantage point you can spot the Train Conductor. He glows white when Eagle Vision is activated. Identify him and you learn that the advantage to speaking to him is his ability to create a big crowd event near your target, giving you more cover where and when needed.

Jump down off the rafters and speak to the conductor. Jacob says "I need to get to the central station." The conductor says it won't happen until he gets his train notices or he'll say he gets his directions from the station chief, the figure you saw prone on the floor and in peril in the last cinematic.

CHALLENGE STEP:
STEAL THE TRAIN SCHEDULE

Look around to the north while in Eagle Vision and you spot the station chief prone on a second story floor. This is where you are headed next. Use the Rope Launcher to return to the rafters and to get back to the rooftop through the same entry point **(2)** you used to get inside.

Once on the rooftop, run north to the glass rooftops on the north wing. Here you find two more open skylight Entry Points. Do not enter the closest one **(3)** as there are too many enemies below to enter stealthily. Instead, stand on the edge of the next closest Entry Point **(4)**. Look below and wait for the Soldier to walk under you. Breach the building by using an Air Assassination on this Blighter.

THE TRAIN SCHEDULE

After taking out the Soldier in the office, look around to spot the *Train Schedule* on a desk inside the same room. Take it. There's also a Chest nearby. Next, activate Eagle Vision and find the remaining enemies in the next room. Use the large mail bin near the doorway as a cover (like a haystack) and whistle for the nearest guard in the next room. Cover Assassinate her when she enters your attack radius.

CHALLENGE STEP:
SPEAK TO THE CONDUCTOR

FREEING THE STATION CHIEF

There are two enemies remaining in the next room where the station chief is located. Throw a smoke bomb into the room and assassinate both the Blighters. And then "Free" the station chief who's on the floor in the back of the room. This completes the first Challenge.

Now simply leave the office and walk down the stairs into the station and speak to the conductor again to give him the train schedule. The conductor now directs the large crowd of travelers to the central station, where all trains are reported to be diverted. You now see the crowd of people slowly making their way to the east side of the station to enter the central station, where Pearl is.

If you follow the crowd to the east a little ways you see Blighters guarding the entrance to the central station. Check out the next area using Eagle Vision. You spot many Blighters and the Security Chief in the distance. There's a lot going on through those doors. We suggest taking a different route. This alternate route satisfies the last Challenge.

USING THE SECRET PASSAGE

From where you spoke to the conductor, turn and face the north. You spot a distant Entry Point blip on the screen in the area below to the north. You'll see a very large set of stairs leading to the street in the tunnel. Follow these stairs down to the street, cross it, and then rush and Double Assassinate the two blighters at the doorway leading back into another wing of the station.

Inside the room is a floor panel, which slides aside to reveal a hidden tunnel entrance in the floor. Enter this tunnel and follow it to a large clearing. Jump down to the lower level and continue following the open tunnel entrance on the opposite end.

Follow the lower tunnel to the right, hop over some low bars and enter another larger conduit area. Climb the wooden scaffolding on the left to reach the continuing tunnel on the second level. At the end of this tunnel is a ladder that leads up to the central station. Press ◎ / ⑧ to open the manhole cover. Exiting the tunnel satisfies the final Challenge.

ASSASSINATING PEARL ATTAWAY
UNIQUE KILL OPPORTUNITY: STEAL THE SECURITY CHIEF'S BLUEPRINTS

Now all that is left is to eliminate your target: Pearl Attaway. If you want to get the unique kill out of her assassination then you must hunt down the Security Chief on the upper balconies and steal his blueprints. A Blighter Soldier leans against a balcony support beam up out of the tunnel and about eight feet away. Come up behind him and assassinate him quietly.

From where the Blighter was standing, pivot to the east and enter the open train car. Head north through the car and exit the other end. This is to avoid the Watcher on the rooftop of the very next car. Continue through the next car the Watcher is patrolling on and exit the other end. Pull yourself up to the edge of the car's rooftop and watch the Watcher. When her back is turned, get to the rooftop of the car and assassinate her.

When the Security Chief walks up the stairs and passes you inside the mail bin, jump out and follow closely behind him while sneaking. When the "Steal" prompt appears, press and hold ⓞ / Ⓑ until the gauge fills to successfully steal the blueprints to Pearl's fortified train car. If you look at the plan closely before closing the message window you can see a window flaw being pointed out on the rooftop of her car. If you look in the direction of her car you can now see a glowing marker indicating the location of the Unique Kill Opportunity. Knock out the Security Chief so he doesn't become a problem.

KILLING PEARL ATTAWAY (UNIQUE KILL OPPORTUNITY)

Head to the south side of the balcony and stand over the two trains below. Shoot the Watcher on top of the train on the right with a dart or a knife. Also wait for a patrolling Soldier to walk into shooting range. He is on the loading zone walkway on the left side of the left train. Hit him with a dart or a knife.

From the top of the train car, Rope Launch to the rafters above and move around on the framework so you can Leap of Faith into the large mail bin below on the balcony walkway.

Rope Launch to the rafters again. Move along the framework until you are directly above the Unique Kill Opportunity marker above Pearl's fortified train car.

DO NOT KILL BLIGHTERS NEAR PEARL

If you kill any of the Blighters directly outside Pearl's car you risk her seeing the body and freaking out. If she moves around then you lose the Unique Kill Opportunity and the marker where you were supposed to enter no longer appears.

Drop from the rafters directly into the Unique Kill Opportunity marker on the rooftop of Miss Attaway's train car. Jacob smashes through the window and Air Assassinates

Pearl. In the Animus white room, Pearl says she was so devoted to her business. She expresses with her dying breath that she doesn't want to lose her busses.

CURRENT OBJECTIVE: ESCAPE WITH THE TRAIN

In order to secure the stolen engines and make sure they do not end up with Starrick, you must now leave the area but take the train with you. Simply start running from Pearl's car heading north through the attached cars until you reach the engine where you see a glowing Reach marker engulfing the train brake. Pull the brake to get the train moving and to complete the mission.

LOCATION: CRAWFORD STARRICK'S OFFICE

In the Sequence 5 ending cinematic, Starrick plays the piano and sings "Then You Will Remember Me" a John McCormack song from Balfe's *The Bohemian Girl* in the year 1916. A guard enters the room and Crawford shoots him dead for disturbing him. Next Lucy Thorne enters and they discuss the Frye twins and the death of his close

friend, Pearl Attaway. He promises that Evie will hang from the gallows and he will personally flay Jacob when he comes to save her.

WALKTHROUGH

SEQUENCE ONE
SEQUENCE TWO
SEQUENCE THREE
SEQUENCE FOUR
SEQUENCE FIVE
SEQUENCE SIX
SEQUENCE SEVEN
SEQUENCE EIGHT
SEQUENCE NINE

A RUN ON THE BANK

ASSASSINATION WALL
LOCATION: TRAIN HIDEOUT

Having uncovered her master plan, Jacob assassinated Pearl Attaway and recovered the internal combustion engines from the Templars. Now a mysterious letter leads Jacob to a plot that could put all of London's gold in jeopardy, while Evie forms a new plan to strike back at Lucy Thorne and reclaim the key to the Shroud of Eden...

AVAILABLE TEMPLAR CONSPIRACY MEMORIES

There are two Templar Conspiracy memories available at the beginning of Sequence 6: *A Case of Identity* in the City of London and *One Good Deed* in Southwark. These two memories launch new (story-related) memories for Jacob and Evie individually. These memory sagas are covered here arranged in their unlocking order—even if that means Jacob's and Evie's missions get shuffled. We start with the closest memory to the train's current location....

LEVEL UP

You should be a level 6 by now and have a decent arsenal and some very adequate Gang Upgrades. We like having our Rooks at level 9 by now so they are performing drive-bys when in carriages and volley some serious firepower when called upon. Make sure you are wearing all the best gear available at this point and use all the Skill Points you can on new fighting upgrades.

A CASE OF IDENTITY

MISSION OVERVIEW

Memory Type: Templar Conspiracy
Suggested Level: 5

ASSASSIN
Jacob Frye

CHALLENGES
Do not kill any policemen

REWARDS
£: 830 + 125 (Full Synch Bonus)
XP: 400 + 150 (Full Synch Bonus)
Kukri: Jade Kukri

LOCATION: ROYAL EXCHANGE, CITY OF LONDON

To begin this memory, find the paperboy **(1)** at the Royal Exchange in The City of London. Jacob snatches the newspaper and opens it. He glances over the top. There are guards everywhere. A man in an expensive suit passes, the Govenor of the Bank of England, Philip Twopenny. He walks with his nose in the air while speaking to another banker trailing behind him. He kicks a beggar's tin bowl sending change everywhere. Instead of apologizing, Twopenny exclaims, "You weak fool, get a job!"

CURRENT OBJECTIVE: LOCATE MR. DREDGE

CHALLENGE: DO NOT KILL ANY POLICEMEN

There's a small gang of your Rooks outside the Royal Exchange doors directly ahead of you. Recruit all of them and from that same spot, activate Eagle Vision and send the gang to attack the policemen through this east entrance. Allow your gang to take out a couple of cops near the doorway before you enter. This does not fail the Challenge because the Rooks are doing your killing.

135

CURRENT OBJECTIVE: KIDNAP DREDGE

Look for Mr. Dredge, the guy that glows yellow. When you enter the exchange, continue east toward your target. Stay away from your gang's activities. Remain anonymous. Sometimes Mr. Dredge will take off running in the street if he gets spooked. Simply chase him and tackle him. There are not as many cops outside. The other option is to walk through the Royal Exchange crowd and "Kidnap" the Dredge.

Tackle Dredge and then press ◎ / ⑧ as soon as he gets his balance back to get his hand behind his back. Accidentally killing him will cause desynchronization.

POLICE BRIBES

If you have not yet spent the money for the Insider Gang Upgrade "Police Bribes" then now would be the perfect time. The cops will not become suspicious of you as quickly, turning a blind eye to your illegal intentions.

CURRENT OBJECTIVE: KIDNAP DREDGE

With Dredge captured, walk slowly to keep the detection zone small around your feet. If a cop gets near, come to a complete stop and then at a snail's pace, edge in the desired direction. If you are in a clearing you can actually walk very quickly using Free Run. Find the nearest unguarded door and walk your victim out into the street and continue until you are clear of the red restriction zone on the Mini-Map.

You have just kidnapped the bumbling Frederick Abberline. He tells you there's to be a robbery in the Bank of England. Jacob assures him he will get all the credit for their arrest if he would only share the name of the guy responsible. Abberline agrees, "The thieves are supplied by Cockham Merchants." In Jacob's next memory, *A Spot Of Tea*, he continues this lead and meets Abberline at the shipyards to dig deeper.

ONE GOOD DEED

MISSION OVERVIEW

| **Memory Type:** Templar Conspiracy **Suggested Level:** 6 | **ASSASSIN** Evie Frye | **REWARDS** **£:** 750 + 150 (Full Synch Bonus) |
| | **CHALLENGES** Do not let the target exit the factory | **XP:** 600 + 150 (Full Synch Bonus) **Schematic:** Mirage Gauntlet Schematic |

CURRENT OBJECTIVE: DEFEND EDWARD

LOCATION: SOUTHWARK

The memory start **(1)** is located on the rooftop of an East Southwark home near the train station. In this memory, Evie visits Southwark after Jacob assassinated Pearl and shut down her omnibus company.

Three Blighter thugs surround Edward Hodson Bayle—a nicely dressed elderly man. He backs away from the gang as they threaten him and his family. Evie drops from a rooftop onto the street behind the gang and yells. The diversion allows the frightened man to get away in a nearby carriage.

PROJECTILES

It's highly recommended that you have your bullets and knives at max capacity before starting this memory. They will be in great demand.

137

While in your carriage, you see Edward Bayle fleeing to the left through the intersection in front of you. A Blighter-driven carriage is hot on his tail. Whip the horse and get after the Blighter carriage. Once in range, begin using the Quickshot pistol feature. Try to take out all three Blighters with bullets. If you run out, fallback to knives.

Bayle's cart is marked with a blue blip and the word "Defend." Race to him directly; the Blighters are drawn to him as well.

There are three carriages with one Blighter each. Not a terribly tough Challenge, unless you are low on ammo. Remember you can also Ram their carriages and then if they survive that you can hijack them out of the carriage and show them your latest knife. If you catch up to Edward, you can board his carriage and take over the driving—it's not a bad idea to do this *while* Blighters are trying to attack Bayle. You will do a much better job of keeping him safe if he's by your side. And the best place for you to be is in control of his vehicle.

CURRENT OBJECTIVE:
REACH THE OMNIBUS FACTORY
DRIVE EDWARD'S CARRIAGE

The objective does not change until all three Blighter pursuers are dead. Then you are to drive Edward in his vehicle to the omnibus factory **(2)**. During the ride Edward expresses his fears for his children's lives. He says since Attaway Transport and the Millner Company went belly-up, with no one to fill their shoes, the gangs made their move. Evie mutters under her breath, "Well done, Jacob."

Edward is the only omnibus builder in the city and they are demanding he work for them. Evie allies with Mr. Bayle to get back a stolen deed that will allow him to start a new, *honest* omnibus company.

CURRENT OBJECTIVE: LOCATE THE DEED
CHALLENGE: DO NOT LET THE TARGET EXIT THE FACTORY
LOCATION: ATTAWAY TRANSPORT, SOUTHWARK

The rest of this mission will seem very familiar to you if you have been conquering boroughs and taking out a lot of child labor factories. There are no children here but the layout of the building is a popular factory design-type and there's a boss glowing yellow inside when searching with Eagle Vision activated. Sounds familiar, right?

So, like most Child Liberation challenges, get to the rooftop before engaging anyone and find the open door to the top floor. In this case, it's on the building's southeast corner. There's a Watcher **(A)** on the balcony outside a door. Air Assassinate her and then cover next to the open doorway. Look into the top floor of the factory.

CURRENT OBJECTIVE: STEAL THE DEED

Sneak into the open factory doorway and continue to cover around the stack of barrels to the left of the entrance. Get to the end of the barrel stack and whistle for the large Brute **(B)** near the balcony rail. There are other Blighters **(C)** nearby so make sure to aim your whistle at the Brute. That's right, "aim." Look directly at the Brute so he is in the center of the screen. Then whistle. This helps focus the sound and helps prevent accidentally alerting others in earshot. After cover assassinating him, throw a knife or two at the head of the last Soldier **(C)** on your floor near the stairs.

Look at the floor using Eagle Vision. Spot the two closest thugs **(D)** & **(E)** patrolling the floors below. Whistle when they are beneath you. One Blighter **(D)** makes the trek up the stairs to find you. Cover Assassinate him from the same location (the barrels near the door).

So believe it or not, you can almost complete this entire Challenge from these same barrels. Continue to look through the floor using Eagle Vision. Soon you see the target with the deed glowing yellow through the floor. Whistle at him and take him out as you did the others. If he's stubborn and doesn't make it all the way to your barrel trap, stealthily throw knives at his head. If you feel like exploring

further and want to catch him patrolling his own floor, you have an opportunity to find a locked Chest. Kill the target and loot the deed from his body.

CURRENT OBJECTIVE: ESCAPE THE FACTORY

Now that you have the deed, you must escape the factory. Simply turn back out the door you entered through, cross the balcony and Rope Launch to the group of houses to the south. By the time you reach the rooftops you escape the restricted zone and receive your next orders.

Find a carriage and follow the route marker back south where this mission began. Pull up next to the omnibus lot **(3)**. You should recognize it as the place where Jacob exploded some busses not too long ago. Hop the surrounding gate to get in the yard and the mission will complete. Evie delivers the deed and receives thanks from Edward and his new omnibus company partners.

A SPOT OF TEA

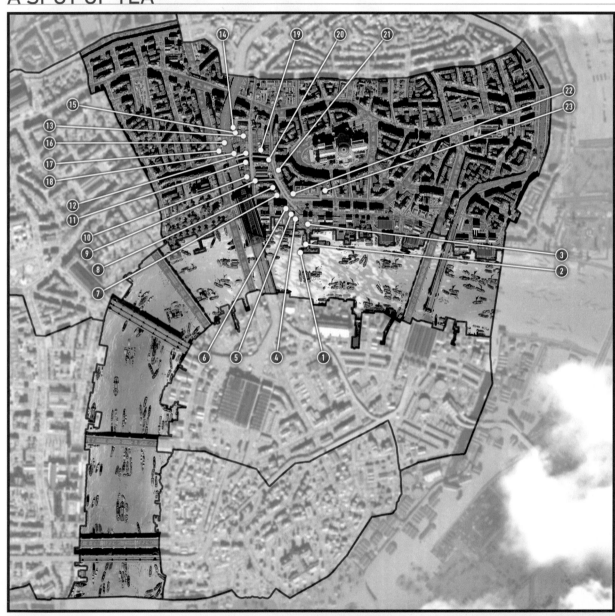

MISSION OVERVIEW

Memory Type: Templar Conspiracy	**ASSASSIN**	**REWARDS**
Suggested Level: 6	Jacob Frye	**£:** 830
		XP: 400
		Belt: Metal Web Belt

CURRENT OBJECTIVE: LOCATE THE SMUGGLED COCKHAM WEAPONS

LOCATION: THE THAMES, SOUTH CITY OF LONDON

Jacob meets Abberline at the end of a pier **(1)** in the City of London on The Thames. Looking out at the sea of shipping vessels, Abberline tells Jacob, "If only I knew which shipment it was, then I could trace the weapons to their owner." Jacob loves this idea and acts on it. He will use his Eagle Vision to locate Cockham's weapon crates.

Head north toward shore. The pier is populated with police and Blighters, so if you don't feel like dealing with them, leap from the pier rail to the mast of the ship **(2)** near your meeting location. Head to the end of the ship and jump to the pier rail and continue to the street.

When you reach the street, activate Eagle Vision and you spot two carriages with suspect cargo. There's one carriage on both sides of the building across the street **(3)**. Neither of these cargos is what you're looking for, so if you don't want to bother with them, walk up to the front of the building and Rope Launch to the rooftop.

From the rooftop of the warehouse **(3)** run to the northwest corner and zipline to the next warehouse **(4)** to the west. With Eagle Vision you'll be able to spot a level 9 Blighter **(A)** in a yard below. You'll be passing over on the zipline. If you can, Air Assassinate this guard from the zipline. The nearby enemies do not have a direct line of sight on him, since he is behind a fence.

From the rooftop of the second warehouse **(4)** walk out onto the hoist on the north side. This vantage point overlooks the carriage with the weapon shipment **(5)**. There are also three more Blighters **(B, C, D)**. When he is alone, Air Assassinate the guard **(B)** around the carriage. Then try to come up behind the last two guards and take them out stealthily or just overpower them in a knife fight. Search the nearby cart.

CURRENT OBJECTIVE: HIDE UNTIL THE CARGO CART'S DEPARTURE

When Jacob inspects the cart **(5)** he finds Cockham's weapon shipment under a tarp. Now you must wait to see who picks it up and then follow them to the group who ordered them. Rope Launch to the top of the building and enter the *Hide* marker. This is located in the northwest corner of the rooftop.

CURRENT OBJECTIVE: TAIL THE CARGO CART

A couple of Blighters arrive and take the reins of the cargo and begin pulling away heading northwest down the street. You must tail this shipment and avoid being seen (don't get too close). Use Eagle Vision to mark the target, making it easier to see. If the cart gets out of your view (blocked by buildings) then a 25 second timer begins ticking down until you get can get a direct line of sight with the cart again. Since the path you must follow takes you through many Blighters on the streets, we suggest that instead of following them in a cart of your own, you instead Rope Launch and parkour your way through this pursuit.

Begin your pursuit by running across the rope suspended between your building and the next to the northwest **(6)**. From the end of the scaffold on the second building, leap to the plank sticking out the north side of the building. This is just around the corner to the right. This allows you to Rope Launch and zipline to the building **(7)** across the street.

Follow the rooftop ledges on the left side of the road. Assassinate the Watcher **(E)** on the house **(10)** with the higher ledge. Continue heading north to the end of the rooftops and then zipline from the end **(11)** to the houses across the street **(12)**.

Follow this building's east roofline ledge. Continue running northward toward the target below. The fog is thick in this memory so keep your eye on the cart (or the orange blip on Mini-Map). Run across the plank between this building **(7)** and the next **(8)**. Rope Launch to the top of the next building's rooftop.

FIRST CHECKPOINT

Follow the rooftops of this building **(8)** as they corner with the intersecting street below. The cart turns left here and stops at a checkpoint **(9)** and the street is full of Blighters. This is why you cannot follow the cart while driving a vehicle. You would run into a lot of trouble here. Continue to follow the roofline ledges around (ziplining where necessary) and start getting ahead of the cart while it prepares to leave the checkpoint.

SECOND CHECKPOINT

About halfway across the long block of houses **(13)** you can begin veering west across rooftops; the cart turns west at the next intersection and circles around the block. You'll be cutting the corner. Do this quickly so you can get the cart back in view before 25 seconds counts down. Now it stops at a second checkpoint **(14)** and picks up the final Blighter delivery driver. You can watch this transaction from the high scaffolding **(15)** above and across the street.

While waiting for the drivers to switch out, look for the rail bridge to the south. The weapons cart will travel under this bridge and circle the next block and come back around to intersect its previous route (see out map). So while waiting for it to move again, look for a Rope Launch lock-on on the top of the railroad lighting truss **(16)**. There's a Watcher on this railroad bridge, but don't worry, she won't be an issue.

From the end of the light truss, Rope Launch to the rooftop of the houses **(17)** to the northwest. Aim for left side as much as possible as the weapons cart is circling around this block and going to pass back under the rail bridge on the next street. So basically, you need to cut the corner and cross back over the rails **(18)**. Get the cart in sight to avoid running the clock down.

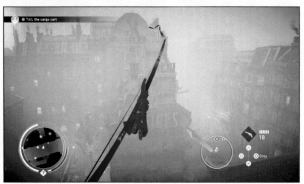

Follow the north side rooftop ledges, chimneys and signs to the next corner **(12)**. You've been here before but this time zipline across the intersection, continuing east past a church bell tower to the next multi-story home **(19)**. From here, zipline across the street to the corner building **(20)**. The weapons cart turns right at this street. Continue to the south edge of your building and zipline across the street **(21)**, getting the farthest Rope Launcher lock-on you can to keep up with the weapons.

Now run along the rooftop ledges heading south until you reach the corner **(22)**. You can continue across one more block of rooftops or jump down to the street and sprint to the next corner where the weapon cart ends its journey in an alley **(23)** to the right.

When the weapons are delivered, a thug tells the driver, "Same routine as before. Mr. Twopenny opens the vault, we robs it and leaves the money in the storehouse." The driver yells, "To the Bank of England." Looks like you've found the guys behind the bank robbery. Nice work.

MISSION OVERVIEW

Memory Type: Templar Conspiracy	**ASSASSIN**	**REWARDS**
Suggested Level: 6	Evie Frye	**£:** 1000 + 150 (Full Synch Bonus)
		XP: 500 + 150 (Full Synch Bonus)
	CHALLENGES	**Outfit:** Master Assassin
	Kill fewer than 5 Royal Guards	

CURRENT OBJECTIVE: REACH THE VANTAGE POINT

CHALLENGE: KILL FEWER THAN 5 ROYAL GUARDS

LOCATION: TOWER OF LONDON, 1868

Take a trip to the train hideout to find Henry Green and the start to this memory. Evie and Henry are surrounded by stacks of books. Evie finds an image of a key in one of her books. Henry says it matches the collection owned by the Queen, kept in the Tower of London.

Hop off the ferry **(1)** and then leapfrog across the bundles of floating crates. Continue following the path of floating debris under the moat tunnel. You reach a slightly opened gate and a set of stairs can be seen through the gap.

Before you climb the stairs, activate Eagle Vision and spot the blue Royal Guards marching on the pathway above. Climb the stairs when they pass and then Rope Launch to the top of the tower. You see a beacon of light radiating from the vantage point marker **(2)**.

Climb to the top of the narrow spire and squat in the vantage point.

VANTAGE POINT VISION
LUCY THORNE: ASSASSINATION TARGET

While in the vantage point you see your assassination target: Lucy Thorne. She's in a chapel yelling at her guards about the Shroud being in a chest that matches the key. She demands they bring it to her.

CHIEF YEOMAN: INFILTRATION OPPORTUNITY

You see Chief Yeoman Warder **(3)** holding the master keys to the Tower of London. Get these keys and you gain easy entry into the tower to get to Thorne. Alternatively, you wont need keys if you simply go for the Unique Kill Opportunity. What the Yeoman's keys guarantees is the Constable's freedom; you won't have to chase after the guard who has the keys to his cell.

ALLIED GUARD: UNIQUE KILL OPPORTUNITY

The Allied Guard is a spy and on your side if you take out some of the disguised Templars for him. They glow red in Eagle Vision so they are easy to spot. He will then allow you to

be taken under (fake) arrest to get marched directly in front of Lucy Thorne. You need only speak to him **(4)** to begin and then kill three Templars dotted around the map. Kill at a safe distance with throwing knives. Once they are dead, return to the Allied Guard and let him take you under fake arrest. Walk yourself directly into the tower and up the stairs to see Lucy. Execute a unique kill ⬜ / ✕ to take Lucy without a fight.

CONSTABLE: ASSISTANCE OPPORTUNITY

The final vision from your Vantage Point is of the Constable **(5)** being locked in a room. If you free him, you have access to a small gang of Royal Soldiers (including the Constable). You can Recruit them and they can aid in your raid on the tower. But for them to be of any use to you, you must first find the Templar holding the key to the Constable's cell. This guy is on a lower floor in the same building. Take him out without much commotion and then return to free the Constable. Alternatively, you can simply unlock the door if you have a Master Key. This is why you should complete the Chief Yeoman's *Infiltration Opportunity* first.

CURRENT OBJECTIVE:
FIND A WAY INTO THE WHITE TOWER
UNIQUE KILL STRATEGY

From the Vantage Point stoop, you have three directions to choose from: Go east and find the Constable; head north and find the Allied Guard; or head west and steal the master keys. You don't have to do it all and you can combine a couple. For example: get the master key and then have a gang of rebellious Royal Guards help you fight your way to Lucy.

Not to worry, the Challenge award has nothing to do with these optional routes, as long as you personally do not kill five of the Royal Guards while doing any of them. We like to take any route that leads us to the Unique Kill Opportunity. So from here we will head west (it's easier than going north to get to the Allied Guard).

Follow the roofline around and start heading north toward the chapel area. You see a large courtyard with many hedgerows and trees. You also see the Allied Soldier's blip **(A)** through this building. Once on the chapel rooftop, drop down to the Allied Guard **(4)** on the ground, investigating the body of the disguised Templar. Talk to him and he asks you to get rid of three Templars that could spot him if he is seen helping you.

SIDE OBJECTIVE: KILL THE THREE DISGUISED TEMPLARS

Completing this objective does not hurt your Challenge goal. These are Templars in disguise so they won't be counted as Royal Guards. The closest Templar **(6)** is in that

hedgerow courtyard in front of the chapel. Get to the rooftop and use the hedgerow as cover to get right up behind him. Stealthily assassinate him.

Head due east from the first Templar Kill location and get to the rooftops to move unnoticed. You spot the next target ahead **(8)** while moving along the north set of buildings. You can tell he's on ground level but there are guards on the rooftop below you. To avoid them, simply Rope Launch to the top of the tallest scaffolds on this building ahead on the left. Move quickly in and out of the zipline to avoid detection. Rope Launch again to the northeast corner lookout tower and then remain there and look at the Templar below. Wait for him to walk under the hanging barrels and get him that way, or throw a knife at his head, or Air Assassinate him.

To get to the last Templar **(9)** quickly, head to the highest point near your last kill and zipline to the very top of a weathervane on one of the tall tower spires. This keeps you out of visual range of the patrolling Royal Guards on the rooftop below. The target patrols the rooftop pathway as well. Where in his patrol he is when you arrive helps you determine if you want to wait until he moves into knife-throwing range or if you want to zipline to the next weathervane to put him in range. Once you execute him with a thrown knife to the head, zipline back to the Allied Guard **(10)** who is now in a new location.

SIDE OBJECTIVE: REACH THE ALLIED GUARD

Zipline to the northwest spire of the tower and you see the Allied Guard behind the shrubs on the west side. Talk to him and then have him take you under false arrest (it works the same way as if you kidnapped someone, but you will be walking in front). Press ◎ / Ⓑ to be kidnapped.

SIDE OBJECTIVE: INFILTRATE THE TOWER

Walk your captor east along the north side of the tower. Just a few yards from where you got arrested you find stairs leading to a locked entrance. Walk slowly up the stairs so your detection zone does not intersect with the Royal Guards on the sidewalk.

CURRENT OBJECTIVE: ASSASSINATE LUCY THORNE

TOWER INTERIOR: FIRST FLOOR

When you reach the door, your Allied Guard screams at the guards inside to open the door. He is bringing Miss Thorne the assassin. Once inside, walk very slowly to keep your detection zone away from the Templars. Walk slowly up the stairs on the right.

TOWER INTERIOR: SECOND FLOOR

Activate Eagle Vision at the top of the stairs to spot the Templars you must avoid. We suggest turning right to follow the hallway on the right. There is a single Blighter **(B)** patrolling this hallway so before heading left at the end of the hallway, wait for him to be on the right side. The passageway is too narrow for three.

TOWER INTERIOR: LUCY THORNE'S ASSASSINATION

When you walk into Lucy's chamber from the right hallway, turn sharply to the left to avoid the Templars **(C)** near the entrance and then follow the red carpet to enter the Infiltrate marker near Lucy.

147

When you enter the marker a cinematic plays. Lucy asks you where the Shroud is located and then says that she'll find it without your help and then strangle you with it. When she turns her back you are prompted to execute her using the ⬤ / ✕ button. If you do not press any button, Lucy orders the Templars to kill you and you get into a fight with the Templars.

In the Animus white room, Lucy questions what good her death does; she does not have the Shroud and tells Evie she hopes she never finds it. Lucy refuses to reveal any information on the Shroud to Evie before she dies.

CURRENT OBJECTIVE: ESCAPE THE TOWER OF LONDON

The tower erupts in battle between Royal Guards and Templars. Run through the chaos to make it back to the lower floor (using the same staircase you used earlier). Once on the lower floor, don't exit through the door you used to enter the tower, instead, turn left (south) and dash to the open doorway **(11)** at the far end of the room.

Do not kill the Royal Guard on the steps, instead Rope Launch to the top of the tower **(12)** and then face south to find the Reach marker on a boat **(1)** in The Thames. Rope Launch to the inner wall **(2)** of the fortress and then zipline to the outer wall and get to the dock. Leap to the boat where the marker is to complete the memory. Evie is seen holding the key taken from Lucy Thorne (the same one she stole from Evie when she made her escape through the window).

LOCATION: STARRICK'S OFFICE

After assassinating Lucy Thorne, a cinematic takes us inside Starrick's office as he dictates a letter to Miss Thorne (he is not yet aware of her demise). In the message, he thanks Lucy for securing the Shroud. But because he does not want to share the powers of the Shroud with her, he dissolves their business relationship. He continues to offer her wealth for life. Just as soon as the dictation ends, a messenger enters the office and delivers the news that Lucy Thorne is dead. And worse news, the key was not found on her body.

A BAD PENNY

MISSION OVERVIEW

Memory Type: Templar Conspiracy **Suggested Level:** 5	**ASSASSIN** Jacob Frye **CHALLENGES** Find the secret passage	**REWARDS** **£:** 2490 + 125 (Full Synch Bonus) **XP:** 3500 + 150 (Full Synch Bonus) **Outfit:** Master Assassin

LOCATION:
BANK OF ENGLAND, CITY OF LONDON

Jacob meets Frederick Abberline on the rooftop of a building **(1)** across the street from the Bank of England. They discuss thwarting Twopenny's bank robbery plans. Jacob assumes that Twopenny is deep in the vault as they speak and asks Abberline how to get into the vault. Abberline explains….

MR. OSBORNE THE BANK MANAGER:
STEALTH OPPORTUNITY

Only Mr. Osborne is allowed free access to the vault. There are other ways into the vault as we will discuss, but if you kidnap the manager you can walk right into the vault through a squad of security guards.

THE VAULT WATCHER:
ASSISTANCE OPPORTUNITY

One man watches the vault like a hawk and if he sees you he is sure to seal it. As a strategy note, you can kidnap the Bank Manager and walk right into the vault under this guy's watch. We suggest taking this guy out first only if you are going in with the intention of eliminating the guards at the vault entrance.

GUS HOWARD THE HEAD OF SECURITY:
UNIQUE KILL OPPORTUNITY

The guard captain, Gus Howard, keeps a tight watch on his men who guard the door. If he leaves, they tend to relax their vigilance.

149

CURRENT OBJECTIVE: REACH THE VAULT

CHALLENGE: FIND THE SECRET PASSAGE

In our strategy we use the Stealth and Unique Kill Opportunity options while the vault watcher's assistance is not needed. The Challenge to "find the secret passage" is utilized during the escape at the end of the mission. Begin the mission by stepping up onto the balcony's rail and use the post jutting from the wall beneath you to perform a Leap of Faith into a haystack below.

SIDE OBJECTIVE: KIDNAP THE HEAD OF SECURITY

Head for the southwest (left) corner of the bank across the street and Rope Launch to the rooftop balcony. Leap from the balcony to the northeast rooftop. Continue northeast across the rooftop until you come to an open skylight (2). There are several Entry Points located on the rooftop and many of them are different entry points into the same main bank chamber. These high, open windows allow direct access to some high trusses which, in turn, allow you to watch over the guards in the bank below while remaining undetected. But that's a different strategy. We've got a plan that utilizes more features than that.

Use the Free Run Down move to run and drop into the open skylight (2). You land on the top of a large chandelier in the office below. Crouch down, activate Eagle Vision and look down into the room. Look to the south and you see Gus Howard, the Head of Security. This is your Unique Kill Opportunity.

Gus walks into the room through the doorway to the south and makes his way to the locked double doors in a small recessed area to the west. He stands there facing those doors with his back to you for a spell. Free Run Down off the chandelier onto the desk below you and then sneak up behind Gus and kidnap him. You don't need to lead him anywhere. You ask him where Twopenny is and he tells you he's in the vault ogling his priceless painting. The Unique Kill becomes available and a location is marked on the Mini-Map. You can choke Gus out now and leave him on the floor.

SIDE OBJECTIVE: KIDNAP THE BANK MANAGER

Stand under the same skylight and Rope Launch back to the rooftop. Pivot to the northeast and walk around the north side of the bank's main lobby. While running along the north ledge you begin to see another Entry Point ahead, but much lower than the others beside you. Follow the rooftop ledge to the next roof.

Once you're halfway across the rooftop **(3)**, drop down and hang from the edge of the roof. You receive an "Enter" prompt over the open window below you. Enter the building now and activate Eagle Vision while on the interior windowsill.

Look directly below you to find the Bank Manager, Mr. Osborne. He ends his patrol route here in this small office. He may not be there for long (or he may not have arrived yet) so when he's present, jump down and kidnap him quickly. There is an open door to the right with five guards standing in front of the vault door looking around for suspicious activity.

To avoid being seen, come up directly behind Osborne, kidnap him, and face this open door. Begin walking very slowly toward the vault.

As you slowly approach the vault, the two guards move a few steps back away from the open door. They are letting you through. They don't give you a very wide path, but there is enough space to fit between them to get through the doorway without anyone entering your detection zone. Walk slowly. Once inside the vault chamber you can choke the manager out. You don't need him anymore and he makes an awful hostage for the Blighters downstairs.

CURRENT OBJECTIVE: ASSASSINATE TWOPENNY

CHALLENGE: FIND THE SECRET PASSAGE
SIDE OBJECTIVE: UNIQUE KILL OPPORTUNITY

Once you are in the vault and have disposed of the manager, walk down the stairs to where the gold is kept. Activate Eagle Vision as you walk into the actual vault. You find yourself on the second level of the two-story vault. There are Blighters peppered everywhere below and you can see Twopenny **(A)** managing the movement of the gold. He glows yellow.

What we are about to walk you through is the route to the painting that you need to hide behind to uniquely kill Twopenny. Oddly enough you need to get by him first. But that's not hard. Here's how. You need to head left when you enter the two-story vault chamber. Two guards **(B & C)** walk up the stairwell in the back of the room heading up and to the right (west) to patrol the west end of the second level. Guard **(D)** walks up the east staircase alone. He is the weak link in their defense.

Head south along the left side of the second floor using the money carts for cover. Remain anonymous to the single Blighter guard **(D)** facing the barred vault near the stairs. Come up behind him quickly and kidnap him. With your hostage, walk down the stairs he just climbed and walk very slowly onto the lower floor to avoid the Brute's **(C)** gaze.

The first floor is the tricky part. Blighters are moving armfuls of loot out of the bank so you need to watch their movement and then fall into a movement pattern with them. Follow closely behind or in front of a guard and move diagonally across the floor to enter the opening between the second and third columns on your left (you often get cornered if you try to hug the outside walls).

Just beyond the second and third columns on the left, veer to the right and follow the path of the loot being moved. Step aside if you need to avoid someone coming in for more loot. Through the back left archway you can see a room across one short hallway. The hiding spot is in this room.

Once inside the vault with the painting in it, choke out the kidnapped Blighter in a corner so no one sees. Approach the painting and press ◎ / ⑧ when prompted. This allows you to hide behind the painting.

Philip Twopenny approaches the painting to admire it and actually reaches out to touch it. You are prompted to press ◎ / ⑧ to assassinate Twopenny. Do so and Jacob tears through the painting and ends Twopenny's greedy life. You join him in the Animus white room where you tell him that he has stolen his last shilling from the people of London.

CURRENT OBJECTIVE: ESCAPE THE AREA
CHALLENGE: FIND THE SECRET PASSAGE

Now that you are back from the Animus, Twopenny is dead at your feet and there's a vault full of unaware Blighters. This is when the Challenge's "secret passage" comes in handy. Cover next to the exit in the painting room and look back into the main vault. Blighters are still loading loot. When no other guards are patrolling the area, sneak up behind the Blighter **(G)** at the archway outside the room and then keep heading straight back following the left wall and either stealthily kill the next Blighter **(H)** near the hallway entrance or just run past him, turning right in the back hallway.

Run through the back hallway heading south and dash into the last open door on the left. You see an intense light being emitted from this room. The back wall has a Slide Under open vent. This is the secret passage. Slide Under to safety.

There's only one way out of the winding tunnel on the other side. Run and follow it until you reach another Slide Under vent. When you slide under this one you end up in a library of stored documents. Enter the open elevator shaft in this room and then Rope Launch to the top of the shaft.

THE ESSENTIALS
WALKTHROUGH
APPENDICES
COLLECTIBLES
REFERENCE & ANALYSIS
INDEX

SEQUENCE ONE
SEQUENCE TWO
SEQUENCE THREE
SEQUENCE FOUR
SEQUENCE FIVE
SEQUENCE SIX
SEQUENCE SEVEN
SEQUENCE EIGHT
SEQUENCE NINE

You reach a two-story room. The open elevator doors are on the second floor. Once on the second floor balcony use Eagle Vision to locate a guard on the first floor. The only reason you may want to spar with him is because there's a locked Chest behind a screen on his floor.

After dealing with the guard and the Chest, pick the locked door in the northwest corner of the room. Once opened, this grants access to the small office where you kidnapped the Bank Manager. Zipline up to the Entry Point window **(3)** in this room to get outside. Once outside simply zipline out of the restricted zone to complete the memory.

Next you see Abberline closing the Bank of England and arresting those involved, taking credit for the bust while Jacob kicks back in a carriage with his feet up and a big smile on his face.

LOCATION: STARRICK'S OFFICE
James Brudenell complains to Crawford Starrick about the financial shape of the city and an arrangement between the two quickly becomes obvious. Starrick threatens to blackmail Brudenell for his involvement in their illegal activities and threatens to offer his body parts to his nemesis, Disraeli. Starrick demands that the halls of parliament be free to govern again. Then he dismisses James Brudenell from his office.

SEQUENCE SEVEN

ALL IS FAIR IN POLITICS

ASSASSINATION WALL

LOCATION: TRAIN HIDEOUT

Jacob and Evie have killed two of Crawford Starrick's agents, Philip Twopenny and Lucy Thorne, but the Templars are far from defeated. A conspiracy to a assassinate the Prime Minister takes Jacob to the Houses of Parliament and, despite Evie's triumph over Lucy Thorne, the quest for the Shroud of Eden takes a dramatic turn…

AVAILABLE TEMPLAR CONSPIRACY MEMORIES

There are three Templar Conspiracy memories available at the beginning of Sequence 7: *Change of Plans* in Whitechapel, *Unbreaking the Bank* in the City Of London, and *Playing Politics* in Westminster. You can play them in any order but we chose to arrange them first by suggested character level and then by which memory is closer to a previously completed memory. *Playing Politics* in Westminster has the lowest suggested level **(6)** so we start there.

PLAYING POLITICS

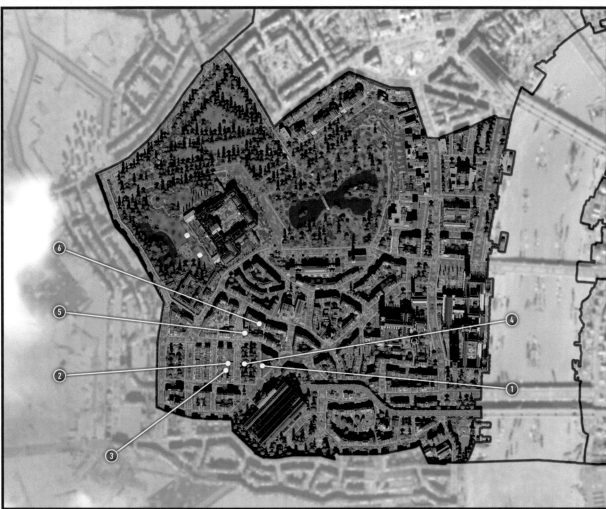

MISSION OVERVIEW

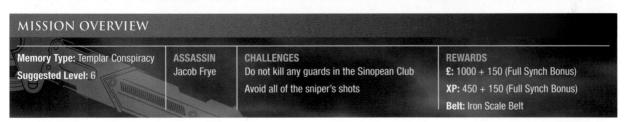

Memory Type: Templar Conspiracy	ASSASSIN	CHALLENGES	REWARDS
Suggested Level: 6	Jacob Frye	Do not kill any guards in the Sinopean Club	£: 1000 + 150 (Full Synch Bonus)
		Avoid all of the sniper's shots	XP: 450 + 150 (Full Synch Bonus)
			Belt: Iron Scale Belt

LOCATION: NEAR VICTORIA STATION, WESTMINSTER

To begin this memory, enter the marker **(1)** at the top of the triangle-shaped building just north of Victoria Station in Westminster. In this memory, Jacob hunts for Prime Minister Disraeli at the Sinopean Club to trace the mysterious "B," who is planning Disraeli's assassination.

CURRENT OBJECTIVE: REACH THE SINOPEAN CLUB

From the rooftop you face west toward the Sinopean Club **(2)** marked in the distance with a green blip around 94 meters away. Jump off the end of the pole sticking out of the building you're on and leap into the haystack below. There's a merchant on the sidewalk below if you need any items.

155

Walk west toward the Sinopean Club across the street. Activate Eagle Vision. Notice the many policemen guarding the entrance and posted at various locations inside. Before you enter the Reach marker in the Sinopean Club courtyard, gather a local Rook gang. You should find some on nearby street corners. Send them inside to attack the policemen before you enter the marker and activate a Challenge that frowns on killing the guards.

LOCATION: SINOPEAN CLUB

Another option is to get onto the Sinopean Club rooftop and look down into the courtyard to assess the situation. Shoot a hallucinogenic dart at a cop and wait for a crowd of cops to form. When a group of them are massed together, shoot a couple more cops in the group with darts to have them kill each other.

While they all fight each other, start throwing Voltaic Bombs on the group until all of the policemen in the group are finished. This does get rid of all the cops in the area and does not stop the policeman that circles the meeting that is about to happen. But it does make the next Challenge a lot easier to deal with.

CURRENT OBJECTIVE: REACH THE SINOPEAN CLUB

CHALLENGE: DO NOT KILL ANY GUARDS IN THE SINOPEAN CLUB

Drop down off the rooftop to the Reach marker inside the courtyard near the round bench enclosure **(3)**. Cover behind the bench enclosure's short walls. While in Eagle Vision you can see the Prime Minister and William Gladstone highlighted yellow. They meet in the middle of the bench enclosure and begin to talk. Remain covered behind the short wall. A new policeman **(A)** arrives to patrol the area. He is located on the west side of the enclosure.

REMAIN WITHIN RANGE TO SPY

You must cover behind the short wall around the meeting at the circle of park benches. Any other location that is out of policemen's sight is too far and a timer activates and counts down from one minute and does not stop until you get within listening range again. If this timer reaches zero, you are desynchronized.

The newly arrived policeman **(A)** patrols around this round park bench wall you are covering behind. So all you have to do is keep Eagle Vision activated so you can locate him clearly and crouch-walk along the wall, always staying on the opposite side as he patrols around it. You do not need to worry about the Prime Minister or Gladstone seeing you in the walkway openings in the short wall. You are of no interest to them. But you do need to make sure the patrolling policeman does not see you cross these openings.

Now you know why we eliminated so many policemen before this Challenge starts (when you enter the Reach marker). Imagine avoiding all the police that were in the area while crouch-walking around the bench walls! At one point, the patrolling policeman **(A)** switches patrol with another **(B)** who was patrolling further north. Just keep an eye on this switch and continue to stay behind the opposite wall from the currently patrolling policeman. Alternatively, you could sneak up behind the policemen as they patrol ahead of you and knock them out. When the second one arrives he inspects the body of the first, which makes him an easy target for another knockout.

CURRENT OBJECTIVE: TACKLE THE SPY

When the heated get-together is over, Benjamin Disraeli walks off and a spy is seen following closely behind him. Jacob begins to pursue the pursuer. You are now supposed to tackle the spy known as "B."

You walk out of the club through the east tunnel and the spy is across the street entering the park **(4)**. When you reach the street, he notices you and starts to run. Give chase into the park.

He's not much of a runner and can usually be tackled before he exits the north end of the park. Once on the ground, Jacob questions the man who exclaims his name is Herbert. When he is about to reveal the name of the man that paid him to follow the Prime Minister, a gunshot rings out and a bullet hole appears in the spy's temple. Sniper!

CURRENT OBJECTIVE: TACKLE THE SNIPER
CHALLENGE: AVOID ALL OF THE SNIPER'S SHOTS

The sniper is spotted on top of the cathedral **(5)** across the street to the north. Run into the gated yard on the right side of the cathedral following the yellow blip that marks the sniper movement along the rooftops. She is now heading north. Rope Launch to the top of the church. If there is still a Helix Glitch located in this area, Rope Launch to the church in the Glitch's location (see the Mini-Map icon). Once on the rooftop you see the sniper now moving east along the rooftops across the yard.

Hop up on the corner railing of the church rooftop and you notice the Helix Glitch floating just in front of the balcony. Get a Rope Launcher lock-on on the chimney of the building **(6)** the sniper is running across. Get a lock-on point on the chimney that, when attached and a zipline is used, Jacob passes through and collects the Helix Glitch.

The sniper stops to shoot at you from the end of the same rooftop. It likely happens when you are ziplining and it's difficult to hit a moving target like that. So if you aren't on the zipline then press ⊗ / Ⓨ to avoid the sniper's bullet.

After the sniper stops to take a shot at you, she turns and runs east along the rooftops, continuing east across three more complexes until she follows the end of the L-shaped rooftop, which now sends her into a southerly direction. She stops on the end of the lower rooftop to set up for another shot. Rush her and tackle her.

CURRENT OBJECTIVE: INCAPACITATE THE SNIPER

Your next objective is to incapacitate her. You can try to choke her out from a kidnapped position or you can just attack her. When her health is low a cinematic takes over. She comes to and is startled to find herself suspended over the edge of the rooftop. She sees Jacob holding her by her jacket collar, temporarily keeping her from falling to her death.

Jacob interrogates the sniper. He asks for the name of the guy she works for. She claims she never got his name. Describes him as an old chap with a big beard and wore some kind of uniform. "Hussars, maybe," she says. She adds that her lads are to attack the Prime Minister's carriage on the way to Parliament. Jacob, getting the info he needs, throws the sniper back onto the safety of the roof. The memory is complete.

MEMORY UNLOCKED

The Bodyguard memory is unlocked after completing *Playing Politics*. This memory's start location is just a few blocks north of where you completed *Playing Politics*. This new memory continues Jacob's Sequence 7 story branch. This is the next memory we cover in the walkthrough.

158

THE BODYGUARD

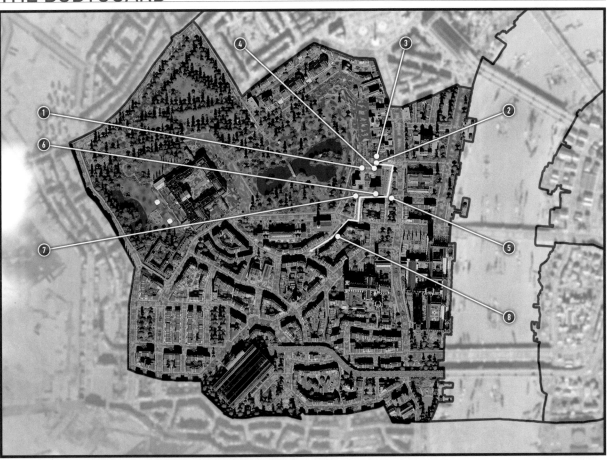

SEQUENCE ONE
SEQUENCE TWO
SEQUENCE THREE
SEQUENCE FOUR
SEQUENCE FIVE
SEQUENCE SIX
SEQUENCE SEVEN
SEQUENCE EIGHT
SEQUENCE NINE

MISSION OVERVIEW

Memory Type: Templar Conspiracy **Suggested Level:** 7	**ASSASSIN** Jacob Frye	**CHALLENGES** Keep the carriage's damage below 50% Hijack the carriage in less than 1 minute	**REWARDS** **£:** 1000 + 250 (Full Synch Bonus) **XP:** 450 + 250 (Full Synch Bonus) **Cape:** Goldred Cloak

LOCATION: THE FOREIGN OFFICE, WESTMINSTER

The memory start location is on a balcony column on the top of The Foreign Office **(1)**. From his perch high above, Jacob spots Benjamin Disraeli and his wife, Mary Anne, leaving their home on 10 Downing St. and entering a chauffeured carriage. A house call is out of the question. You must infiltrate the carriage if you want to warn the Prime Minister about a viable threat on his life.

159

CURRENT OBJECTIVE: INFILTRATE THE DISRAELIS' CARRIAGE

The Disraelis enter the carriage **(2)** in front of their house and remain there until you infiltrate it. So you have time to strategize. There are policemen across the street and a couple that patrol the sidewalk near the carriage. The only way to enter the carriage is to remain anonymous. Zipline to their house's rooftop **(3)** and look over the edge to the top of their carriage. Watch the patrolling police below. When they have passed the carriage, look to the buildings **(4)** directly across the street and find a low Rope Launch lock-on that allows you to drop to the sidewalk right beside the carriage's door. Quickly open the door before any of the cops see you.

Inside the carriage, Jacob warns the Prime Minister about the threat on his life. As the Prime Minister begins to question the validity of this news, a gunshot rings in the distance. Jacob leaps out of the carriage and into action.

CURRENT OBJECTIVE: DEFEND THE DISRAELIS
CHALLENGE: KEEP THE CARRIAGE'S DAMAGE BELOW 50%

When you exit the carriage you are tasked with defending it from attacking Blighters. The Challenge is to keep its damage below fifty percent. A damage gauge appears on screen. Currently there are four aggressors on two high balconies **(4)** on the building across the street from the carriage. Quickly Rope Launch to the rooftop of the building the Blighters are on. Accessing the rooftop puts you above them, giving you the height advantage.

You may be able to achieve a Double Air Assassination on the Watchers on the balcony below, but don't waste too much time trying to achieve this as the Challenge does not leave much time for flawless execution. Defeat the Watchers on the first balcony and then Rope Launch back up to the rooftop and perform a similar attack on the Watchers on the second balcony.

WALKTHROUGH

SEQUENCE ONE
SEQUENCE TWO
SEQUENCE THREE
SEQUENCE FOUR
SEQUENCE FIVE
SEQUENCE SIX
SEQUENCE SEVEN
SEQUENCE EIGHT
SEQUENCE NINE

As soon as you kill the fourth Watcher on the balconies, two more Watchers and a Brute appear on the sidewalk below. Free Run Down to the lower balcony above these enemies. You can acquire an Air Assassination target lock on the nearest Watcher. Execute her this way and then use your fighting skills to eliminate the Brute and other Watcher.

After defeating the first seven attackers, three more come running into action from the west end of the street. Rush them and attack using a smoke bomb and your blade. Defeating all of these Blighters triggers a cinematic. In it, a Blighter takes control of the Prime Minister's carriage and begins speeding off with the Disraelis inside.

CURRENT OBJECTIVE: HIJACK THE CARRIAGE

CHALLENGE: HIJACK THE CARRIAGE IN LESS THAN ONE MINUTE

The Challenge for keeping the carriage's damage below 50% is over. To fulfill the next Challenge, you must hijack the Prime Minister's carriage in less than a minute. It races east down the street. There is an unoccupied parked carriage beside you. Take it and give chase.

Two Blighters in a single carriage join the Challenge when you follow the Disraeli's carriage as it turns west around the next corner **(5)**. As you race after the carriage on this street, you pass a single Blighter in a carriage **(6)** who is alerted to this chase. He turns around and tries to attack you. In the next turn **(7)** one more Blighter carriage enters the chase. Now there are three Blighter carriages after you and you should be very close to the Prime Minister by now.

Equip your pistol and use Quickshots to fend off the enemy while continuing to focus on your driving and catching up to the Disraeli's carriage. You should be able to catch up with it when you reach the road heading southwest. Drive up beside the carriage, go to the roof, jump to the Prime Minister's carriage, and then hijack the driver.

CURRENT OBJECTIVE: HIJACK THE CARRIAGE

There are likely Blighters still hot on your tail, so use Quickshots and carriage ramming to get rid of them. You must now become anonymous; so watch the Mini-Map to help you drive out of the red zones. The red zones turn to green zones. Drive out of the green zone to become anonymous.

In a cinematic, Jacob returns the Disraelis to their home. The Prime Minister curses the name of Gladstone, swearing, "He will pay for this!" Jacob asks Mary Anne Disraili if she knows of a man that fits the sniper's description of her contact. Mary Anne does not answer the question directly and asks Jacob if he would give her a tour of slums, the "Devil's Acre" to see how bad it really is and if you agree, she will assist you with your inquiry.

DRIVING MRS. DISRAELI

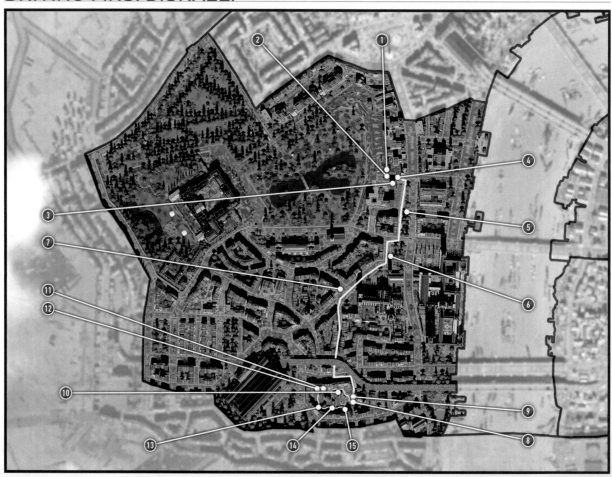

MISSION OVERVIEW

Memory Type: Templar Conspiracy	ASSASSIN	CHALLENGES	REWARDS
Suggested Level: 7	Jacob Frye	Distract the reporters with an ally	**£:** 1000 + 250 (Full Synch Bonus)
		Do not get detected by Thugs in the slum	**XP:** 450 + 250 (Full Synch Bonus)
			Schematic: Iron Death Gauntlet Schematic

LOCATION: 10 DOWNING ST., WESTMINSTER

Enter the memory marker **(1)** in the Disraeli's backyard on 10 Downing St., Westminster. Jacob meets Mary Ann Disraeli at night on a park bench with her small dog, Desmond, in a bag. Jacob is exaggeratedly polite and courtly to the Prime Minister's wife as he asks if she is ready to tour Devil's Acre. She tells Jacob she's afraid she'll have to cancel their engagement; there are scandal-hunting reporters crawling outside her door. She can't risk being seen with Jacob. Jacob tells her that he will take care of them, discreetly.

CURRENT OBJECTIVE:
USE TOOLS TO DISTRACT THE REPORTERS

CHALLENGE: DISTRACT THE REPORTERS WITH AN ALLY

When you gain control of Jacob, walk through the concrete archway in the yard and head south through the yard to the open metal gate near a haystack. Now you are at the street. To your right are the reporters **(2)** and police at the Disraeli's front door. Across the street is a small girl **(3)** sitting on a stoop. She glows white when Eagle Vision is activated. Walk up to this small girl and speak to her.

Jacob pays the small child to distract the reporters. She stands up and raises her arms and screams, "Blimey, look! It's Squire Bancroft!" The reporters come running looking for an interview with the famous actor.

CURRENT OBJECTIVE: ESCAPE THE JOURNALISTS

With the reporters chasing you, simply Rope Launch to a nearby rooftop and then zipline again to another distant rooftop to escape them.

CURRENT OBJECTIVE:
REACH MRS. DISRAELI'S CARRIAGE

Once you have lost the reporters, head back to the carriage **(4)** outside the gate near the Prime Minister's house. Get into the driver's seat. Mrs. Disraeli enters the carriage.

CURRENT OBJECTIVE:
ESCORT MRS. DISRAELI TO THE DEVIL'S ACRE

Follow the white route marker on the road to reach Devil's Acre. A reporter in a carriage **(5)** is spotted about a block south from the Disraeli's home.

CURRENT OBJECTIVE: ESCAPE THE JOURNALISTS

When you spot the journalist on the corner on your route to Devil's Acre, just whip the horse and continue to blaze southward on the same street. When you reach the next intersection take a sharp right and then the next possible left and you lose the tail about halfway down the block **(6)**.

CURRENT OBJECTIVE: ESCORT MRS. DISRAELI TO THE DEVIL'S ACRE

Continue following the white route marker to the destination **(8)**. About halfway there, another journalist in a carriage **(7)** spots you and begins to chase you. As soon as you spot him, veer left down the next side street (the same one marked on our map) and keep boosting until you have lost him, which only takes a few seconds. When you reach Devil's Acre, stop in the Reach marker **(8)** and Mary Ann exits the carriage and energetically starts for the slums.

CURRENT OBJECTIVE: ESCORT MRS. DISRAELI THROUGH THE SLUM

CHALLENGE: DO NOT GET DETECTED BY THUGS IN THE SLUM

Follow Mary Ann down the stairs into the slums. She stops at the bottom of the stairs **(9)**. Activate Eagle Vision and look west to mark Blighters.

There's a Blighter Brute standing near a barrel fire just beyond the first Reach marker at the gate opening. Leave Mary Ann behind and run up behind this Brute and dispatch him. He keeps his back to you, so this is an easy kill.

Approach Mary Ann and press ◎ / Ⓑ to escort her to the west towards the next Reach marker **(10)**. Halfway to the marker her dog, Desmond, starts barking. Her dog growls when approaching danger. This causes a very wide, red detection ring to appear beneath your feet. You cannot have this. Stop your progression and stay away from Blighters to avoid being noticed. If you can remain undetected you can pass through the slums without killing anyone.

Go back for Mary Ann and take her arm. Walk through the Reach marker **(10)** and veer right to hug the right walls. Continue west through a narrow opening in a wooden fence near a lantern on the barrels. As soon as you pass through the fence opening, activate Eagle Vision and scan the area ahead for more Blighters.

As you pass under a clothesline you can spot a couple of Blighters to your left through a passage between two buildings. Time your passage through this area when the nearest Blighter is facing away from you. Pass under a wooden scaffold bridge and you soon spot a haystack and a Blighter Soldier near some stairs ahead.

As you approach the haystack the Soldier walks away, through the next Reach marker **(12)**, and continues farther to the east and joins a Brute. They both stand side-by-side for a while. Leave Mary Ann near the stairs **(11)** and the haystack and move silently to the back or side of the house the two Blighters are standing in front of. Rope Launch to the rooftop and use the lamppost jutting out of the building above them to launch a Double Air Assassination on them.

After killing the two Blighters, look to the northeast and find two Blighters standing under hanging barrels. Get close enough to get the barrels in knife-throwing range and take them out. Return for Mary Ann and Desmond **(11)** and move them forward through the next marker **(12)**.

Walk over the dead bodies and head for the next marker **(13)** to the south, through a fence and behind some stairs and another house. Leave Mary Ann here in this shady area while you move ahead to clear the way again.

Return for Mary Ann and now walk her safely the rest of the way to the last marker where the outside bar is located **(15)**.

Move up to the next fence behind the house and, using Eagle Vision, look east to spot two Blighters that will be an issue. There's a Brute patrolling on the right under hanging barrels

and a Soldier just standing with his back to you on the left. Wait for the Brute to walk under the barrels **(14)** and drop them on him and then just throw a knife at the head of the Soldier or come up behind him and execute him.

While sitting down to share a couple of pints, a Blighter sitting nearby takes notice of the odd couple and their dog in a bag at the next table. He promptly gets up, walks over to your table, and steals the puppy and bag.

THE ESSENTIALS
WALKTHROUGH
100% OBJECTS
COLLECTIBLES
INDEX

SEQUENCE ONE
SEQUENCE TWO
SEQUENCE THREE
SEQUENCE FOUR
SEQUENCE FIVE
SEQUENCE SIX
SEQUENCE SEVEN
SEQUENCE EIGHT
SEQUENCE NINE

CURRENT OBJECTIVE: FOLLOW DESMOND'S BARKS TO FIND THE DOGNAPPER

You are tasked to follow Desmond's barks to find the Blighter who stole him. Look onscreen to find the green blip on the ground and pass through it. When you can't see the next green blip visually, glance at the Mini-Map to locate the next closest blip. Continue to follow the green blips until you run into the Blighter with the pup. The final location is where the first Reach maker appeared in the slums **(10)**.

When you catch up with the thief he threatens you, but throws you the dog in the bag. Jacob suddenly realizes he just left the Prime Minister's wife alone in one of London's most dangerous pubs. He rushes back to see that she is doing fine holding her own with the locals.

CURRENT OBJECTIVE: ESCAPE WITH MRS. DISRAELI

After the cinematic, Mary Ann, Desmond, and you are back at the carriage **(8)**, but the dognapper and his Blighter friends are quickly approaching and they won't be messing with the pooch this time. You can either stand and fight or jump into the driver's seat of the carriage and take off for Mary Ann's home. If you decide to stand and fight, begin the battle by throwing a smoke bomb down on the ground around you. This helps you make quick work of the three level 8 and one level 9 Blighters.

CURRENT OBJECTIVE: ESCORT MRS. DISRAELI BACK TO 10 DOWNING STREET

After the you have dealt with the Blighters or have chosen to escape in the carriage immediately, once you drive Mrs. Disraeli out of the red restricted zone you simply have to take her back home **(4)**. Just before you reach her house she gives up the name of the man you seek: Lord Cardigan. She says you can find him at the Palace of Westminster.

CHANGE OF PLANS

THE ESSENTIALS
WALKTHROUGH
SIDE QUESTS
COLLECTIBLES
GAMES CONNECTED
INDEX

SEQUENCE ONE
SEQUENCE TWO
SEQUENCE THREE
SEQUENCE FOUR
SEQUENCE FIVE
SEQUENCE SIX
SEQUENCE SEVEN
SEQUENCE EIGHT
SEQUENCE NINE

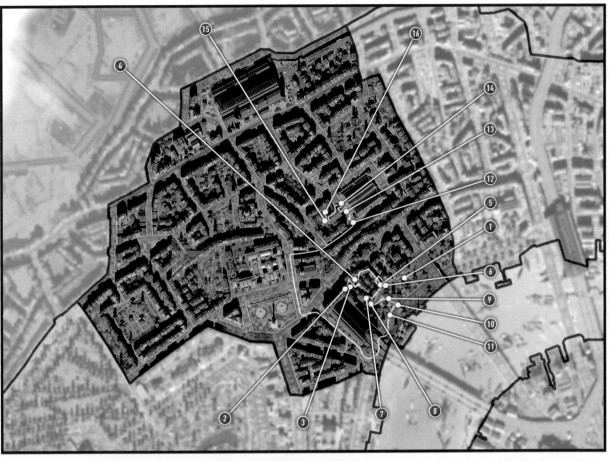

MISSION OVERVIEW

Memory Type: Templar Conspiracy **Suggested Level:** 7	**ASSASSIN** Evie Frye	**CHALLENGES** Use Henry's distraction twice Kill guards using hanging barrels	**REWARDS** **£:** 1200 + 250 (Full Synch Bonus) **XP:** 600 + 250 (Full Synch Bonus) **Schematic:** Nightshade Cloak Schematic

DULEEP SINGH

Duleep Singh was the last Maharaja of the Sikh Empire and at this time is living in exile in England and has been since he was very young. He was initially quite the man about town, and a good friend of the Queen and Prince Albert. However, after he was reunited with his mother in 1863, he began to reclaim his crown, eventually leaving London for an unauthorized return to India in 1883. Here in 1872, he's between those two positions—not yet decided on returning to India and reclaiming his rightful place, but also not the contented showpiece he once was. Henry sees Duleep as someone who has sold out—making a fortune in England and playing the exotic foreigner for years. Duleep sees Henry as someone who is too willing to work outside the system—he knows of the Assassins and disapproves of their methods. However, as each needs contacts and information, they often have much to offer one another. They're not enemies, but neither are they friends.

LOCATION: THE STRAND

Evie meets Henry at the square **(1)** in The Strand. Evie and Henry are walking together across the square, Henry strides with a purpose. Evie tries to keep up. Henry has found a letter from the Prince Consort among Lucy Thorne's research dated 1847. The year the Prince began renovations to Buckingham Palace. They think maybe he added a vault for the Shroud of Eden.

They reach Dupleep Singh on a park bench and introductions are made. He tells Henry the plans have been removed by Crawford Starrick, but he knows where they are, but it's heavily guarded.

CURRENT OBJECTIVE: FIND THE DOCUMENTS

CHALLENGE: USE HENRY'S DISTRACTION TWICE
LOCATION: CHARING CROSS STATION, THE STRAND

You begin this memory crouched on the edge of a high, hanging scaffold **(2)** on the northeast side of Charing Cross Station. You face a courtyard of Templars below and Henry Green **(B)** can be seen on a rooftop below and to your right (he glows yellow with Eagle Vision activated). There are also a couple of Watchers on rooftops in the area that you need to deal with before you ask Henry to distract the Templars around the first location **(3)** to search for the documents.

Rope Launch to the chimney on the rooftop to your left and then immediately perform an Air Assassination on the Watcher **(A)** standing on this rooftop. Rope Launch to Henry's **(B)** rooftop then walk down the east side. Leap to the rooftop across the alley and come up behind the Watcher **(C)** and silently assassinate her.

Return to Henry and speak to him. He says he'll distract the guards and start a fight. That's when you throw a smoke bomb on the scene, check the crate **(3)** for the documents, and escape. The crate is at the base of the statue in the middle of the courtyard and is marked with a green blip. So focus on the enemies below and press the **R1 / RT** button to send Henry after them to distract them.

Watch Henry move to the ground and to the Templars below. He is marked with a blue blip. Throw a smoke bomb when he reaches the Templars. Jump down to the smoky courtyard, search the crate, and escape to the rooftops again. The crate does not contain the documents you were looking for but does contain the Upgraded Throwing Knife Schematic III.

There are two more locations to search. Continue the search by getting to the rooftop **(4)** to the east. Sneak up behind the Watcher on this rooftop and assassinate her. Follow the rooftops around until you reach an area **(5)** with a good view of another large group of Templars standing around an alarm bell in the northeast section of the block.

Select the Templars and press the **R1 / RT**
button to send Henry after them to distract them.
This completes the Challenge for Henry's two
distractions. Throw a smoke bomb to help him
escape and to allow you to jump to the building
with the open window to the east of this group.
Enter the window and search the crate **(6)**. It does
not contain the documents either.

Exit the house through one of the Entry Point
windows and work your way to the final Chest **(8)**,
which is inside a house in the southeast corner of
the block. From the rooftop **(7)**, call Henry Green
to distract the Templars in the courtyard below and
throw a smoke bomb to further distract the Thugs
as you make your way into the top open window
(Entry Point) below.

Once inside the top floor of the house with the last Chest **(8)**, rush the Templar near the Chest and assassinate him. Search the Chest. You find this Chest empty
as well. Evie concludes that she's going to have to interrogate someone to figure out where the plans are.

CURRENT OBJECTIVE: KIDNAP A NEARBY TEMPLAR

Before you leave the room with the last Chest **(8)**, cover at the bedroom
doorway and whistle for the Templar directly below you on the first floor. Cover
Assassinate him when he comes up to investigate. Head downstairs and you
see a Templar with his back to you guarding the exit. He is perfectly positioned
for a kidnapping.

Kidnap the Templar in the doorway and walk him back inside the house. He
tells you that Henry has been taken but knows nothing about the documents.
Choke the Templar out or assassinate him (slice his throat while you have him
kidnapped) and leave him there.

CURRENT OBJECTIVE: FIND HENRY

Exit the front door where you kidnapped the Templar and head east on the sidewalk following the distant green blip **(9)**. When you reach the park, head to the northeast side of the gazebo to find your first clue to Henry's disappearance.

CURRENT OBJECTIVE: INVESTIGATE HENRY'S DISAPPEARANCE

There is a search icon on the ground between two dead Blighter bodies. Search this glowing marker. The dead bodies clearly show that Henry fought back. You begin to hear a little girl **(10)** at the street calling for you. Search the second clue just feet away from the first on your way to talk to the little children. These are visible footprints that indicate Henry might have been carried away.

With Eagle Vision activated you can see the footprints glowing and leading out of the park past the children you need to speak with next. The children say that Henry was taken off in a carriage and that the carriage was badly damaged and leaving tracks. He points to the south where another marker appears. Investigate this corner **(11)** next.

CURRENT OBJECTIVE: FOLLOW THE KIDNAPPERS' CARRIAGE

Activate Eagle Vision once you reach the marker on the street corner **(11)** the children pointed out. You spot yellow highlighted carriage tracks heading across the street. From here follow these tracks for blocks finding the wreckage it left in its wake. Follow the route marked on our map if you lose sight of the tracks.

CURRENT OBJECTIVE: FIND HENRY

CHALLENGE: KILL 2 GUARDS USING HANGING BARRELS
LOCATION: STREET MARKET, THE STRAND

The tracks lead to a market square a few blocks north. Assassinate the Blighter near the entrance and parked carriage and then speak to the first of a few civilians that may be able to help in the investigation. These people are highlighted yellow in Eagle Vision and appear on the Mini-Map as green blips. The first lady **(12)** near a flower cart only talks about the number of armed Thugs in the area.

THREE GREEN BLIPS

When you reach the market, you see four green blips representing people to talk to that can help you find Henry. You can talk to all of them, or just cut to the chase, skip the market, and go straight to the man **(15)** behind St. Paul's Church. This guy points you to the sewer where Henry was taken.

Sneak south and hide behind a cart near a small booth. You spot a couple of Thugs further to the south. They block you from reaching the next civilian to speak to **(13)**. Whistle for the nearest Thug and assassinate him when he investigates. Approach the second civilian **(13)** and talk to him about Henry. This guy (near the hiding booth) saw them carrying him from the carriage to the church.

Climb to the top of the shelter to the south of the man you just spoke with. From the rooftop of this shelter you can throw knives at the heads of the many Templars around the third civilian **(14)**. Before you approach and talk to this woman, Rope Launch to the rooftop of St. Paul's Church (next to the shelter you were on) and get rid of the Watcher on the rooftop. Take out the two Templars on the sidewalk to the north as well. Now you can speak to the woman at the fruit stand **(14)** without interruptions.

LOCATION: ST. PAUL'S CHURCH, THE STRAND

This lady thinks Henry was drunk and says they carried him off to the churchyard to sleep it off. There is one green blip remaining in the area. It's to the south in the churchyard **(15)**. Rope Launch back up to the rooftop of St. Paul's Church and head to the southern edge of the rooftop. Perform a Leap of Faith into the haystack below. Immediately Cover Assassinate the Brute standing next to the haystack.

Whistle for the second Brute to come to the haystack and then execute him. Exit the haystack and talk to the man **(15)** in the hat in the middle of the courtyard. He talks about a gate being unlocked and points north. Find the Pressed Flower on the bench nearby (flower icon on the Mini-Map).

Look at the Mini-Map and you notice a small green patch highlighted in the red restriction zone you're currently in. Head to this green area to the north and you find a Templar guarding an open well **(16)**. Instead of entering through the open gate where the Templar Brute and Solider can spot you, hop over the fence beside the open well and either drop into the well or assassinate the Templars and then enter the well.

LOCATION: SEWERS BELOW ST. PAUL'S CHURCH

Examine your Mini-Map when you jump down into the well. The accessible pathway is highlighted green. Head down the stairs on the left at the end of the first sewer tunnel. Assassinate the Brute standing with his back to you at the bottom of the stairs.

Follow the lower tunnel heading south. The tunnel bends left and reveals a door guarded by a Templar. He patrols this tunnel section and ends up approaching you. Back up to the previous corner and then come up behind him when he turns back towards the doorway.

In the next clearing, and with Eagle Vision activated, you see Henry (yellow) slumped over in a chair, with three Templars and barrels hanging in the middle of the chamber. If you miss this opportunity to drop barrels on two guards, there is another chance as you leave the sewers. Defeat the three Templars and free Henry.

172

CURRENT OBJECTIVE: ESCORT HENRY OUT OF THE AREA

CHALLENGE: KILL 2 GUARDS USING HANGING BARRELS

Untie Henry's ropes and he tells you they sent someone back to move the architectural plans. He asks if you have them. You do not. Open the Chest in the room and then follow Henry out of the sewer. In the next tunnel are two Templars. Henry throws down smoke as he runs past them. You can easily Double Assassinate them as you pass by them in the cloud of smoke.

Continue to follow Henry as he climbs stairs out of the sewers and enters Charing Cross Station. At the top of the first set of stairs in the station you can spot Templars on the left standing under hanging barrels. Quickly throw a knife at the barrels as you ascend the stairs. This completes the Challenge if have not completed it yet.

Henry turns right at the top of the stairs and throws a smoke bomb at the entrance of the next passage. Take out these two Templars. Henry runs into the next side of the station and attracts the attention of a group of four Templars. Henry runs back into the tunnel passage seeking your help with the battle. Drop your own smoke if you have some and quickly annihilate the threat.

Henry does it again…he runs south through the terminal and runs right into a large group of level 7 Templars. Throw a smoke bomb and help Henry take them out. It's likely this is a two-smoke bomb battle, as there are many high-level Templars to fight. Switch to knives or have your pistol available for Quickshots or combos that include weaponry. Luckily, there is a small gang of Rooks nearby that lends a hand—and a bullet or two.

Follow Henry across the street to complete the memory. Evie tells Henry to get Miss Nightingale to look at the wound on his forehead. She tells him that she must find the vault before Starrick secures the Shroud. Henry apologizes for his capture messing up her plans. Henry tells Evie, even if she finds the vault, she can't just walk into Buckingham Palace alone. She reassures him that she won't be alone and tells him she'll see him back on the hideout train.

UNBREAKING THE BANK

MISSION OVERVIEW

Memory Type: Templar Conspiracy Suggested Level: 7	ASSASSIN Evie Frye	CHALLENGES Burn the counterfeit money Let the civilians into the Bank	REWARDS £: 900 + 250 (Full Synch Bonus) XP: 700 + 250 (Full Synch Bonus) Firearm: M1877 "Lightning"

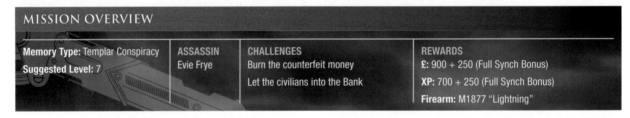

LOCATION: ROYAL EXCHANGE, CITY OF LONDON

Evie meets Frederick Abberline in an alley near the Royal Exchange in the City of London. There's a market riot going on and Abberline looks angry. He pokes a finger at Evie saying her brother is behind this chaos. The newspapers are all over Twopenny's murder and if that weren't enough, someone has stolen the currency printing plates. Abberline believes Jacob was behind this. Abberline fears inflation, riots, and possibly manufacturing jumping to America for cheap labor. Evie tells Abberline that she will fix everything by sneaking the plates back into the bank. He also asks her to destroy the counterfeiting plates if she comes across them.

CURRENT OBJECTIVE: FOLLOW ABBERLINE

Walk with Abberline as he escorts you through the chaos in the street. There's a couple of cops to pass (they're with Abberline) but they won't be a problem as you walk through the crowded street. Abberline loudly and nervously bickers about the counterfeit plates. All the while, Evie tries to remain cool and quiets him under her breath. Don't worry; you'll leave him behind soon enough.

CURRENT OBJECTIVE: LOCATE THE COUNTERFEITER

When you reach the next street **(2)**, Abberline stays behind. You see the Royal Exchange ahead and a green blip inside. Walk right in through that south doorway while walking upright like the rest of the public. There's no worry…yet. Once inside, activate Eagle Vision and look to your right to spot the counterfeiter. He glows yellow and has been labeled "Tail."

CURRENT OBJECTIVE: TAIL THE COUNTERFEITER

With Eagle Vision activated you can see two red Blighters and the yellow counterfeiter. They join together and walk out the north doorway—a straight shot from the south doorway you entered. Beat them to it. Just walk right through that building and keep your eye on the "Tail." When you take your eyes away a timer appears and starts counting down from 15 sec before you are desynchronized. So when you just walk through the Royal Exchange, enter the carriage **(4)** parked outside at the curb. Enter the hiding spot inside the carriage, not the driver's seat. This keeps you hidden from all the threats on the street and from the two escorting the counterfeiter to his carriage. His carriage **(5)** is just a few yards away from you to the west.

If you take out his bodyguards it always turns out badly; the counterfeiter notices you eventually and you are desynchronized. You also see a group of Rooks across the street from your hiding carriage. Don't call on them yet. They can just foul things up too.

When the counterfeiter reaches his carriage, exit your hiding spot inside and quickly take the driver's seat. Begin following your Tail. Do not follow too closely, but get moving if a cop or Thug starts looking at you for too long. Follow the counterfeiter as he gets driven only a few blocks away to the south. It's a short trip. They stop at some ramshackle building **(6)**. Exit your vehicle a good distance away and get to the rooftops **(7)** across the street from where the target's carriage parked. Your objective changes when he reaches this destination. You no longer have to worry about being seen. But let's remain anonymous.

CURRENT OBJECTIVE: LOCATE THE PRINTING PLATES

CHALLENGE: BURN THE COUNTERFEIT MONEY

From the rooftops **(7)** across the street, get a Rope Launch lock on to the rooftop of the target building **(8)** with the printing plates.

Get to the west side of this corner unit apartment building and look over the edge. You see a haystack and three Blighters around a barrel fire (use Eagle Vision). To your left you can see a few Blighters inside an apartment and an item that has a "Steal" blip. Walk along the rooftop until you are next to the open window on the second floor. The Blighters do not spot you if you go no lower than the second floor.

BURN COUNTERFEIT MONEY

Enter the only open room on this floor and you find the counterfeit money to burn on a desk inside. Burn it to complete the Challenge.

Head downstairs and assassinate the Brute if you have not already (on the stairs) and then silently dispatch the Enforcer on the lower floor where the printing plates are. The plates are on a desk near the stairs. Take them. Exit out of the apartment by heading back upstairs and going through the window in the room where you found the counterfeit money that you burned.

There is a Watcher guarding this window, but if you enter using the **L1 / LT** button then you can move right to an attack as you are passing through and get an assassination. If you miss, the Watcher is so off guard that you can take her out before she gives you away. You can wait to do this move when the nearby Brute is not on the stairs or just go in and take them both quickly. It won't escalate to reinforcements.

176

CURRENT OBJECTIVE: REACH THE BANK OF ENGLAND

CHALLENGE: LET THE CIVILIANS INTO THE BANK

Exit the south side of the counterfeit house and look for the green blip on your map that represents the Bank of England. Rooftop hop and zipline to get there. When you reach the bank **(9)**, you discover a huge crowd at the southern entrance and security holding them back. No one is allowed inside. Look further east on the corner and you find a gang of Rooks **(10)**. Recruit them and then come back to the crowded doorway.

Have your Rooks take out the cops near the door and then enter the bank through this doorway and order your Rooks to take out any other nearby threats. Stand in the lobby just through the doors and watch the crowd from the street start spilling into the bank. This completes the Challenge.

CURRENT OBJECTIVE: RETURN THE PRINTING PLATES

You've been in the bank before as Jacob so you probably know its layout pretty well by now. Just walk into the main lobby, continue north to the vault, take a right into the office (not into the vault) where Jacob kidnapped the Bank Manager. Unlock the door and enter the next room with the open elevator shaft. Return the plates to the table near the windows on the left side of the room.

CURRENT OBJECTIVE: ESCAPE THE BANK OF ENGLAND

To escape, just run out the front door. You could use the Entry Point in the small office where you just unlocked the door, but it's just as easy to run out the front door and lose any followers you might have picked up.

CURRENT OBJECTIVE: SPEAK TO ABBERLINE

Abberline stands near a lamppost **(11)** on an island in the cobblestone street in front of the Royal Exchange.

Abberline thanks you for cleaning up Jacob's mess. He says the papers are running the story of how it was all a hoax. No more riots! Faith in the bank restored!

177

MOTION TO IMPEACH

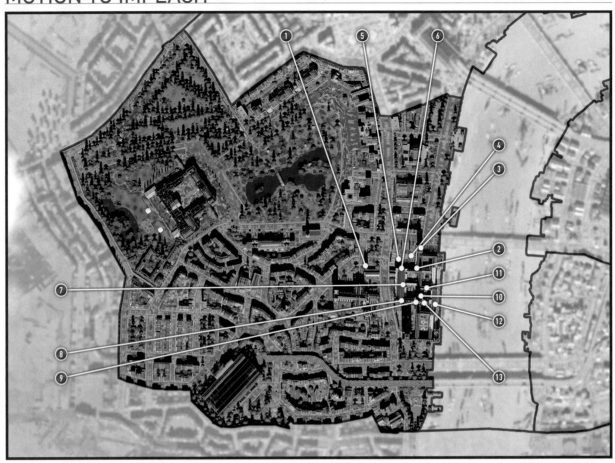

MISSION OVERVIEW

		CHALLENGES	REWARDS
Memory Type: Templar Conspiracy	**ASSASSIN**	Don't kill any policemen	**£:** 3480 + 250 (Full Synch Bonus)
Suggested Level: 7	Jacob Frye	Do not get detected by the target	**XP:** 4000 + 250 (Full Synch Bonus)
			Outfit: Blackguard's Suit

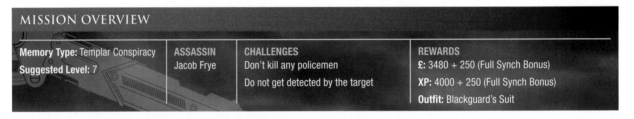

LOCATION: ST. MARGARET'S, WESTMINSTER

You can start this memory by entering the marker at the top of St. Margaret's church **(1)** in Westminster. The marker is at the top of the clock and bell tower. In the beginning of the mission, Jacob sits on the side of the bell tower strategizing his next move regarding Lord Cardigan, currently inside the House of Parliament.

CURRENT OBJECTIVE: FIND THE EARL OF CARDIGAN

CHALLENGE:

DO NOT KILL ANY POLICEMEN

CHALLENGE:

DO NOT GET DETECTED BY THE TARGET

Jacob starts this Challenge by sitting on St. Margaret's bell tower while studying the activity across the street around Big Ben and the House of Parliament. You have three tactical options with this memory: a Unique Kill Opportunity **(A)**, a Stealth Opportunity **(B)**, and an Assistance Opportunity **(C)**. We use all three in our strategy and in the order they are introduced in the beginning of the memory.

Start by getting the password from the Minister **(A)** in the courtyard below Big Ben. This gives you a Unique Kill Opportunity on the Earl of Cardigan. Next, kidnap the corrupt policeman **(B)** in the same courtyard to stealthily gain entry into the House of Parliament without harming any policemen. Once inside, talk to a politician **(C)** to get an assistance opportunity allowing you to be guided to the door where the password is used.

Zipline to the rooftop of the House of Parliament and make your way to the lowest rooftop (balcony) in the southeast corner **(2)** of the Big Ben courtyard. Use Eagle Vision to spot the many policemen patrolling the area and to locate the Minister **(A)**. Notice the policeman **(D)** patrolling under your balcony. This is your first target.

LOCATION:

HOUSE OF PARLIAMENT COURTYARD

OPTIONAL OBJECTIVE: STEAL LORD CARDIGAN'S PASSWORD

Drop down off the balcony when the policeman **(F)** near the middle of the courtyard is walking west and away from you on his patrol. Drop down and hide behind the south side of the second column in the hallway below the balcony to hide from the patrolling policeman **(D)** under the balcony. He stops just on the other side of this second column then walks north toward a second patrolling policeman **(E)** at the far end of the balcony hallway.

Knock out the cop **(D)** when he is walking past the next column so that none of the policemen, especially the closest one **(F)** see you or his body when you have dropped him. Only knock out the policemen; do not assassinate them or you fail the Challenge.

179

We also suggest you make the trek to the end of the Big Ben hallway to choke out the policeman **(E)** patrolling the far end. He could possibly see you steal the password from the Minister, which you will work on getting next.

With the two hallway patrols out of the way and while policeman **(F)** is walking away to the north, you can now move from behind a nearby column to approach the Minister **(A)** on the middle sidewalk when he walks north towards the fountain. Quickly come up behind him, acquire the *Steal* prompt, press and hold ◎ / Ⓑ until the Steal gauge fills and then quickly walk away, back under the column you just left to hide again.

OPTIONAL OBJECTIVE: KIDNAP THE CORRUPT POLICEMAN

From behind a column under the balcony where you knocked out two policemen, wait for policeman **(F)** to walk north on the sidewalk he patrols. Come up behind him quickly before he gets too far north that the corrupt policeman sees and knock him out. You can leave him on the sidewalk.

After knocking out the policeman **(F)** sneak north along his sidewalk and cover behind the north side of the hedgerow that gives you a clear view of the House of Parliament's north entrance and the patrolling Minister **(G)**.

To kidnap the corrupt policeman, make your move when the policeman **(G)** walks away from the House of Parliament entrance and moves towards your hiding place behind the hedgerow and then turns north (right), continuing his patrol. Sneak around the end of the hedge and come up behind him and kidnap him.

OPTIONAL OBJECTIVE: REACH WESTMINSTER HALL

Walk the corrupt policeman through the front entrance of the House of Parliament **(6)**. Sometimes the guards at the door move far away from the entrance and sometimes they leave little room for you to get past them. Regardless, they move enough for you to slowly walk past them without your detection ring intersecting with their feet.

LOCATION:
HOUSE OF PARLIAMENT INTERIOR
OPTIONAL OBJECTIVE:
FOLLOW THE POLITICIAN

Once inside Parliament, walk the policeman into the left corner and knock him out. Now walk up to the politician just a couple of yards away along the left wall. Talk to him and he has you follow him to Lord Cardigan's office where you are to use the password you acquired.

As the politician heads to the south end of the hall you quickly notice a patrolling Brute **(H)** near some pews. You do not have the politician kidnapped so you currently have no stealth opportunity. If the Brute sees you, you instinctively run for cover into the open hallway **(7)** on the left. If you do this, you run right into a couple of patrolling Blighters. To deal with this issue, quickly throw a knife at the Brute's **(H)** head to get rid of him.

Rejoin the politician at the north end of the room (open the Chest to the right of the hiding booth) and follow him as he enters the left (east) hallway **(8)**. There is a Templar Brute in this hallway. Throw a knife or wait and sneak up behind him and assassinate him. Enter the room **(9)** at the end of this hallway and Double Assassinate the two Blighters standing next to each other with their backs to you.

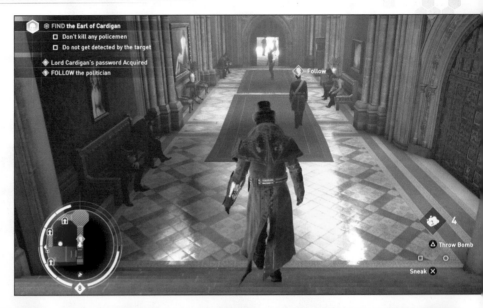

Follow the politician into the north hallway **(10)** where you face four level 7 Templars. Use a smoke bomb and have fun eliminating the confused gang while the politician enters the hallway to the right **(11)**.

In the hallway to the right is a mixture of level 7 and 8 Templars. There's a total of six Templars in all. Throw a few smoke bombs during this battle. Eliminate them all. It's fun. There are ways to do this stealthily using the hiding booth at the beginning of the hallway or by opening the exterior door on the left side of the hallway, but it's much more fun just to have a big brawl and use your awesome fighting skills to own this crowd.

Loot all the bodies and continue to follow the politician to Cardigan's Office **(12)**. His office is at the end of the southeast hallway. There's an intersecting hallway with Templars (to your right) that could be an issue. Either sneak past them when they are not facing your way or just eliminate them. But when you reach Cardigan's office you must be anonymous to give the password. When you are anonymous and at the doorway, simply press the ⊚ / ⑧ button to give the password. Make sure you do not hold the button or you unlock the door and cancel your Unique Kill Opportunity.

Jacob gives the password: Balaclava. The guard opens the door and Jacob silently executes him then sneaks up behind the Earl of Cardigan, whose back is turned, preoccupied with something at a desk. Press the ⚪ / ✕ button when prompted to assassinate the Earl using the Unique Kill Opportunity. Jacob gets no usable information out of the stubborn old man in the Animus white room and when you return from the white room you must escape the Houses of Parliament.

WALKTHROUGH

SIDE QUESTS

COLLECTIBLES

REFERENCE & ANALYSIS

INDEX

SEQUENCE ONE

SEQUENCE TWO

SEQUENCE FIVE

SEQUENCE SIX

SEQUENCE SEVEN

SEQUENCE EIGHT

SEQUENCE NINE

CURRENT OBJECTIVE: ESCAPE THE HOUSES OF PARLIAMENT

When control returns to you, head for the Templar at the open door on the northwestern side of the office. Come up behind the Templar and silently assassinate him. There are three Templars guarding the door **(13)** to the left as you enter the hallway. Throw a smoke bomb and eliminate them.

Enter the chamber **(9)** (the hallway junction with the statue in the middle of the floor) these Templars were guarding and then head to the Entry Point you can see in the hallway to the right **(10)**. Rope Launch to the rooftop of the building and travel along the rooftops to reach The Thames where you can exit the restricted zone and complete the mission.

THE JOYS OF FREEDOM

Now that Jacob and Evie have conquered three of London's boroughs, they have attracted the attention of the most powerful kingpin in London. Meanwhile, Evie becomes disillusioned after Henry's mistakes cause her to lose ground in the search for the Shroud of Eden.

TAKE THE STREETS!

To unlock Sequence 8 you must control at least three boroughs.

STRANGE BEDFELLOWS

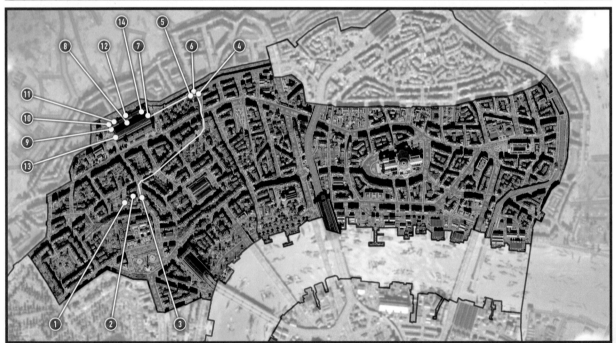

MISSION OVERVIEW

Memory Type: Templar Conspiracy	**ASSASSIN**	**CHALLENGES**	**REWARDS**
Suggested Level: 7	Jacob Frye	Use the moving train	**£:** 1160 + 250 (Full Synch Bonus)
		Destroy all dynamite by igniting it	**XP:** 500 + 250 (Full Synch Bonus)
			Cape: Lady Cyrielle's Shawl

THE ESSENTIALS
WALKTHROUGH
SIDE QUESTS
COLLECTIBLES
REFERENCE & ABILITIES
INDEX

SEQUENCE ONE
SEQUENCE TWO
SEQUENCE THREE
SEQUENCE FOUR
SEQUENCE FIVE
SEQUENCE SIX
SEQUENCE SEVEN
SEQUENCE EIGHT
SEQUENCE NINE

LOCATION: ALHAMBRA MUSIC HALL, THE STRAND

Find the start marker **(1)** for this Jacob-only memory at the Alhambra Music Hall in The Strand. This is just next door to Leicester Square. When this memory begins, you must first locate the back entrance before the intro cinematic. There's someone you have to see.

CURRENT OBJECTIVE: LOCATE THE BACK ENTRANCE

When you try to enter the front door of the Alhambra Music Hall, you find the door locked. Your Mini-Map is lit with a small green square representing the search radius. The "back" door is on the north side of the building. There you find a doorman in a very nice derby **(2)**.

CURRENT OBJECTIVE: SPEAK WITH THE DOORMAN

Speak to the doorman with the derby. You tell the doorman you are there to speak with Mr. Roth. The doorman kindly asks "weapons?" and Jacob returns a smart reply. He tells Jacob he should be on the stage and lets him inside.

CURRENT OBJECTIVE: REACH ROTH

Once inside, use Eagle Vision to quickly spot Roth backstage behind a room full of stage props. Follow the green blip to find Roth.

Maxwell Roth and Jacob manage to have a civil conversation between enemies. Max admires Jacob's heroics in battling their common enemy Crawford Starrick.

Jacob is surprised at Roth's candor since he has picked off so many of his soldiers. In they end they surprisingly agree to work together to take out Starrick. Won't Evie be pleased.

CURRENT OBJECTIVE: DRIVE TO THE DESTINATION WITH ROTH

Once out of the theatre, follow Roth to his carriage **(3)** parked outside the gates. He has you take the reins and directs you to drive to St. Pancras **(4)**. Follow the route marker to reach this destination. Along the way, Roth explains that this station they are headed to contains a large shipment of explosives to be dispatched straight on to Starrick & Co. They intend to blow it up.

CURRENT OBJECTIVE: FOLLOW ROTH

Once at the destination **(4)**, Roth jumps out and climbs to the top of a building. Follow him. Once there you find yourself within jumping distance to a set of raised tracks. Roth speaks….

CURRENT OBJECTIVE: LOCATE AND DESTROY THE 5 EXPLOSIVES

CHALLENGE: USE THE MOVING TRAIN

While on the rooftop **(5)**, Roth explains that there is a train inside St. Pancras station that he needs you to bring to him. While there, you can blow up his merchandise. A train moves toward you from the east. Turn the camera during the conversation so you can see it coming. Roth says, "As we speak, the up train **(6)** is headed to St. Pancras that, should you choose to ride it, may help you enter the station unseen."

As soon as the train rolls by, turn, run, and jump onto the train. It doesn't matter what car you ride in; you remain concealed no matter which car you choose. We suggest jumping into one of the last cars so you can get inside a covered car.

Activate Eagle Vision as you enter the train station **(7)**. You spot Templars all over the station, including the catwalks, and you see five green blips peppered on the screen. These mark the locations of the crates you must ignite.

It's much easier to eliminate anyone that gets in your way in this memory as opposed to hurting few. But if you do it silently and without attracting too much attention, you can complete this memory rather quickly.

THE COVERED CAR ADVANTAGE

To take out a high number of enemies right in the central docking area get into the covered car on the train you are riding on and ride that until it is stopped. Cover under or beside a window on the north side and the train stops next to many Templars.

Throw a knife at the head of the Templar Leader with the yellow 7 over his head. That's a good start. Make sure you are covered, as there will be some curiosity from more of the five other Templars in the area. You can kill up to three Templars from this location. Exit the car launch to the high rafters as soon as possible and before being spotted by the Snipers on the catwalks.

From the high framework you can move over the Snipers on the catwalks and get within knife-throwing range. Save a knife and Air Assassinate the final catwalk Templar.

Continue moving all around this side of the train station taking out Templars from above, like a spider attacking prey, then springing back up to the rafters. Once you have eliminated most (or all) of them, you can focus on the explosive crates.

EXPLOSIVES 1

The first crate of dynamite **(8)** you usually find is the one inside the train car on the opposite tracks you rolled in on. Hold to ignite them until the gauge is full and then clear out. We suggest Rope Launching back up to the rafters.

EXPLOSIVES 2

Head all the way to the northwest end of the train station and defeat the guards on the upper balcony. Drop down to the lower floor (where the trains are) and you find dynamite **(9)** along the northern wall behind a desk. Use the desk for cover as you take out the Brute, then ignite the dynamite.

EXPLOSIVES 3

Now head around the corner to enter the most northwestern corner of the train station on the first floor to find the third crate of dynamite **(10)**. Defeat the nearby Templars and ignite these explosives.

EXPLOSIVES 4

Follow the red blip **(11)** on your Mini-Map to the last red blip in the area. This is on the eastern branch of the second level balcony on the northwest end of the train station. There's a slow Templar Sniper and a Templar Soldier. Easy pickings. Take them out by sneaking up on them from pretty much any angle and then ignite the crates (don't shoot them).

EXPLOSIVES 5

The last crate of explosives **(12)** is located in the north wing of the station—the north hall just outside the track loading area. You can reach this area through a large open archway-like window near the ceiling to take the Templars around it by surprise. The explosives are behind the newsstand. Igniting (and not shooting) the final crate of explosives completes the Challenge.

CURRENT OBJECTIVE: FIND AND KIDNAP A DRIVER

Now to get the train that Roth wants. To get a train you're going to need an engineer. Look at the Mini-Map and spot the green blip on the map in the southwestern side of the station, in the main loading area. Head there now. Defeat any Templars in your path. Having most of the Templars dead in the main station makes this next objective much easier.

As you get close to the driver the blip on the Mini-Map turns to a search area green circle and then, even closer, you spot the driver and he appears as an orange blip on the Mini-Map. Kidnap this man **(13)**.

CURRENT OBJECTIVE: REACH THE LOCOMOTIVE WITH THE DRIVER

Now walk the kidnapped driver to the north side of train station **(14)** to access the northern loading area. Move slowly to sneak past any surviving Templars. Walk the driver into the glowing reach marker next to the train engine. Ignore the nearby Brute (if he's still living). The driver gets the train moving as you leave the station.

When the train reaches Maxwell Roth, it slows to allow Jacob off and everyone else on. They continue to hold the driver at gunpoint. Jacob looks as if he's already starting to regret this working relationship. Roth yells back to Jacob, "Splendid, Starrick will be on his knees in no time. My hat is off to you." "…Do come see me again."

TRIPLE THREAT

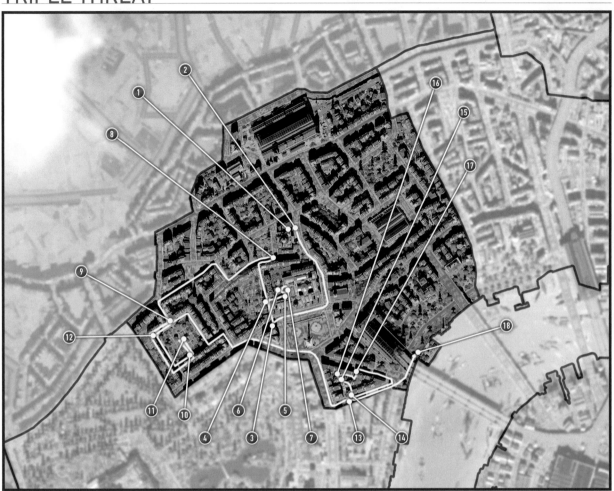

MISSION OVERVIEW

Memory Type: Templar Conspiracy	**ASSASSIN**	**CHALLENGES**	**REWARDS**
Suggested Level: 7	Jacob Frye	Do not kill anyone inside the Target locations	**£:** 1160 + 250 (Full Synch Bonus)
		Don't let any target escape from being kidnapped	**XP:** 500 + 250 (Full Synch Bonus)
			Schematic: Assassin Gauntlet Schematic

LOCATION:

ALHAMBRA MUSIC HALL, THE STRAND

Return to the Alhambra to talk to Roth. This time you know where to enter—the back door **(1)**, where you met the doorman last time.

When Jacob finds Roth, he's absorbed with a birdcage on a low table and doesn't even look up when Jacob enters the room. The baby crow draws his attention until he warmly looks up to Jacob and turns on the excitement like a switch. He wants you to ride with him to take out three of Starrick's top henchmen.

CURRENT OBJECTIVE:
REACH THE NATIONAL GALLERY

> CHALLENGE: DO NOT KILL ANYONE INSIDE THE TARGET LOCATIONS
>
> CHALLENGE: DON'T LET ANY TARGET ESCAPE FROM BEING KIDNAPPED

Once outside the Alhambra **(1)**, follow Roth to his carriage **(2)** at the street. And of course, he wants you to drive. Take the reins. Follow the route marker to the National Gallery and stop in the glowing white marker in the street **(3)**.

Step onto Roth's carriage to resume

CURRENT OBJECTIVE: FIND CLUES TO HATTIE'S WHEREABOUTS

Just before you reach the first stop **(3)**, Roth explains Starrick's interest in art. Hattie Cadwalleder has exquisite taste in art, so much so that Starrick has hired her to be the keeper of his extensive personal collection. She also scouts out the National Gallery shipments and organizes art thefts based on the Gallery's schedule and incoming shipments. Roth wants you to kidnap her. Leave the carriage, walk north down the alley, and talk to the little girl at the gate **(4)**.

The girl points you through the gates behind her when you ask her about Hattie's whereabouts. Head east into the courtyard. Don't stop walking until you are right up on a policeman **(5)** who is preoccupied with some art pedestal in front of him. Come up behind the policeman and knock him out and then investigate the pedestal.

Turn north from the pedestal and talk to the little boy at the next gate **(6)**. He points you to the sewers on the other side of that short wall beside you **(7)**. Quickly follow the policeman in this yard around the circular wall/island in the middle. Come up behind him and knock him out. You can leave him where he falls.

CURRENT OBJECTIVE: KIDNAP HATTIE CADWALLADER

After speaking to the boy at the gate, your objective is to go get Hattie and take her back to Roth's carriage. Enter the sewers found behind the short wall. Climb down the stairs and stop at the second right corner turn to study the movements of the Templars below.

A Templar soldier enters the tunnel you are facing and walks toward you. When he does this and turns back to head back the way he came, make your move. Come up behind him and knock him out. Do not kill him so you can follow the Challenge rules (do not kill anyone in the target zone). You can see the sewer tunnels are highlighted red on the Mini-Map. You are again in the target zone.

After knocking out the first **(A)** soldier, take the first left possible in the tunnel and quickly kidnap the guard on the left side of the room. Now stand facing the second guard **(B)** walking your way from the back of the tunnel to the north. Choke out the first guard as soon as the second guard passes you, then come up behind him and choke the second guard out.

Head north into the tunnel the second soldier **(B)** was guarding and turn left. Use Eagle Vision and you can see your kidnap victim in the next room. We suggest heading straight to the target and knocking her out. This way she has no chance of escape. She is not dead when you do this (unlike with Bounty Hunts); Roth and the Challenge accept your kidnapped victims knocked out. Pick up Hattie. Exit the tunnel the way you came in and continue through the yard to the point where you talked to the girl at the first gate **(4)**. There are no cops to be concerned about because you knocked them out on the way in.

CURRENT OBJECTIVE: DELIVER HATTIE TO ROTH

When you reach the girl at the gate **(4)**, instead of heading left the way you came, head right instead. Roth has moved the carriage to the other street **(8)**. Walk down the alleyway and take a right at the street to reach Roth. It's much easier this way than going through the police in the courtyard. Avoid running into people; that causes you to drop the body. Also, run in the street to avoid the sidewalks but weave in and out of the carriage traffic. Put the body in Roth's carriage.

CURRENT OBJECTIVE: REACH SAINT JAMES PARK

This memory is called "Triple Threat," which means you have two more kidnappings like this one to make. Take the reins of Maxwell Roth's carriage **(8)** and drive you, Roth, and Hattie to the next destination, Saint James Park **(9)**.

CURRENT OBJECTIVE: KIDNAP BENJAMIN RAFFLES

When you arrive at the Reach marker across the street from Saint James Park, Roth tells you to be careful and that Raffles' guards are never far away. The park's north entrance has two guards, as do the west and east. Use the rooftops to reach the south entrance **(10)** where no guards stand or patrol. Raffles has a short patrol route to and from the east side of the gazebo **(11)**. When he walks away from the gazebo, move to the opposite side of it (west) and wait for him to come and turn away again.

CURRENT OBJECTIVE: DELIVER BENJAMIN TO ROTH

Come up behind Raffles when he is facing away from the gazebo and kidnap him. Walk him back through the south exit **(10)**. This is the least guarded area. Now work your way carefully back through the street to Roth, avoiding the patrolling Blighter carriage and the Blighters on a street corner **(12)** to the north.

CURRENT OBJECTIVE: REACH SCOTLAND YARD

With two henchmen in the carriage, time to get the last one. Drive everyone to Scotland Yard **(13)** following the route marker on the road or Mini-Map. Blighters on the road generally leave you alone while you are with Roth, but don't push your luck. Drive cool and get to the destination without having to kill anybody.

CURRENT OBJECTIVE: KIDNAP CHESTER SWINBOURNE

Parked in the marker outside Scotland Yard **(13)**, turn and face the yellow-bricked building to your north and Rope Launch to the top.

Activate Eagle Vision once on the rooftop **(14)** and you spot Chester (the yellow figure) in a room two buildings away. Hop from your rooftop to the next and then to Chester's building.

Climb on the exterior wall to his open window on the fourth floor. Wait beside the window **(15)** until Chester walks away from this open window. When he does, walk in and kidnap him.

CURRENT OBJECTIVE: DELIVER CHESTER TO ROTH

LOCATION: SCOTLAND YARD; FOURTH FLOOR

This is the trickiest delivery so keep him conscious. Do not knock Chester out until you are in the clear, out of Scotland Yard security.

With Chester kidnapped, walk him down the stairs in the next room (avoiding the cop at the window to the left) to reach the third floor. Walk him very slowly so he does not escape on the stairs.

LOCATION: SCOTLAND YARD; THIRD FLOOR

On the third floor, wait for the guard **(C)** to walk from the right side of the room to the window on the left. Walk past him and the civilians to reach the stairs on the right side of the room. Head down the stairs to the second floor.

LOCATION: SCOTLAND YARD; SECOND FLOOR

On the second floor, stop at the bottom of the stairs and wait for the patrolling policeman **(D)** to move away from the window and stair entrance. Just keep to the left and walk down the stairs in the middle of the room. Do this slowly so the second policeman **(E)** leaning on the other side of the railing does not cross your detection zone.

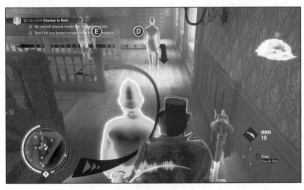

193

LOCATION: SCOTLAND YARD; FIRST FLOOR STAIRWAY

On your way down the stairs from the second floor you spot a guard **(F)** at the door at the bottom of the stairs and another guard outside the door **(G)**, blocking it completely. There's no way to squeeze through. Stop on the stairs and wait for the guard **(F)** at the bottom of the stairs to walk into the room on the left and then walk Chester to the bottom of the stairs and take a right at the doorway to enter the room to the right of the stairs. Continue around a desk and out a backdoor.

LOCATION: SCOTLAND YARD EXTERIOR

Once outside **(16)**, turn right and pass the alarm bell and hiding booth on your right and continue through the concrete gate archway. There are two guards behind you to your west that patrol these grounds. Keep moving and, if they get close, walk out of their pathway to keep them out of the detection zone. This zone becomes smaller when you walk slowly as opposed to standing in one place.

Continue along this path through the archway. Slowly pass two guards on the right side of the pathway. One more policeman patrols ahead near the next gate opening. He walks away to the right. When he does, pass through the gate and turn left toward the street **(17)**.

Once in the street, check your map and you see you are on the opposite side of the block from Roth **(13)** so walk Chester through the street around the east corner

and back to the carriage. If you don't want to risk him getting away now, you can knock him out and carry him from here.

CURRENT OBJECTIVE: REACH THE DELIVERY POINT

With everyone in the carriage, drive to the delivery point **(18)** just southeast of the Charing Cross Station, just a few blocks away to the northeast.

When you reach the docks, Roth's men load the three kidnapped henchmen onto a boat. Roth congratulates you and tells you to come see him again at the Alhambra.

FUN AND GAMES

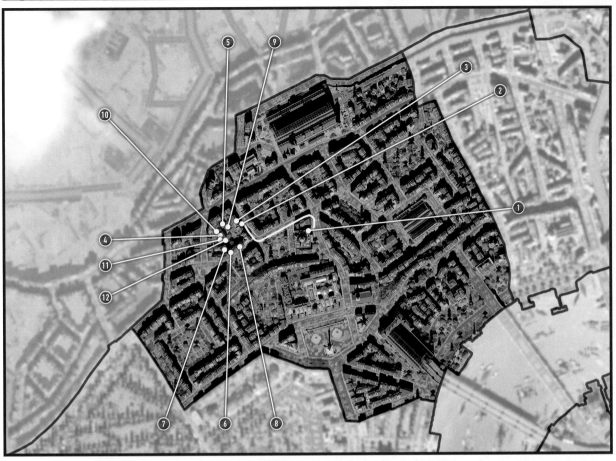

MISSION OVERVIEW

Memory Type: Templar Conspiracy **Suggested Level:** 7	**ASSASSIN** Jacob Frye	**CHALLENGES** Do not kill anyone while placing explosives	**REWARDS** **£:** 1160 + 250 (Full Synch Bonus) **XP:** 500 + 250 (Full Synch Bonus) **Brass Knuckles:** Copper Love

LOCATION: ALHAMBRA MUSIC HALL, THE STRAND

Return to the Alhambra to talk to Roth. Again, start this memory from the back door **(1)**. This time Roth meets you at the door and directs you to his carriage in the street. He has something to show you.

CURRENT OBJECTIVE:
REACH STARRICK'S WORKSHOP

Enter the carriage in the street next to the Alhambra. Drive Roth to Starrick's workshop compound about a block away to the west **(2)**.

15
XP
WANTON DESTRUCTION
55 / 75 Performed

10

Ram □   ○ Exit

Boost ✕

CURRENT OBJECTIVE: FOLLOW ROTH

LOCATION: STARRICK'S WORKSHOP, THE STRAND

Once you enter the Reach marker outside Starrick's compound **(2)**, Roth hops out of the carriage and enters a short covered alleyway and climbs to the rooftop **(3)** of a building on the right. Follow him.

Enter Eagle Vision while standing on the edge of the rooftop with Roth. Notice the Templars all around the workshop to the west **(4)** across the street.

CURRENT OBJECTIVE: RIG THE WORKSHOP WITH DYNAMITE

CHALLENGE: DO NOT KILL ANYONE WHILE PLACING THE EXPLOSIVES

There are multiple crates of dynamite around the workshop that are easily spotted; they appear as orange blips onscreen and on the Mini-Map. There are four locations where you need to place the dynamite around the building. Walk to the edge of the rooftop to get as close as you can to the building **(5)** to the north of the workshop.

Acquire a Rope Launch lock-on on this building's chimney and zipline there. Your target is the rooftop sniper that must be dealt with first. Walk over the peak of the rooftop and knock out the Sniper from behind. Kill no one to obey the Challenge rule.

Move to the south edge of this rooftop and Rope Launch to the northwest edge of the workshop's **(4)** rooftop to get behind the Templar on the rooftop. Knock this Templar out. There's one more rooftop Templar **(C)** to deal with.

Move to the southwest corner of the workshop rooftop **(4)** and zipline to the buildings **(6)** on the southern edge of the workshop compound. You pass the last rooftop Templar who is on a building on the right **(7)**. Now zipline to the south edge of the rooftop Templar's building and come up behind her and knock her out.

From the corner of this rooftop **(7)** you can look down to the alley and sidewalks around the workshop and spot about five or six of the Templars guarding the workshop. We will walk you through taking out every Templar down there. Taking them all out makes the Challenges in this memory much easier to deal with.

Return to the previous rooftops **(6)** and walk along the north edge heading to the end of the building **(8)** to the northeast. Drop down to the alley and knock out the Templar **(D)** that patrols the alley below.

THE ESSENTIALS
WALKTHROUGH
SIDE QUESTS
COLLECTIBLES
REFERENCE & ANALYSIS
INDEX

SEQUENCE ONE
SEQUENCE TWO
SEQUENCE THREE
SEQUENCE FOUR
SEQUENCE FIVE
SEQUENCE SIX
SEQUENCE SEVEN
SEQUENCE EIGHT
SEQUENCE NINE

Get back to the rooftops and travel back to where Roth is standing **(3)**. Rope Launch back to the rooftop of the small house **(5)** north of the workshop. Drop down to the red awning on the house's east side. Wait for the patrolling Templar **(E)** below to walk south toward the nearest dynamite cache. Drop down and knock him out before he reaches the cart where the dynamite is located (there's another Templar standing behind this cart at a gate entrance).

Now take cover at the northeast corner of this same house **(5)**. While under the awning you dropped down from, look north for the patrolling Templar **(F)**. He patrols from west to east and stops near the parked carriage near this house. When he turns back west on his route, sneak up behind him and knock him out.

Again, return to the east side of the house **(5)** and sneak up beside the cart **(9)** near the explosives. Use Eagle Vision to spot the patrolling Templars in the yard around the workshop. The Templar **(G)** standing with his back to you at the end of the cart near the explosives does not patrol. The Brute **(H)** closest to him in the yard patrols from just beside this Templar to a haystack next to the house **(5)**. A Templar Leader **(I)** also needs to be watched, as he stops near the haystack at the end of his patrol. When the Leader **(I)** is far away from the haystack and the Brute **(H)** is walking toward the haystack, sneak around the corner of the cart and knock out the Templar Soldier. There's enough time to pick him up and hide his body behind the cart.

Do not interact with the explosives yet. Instead, get to the house **(5)** rooftop and perform a Leap of Faith into the haystack on the south side. When the Templar Leader **(I)** is walking away from the haystack and the Brute **(H)** turns and walks away from the haystack, silently exit the haystack and knock the Brute out. Hide his body behind the cart **(9)** so the Leader does not see it.

Renter the haystack when the Leader **(I)** is not looking and then wait for him to come and go again and sneak up behind him and knock him out. Do this quickly before he walks too closely to the Templar Soldier **(J)** guarding the small toolshed to the west. Hide his body behind the cart **(9)**.

Rope Launch to the rooftop of the workshop **(4)** then Leap of Faith into the haystack (next to the toolshed). Exit the haystack and sneak around the north edge and come up behind the Templar **(J)** standing in front of the shed and knock him out.

Creep up and cover next to the southwest corner **(11)** of the workshop. Look around the corner and observe the Templar **(L)** leaning on the stack of barrels on the south side of the workshop. This Templar Soldier does not move unless alerted. Come up beside him and knock him out. The Templar **(M)** walking a patrol route on the other side of the nearby fence does not see you through the fence, so you do not need to wait for him to walk by.

Cover beside the north fence and the toolshed **(10)** and watch the Brute **(K)** patrolling the yard to the south. When he walks away from you heading south, come up behind him and knock him out. You can leave his body where it falls. You're almost done; only a couple more to go.

Hop up on the fence and then leap over when the patrolling Templar **(M)** walks by. Come up behind him and knock him out.

PLACE FOUR CRATES OF DYNAMITE IN FOUR LOCATIONS

Now that all the enemies are knocked out, follow the yellow blips on the map around the yard to find the dynamite caches. When you pick up a crate of dynamite four green drop-off locations appear around the workshop **(4)**. Place a crate of dynamite in each of these for locations (blipped green on the Mini-Map). Do not ignite or shoot the crates once placed.

CURRENT OBJECTIVE: SPEAK TO ROTH

Once you have delivered one crate of Dynamite in each of the four locations, return to Roth on the rooftop **(3)**.

While talking to Roth on the rooftop, Jacob sees children entering the workshop that he just set explosives around to detonate. Jacob screams at Roth to stop his men from detonating the building. Roth has no concern for the children, so Jacob leaps from the rooftop and kills two of Roth's men headed for the detonation switch.

CURRENT OBJECTIVE: RESCUE THE CHILDREN

CHALLENGE: RESCUE ALL CHILDREN IN UNDER 2 MINUTES

Three minutes tick away on a clock at the top of the screen. But you have less than two minutes to rescue the children from the doomed workshop **(4)**. The building erupts in flames as you approach the front door and the concussion knocks you on your butt.

Get up off the ground and enter the rightmost first floor window that has been blown out.

Activate Eagle Vision once inside the burning workshop to quickly spot the children (glowing yellow). There are three on the floor and four others still conscious.

The first thing you need to do is head to the back (west) side of the room and kick the backdoor open. Four of the conscious children run out the door to safety. This leaves three to pick up and carry out one at a time.

Pick up the closest child to the door and head though the doorway you opened. Run to the end of the walkway following the escaping children and place the unconscious child in the glowing Deliver marker at the gate. When you return to the burning workshop you spot a Templar nearby. Go ahead and kill him quickly (the "do not kill" Challenge is over).

Now run into the burning building and save the last two children, picking each one up and bringing them to the delivery point. When the last child passes through the doorway the memory is completed.

Roth's doorman arrives on the scene and hands you a box with your "gift" from Roth inside. The The attached letter is an invitation to Roth's play.

FINAL ACT

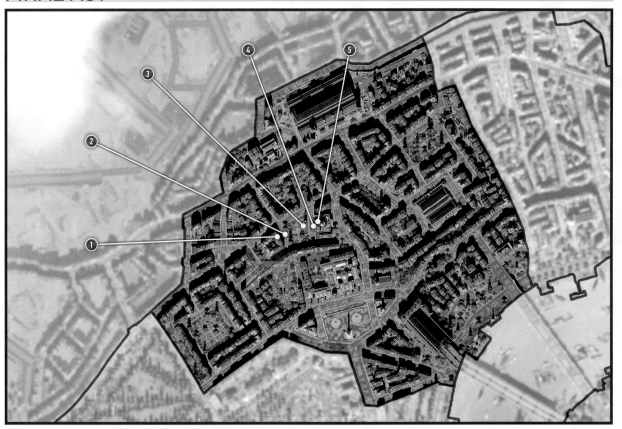

MISSION OVERVIEW

Memory Type: Templar Conspiracy	**ASSASSIN**	**CHALLENGES**	**REWARDS**
Suggested Level: 8	Jacob Frye	Do not use ranged weapons to kill the decoys	**£:** 1160 + 250 (Full Synch Bonus)
		Escape the Alhambra in less than 90 seconds	**XP:** 500 + 250 (Full Synch Bonus)
			Schematic: Maximum Dracula Schematic

LOCATION: NEAR LEICESTER SQUARE, THE STRAND

The start location for this memory is on a high wooden platform **(1)** near the rooftop on the east side of the houses facing Leicester Square. This park stands between you and the Alhambra Music Hall where you find Roth.

CURRENT OBJECTIVE: INFILTRATE THE ALHAMBRA MUSIC HALL

In the opening cinematic you are shown the optional tasks involved in this memory. There's a Stealth Opportunity with an Usher, an Assistance Opportunity with a Waitress, and a Unique Kill Opportunity with the assistance of a Machinist. We will use all of these opportunities in this walkthrough.

Begin by ziplining down to the park using the park entrance archway **(2)** as a Rope Launch lock-on.

Head east through the park and kill the two Blighter Soldiers with their backs to you near the exit **(3)**.

Loot the mask from one of the dead Blighters. With your newfound mask you experience a certain degree of stealth without having to sneak around.

OPTIONAL OBJECTIVE: FOLLOW THE USHER TO ENTER THE MUSIC HALL

Leave the park and find the female usher **(4)** to the right of the music hall's entrance. With the mask on your face already, she begins to move to the front door as soon as you reach her. She appears with an assassin icon near her head and the icon is also reflected on the Mini-Map.

Walk in the middle of the crowd she leads through the front door to avoid the Blighter guards around the entrance **(5)**.

CURRENT OBJECTIVE: REACH THE MUSIC HALL'S VANTAGE POINT

Once inside the main lobby, you can see the vantage point icon up high through a wall behind the main counter. The vantage point is on a higher level. Turn left in the lobby and climb the stairs to the east to reach the second floor. The mask keeps you undercover as long as you don't raise suspicion by doing things like killing in front of other Blighters or Rope Launching to different floors while in sight of the guards.

ALHAMBRA MUSIC HALL: SECOND FLOOR

At the top of the stairs on the second floor, continue down the hallway and enter the first open room on the right.

Inside you see a Blighter behind the bar and another at the second level balcony entrance ahead. Ignore these guys for now and just head up the next set of stairs on the right to reach the third level.

ALHAMBRA MUSIC HALL: THIRD FLOOR

At the top of the stairs on the third floor, again head through the first open door on the right. This puts you on the third floor balcony and you see the Vantage Point marker above the balcony rail.

Climb and perch on the top of the third floor balcony rail in the Vantage Point marker. All the while you can hear Roth announcing tonight's show and by the time you reach the Vantage Point following our direct route, Roth mentions the show being dedicated to you. The optional tasks are reviewed again in a cinematic while you are perched in the vantage point.

CURRENT OBJECTIVE: KILL ROTH'S 4 DECOYS

CHALLENGE: DO NOT USED RANGED WEAPONS TO KILL THE DECOYS

The first thing you need to do is eliminate Roth's four decoys, which glow yellow when using Eagle Vision. You can see three of them on the left side of the music hall and the fourth on the right side. The Challenge is not to use ranged weapons on the "decoys." This does not mean you cannot use them on anyone else. Remain on your perch in the vantage point location until the first decoy **(A)** on the lowest floor walks from the left hallway, across the dining area below you and eventually stops near a table on the right side of the room.

Look down and throw a knife at the head of the Blighter **(B)** following the first decoy **(A)**.

THE ESSENTIALS
WALKTHROUGH
SIDE QUESTS
COLLECTIBLES
TROPHIES/AWARDS
INDEX

SEQUENCE ONE
SEQUENCE TWO
SEQUENCE THREE
SEQUENCE FOUR
SEQUENCE FIVE
SEQUENCE SIX
SEQUENCE SEVEN
SEQUENCE EIGHT
SEQUENCE NINE

DECOY 1

From your perch in the Vantage Point, acquire a Rope Launch lock-on across the room that allows you to pass over the target to perform an Air Assassination on the decoy **(A)** on the first floor. That's one decoy dead.

WAITRESS: ASSISTANCE OPPORTUNITY
DECOY 2

Get to the second floor balcony on the west side of the music hall and activate Eagle Vision. You spot a waitress **(C)** serving drinks to one of the decoys **(D)**. Wait for the waitress to exit the bar area so you don't have to walk past the Blighter at the stairs guarding the area. Walk up to her and speak to her. When you ask where the bathroom is, she turns and points and Jacob slips poison into her pitcher. Watch her as she returns to the table to serve the decoy **(D)** again. A few moments later the decoy and the Blighter next to him suffer the hallucinogenic effect and start killing other Blighters around. Leave the area while this commotion is happening, but make sure to watch.

203

DECOY 3

The waitress's assistance works for two decoys on this floor but it takes some time. The waitress has to return to the bar, refill her pitcher and head to the second decoy on this floor. Watch as she poisons the decoy and his comrade drinking with him.

FREE THE MACHINIST BEFORE YOU KILL THE LAST DECOY

Before you kill the last decoy, make sure to free the Machinist from the backroom behind the stage to get the Unique Kill Opportunity. It is still possible to do afterward, but it's much easier to get to free him before.

MACHINIST: UNIQUE KILL OPPORTUNITY

Head to the northwest end of the second floor balcony to reach the backstage. Here you can see a Blighter (F) with his back to you just through the open doorway. Silently assassinate him.

Face north in the hallway with Eagle Vision engaged. You see two Blighter guards (G) & (H) standing between you and freeing the Machinist (I), which you can see standing in a room through the nearby wall. The Brute (H) walks off the raised area where the prisoner is being held. You can throw a knife at his head when he stands at the bottom of the stairs. Rush up and take the Blighter Soldier (G) standing guard at the locked door by surprise and eliminate him before he calls for help.

Unlock the door and free the Machinist inside (I). When you free the Machinist, he works on lowering the rafter platform. This is the key to your unique kill on Roth. You must wait for him to lower the platform above the stage before you can take advantage of the opportunity. However, if you have saved the last decoy until now, by the time you kill the last decoy, the rafter is ready.

Leave the Machinist's room and walk back down the small set of stairs headed for the backstage area. You spot the final decoy around the set backdrops ahead (J). Walk up behind the target while disregarding all the remaining Blighters around and silently assassinate the last decoy. When the rafter is lowered a cinematic with Roth as the star attraction is triggered.

THE ESSENTIALS
WALKTHROUGH
SIDE QUESTS
COLLECTIBLES
REFERENCE & ATLAS
INDEX

SEQUENCE ONE
SEQUENCE TWO
SEQUENCE THREE
SEQUENCE FOUR
SEQUENCE FIVE
SEQUENCE SIX
SEQUENCE SEVEN
SEQUENCE EIGHT
SEQUENCE NINE

CURRENT OBJECTIVE: ASSASSINATE MAXWELL ROTH

UNIQUE KILL OPPORTUNITY: CUT THE ROPE TO ASSASSINATE ROTH

Roth addresses the audience and shortly after commands his guards to light the stage and music hall on fire, trapping everyone inside his performance art of death. He then dares Jacob to escape.

This assassination is very easy if you have used the Machinist's help. Simply run to the back stage below the rafter platform and Rope Launch to the top. In the rush of things it's difficult to get a lock-on on the rafter so you may have to launch to the top of the background set pieces and jump from the top of those to the rafter platform.

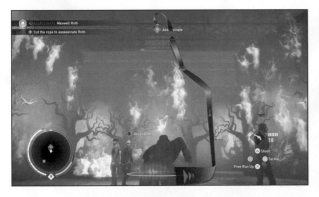

You may have incurred a degree of notoriety doing this, depending on where you were when the cinematic started. Before you can cut the rope on the rafter you must become anonymous. So crouch down and this will happen not too long after you reach the rafter. Stand near the rope (assassinate icon) and cut it the moment you become anonymous. A sandbag weight with a rope tied around it drops. The other end of the rope wraps around Roth's foot and sends him up in the air directly in front of the rafter. Jacob lifts him onto the rafter and puts a knife through his throat.

CURRENT OBJECTIVE: ESCAPE THE ALHAMBRA

CHALLENGE: ESCAPE THE ALHAMBRA IN LESS THAN 90 SECONDS

When you return from the Animus white room you are Challenged to reach the exit in less than 90 seconds. Drop off from the rafter platform and land on the stage below. Face the front of the stage and run through the dining tables where the audience used to be. Rope Launch to the second floor balcony.

Once on the second floor balcony, run through the open door and south through the bar area. You reach the lobby balcony at the front of the music hall. Hop off the balcony and run into the entry point to escape safely and complete the mission.

SHALL WE DANCE?

Crawford Starrick's servant helps him dress for a formal party. He grumbles about Twopenny, Lucy, Brudenell, Elliotson, and Pearl all failing him and how everything rests on his shoulders now. He takes a knife from his desk and slips it into his jacket before he leaves the room muttering, "London must be reborn."

DOUBLE TROUBLE

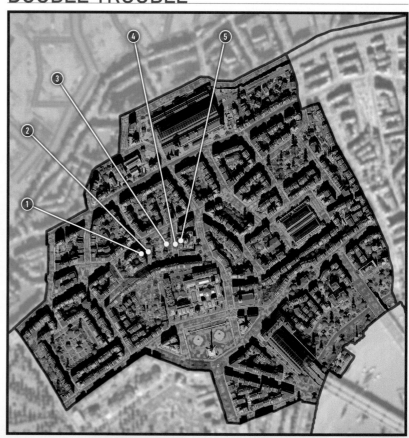

MISSION OVERVIEW

Memory Type: Templar Conspiracy	**ASSASSIN**	**CHALLENGES**	**REWARDS**
Suggested Level: 8	Jacob Frye	Don't kill any policemen	**£:** 1330 + 250 (Full Synch Bonus)
		Do not damage the Gladstone's carriage	**XP:** 600 + 250 (Full Synch Bonus)
			Schematic: Devil's Handshake Schematic

LOCATION: TRAIN HIDEOUT

Tensions between Evie and Jacob are at an all time high. Evie is tired of cleaning up the mess Jacob leaves in his wake. She tells Jacob that Starrick is making his move and that the Piece of Eden is somewhere inside Buckingham Palace. They begin to fight like children as Henry Green enters in time to break it up. He tells the twins he heard from his sources that Starrick plans to steal the Piece of Eden at the ball tonight and then eliminate the heads of church and state. The twins agree to work together one last time…then call it quits.

Mary Anne Disraeli enters the car. Jacob asks the Prime Minister's wife for entrance into the ball tonight. As Mary Anne starts in with how impossible that would be, her husband Benjamin butts in and guarantees them entry. Evie suggests that Jacob steal the Gladstones' invitations. Everyone agrees to that delightful plan.

CURRENT OBJECTIVE: REACH THE GLADSTONES' HOUSE

CHALLENGE: DO NOT KILL ANY POLICEMEN

LOCATION: GLADSTONES, WESTMINSTER

Since you were on the train, there's really no telling where you will be when you begin this memory. Hop off the train and take a carriage to the Gladstone's **(1)** in Westminster. The carriage you were hoping would be outside their house is missing.

CURRENT OBJECTIVE: SPEAK WITH THE KID

Head south down the sidewalk from the previous Reach marker to find, just a few houses away, a child standing in an open doorway **(2)**. Talk to her. She tells you she saw the two carriages heading south and points in the correct direction. Open the chest in this office before you leave on your quest.

CURRENT OBJECTIVE: REACH MR. GLADSTONE'S LOCATION

Get in a carriage and drive just south of Westminster Abby and stop in the street near the Reach **(3)** marker. Walk through the short covered alley and you see an open courtyard to the right (north).

CURRENT OBJECTIVE: STEAL MR. GLADSTONE'S INVITATION

Activate Eagle Vision to spot many policemen around the courtyard, maintaining order during the festivities. You also spot a yellow blip. This indicates the location of the invitation you are to steal. The Challenge is to not kill any coppers while stealing the invitation. If you have to get rid of a policeman, then knock him out.

Begin the task by Rope Launching to the rooftop on your right. There's a policeman **(4)** there facing the courtyard that needs to be dealt with first. Come up behind him and knock him out. There's a Helix Glitch nearby, but we suggest leaving it there as it seems it's ideally located to alert police as you attempt to retrieve it.

From the north edge of the rooftop **(4)**, look down into the courtyard. You see a circus tent **(7)** in the middle; the invitation is under the tent. Acquire a Rope Launch lock-on on the rooftop of the building behind the tent. Zipline over the tent to that rooftop **(5)**.

Move to the northeast side of the rooftop **(5)** and perform a Leap of Faith into the haystack **(6)** near Westminster Abby. Once in the haystack, activate Eagle Vision to spot the nearby police. There's one with his back always to you at the gate **(A)** and another that patrols back and forth around the haystack. Jump out of the haystack and knock out the patrolling policeman **(B)** when his back is to you and no other guards are in view.

Leave his body and enter the hiding booth and wait for the patrolling policeman **(C)** under the tent to walk past the crate stacks. Come out of the booth and knock this guard out as he reaches the end of his patrol behind the crate stack.

Now simply walk up to the table with the invitation on it and press and hold the ⊙ / ⓑ button. Wait for the gauge to fill up to steal the invitation.

365 m

WALKTHROUGH

SIDE QUESTS
COLLECTIBLES
REFERENCE & ANALYSIS
INDEX

SEQUENCE ONE
SEQUENCE TWO
SEQUENCE THREE
SEQUENCE FOUR
SEQUENCE FIVE
SEQUENCE SIX
SEQUENCE SEVEN
SEQUENCE EIGHT
SEQUENCE NINE

CURRENT OBJECTIVE: STEAL MRS. GLADSTONE'S INVITATION

That's one invitation down. Now you need one for Evie. A yellow blip appears on Victoria Station **(9)** to the southwest. Get to the rooftops and out of the restricted zone.

LOCATION: VICTORIA STATION, WESTMINSTER

Enter the northeastern entrance of the train station and walk among the civilians along the passenger loading area. Activate Eagle Vision to spot the cops at the south end of the station. Rope Launch to the top of the rafters and follow the framework until you are directly above Mrs. Gladstone (a yellow glowing figure while Eagle Vision is on).

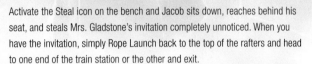

Activate the Steal icon on the bench and Jacob sits down, reaches behind his seat, and steals Mrs. Gladstone's invitation completely unnoticed. When you have the invitation, simply Rope Launch back to the top of the rafters and head to one end of the train station or the other and exit.

When you get near Mrs. Gladstone she begins moving and then sits on a bench. You are heard saying to yourself to not make a move until she's alone. Listen to your inner voice. Move down to the lower network of rafters and then drop down to the top of the nearby sign. Drop to the floor. To avoid being spotted by her police escort, move quickly to the seat. If you miss her at the bench, she moves into the nearby hiding booth. If this happens, stealthily enter the booth with her and steal the invitation while inside.

CURRENT OBJECTIVE:
HIJACK MRS. GLADSTONE'S CARRIAGE

CHALLENGE: DO NOT DAMAGE THE GLADSTONES' CARRIAGE
LOCATION: VICTORIA STATION, WESTMINSTER

Mrs. Gladstone's carriage **(10)** is parked just outside the station on the north side. Enter the carriage and drive extremely carefully, so as not to scratch the carriage. Avoid collisions with anything. Park the unscathed carriage in the Reach marker to the northeast **(11)**. The next memory, "Dress to Impress" is started where you parked the carriage.

DRESS TO IMPRESS

MISSION OVERVIEW

Memory Type: Templar Conspiracy
Suggested Level: 8

ASSASSIN
Jacob Frye

CHALLENGES
Do not kill anyone

Hide the body in a carriage

REWARDS
£: 1330 + 250 (Full Synch Bonus)

XP: 600 + 250 (Full Synch Bonus)

Belt: Master Assassin's Belt

LOCATION: WESTMINSTER

This memory starts where Jacob left the Gladstone's carriage **(1)** in Westminster at the end of the last memory. When you reach the carriage, you find a disguised Frederick Abberline sweeping the street. Speak to him to begin the memory.

Jacob tells the detective that he has an invitation to the Queen's ball tonight and that there's to be an attack. He asks Frederick if he can

smuggle some weapons inside to help him prevent it. He tells Jacob that he needs a Royal Guard's uniform in order to that pull off.

CURRENT OBJECTIVE: REACH ST. MARTIN CHURCH

When you enter the street near where Abberline was sweeping, look up to the sky to spot a green marker at the top of the church steeple **(2)** across the street. Rope Launch to the steeple.

CURRENT OBJECTIVE: SEARCH FOR ROYAL GUARDS

Once on top of the steeple, press ⊚ / **Ⓑ** to search for Royal Guards.

CURRENT OBJECTIVE: KNOCK OUT A ROYAL GUARD

CHALLENGE: DO NOT KILL ANYONE

Look down to the west at Wellington Barracks. You see five orange blips appear on screen. These are royal guard locations. You only need to steal one of their uniforms. Picking the easiest guard is key.

While on the very top of the steeple, acquire a Rope Launch lock-on on the edge of the Wellington Barracks' southeast rooftop **(3)**. Zipline there. Follow the roofs to the westernmost edge **(4)**. Activate Eagle Vision to spot the police in the area. You also find a Royal Guard to the north and one to the south. The royal guard we have our eye on patrols the area to the north.

Zipline to the wooden platform **(5)** on the west wall inside the small courtyard. Jump to the top of the short wall **(6)** just above the two policemen **(A)** & **(B)**.

From this perch, wait for the royal guard **(C)** to the north to walk toward the courtyard you're squatting over. Prepare to throw a smoke bomb. When the guard passes under you and enters the courtyard, drop the smoke bomb close to his feet. Quickly drop down and kidnap him.

Now simply walk your kidnapped victim out the main north exit **(7)** past all the cops. Continue walking him across the street (while avoiding police or Blighters passing by) and walk him directly into the park **(8)**. Look around with Eagle Vision to make sure no police or Blighters are around and then knock him out.

CURRENT OBJECTIVE: STEAL A ROYAL GUARD UNIFORM

With the royal guard knocked out on the ground, inspect his body and loot it for the garments.

CURRENT OBJECTIVE: HIDE THE BODY OF THE ROYAL GUARD

CHALLENGE: HIDE THE BODY IN A CARRIAGE

Now to fulfill the Challenge, pick up the royal guard and walk through the park heading east to avoid police and Blighters on the street and sidewalks. Continue east until you see a covered carriage in the street where you can hide the unconscious body. You could always put the guard down and hijack one as it goes by, but you can usually find a parked one near Saint Martin **(2)**.

CURRENT OBJECTIVE: SPEAK WITH ABBERLINE

Resist the urge to kill any Blighters you may randomly see on your way back to where you left Abberline **(1)**. It would be a shame to waste all that hard work on not killing anyone only to lose the Challenge because of a lowly Blighter. Return to Abberline and talk to him to complete the memory. Jacob hands over the uniform and Frederick promises to meet Jacob on the rooftop of Buckingham Palace.

FAMILY POLITICS

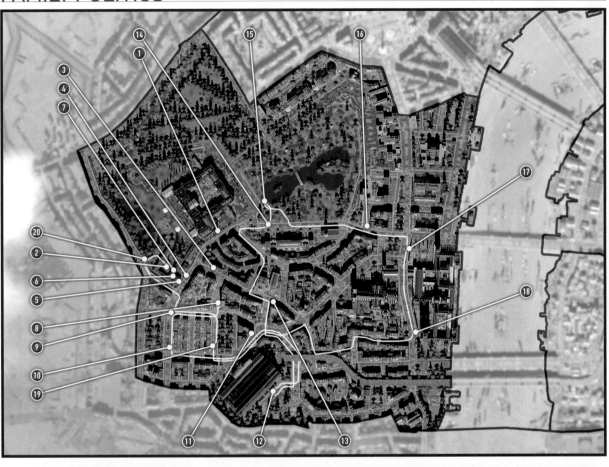

MISSION OVERVIEW

		CHALLENGES	REWARDS
Memory Type: Templar Conspiracy	**ASSASSIN** Evie Frye	Steal a carriage without entering the courtyard	**£:** 2830 + 250 (Full Synch Bonus)
Suggested Level: 8		Don't let the royal carriage's condition drop below 50%	**XP:** 1350 + 250 (Full Synch Bonus)
			Cape: Cloak Of Victory

LOCATION: BUCKINGHAM PALACE, WESTMINSTER

Evie meets Duleep Singh outside Buckingham Palace in Westminster. She apologizes to the Maharaja for not having Buckingham Palace's renovation plans. Duleep eases her mind, telling her that there are copies to be had. He asks her to quickly and stealthily acquire an official carriage, which they could use to deliver politicians to their destinations. Along the way, the Maharaja can hold political meetings with them. Do this for him and he will help you find the renovation plans you need.

CURRENT OBJECTIVE: BORROW A ROYAL CARRIAGE

CHALLENGE: STEAL A CARRIAGE WITHOUT ENTERING THE COURTYARD

Head west along the sidewalk to reach the heavily guarded compound on the corner **(2)**. Make sure you have a smoke bomb before getting too far. There is a merchant a block away if you need one **(3)** or you can defeat some random Blighters walking around with hopes they're carrying smoke bombs. Walk past the open gate **(4)** with Eagle Vision activated and you see multiple royal guards around, including some on nearby rooftops. Through an open gate you can see a beam of light in the middle of the courtyard indicating the location of an official carriage **(2)** to hijack.

213

The following tips allow you to beat the Challenge of stealing the carriage without entering the courtyard. Walk up to the knee-high gate **(5)** between the front door of the southwest building and the column that connects the metal fencing to the large gate entrance **(4)**. From this position you can acquire a Rope Launch lock-on to the rooftop of the building. The royal guard at the front door does not notice your activities.

Head to the northwest side of the rooftop, being careful not to attract the attention of the rooftop royal guards to your left. Jump to the next rooftop **(6)** to the northwest and sneak to the northern edge **(7)** and look for the carriages below **(2)**.

There are three carriages, each marked with an orange blip. Throw a smoke bomb at one of the three to spook the horse. The carriage typically takes off through the southeast gate **(4)**.

The carriage does not go too far away if you end up chasing it. It is possible that the carriage will return to the courtyard again. In that case you must repeat the smoke bomb process and catch it more quickly the next time. Most of the time, the horse calms down and stops in a nearby street. Jump up onto the carriage and hijack it. If you acquired some attention from nearby Blighters, Police, or Royal Guards, become anonymous and the next objective occurs.

CURRENT OBJECTIVE: REACH DULEEP

CHALLENGE: DON'T LET THE ROYAL CARRIAGE'S CONDITION DROP BELOW 50%

LOCATION: BUCKINGHAM PALACE, WESTMINSTER

You are directed to meet Duleep a block from Buckingham Palace. The carriage's health gauge must not dive below 50% or you fail the current Challenge. This gauge  remains active until the end of the memory. The carriage's health is at 90% when you first obtain it. So drive extremely safely. You are about to make multiple stops for Duleep. During these cab rides, there will be timers counting down from time to time but you rarely need to use a speed boost. So there's no need to whip the horse.

CURRENT OBJECTIVE: REACH THE FIRST POLITICIAN

Try not to scratch the carriage once on your way to pick up the Maharaja **(8)**. Duleep wants to conduct his first mobile meeting with the politician **(10)** waiting near Belgrave Square.

LOCATION: HOUSE FIRE

So now that you have to take care of a carriage, you don't think that the game is going to play nice, do you? Along the route you experience some abnormal traffic behaviors. The first very noticeable one is the fire truck that comes racing at you in an intersection. Slow down and let it pass. It's on its way to a fire down the street. You pass this commotion several times on your trips back and forth, so be especially careful in that house fire area **(9)**.

CURRENT OBJECTIVE: REACH VICTORIA STATION

TIME LIMIT: 1:30

Stop in the Reach marker and allow the politician to enter the carriage with the Maharaja. While Duleep converses with the politician **(10)**, you are to drive them to Victoria Station **(12)**. You have one minute and thirty seconds to get to the train station. The fire truck that passed you earlier is now blocking your path. Maneuver around it carefully. When you reach a few blocks to the east you get to see what all the commotion is about.

The house burns on the triangle intersection **(11)**. You need to go at a turtle's speed through the scene so you can squeeze through all the fire trucks. Turn right at this intersection and things clear up and you can reach the station on time. The politician leaves the carriage and you begin your trip to the next one.

THE ESSENTIALS
WALKTHROUGH
SIDE QUESTS
COLLECTIBLES
REFERENCE & ANALYSIS
INDEX

CURRENT OBJECTIVE: REACH THE NEXT POLITICIAN

LOCATION: VICTORIA STATION

There's no time limit to reach the next politician so take it really easy on the way, as not to damage the carriage. You pass the house fire area **(11)** on your way to St. James's Park **(14)**. Once you are past the fire and approaching the next intersection, another fire truck **(13)** comes at you on it's way to the fire. Allow this truck the right of way and continue cautiously. You might get stuck behind a slow cart on a narrow road, but the rest of the way is smooth sailing.

When you reach the park, the next marker appears *inside* the park so this means you are about to do a little off-roading. But not to worry, the dirt pathway through the park is a smooth one, unless you run over some pedestrians. You pick up the next politician **(15)** from near the pond.

CURRENT OBJECTIVE: REACH PARLIAMENT

TIME LIMIT: 1:24

From the park, you are to take the politician to parliament **(17)** while Duleep has his mobile meeting with another person who refused to meet with him in the past. Turn the carriage on a dime and return the way you came, but veer left at the dirt path intersection to exit the park closer to your destination. Weave through the heavy traffic just outside the park.

In an intersection **(16)** just before you reach Parliament an actual carriage police chase is happening. Slow down and let the crooks continue to escape the police carriage, which is hot on their tail.

You can reach Parliament **(17)** without anything more than some overly aggressive drivers and the annoyingly slow drivers (nothing's changed

with traffic over time). Drop off the politician with time left on the clock.

CURRENT OBJECTIVE: REACH MR. GLADSTONE

LOCATION: HOUSE OF PARLIAMENT

You pick up your last rider, Mr. Gladstone **(18)**, at the other end of the House of Parliament.

CURRENT OBJECTIVE: REACH THE GENTLEMEN CLUB

TIME LIMIT: 2:26

Mr. Gladstone has some serious business to attend to at the gentlemen club **(19)**. And he has to be there in two minutes and twenty six seconds! Allow Gladstone to enter the carriage and then take him there pronto…but safely. You don't run into anything out of the ordinary until you have to cross the house fire **(11)** intersection again. But that's not bad because your destination is right around the corner.

Drop Gladstone off at his destination **(19)**. Surprisingly the Maharaja will also be joining Gladstone at the club. Evie and Duleep say their goodbyes. He thanks you for forwarding his cause and tells Evie where she can find the copies of the Buckingham Palace plans.

CURRENT OBJECTIVE: RETURN THE ROYAL CARRIAGE

After dropping off the boys **(19)**, jump back in the carriage and return it to the courtyard where it was originally parked. There's no time limit and the Challenge still stands, so be very careful on this final trek. You enter the compound **(20)** from the west entrance and then pull through to drop it off further inside **(2)**.

CURRENT OBJECTIVE: ESCAPE THE AREA

Exit the carriage and quickly run to the nearest wall to avoid the guards. Rope Launch to the rooftops. Running southeast for the street **(4)** has you out of the restricted zone in no time. This completes the memory.

THE ESSENTIALS

WALKTHROUGH

SIDE QUESTS

COLLECTIBLES

REFERENCE & APPENDIX

INDEX

SEQUENCE ONE

SEQUENCE TWO

SEQUENCE THREE

SEQUENCE FOUR

SEQUENCE FIVE

SEQUENCE SIX

SEQUENCE SEVEN

SEQUENCE EIGHT

SEQUENCE NINE

A NIGHT TO REMEMBER

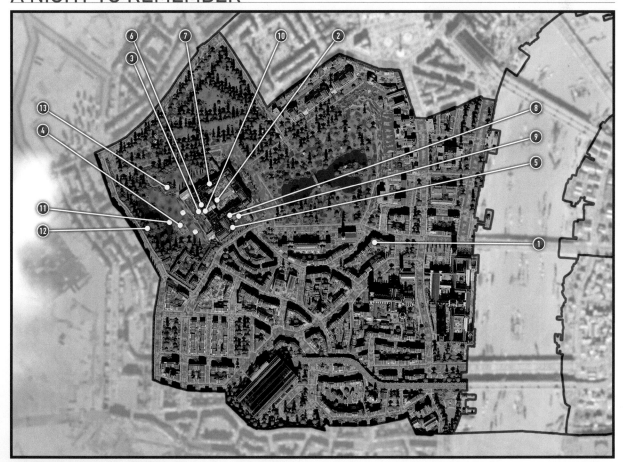

MISSION OVERVIEW

Memory Type: Templar Conspiracy	**ASSASSIN**	**CHALLENGES**	**REWARDS**
Suggested Level: 8	Jacob & Evie Frye	Free all captive royal guard groups	**£:** 3990 + 250 (Full Synch Bonus)
		Use a key to enter the White Drawing Room	**XP:** 4500 + 250 (Full Synch Bonus)
			Schematic: Legendary Assassin Belt Schematic

LOCATION: WESTMINSTER

The start marker for the final story memory is located at a suitcase behind a building **(1)** in Westminster.

Jacob and Frederick Abberline roll up to Evie in the Gladstone's carriage. Tensions still surround the twins. Frederick is in his royal guard disguise and Jacob asks Evie to hand over her weapons; they must enter Buckingham Palace unarmed. Her bag of weapons is at her feet ready for the taking.

LOCATION: BUCKINGHAM PALACE, WESTMINSTER

They all enter the carriage together and roll through security at the palace. Security takes a look into the carriage and sees the nicely dressed Evie Frye. He waves their carriage through the gates. The Gladstones are seen having difficulty making it past the second guard at the gates as your team rolls through with their carriage and invitations.

CURRENT OBJECTIVE: FOLLOW JACOB INTO THE BALLROOM

You begin this memory as Evie Frye, who is dressed in a very beautiful, yet restrictive, ballroom dress. She cannot climb nor can she run. Follow Jacob straight into the palace, through the anteroom and out the backdoor to reach the festivities **(2)** in the backyard.

Once on the back porch **(3)**, Jacob says he's off to meet Freddie to pick up their weapons. You are shown the locked drawing room containing the plans.

CURRENT OBJECTIVE: REACH THE SECOND FLOOR

When you activate Eagle Vision you see blue glowing royal guards and red glowing royal guards. The red ones are Starrick's gang in disguise. Kidnap one of the two guards in front of you with a key icon above their head, which you can see while using Eagle Vision.

Walk the kidnapped soldier through the backdoor and into the first hallway, turn right, and head toward the two royal guards guarding the stairs. As you get close, your hostage tells them, "The lady is with me." They don't move but they let you pass. Walk slowly so that your detection ring does not touch the guards.

At the first stairway landing, turn left or right at the ropes to continue up the winding staircase to the second floor. Enter the marker on the second floor landing.

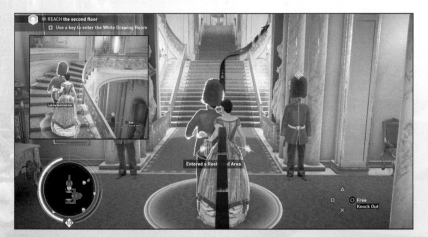

218

CURRENT OBJECTIVE: STEAL THE PLANS

CHALLENGE: USE A KEY TO ENTER THE WHITE DRAWING ROOM
LOCATION: BUCKINGHAM PALACE: SECOND FLOOR

Keep the guard in your control and walk him to the end of the long hallway, passing the multiple guards at various doors along the way. As you pass through the hallway you can spot a yellow "Steal" icon marking the plans through the walls on the left. Continue into the open doorway at the end of the hallway.

Turn left in the open room at the end of the hallway. There are a couple of guards at the windows behind the low screens. Keep your captive with you until you reach the adjoining room. Move your victim behind the screens in the middle of the second room and knock him out.

Open the chest near the window and find the Memory Item (letter) on the small table on your way to the locked door. Approach and unlock the door in this room using the key automatically obtained from the captive guard. In the drawing room, steal the plans from the chest to the left near the screens.

CURRENT OBJECTIVE: REACH THE VAULT ENTRANCE

There are two more locked doors in the drawing room. Do not open the one on the east wall; there are two guards on the other side that will see you open it. Instead, unlock the door on the south (narrow) wall. There are two guards in the next room but they face a window behind a piano and never turn around.

Use Eagle Vision to look through the left wall. Make sure the guard patrolling the hallway is nowhere near. Pass through the open doorway and enter the hallway. The guards are much farther left but make a beeline to the right for the staircase to the first floor.

When you reach the bottom of the stairs notice that the two royal guards who used to be there are now gone. You can safely reach the marker in the first floor anteroom without using a kidnapped guard.

LOCATION: BUCKINGHAM PALACE: FIRST FLOOR

Mrs. Mary Ann Disraeli stops Evie on her way to the vault. She has someone that she is just dying to introduce to you. She walks you to the festivities in the backyard and introduces Evie to Queen Victoria.

The Queen, surprisingly connected to the day's events, asks you about your involvement in the Gladstones' invitation mishap, but tells you the cake is good and to enjoy the evening.

Before Evie can return to her mission, none other than Crawford Starrick grabs her by the hand and leads her to the dance floor **(4)**. As not to blow her cover, she holds back her rage and dances with the villain and hears him out. Adding support to her forced composure are Starrick's rooftop snipers. As the two enemies dance together, Crawford promises Evie that her time will be up by the end of the dance.

CURRENT OBJECTIVE: REACH ABBERLINE

LOCATION: BUCKINGHAM PALACE: BACKYARD

Now you control Jacob Frye who is still on the back porch **(3)** on his way to find Abberline with the weapons. Look up to the rooftops to the southeast and you see the green blip representing Abberline's location on a distant rooftop. To avoid most of the guards, do not climb up to any of the nearby rooftops (they are heavily guarded). Instead, head south around the palace through the side yard. Once on the south side, climb the walls to the rooftop to find Abberline **(5)** in the royal guard disguise you stole for him.

CURRENT OBJECTIVE: REACH THE HIDING SPOT TO RETRIEVE YOUR GEAR

LOCATION: BUCKINGHAM PALACE: ROOFTOP

Just a few feet away from where Abberline stands is a hiding booth where your weapons and gear are hidden. Enter the booth to retrieve both Evie's and your weapons. After gearing up you speak to Abberline; he points out the imposter guards on the rooftops who are currently watching Starrick dance with Evie.

CURRENT OBJECTIVE: KILL THE SIX SNIPERS

TIME LIMIT: 3:00

You have three minutes to make it to the rooftops where the six snipers are located **(6)**. This is not a difficult task given your experience at this point in the game. How you

chose to take out the snipers is your choice. You can use smoke grenades to cover the battle or you can shoot a few imposters with hallucinogenic darts… or do both. Just take them all out in the time allotted.

CURRENT OBJECTIVE:
LOCATE AND KILL STARRICK'S 16 IMPOSTERS

CHALLENGE: FREE ALL CAPTIVE ROYAL GROUPS

Once the six snipers are dead you must locate and kill Starrick's 16 imposters and free the captive royal guards. Two green blips appear on the map; one each on the north and south end of the palace grounds. The one to the north **(7)** is closer. Head there now via rooftop travel.

Get to the north rooftop edge where you overlook a balcony with a single patrolling imposter **(A)**. Air Assassinate this imposter. From the edge of his balcony railing you can overlook the remaining seven imposters. Shoot some with darts, knives, or bullets, or use smoke and an Air Assassination. Defeat these targets and then look for their captives.

Find the captives **(6)** tied to a pole near the north wall under the balcony. Walk up to them and cut the rope that binds them. Recruit them. Use them to defeat any of the eight remaining imposters in this area before heading to the remaining eight on the south side.

You spot the captives **(7)** and the surrounding eight imposters in a courtyard on the south side of the palace. Use your recruited gang to help you take out the remaining eight imposters or take them out one at a time yourself. Drop down in the courtyard **(9)** and spot a patrolling imposter **(B)** under the shelter. Defeat this guard or allow him to leave the area on his normal patrol and head to the narrow alley behind the shelter.

Sneak up behind the imposter guarding the captive royal guards in the back alley **(8)**. Silently assassinate the imposter and free the guards. Have them join your party and send them to attack what remains of the imposters in the area.

THE ESSENTIALS
WALKTHROUGH
SIDE QUESTS
COLLECTIBLES
REFERENCE & ANALYSIS
INDEX

SEQUENCE ONE
SEQUENCE TWO
SEQUENCE THREE
SEQUENCE FOUR
SEQUENCE FIVE
SEQUENCE SIX
SEQUENCE SEVEN
SEQUENCE EIGHT
SEQUENCE NINE

CURRENT OBJECTIVE: REACH THE ROOFTOP TO SIGNAL EVIE

With all 16 imposters dead and the captives saved, return to the rooftops and head to the south edge of the palace rooftops where the imposter snipers were located. Here you find a marker **(10)**. Step into it and press ◎ / ⑧ to warn Evie, who is still on the dance floor with Starrick. Evie receives Jacob's signal from the rooftop and with that, she stomps on Starrick's foot, sending him to his knees in front of everyone.

Distracted by partygoers' sudden concern for Crawford, Evie turns around and Starrick and her necklace are gone. Jacob quickly arrives and Evie hands him the plans, which will help him locate the vault. She tells him to go and to hurry. He's concerned that Evie has no time for an execution plan. She says she'll catch up as soon as she changes into her gear.

CURRENT OBJECTIVE: REACH THE VAULT ENTRANCE

LOCATION: BUCKINGHAM PALACE: BACKYARD

You gain control of Jacob while he wades in shallow pond water **(11)** behind the palace. Swim to the other side of the pond following the distant green blip signifying the vault's entrance **(12)**. Run from the shore into the thick woods heading toward the flames you see in a clearing. Drop into the paved tunnel entrance in the ground.

You begin to slide down a steep set of narrow stairs. So steep that you slip down the passageway like a giant theme park ride. Press and hold **R2 +** ◎ **/ RT +** ⑧ to slide down the passage faster.

At the end of the stairs you reach a room that looks like it collapsed on itself. Climb the back wall to locate the Reach marker above in the vault entry point.

CURRENT OBJECTIVE: KILL CRAWFORD STARRICK

LOCATION: VAULT INTERIOR

STAGE 1: JACOB'S ATTACK

You stand on a high ledge at the entrance to a large hall with many columns and a high ceiling. Crawford Starrick stands at an altar at the far end with his back to you.

Jump down to the floor and run at Starrick. A cinematic triggers when you reach him. Starrick counters Jacob's attack and grabs him by the neck. The shroud draped around Starrick's shoulders glows with some mystical powers. Jacob seems helpless in its presence.

CURRENT OBJECTIVE:
RESCUE JACOB

TIME LIMIT: 3:51

When the cinematic ends you find yourself in control of Evie who has just changed into her gear. She's behind Buckingham Palace and has to swim across the pond to reach the same vault entrance Jacob found. You have 3 minutes and 51 seconds to rescue Jacob.

When you reach the woods, activate Eagle Vision so you can spot the Templars around the vault entrance **(12)**. Just stab the one crouched over at the vault entrance in the back and ignore the others. Free Run Down into the hole. Slide down the stairs as you did with Jacob.

Inside the vault, you spot Starrick with Jacob in his grasp. A laser security system activates and a triangular beam of light shines down to the floor from the ceiling. The light approaches you as if on a rail. If it touches you, it does damage and throws you back. Unless you want to get damaged by each laser beam, you're going to have to find a way around them.

CURRENT OBJECTIVE: KILL CRAWFORD STARRICK

LOCATION: VAULT INTERIOR
STAGE 2: EVIE'S ATTACK

FIRST LASER GRID ESCAPE PLAN

You can actually remain on the ground and just run around the first laser grid pattern and then rush to Jacob's rescue.

Three triangular laser beams shoot from three different locations from the vault ceiling. Use the Rope Launcher to get beyond the nearest beam by attaching to one of the high poles sticking out of the columns.

From atop the first pole you launched to, quickly obtain a lock-on to a column behind Starrick and zipline until you are above him. Drop off the zipline at his feet.

THE ESSENTIALS
WALKTHROUGH
SIDE QUESTS
COLLECTIBLES
REFERENCE & ANALYSIS
INDEX

SEQUENCE ONE
SEQUENCE TWO
SEQUENCE THREE
SEQUENCE FOUR
SEQUENCE FIVE
SEQUENCE SIX
SEQUENCE SEVEN
SEQUENCE EIGHT
SEQUENCE NINE

When you drop down to rescue Jacob one of the security orbs shoots Jacob and throws him to the back of the chamber near the entrance.

Control returns to Evie. Move in quickly and start throwing attack combos at Starrick. The Shroud of Eden protects the wearer from any firearm or ranged attack, so throwing knives or shooting bullets at Starrick is be a waste of time and ammo. Continue performing normal Attack combos and start countering as soon as Starrick breaks out of your combo. Counter and attack.

What happens next is reminiscent of the battle with Lucy Thorne. The camera pans in close to Starrick as he prepares to launch a volley of combos that you must block one after the other—similar to the attack sequence that Thorne used. His third swing is always a fake that is followed by a quick left swing. Counter all of these moves, then follow up with another attack combo, and then end your attack with as many rounds from your firearm as you can fit in.

After the second round of attacks, Evie lands a stabbing attack. Blood pools around Crawford's wound but with the power of the Shroud of Eden, the wound miraculously heals. While Evie is completely shocked and caught off guard, Crawford grabs her by the throat and holds her there as he did her brother moments earlier.

STAGE 3: JACOB'S 2ND ATTACK
TIME LIMIT: 1:30

Control switches to Jacob who's getting to his feet at the back of the vault. The beginning of this stage starts like the beginning of Evie's battle: three triangular laser beams sweep across the vault heading your way. Move to the extreme left or right side of the chamber and you see a clear path that you can run through to avoid the lasers while simply running along the floor.

When you reach Starrick, Evie gets laser zapped to the back of the vault just as Jacob was moments earlier.

As Jacob, tear right into Crawford with your best blades and pull off the longest attack combo possible. Within this combo a short cinematic is triggered and in it, Starrick gets hit with a very damaging knife puncture.

Starrick recovers from this attack using the power of the shroud. He grabs Jacob's knife hand and laughs as he lays a fist across his chin. The battle ends with Jacob at a disadvantage.

STAGE 3: EVIE'S 2ND ATTACK

TIME LIMIT: 1:30

Evie wakes up and pulls herself off the floor. Now you control Evie as she comes to and sees Jacob in Starrick's clutches. You have a minute thirty to get to Starrick again and save your brother.

Again with the lasers! You must dodge lasers to get to the other side of the room. This time the laser beam shape has changed, forcing you to use a different route to get through. All three lasers are side-by-side so there's no space to slip between them. This time you must just get over the highest line of beams.

Rope Launch upwards to a column pole and stay there for a second. Once over the first wall of lasers a second one is right behind it but this time covering the upper level of the room—which is where you are right now. Drop down off the pole when the first wall of lasers has passed under you.

Once you are on the floor and the high lasers have passed, there's one more wall to go. It's a low one again so just Rope Launch up to a column and jump over it to reach Starrick.

When you reach Starrick, Jacob is thrown back in a flash of light. Move in quickly with an attack combo and shortly after you enter the attack sequence that tests your countering reflexes. His attack pattern is the same and should be fresh in your memory. Counter his attacks and then in a cinematic, Evie slips a knife into Starrick's side. He brushes it off, slaps Evie, and takes her by the neck.

STAGE 4: JACOB'S 3RD ATTACK
TIME LIMIT: 1:30

Jacob wakes up and pulls himself off the floor. Now you control Jacob who is now looking at his sister in the same position he was in when she came to his rescue. You have one minute and thirty seconds to get to Starrick through his new laser defense pattern. The first wall of lasers collapses into a small gap you can get through near the floor. So stay on the ground and run forward through the first wall. Even if the gap seems too small, go for it; you are not hurt if the laser does not hit your feet.

Zipline up to a column as the second wall approaches. It's triangular shaped and points at the top so you can get on a perch above and drop down on the floor when it passes.

As soon as you drop, the next laser wall passes your head above (they were close together). But the next wall behind that one is also very close. Continue by Rope Launching over the wall and down again. Run at Starrick in the clearing.

When you reach Starrick you immediately enter a cinematic where both twins end up hanging from the ends of Starrick's grasping hands. When all hope seems lost, a knife zips through the air and Starrick crouches backward. You see Henry in the distance. It was his blade. Starrick throws Evie back a few yards.

Henry rushes at Starrick as he pulls his knife out of his back and tosses Jacob aside like a ragdoll. Crawford blocks Henry's attacks and Starrick lands a nice backhand across Henry's jaw. Henry recovers and slashes Crawford. Now Henry is surprised when he sees how quickly he heals. Henry is thrown aside and you gain control of Jacob.

Move right in and get your combos in, Crawford lets this slip through his defense. He should be at half health by now. When you get him down to about 25% health a cinematic triggers.

THE ESSENTIALS
WALKTHROUGH
SIDE QUESTS
COLLECTIBLES
REFERENCE & ANALYSIS
INDEX

SEQUENCE ONE
SEQUENCE TWO
SEQUENCE THREE
SEQUENCE FOUR
SEQUENCE FIVE
SEQUENCE SIX
SEQUENCE SEVEN
SEQUENCE EIGHT
SEQUENCE NINE

STAGE 3: EVIE'S 3RD ATTACK
Evie gets her chance to get in a third attack. There's no time limit. Run to Jacob and Starrick— and yes, to Henry too. One good strike on Starrick triggers your opportunity for the finishing move….

Evie has Crawford on the ropes and screams for Jacob's help. He rushes in and lands a flying right hook.

Jacob follows the punch with a stabbing and yells, "Evie, NOW!" Without a plan made in advance, Evie strikes a sweeping knife attack across Crawford's chest that sends the Shroud flying to the floor behind him.

Crawford is in a bad way now. They throw him behind the altar and he pulls himself across the floor. He struggles to his feet. You are prompted to perform an Assassination ⊡ / ⊗. Do so and both Evie and Jacob double-team the wounded Templar.

They deliver death to Crawford Starrick together as an assassination team. All three are transported to the Animus white room. Crawford, still tying to defend himself finally dies, allowing the twins to get in the last word.

ASSASSINATE

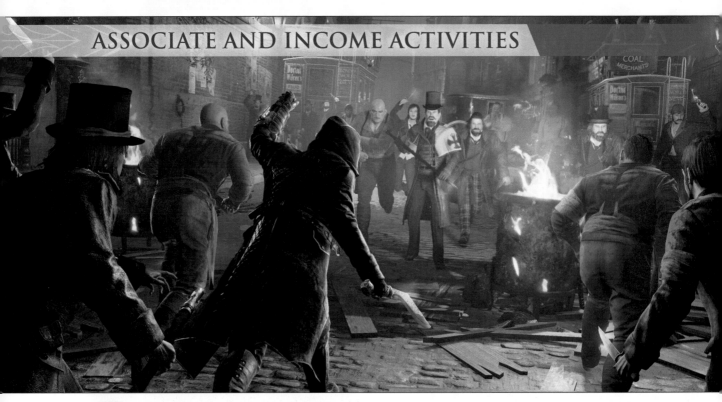

ASSOCIATE AND INCOME ACTIVITIES

 ## GANG STRONGHOLDS

While the main objective of every stronghold is to clear out the Blighter presence, 100% completion of the memory requires you to complete a few Challenges that differ between each stronghold. For a general completion, stealth is not necessary, but it is recommended to always enter from the top of the buildings surrounding the strongholds. If you are looking to get 100% synchronization on each of these activities, use the tips below to complete the required Challenges. Each Challenge can be completed separately so if you are having trouble completing two Challenges at once, try to complete one, then complete the memory, and then play it again to complete the other Challenge. While completing each Challenge separately rewards 100% synchronization for the memory, you do not get the 100% completion bonus.

ACTIVITIES	
⦿	Gang Strongholds
⦿	Templar Hunts
⦿	Bounty Hunts
⦿	Child Liberations

THE ESSENTIALS
WALKTHROUGH
SIDE QUESTS
COLLECTIBLES
REFERENCE & MAPS
INDEX

ASSOCIATES & INCOME
LONDON STORIES
WAR TIME ANOMALY
TRACK HUNT LIST
DREADFUL CRIMES

BURN BLIGHTER HEIST PLANS

Blighter Heist plans can be located with Eagle Vision. This usually requires searching the open floors of different buildings in the stronghold. There are often guards in the same room as the plans. Make sure to eliminate any enemies before destroying the plans as the action performs a small cut scene, making you extremely vulnerable.

You can locate and burn the plans at any time, but it is much easier to just kill all but one enemy and then search for them, allowing you to get around without much effort.

DO NOT LET THE LOOKOUTS CALL REINFORCEMENTS

The easiest way to prevent lookouts from calling reinforcements is by killing them before they catch wind of your actions in the stronghold. When using Eagle Vision you will notice that Lookouts have a different Icon above their heads which lets you single them out of the crowd quickly. If you are spotted by a lookout the icon above their head changes colors; quickly kill them before they can get to a door to summon more enemies.

FREE AND PROTECT CAPTURED ROOKS/CLINKERS

There are groups of Rooks being held hostage in the stronghold. Stealthily kill the enemies guarding them and they join your cause, immediately fighting any enemies in the nearby areas. Make sure to kill off any rooftop enemies before dropping down into the areas with the Rooks, as Scouts can easily pick off the Rooks (and you) with their heavy ranged attacks. If any Rooks die, this bonus objective fails, so be sure to stay near them after freeing them.

KILL THE LEADER UNDETECTED

Locate the Leader with Eagle Vision. They are outlined in yellow while the rest of the enemies are the standard red color. The easiest way to accomplish this early in the game is to stick to the rooftops, eliminating any enemies that inhabit the area. Then either use your Throwing Knives or a quick Air Assassination to kill the Leader. Once you've eliminated the Leader, you no longer have to worry about the Challenge as it is already complete. This may be the easiest Challenge to accomplish once you unlock hallucinogenic darts after Sequence 4. Hallucinogenic darts allow you to effectively "recruit" any enemy in the stronghold, so aim for the ones closest to the Leader. Once affected by the dart, they break into a blind violent rage, and begin to attack the enemies next to them. Use this to your advantage by targeting a Brute as they have high enough health to easily outlast the Leader. It's also important to note that killing the Leaders in a stealthy way causes any witnesses to flee.

STRONGHOLDS

MAP	LVL	BOROUGH	NAME	CHALLENGES	REWARDS/100%
8	6	City Of London	Rosemary Lane	Free and protect captured Rooks. Kill the Leader undetected.	£: 400 + 150 XP: 300 + 150
6	6	City of London	Field Lane	Kill the Leader undetected. Burn Blighter Heist Plans.	£: 400 + 150 XP: 300 + 150
7	6	City Of London	Black Swan Yard	Do not let the Lookouts call reinforcements. Kill the Leader undetected.	£: 532 + 150 XP: 360 + 150
12	4	Lambeth	Echostreet Alley	Burn Blighter Heist plans. Free and protect Captured Rooks.	£: 400 + 100 XP: 300 + 125
11	3	Lambeth	Battersea Bellows	Kill the Leader undetected. Free and protect Captured Rooks.	£: 264 + 75 XP: 250 + 100
10	5	Southwark	The Mint	Do not let Lookouts call reinforcements. Burn Blighter Heist Plans.	£: 400 + 125 XP: 300 + 150
9	5	Southwark	Jacob's Island	Do not let Lookouts call reinforcements. Kill the Leader undetected.	£: 532 + 125 XP: 360 + 150
5	2	Whitechapel	Spitalfields	Free and protect captured Clinkers.	£: 264 + 75 XP: 250 + 100
1	9	Westminster	Devil's Acre	Free and protect captured Rooks.	£: 600 + 350 XP: 430 + 300
2	9	Westminster	Blue Anchor Alley	Burn Blighter Heist Plans. Kill the Leader undetected.	£: 600 + 350 XP: 430 + 300
3	8	The Strand	Clare Market	Burn Blighter Heist Plans. Do not let Lookouts call reinforcements.	£: 532 + 1330 XP: 360 + 600
4	8	The Strand	St. Giles Rookery	Free and protect captured Rooks.	£: 532 + 1330 XP: 360 + 600

BOUNTY HUNTS

Bounty Hunting requires you to bring the target back to a secure location dead or alive. The target is surrounded by his allies and attempts to run if you are detected.

LOCATING THE TARGET

Use Eagle Vision to locate your target. Enemies appear as red, while your target appears as yellow. Ziplining from roof to roof over the Bounty Hunt area helps you quickly locate the target. Locating the target before making your approach is crucial as this helps you plan the escape and prevents you from killing them accidentally.

CHOOSING YOUR APPROACH

For 100% completion you must bring the target back alive. This leaves you with two general ways of going about securing the target and then extracting them to the specified location. Killing the target only grants you 90% completion.

GRABBING THE TARGET

When deciding to grab the target you have three options.

❖ Killing the target and moving their dead body into the carriage is easy, but you do not get the 100% synchronization bonus, so avoid this if at all possible.

❖ Knocking the target out is the easiest way to move them. This allows you to engage in combat with any enemies that may be in between you and your way out. This also leaves your target incapacitated so you don't have to worry about them running away during any accidental combat.

❖ The last option is kidnapping the target. While this may help you navigate through the maze of enemies, it can get complicated when exiting one of the small alleys on the way to the carriage.

THE LOUD WAY

Going in "Loud" favors the gameplay of Jacob as you are going to be inviting all of the enemies in the area to fight you. Once the target learns of your presence they begin to flee the area. Quickly run and tackle them, being careful not to assassinate them. To kidnap or knock out the target you must not be in combat mode, which makes this method a little bit complicated. Wandering too far from the target during the fight may let the target begin to run away again so try your hardest to stay near the target. Knock out the target quickly before the main fight begins by utilizing hiding spots and high ground to get in close.

KEEPING IT QUIET

Evie is the best option for this approach, as her skills are more stealth oriented. Use high ground and throwing knives to pick off lone enemies, making an effort to clear your way to the target. Once you have a path to the target set, plot your exit before making contact. Make sure no enemies are between you and your way out as they are likely to spot you with the target. If you've eliminated a good amount of enemies, kidnapping the target makes it easy to work past the remaining enemies.

THE GETAWAY

Once the target is either kidnapped and walking with you, or you have their body slung over your shoulder, you need to head for the nearest carriage. Luckily for you, the Rooks always have one parked nearby. Locate the cart by finding the small green icon on your map. If you are confronted you need to kill off any enemies in the area before you can put the target in the cart. Once the target is in the carriage, follow the GPS to the drop off point. Make sure to either wreck or lose any of the enemies chasing you as you need to be out of combat to complete the memory.

If you have enemies closing in on you, drop a smoke bomb while sitting in the cart at the drop off. If enemies followed you all the way to the drop off, get out and kill any who dared to follow you all the way. Once they are dead the memory completes.

BOUNTY HUNTS

MAP	LVL	BOROUGH	NAME	CHALLENGES	REWARDS/100%
3	9	Westminster	Ivan Bunbury	Bring back the target Alive.	£: 600 + 350 / XP: 430 + 300
7	5	City of London	Harvey Hughes	Bring back the target Alive.	£: 264 + 125 / XP: 250 + 150
8	6	City of London	Maude Foster	Bring back the target Alive.	£: 400 + 150 / XP: 300 + 150
9	6	City of London	David O'Donnell	Bring back the target Alive.	£: 400 + 150 / XP: 300 + 150
13	3	Lambeth	Leopold Bacchus	Bring back the target Alive.	£: 264 + 75 / XP: 250 + 100
14	3	Lambeth	Mildred Graves	Bring back the target Alive.	£: 400 + 75 / XP: 300 + 100
15	3	Lambeth	Jesse Butler	Bring back the target Alive.	£: 264 + 75 / XP: 250 + 100
6	8	The Strand	Sylvia Duke	Bring back the target Alive.	£: 532 + 250 / XP: 360 + 250
4	8	The Strand	Milton King	Bring back the target Alive.	£: 532 + 250 / XP: 360 + 250
5	8	The Strand	Gilbert Fowler	Bring back the target Alive.	£: 532 + 250 / XP: 360 + 250
16	5	Southwark	Anna Abramson	Bring back the target Alive.	£: 400 + 125 / XP: 300 + 150
17	5	Southwark	Albie Vassell	Bring back the target Alive.	£: 400 + 125 / XP: 300 + 150
12	4	The Thames	Simon Chase	Bring back the target Alive.	£: 264 + 100 / XP: 250 + 125
11	3	The Thames	Emmet Sedgwick	Bring back the target Alive.	£: 400 + 75 / XP: 300 + 100
10	4	The Thames	George Scrivens	Bring back the target Alive.	£: 264 + 100 / XP: 250 + 125
18	2	White Chapel	Homer Dalton	Bring back the target Alive.	£: 132 / XP: 200
1	8	Westminster	Harrison Harley	Bring back the target Alive	£: 532 + 250 / XP: 360 + 250
2	9	Westminster	Wade Lynton	Bring back the target Alive.	£: 600 + 350 / XP: 430 + 300

CHILD LIBERATIONS

Child Liberations task you with assassinating the Foreman and freeing the children inside a factory.

GAINING ENTRY

Each factory has a roof entrance that might be guarded by a scout, so use Eagle Vision and a bit of caution before haphazardly using your Rope Launcher to get to the top of the building. Use throwing knives to clear out the top level to make the jump down into the building easier. Don't knock any bodies off the roof or down into the center of the factory as that is a sure way to set off the alarm.

KEEPING THE ALARMS QUIET

If you alert an enemy, all is not lost if you act quickly! Once they have a bell appear above their head, they begin to run for the Alarm Bell. Use throwing knives to quickly stop them if they are out of reach, as using your pistol results in other enemies noticing you.

Another option is using a hallucinogenic dart on an enemy on the main floor. This pulls some enemies from the surrounding area, giving you the opportunity to sneak in and disable the bell. With the bell disabled you are free to move around without risking the alarm being raised.

FREEING THE KIDS

The kids may be guarded by enemies, though often there is only one nearby. The majority of the enemies are located on the main floor of the building near the Alarm Bells. When you free a group of children, they do not trigger alarms or raise attention as they run away, so don't be afraid to stealthily release them when an enemy has their back turned.

The groups of children are usually crouched down and show up as green when you are using Eagle Vision to locate them.

KILLING THE FOREMAN

There are a variety of ways to kill the Foreman. As in the Gang Strongholds, killing the Foreman in a stealthy manner causes any witnesses to flee.

USE THE ENVIRONMENT

Factories are a dangerous place regardless of age. Hanging crates and dynamite are commonly found around the factory. If the opportunity presents itself, use objects in the environment to kill enemies as well as the foreman.

THROWING KNIVES

Depending on your level and upgrades, you may not be able to headshot kill the foreman on the first try, so be ready to land a few follow up shots if need be.

HALLUCINOGENIC DARTS

Hit one of the enemies near the Foreman and let them do the dirty work for you. The hallucinating enemy will either kill the Foremen or injure him enough to make your follow up attacks lethal.

ASSASSINATION

The easiest way to assassinate the Foreman is to hide behind one of the stacks of crates nearby, and then whistle to attract him over. Once he is just around the corner form you, jump out and assassinate him.

CHILD LIBERATIONS

MAP	LVL	BOROUGH	NAME	CHALLENGES	REWARDS/100%
4	6	City of London	Wolfshead Brewing Co.	Do not trigger the alarm.	£: 400 + 150 XP: 300 + 150
5	6	City of London	Outterridge Manufacturing	Do not trigger the alarm.	£: 400 + 150 XP: 300 + 150
6	5	City of London	Spindles and Looms	Do not trigger the alarm.	£: 332 + 125 XP: 280 + 150
10	4	Lambeth	Strain & Boil	Do not trigger the alarm.	£: 264 + 100 XP: 250 + 125
3	8	The Strand	Lynch's Fine Ornamentation	Do not trigger the alarm.	£: 532 + 250 XP: 360 + 250
8	4	Southwark	Cotton Mill	Do not trigger the alarm.	£: 264 + 100 XP: 250 + 125
7	5	Southwark	Blackburn Bellows	Do not trigger the alarm.	£: 332 + 125 XP: 280 + 150
9	5	Southwark	Hightower Coal	Do not trigger the alarm.	£: 332 + 125 XP: 280 + 150
11	2	Whitechapel	Radclyffe Mill	Do not trigger the alarm.	£: 132 XP: 200
2	9	Westminster	Goodfellow's Brewery	Do not trigger the alarm.	£: 600 + 350 XP: 430 + 300
1	9	Westminster	Red Growler Distillery	Do not trigger the alarm.	£: 600 + 350 XP: 430 + 300

TEMPLAR HUNTS

Templar Hunts require you to eliminate the target, using specific methods to complete the Challenges successfully.

HAROLD DRAKE

Memory Type: Associate Activity / Templar Hunt
Suggested Level: 2
Challenges: Kill Target with a crate of dynamite.
£: 132 + 75 (Full Synch Bonus)
XP: 200 + 100 (Full Synch Bonus)
Location: Whitechapel

Sneak into the market, working your way toward Harold. You find him in a secluded area walled in by pallets of food and other supplies. On the outside of this small area are some boxes of dynamite.

Ignite one of the boxes and then run away as fast as you can out the exit of the market. Harold is killed by the explosion and you can almost clear the area to complete the mission by the time the crate detonates.

MARTIN CHURCH

Memory Type: Associate Activity / Templar Hunt
Suggested Level: 3
Challenges: Kill Martin with the Hidden Blade
£: 400 + 75 (Full Synch Bonus)
XP: 300 + 100 (Full Synch Bonus)
Location: Lambeth

Climb the wall nearest the church and then continue up to the top of the church building. A scout is perched on the roof. Sneak up behind him and assassinate him before

taking a dive into the cart full of leaves below. Wait for the target to come close to the pile of leaves and then whistle. Once he is within range, quickly grab him to kill him with the hidden blade and pull him into the pile.

> ### WHISTLE WISELY
> When using whistle make sure that your target is the closest enemy to you, preventing you from accidentally calling the wrong enemy over.

Run back out of the pile and back up to the rooftop of the church and out of the church's complex to escape and complete the memory.

THE LAMBETH BULLIES (CLYDE AND ADA)

Memory Type: Associate Activity / Templar Hunt
Suggested Level: 3
Challenges: Do not let the Bullies kill more than two civilians.
£: 264 + 75 (Full Synch Bonus)
XP: 250 + 100 (Full Synch Bonus)
Location: Lambeth

Get on top of the buildings that surround the courtyard containing the Bullies. From there jump onto the connecting buildings. The rope allows you to drop down and kill Clyde before rushing over to kill Ada. They are the only two that kill civilians. If you act quickly, the enemies can't join the fight before you've killed both targets.

Once you've killed the targets there's no need to stick around; the captured civilians are no longer at risk. Quickly flee the area to complete the mission.

THE FLETCHERS

Memory Type: Associate Activity / Templar Hunt
Suggested Level: 3
Challenges: Kill both targets at the same time.
£: 264 + 75 (Full Synch Bonus)
XP: 250 + 100 (Full Synch Bonus)
Location: Lambeth

Stick to the roofs, moving from roof to roof when needed to keep track of the Fletchers. Eventually they move to the south side of the area. If you are on the roof you have two options, use the Nitro crate provided to kill them with an explosion, or attempt to perform a double assassination.

Killing them with the Nitro is a safer bet as they can be further away, however it attracts a lot of attention if you fail, so be ready for a fight if you didn't take out both of the Fletchers in the blast. With both Fletchers dead, jump the fence and escape.

THE JEKYLL BROTHERS

Memory Type: Associate Activity / Templar Hunt
Suggested Level: 3
Challenges: Have a police officer kill one of the targets.
£: 132 + 75 (Full Synch Bonus)
XP: 200 + 100 (Full Synch Bonus)
Location: The Thames

This fight takes place down on the docks, so high ground is out of the question. Before running in, use your Eagle Vision to pick out the target. Make a dash straight for them, bumping into them and forcing them to chase you. With one of the brothers chasing you, head straight for a police officer.

Make sure to avoid attacking anyone or bumping into the police officer until he has started fighting the Templars. With one brother now tied up in a losing fight with the officer, locate the other brother and kill him. For an easy escape, jump into the water and swim away.

CAPTAIN HARGRAVE II

Memory Type: Associate Activity / Templar Hunt
Suggested Level: 4
Challenges: Dispose of the target's body in the Thames River
£: 264 + 100 (Full Synch Bonus)
XP: 250 + 125 (Full Synch Bonus)
Location: The Thames

Captain Hargrave II is aboard his ship in the center of the Thames. Get to the high mast of one of the ships surrounding him. Use the water to help you sneak to a good lookout point. Once you have some high ground take a look down into the mess of ships, noting the location of Captain Hargrave. Set up your Rope Launch to cross directly over the top of him.

Assassinate Captain Hargrave from above. Quickly kill the other enemy on his boat before throwing the Captain's body into the river. Once you've tossed the body, swim away and nobody is able to chase you.

TOM ECCLESTON

Memory Type: Associate Activity / Templar Hunt
Suggested Level: 4
Challenges: Kill the target by performing an Air Assassination
£: 264 + 100 (Full Synch Bonus)
XP: 250 + 125 (Full Synch Bonus)
Location: The Thames

Stay on the upper walkway near the road and head south to the end of the restricted area before jumping up on the ledge. Once on the ledge look for the end of the dock below. It should line up with a planter box that is hanging from the ledge.

Use your Eagle Vision to spot Tom, and then wait for him to walk into range for an Air Assassination. Once you've killed him, head back up the wall and run across the street to get away.

THE SLAUGHTERHOUSE SIBLINGS

Memory Type: Associate Activity / Templar Hunt
Suggested Level: 5
Challenges: Have Charlie kill her brother.
£: 264 + 125 (Full Synch Bonus)
XP: 250 + 150 (Full Synch Bonus)
Location: City of London

Start at the top of the house in the center of the courtyard, killing the scout on the roof, then the one on the outside balcony. After they are dead, use ledge assassinations to kill a few of the enemies inside, leaving the Siblings alive. Be warned that there are police patrolling below. If they spot you after seeing a dead body, they begin to attack.

Once you've cleared some room in the house, head in with your hallucinogenic dart ready. Shoot the woman, Charlie, then exit the house and let the dart do the rest. She freaks out and her brother runs up into the room from the floor below if he wasn't already in the room by the time you shot her.

Once her brother is dead, hop back in and finish her off with a quick attack or use a ranged attack to kill her through the window. Head back out to the streets to get away.

THE ESSENTIALS
WALKTHROUGH
SIDE QUESTS
COLLECTIBLES
REFERENCE & ANALYSIS
INDEX

ASSOCIATES & INCOME
LONDON STORIES
WWI TIME ANOMALY
TRAIN HIDEOUT
DREADFUL CRIMES

MYRTLE PLATT

Memory Type: Associate Activity / Templar Hunt
Suggested Level: 5
Challenges: Kill the target using hanging barrels
£: 400 + 125 (Full Synch Bonus)
XP: 300 + 150 (Full Synch Bonus)
Location: Southwark

Rope Launch to the top of the factory. Enter through the door on the roof that leads into the top floor. There is one enemy there; kill him and then move down to the next level. Here you also encounter one enemy; use a throwing knife or sneak over to kill him.

The next level contains two enemies and Myrtle. Myrtle does not walk underneath the hanging barrels, so you need to take out the two other enemies on the level before moving into position to whistle Myrtle over to the barrels.

To release the hanging barrels use a throwing knife or your gun. Once you've crushed Myrtle, run out the open window onto the pipes, following them across the street to freedom.

PHILLIP BECKINRIDGE

Memory Type: Associate Activity / Templar Hunt
Suggested Level: 5
Challenges: Run over the target with a carriage
£: 400 + 125 (Full Synch Bonus)
XP: 300 + 150 (Full Synch Bonus)
Location: Southwark

Grab a nearby carriage and slowly drive on the road. The road is not in the restricted area, so driving on the far side does not draw an attack.

Use Eagle Vision to find Phillip, wait for him to come to the lower level of the small market. Once he is there, line up your cart and run him over at full speed. Don't worry about missing, he stays on the low ground and the enemies slowly gather around him. Keep taking runs at him until you kill him, then stay in the carriage and ride away.

EVELINE DIPPER

Memory Type: Associate Activity / Templar Hunt
Suggested Level: 6
Challenges: Kill the target while she is under the smoke bomb effect
£: 400 + 150 (Full Synch Bonus)
XP: 300 + 150 (Full Synch Bonus)
Location: City of London

Rope Launch to the top of any of the surrounding buildings from the street. There is one enemy lookout on the rooftop; quickly kill them and then focus on the courtyard below. Using Eagle Vision, locate Eveline, and line yourself up for a Leap of Faith down into the cart below. Once you're lined up for the jump, aim and throw the smoke bomb down onto Eveline.

Take the Leap of Faith, quickly hop back into action, and run over to assassinate her while she is under the effect of the smoke. Quickly Rope Launch back up to the nearest roof, then zipline to a building across the road for a quick getaway.

THOMAS BLACKROOT

Memory Type: Associate Activity / Templar Hunt
Suggested Level: 6
Challenges: Bury the target in a nearby grave
£: 400 + 150 (Full Synch Bonus)
XP: 300 + 150 (Full Synch Bonus)
Location: City of London

A few scattered enemy patrols pace around the outside of the small graveyard. You have the choice of killing them off, or sneaking past them and into the graveyard containing Thomas. Once in the graveyard eliminate Thomas. This may cause the nearby enemies to attack, so be ready for a short fight as there are only five other enemies in the area.

One of the graves near the building is marked with a floating Glitch. Simply pick up Thomas's body, walk over to the grave, and drop it in. You do not need to actually bury the body. If there aren't any enemies remaining, walk out of the zone to finish the mission. If you are being attacked, Rope Launch quickly to the top of the church to get away.

THE ESSENTIALS

WALKTHROUGH

SIDE QUESTS

COLLECTIBLES

DATABLOCK & ANALYSIS

INDEX

ASSOCIATES & INCOME

LONDON STORIES

WORLD TIER 400 MAP

TRAIN HIDEOUT

DREADFUL CRIMES

PETER NEEDHAM

Memory Type: Associate Activity / Templar Hunt
Suggested Level: 7
Challenges: Kill the target using explosives.
£: 400
XP: 300
Location: The Strand

Rope Launch to the top of the yellow brick building on the south side of the Templar Hunt area. Drop down into the courtyard behind the tree. You see Peter making his rounds up and down a set of stairs. Wait until he walks away from you toward the set of stairs that he walks up. Move into position, grabbing the Nitro bottles. Make sure that you have the explosive crate full of Nitro bottles and not the crate with TNT sticks. The sticks do not explode on impact.

When Peter comes down the steps, throw the explosives at him to kill him. This attracts all enemies in the area, so Rope Launch back up to the roof you entered from, then across the road to freedom.

LOUIS BLAKE

Memory Type: Associate Activity / Templar Hunt
Suggested Level: 8
Challenges: Kill the target by headshot
£: 532 + 250 (Full Synch Bonus)
XP: 360 + 250 (Full Synch Bonus)
Location: The Strand

Before running straight into the park to take on Louis Blake, walk around the outside fence with Eagle Vision active. You find Louis flanked by two guards, with a scout blended into the crowd.

While you are still on the outside of the fence you find a part of the fence near a tree that is almost in line with him. Make sure you are in stealth mode and climb onto the fence, moving in toward Louis. With your throwing knife equipped, use Eagle Vision and aim for his head.

Once he's dead, quickly turn around, cross the street, and Rope Launch to the rooftops. Any enemy that was alerted to your actions can't keep up, making your escape incredibly easy.

ARGUS AND ROSE BARTLETT

Memory Type: Associate Activity / Templar Hunt
Suggested Level: 8
Challenges: Perform a cover kill on one of the targets
£: 532 + 250 (Full Synch Bonus)
XP: 360 + 250 (Full Synch Bonus)
Location: The Strand

Enter through the North alley. From there slowly work through the maze of small walls and scattered cargo. Kill enemies while working your way clockwise around the courtyard. When you near Argus or Rose, watch their route and try to cut them off while hiding behind a wall. If they are close to your cover spot, whistle to pull them the rest of the way to you. Be careful though, whistling may attract a different enemy.

Throwing knives are a good way to pick off enemies in this courtyard, making it easier for you to focus on the targets. If you missed the cover kill on the first attempt, don't worry, you only need to kill one of the targets from cover! After you've killed the targets, Rope Launch to the nearest roof and begin your escape.

WALLACE BONE

Memory Type: Associate Activity / Templar Hunt
Suggested Level: 8
Challenges: Kill the target from a hiding spot.
£: 532 + 250 (Full Synch Bonus)
XP: 360 + 250 (Full Synch Bonus)
Location: Westminster

Get onto the east rooftops and locate Wallace. There is one enemy looking directly at a hiding spot, while two groups of enemies flank the north and south sides of the alley. From the roof use a hallucinogenic dart on the Brute in the north group of enemies. When doing this, make sure that Wallace is at the farthest south end of his walking route. If Wallace is not as far south as possible, he also joins the fight where he can potentially die, preventing you from getting 100% synchronization.

The fight between the north group of enemies pulls the foe guarding the hiding spot away from his position. If you're lucky he will die in the fight.

Wallace begins to walk his route back toward the north side of the alley and directly in front of the hiding spot. Quickly grab him and pull him in to assassinate him, then head for the rooftops to escape.

BEATRICE GRIBBLE

Memory Type: Associate Activity / Templar Hunt
Suggested Level: 9
Challenges: Kill the target with a Voltaic Bomb
£: 600 + 350 (Full Synch Bonus)
XP: 430 + 300 (Full Synch Bonus)
Location: Westminster

Beatrice is located in the back of the small park. You can sneak around on the side near the edge of the water until you locate her. You need multiple voltaic bombs to kill her from a full health state. Voltaic Bombs also stun enemies around the point of impact. Use this area attack to stun any other groups of enemies who approach.

Due to the lack of high ground and buildings, you are likely to encounter open conflict with the enemies in the park, so be ready for a fight but keep your eye out for the target. If you accidentally bring Beatrice near death, quickly switch to the Voltaic Bomb to finish her off. The killing blow is what counts to complete the Challenge.

EDGAR COLLICOTT AND BODYGUARD

Memory Type: Associate Activity / Templar Hunt
Suggested Level: 9
Challenges: Kill Edgar or his bodyguard by Air Assassination
£: 600 + 350 (Full Synch Bonus)
XP: 430 + 300 (Full Synch Bonus)
Location: Westminster

Edgar and his bodyguard are located on the rooftop surrounded by five scouts. Use your Rope Launcher to get to the rooftop before assassinating the scouts. Edgar's Bodyguard is female; use this fact to differentiate her from the other nearby male enemies when using Eagle Vision. Get above Collicott or the bodyguard and perform an Air Assassination. To complete the Challenge you only need to get one of them with this move, then you can finish the other one off however you choose.

THE ESSENTIALS

WALKTHROUGH

SIDE QUESTS

COLLECTIBLES

RESOURCES & FINANCES

REFERENCE

ASSOCIATES & INCOME

LONDON STORIES

WORLD TIER, CRIMINAL

CRIME REVEALED

DREADFUL CRIMES

GANG WARS

Want to be the Boss of the Borough? Once you've completed all of the conquest activities in a Borough, a Gang War unlocks. Gang Wars pit you against the toughest Crime Bosses and their crews. Fight side by side with your Rooks until you've earned your one on one showdown with the Boss.

> **STOCK UP!**
>
> Make sure that you are topped off on all of your consumables (Medicine, Bullets, Throwing Knives, Smoke Bombs…)

WINNING THE FIGHT

Unlike other activities, there is no challenge requiring you to complete this memory a specific way. All you have to do is kill all of the Blighters, then kill their boss. This leaves you to rely heavily on your combat abilities to get through this fight.

SMOKE THEM OUT

During the initial confrontation, your gang of Rooks throws some smoke bombs putting up a wall in front of the advancing enemies. Run in and assassinate as many enemies as possible before the smoke dissipates.

UPGRADES

Gang upgrades within the Ringleader tree help strengthen your Rooks. Other upgrades in the tree take health away from the Blighters, as well as make their ranged attacks much less effective.

KEEPING YOUR DISTANCE

If you are facing the Gang Leader and you aren't doing much melee damage, resort to you ranged weapons. Circle around your foe, keeping yourself far enough away to force them to range attack you. Use Counter-Shot to either fire your pistol or throw knives at the target. When they are stunned from the counter, quickly aim for a headshot and deal some extra damage.

UP CLOSE AND PERSONAL

Be ready for a fight. Gang bosses hit incredibly hard, so you need to be ready to counter their attacks at all times. The counter window is much shorter with gang bosses. Throw in some Guard Breaking moves while comboing on the boss. This keeps them from regaining their composure and allows your onslaught of attacks to continue.

END OF THE FIGHT

With the exception of the first Gang War, discussed during Sequence 3 of the Story Walkthrough, the boss comes to fight you in the same arena as the initial battle. Once the boss is dead, that's the end; the turf is yours. Rook presence increases in the area as now most of the Blighters in the area have decided to join.

GANG LEADER ELIMINA

> **CUT OFF THE HEAD**
>
> Though it is often difficult, you can choose to take out the Gang Boss before Gang War starts. If you succeed at taking them out, you only have to clean up the remaining Blighters to secure the territory.

MAP	LVL	BOROUGH	GANG LEADER	REWARD
1	2	Whitechapel	Rexford Kaylock	£: 164 XP: 200 Adept Cane-Sword
2	9	The Strand	Victor Lynch	£: 532 XP: 360 Black Death Belt
3	7	City of London	Bloody Nora	£: 532 XP: 360 M1877 "Thunderer" (Firearm)
4	5	The Thames	Edith Swinebourne	£: 234 XP: 250 Gold Blessing Kukri
5	6	Southwark	Octavia Plumb	£: 400 XP: 300 Smoke Bomb Upgrade II Schematic
6	4	Lambeth	Cletus Strain	£: 400 XP: 300 Voltaic Bomb Upgrade II Schematic
7	10	Westminster	Lilla Graves	£: 600 XP: 430 Eagle's Splendor Knuckles

INCOME ACTIVITIES

Running low on resources or money? Participate in the various income activities scattered around the city! Each activity is replayable, so grinding out some money and materials is a piece of cake if you're game.

FIGHT CLUBS

Each borough houses a fight club with increasing difficulty, offering rewards for each round that you defeat the other competitors. Fight Clubs are unlocked after speaking to Robert Topping, which becomes available after Sequence 3.

FIGHTING

The basics section will give you a good run down on how to fight effectively but let's touch on a few things.

NO WEAPONS OR CONSUMABLES

The only thing you can bring into the ring is your fists. This means no medicine to heal you when you are injured, no quickshots to hit enemies at a distance, and no smoke bombs to disorient groups of enemies.

NO HIDING

Since you can't retreat from combat, you cannot heal. No health is gained between rounds, so try and keep your face pretty by countering opponents' attacks.

ODD MAN OUT

While there are other competitors in the ring with you, they do not fight each other. This means you fight multiple enemies at once. Focus on killing one enemy at a time, but don't let this stop you from countering other enemies who try to attack you.

When deciding on which enemy to attack, chose an enemy who is not in a guarded stance. While you attack one of the other enemies in the ring he will most likely try to attack. Once he begins his attack, counter then attack. This breaks his guarded stance without you breaking your combat flow to take an enemy out of a guarded stance.

If you're fighting just one enemy, let them swing first. Counter the first attempt at an attack and then unleash a fury of punches to debilitate them.

FIGHT CLUB

MAP	LVL	BOROUGH	ROUNDS	MAX REWARD
1	2	Whitechapel	4	£: 1250 XP: 300 Leather: 38 Chemical: 20
2	2	City of London	4	£: 1250 XP: 300 Metal: 20 Chemical: 20 Leather: 18
3	8	The Strand	7	£: 4000 XP: 1000 Metal: 90 Chemical: 75 Leather: 45
4	4	The Thames	5	£: 1850 XP: 500 Metal: 37 Silk: 45 Leather: 27
5	5	Southwark	6	£: 3500 XP: 600 Leather: 60 Chemical: 52 Metal: 37
6	3	Lambeth	5	£: 1850 XP: 500 Leather: 37 Silk: 45 Metal: 27
7	9	Westminster	8	£: 6000 XP: 2000 Metal: 150 Chemical: 75

STREET RACING

Each race, you are either racing against other drivers, trains, or the clock. No matter what you are racing against you want to have the lead.

TAKING THE LEAD

In Lap and A to B races, you start in the back of the starting lineup. Use a well-timed boost to split the two front runners right away, using your cart to ram them to the left or right if necessary.

Taking the inside of the turn and then ramming the other carts outward is extremely effective. When taking corners, don't be afraid to hit a small post or other small object, these won't slow you down enough to make them worth avoiding.

KEEPING THE LEAD

Once you are in the lead, watch the Mini-Map to get a sense for how close the other drivers are. Don't get too locked in on the map, doing so may cause you to crash, a surefire way to give up your lead. When you begin to see the front of another driver's horse at the bottom of your screen, try to force them into a carriage on the road, or cut them off at the turn.

THE RACES

There are four different types of races. While there is no level suggestion for completing the races, you still gain a benefit from being higher level and having upgrades researched for your carriage.

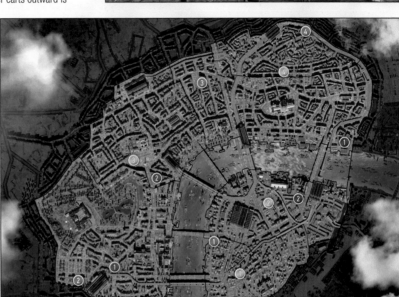

STREET RACING	
◉	Lap Race
◉	Exotic Race
◉	Triathlon
◉	A to B Race

LAP RACE

Lap Races pit you up against three other drivers, racing to finish all three laps first.

MAP	BOROUGH	REWARD
1	Lambeth	£: 600 XP: 140 Metal: 22 Leather: 22 Chemical: 30
2	Southwark	£: 800 XP: 165 Leather: 60 Chemical: 22
3	The Strand	£: 1200 XP: 200 Leather: 37 Metal: 37 Chemical: 30
4	Whitechapel	£: 450 XP: 125 Metal: 37 Chemical: 22

EXOTIC RACE

Its horse vs. machine in the Exotic Races. Your goal is to reach the train station before the train arrives, following all of the checkpoints along the way. The exotic race is much like the A to B race, however instead of racing from point to point against drivers, you are racing a train.

MAP	BOROUGH	REWARD
1	City of London	£: 600 XP: 140 Leather: 44 Chemical: 30
2	Southwark	£: 800 XP: 165 Leather: 60 Chemical: 22

A TO B RACE

An A to B race is a non-looping race, going from one point on the map to the other. This is a competitive race, so you will be racing against three other carriage drivers. View the amount of checkpoints left on the top left of the screen to keep track of how close you are to the finish line.

MAP	BOROUGH	REWARD
1	Lambeth	£: 600 XP: 140 Leather: 44 Chemical: 30
2	Westminster	£: 1400 XP: 215 Leather: 84 Silk: 30

TRIATHLON

Starting out in a cart, you race down the road, until you have to jump off. Then you'll be free running, climbing, and taking Leaps of Faith to follow the check points. When approaching the start of a running checkpoint, climb to the roof of your carriage, then free run off of it and into the checkpoint.

MAP	BOROUGH	REWARD
2	The Strand	£: 1200 XP: 200 Leather: 37 Metal: 37 Chemical: 30
1	Westminster	£: 1400 XP: 215 Leather: 84 Silk: 30

MAP	BOROUGH	REWARD
3	City of London	£: 800 XP: 165 Leather: 30 Metal: 30 Chemical: 22
4	Whitechapel	£: 450 XP: 125 Metal: 37 Chemical: 22

CARGO HIJACK

Cargo Hijacking is simple: get in, get the cargo, and get out. There are static Cargo Hijack Activities that can be played once only in each of the land-based Boroughs.

However, there is also a chance that you find a random Cargo Carriage with Blighters at the helm. These do not have a level suggestion and the reward is much lower. The non-static Cargo Hijacks appear frequently, allowing you to gain more Influence with Ned Wynert, while providing you with bits of resources and money. The resource reward can be viewed by hovering over the Icon on the map.

SECURING THE CART

There are multiple ways to secure the cargo carriage that is being guarded by the Blighters. While a stealth approach is possible, the more action oriented "smash and grab" technique speeds up completion drastically while offering the same rewards.

THE STEALTH APPROACH

Seek the highest ground near the restricted area, using Eagle Vision to scout it out. Look for enemies that are either between you and the cart, or enemies that you have to get through once you have the cart secured. In most cases all of the enemies in the area need to be eliminated, and unlike strongholds, there aren't usually many Blighters lining the roofs.

When killing enemies from a rooftop, be extra careful not to raise the alarm of any remaining enemies. If they are alerted and you are not near them, they grab the cart and begin to drive away. If the enemy drives off with the cart, the mission does not end until they gain enough distance from you to count as a failure.

SMASH AND GRAB

If the Cargo Carriage is in a courtyard, use your zipline to line yourself up with the carriage. Once you are above the carriage, drop down and quickly take the driver's seat. Throw a smoke bomb down to immediately send your horses running, and obscure the view of any enemies that are close by.

For carts that are in a lumberyard or outdoor area not surrounded by buildings, scout the area, finding the fastest way to get to the cart. This often requires jumping a fence. Once you have your route set, free run as fast as you can to get inside. Jump into the driver's seat, throw a smoke bomb, and get the heck out of there.

SMOKE THEM OUT

If you've got a carriage of your own, line yourself up so you are blocking a nearby exit. Hop on top of your carriage and then throw a smoke bomb at the horses leading the cargo cart. This causes the horses to run off by themselves. Then all that's left is to chase the cart down.

Once you've caught up to the cart, either cut it off, forcing it to stop, or jump from the roof of your carriage, landing on the cart and then taking the driver's seat.

THE ESSENTIALS
WALKTHROUGH
SIDE QUESTS
COLLECTIBLES
RESOURCE & UPGRADE
INDEX

ASSOCIATES & INCOME
LONDON STORIES
WAR-TIME ANOMALY

THE DELIVERY

Once you have the cart in your possession, follow the GPS to the Rook's drop off location. On the way you may attract the unwanted attention of some Blighters who try and stop you from stealing their cargo.

Keep going toward the drop off point. Although you cannot drop off the cargo until you are incognito, the nearby Rooks help you kill off any Blighters who dared follow you the entire way there.

If you have a cart on your tail when you pull up, use a Smoke Bomb to frighten the horses of the other cart, forcing them to pull the enemy away and masking your location which, in most cases, makes you incognito instantly and allows you to deliver the cargo immediately.

CARGO HIJACK

MAP	LVL	BOROUGH	REWARD
1	2	Whitechapel	£: 900 XP: 450 Leather: 54
2	2	Whitechapel	£: 900 XP: 450 Metal: 54
3	2	Whitechapel	£: 900 XP: 450 Metal: 27 Leather: 27
4	6	City of London	£: 2200 XP: 500 Metal: 45 Leather: 45 Chemical: 18
5	6	City of London	£: 2200 XP: 500 Metal: 90 Chemical: 18
6	5	City of London	£: 1550 XP: 450 Leather: 90 Silk: 18
7	8	The Strand	£: 2900 XP: 560 Leather: 108 Silk: 18

MAP	LVL	BOROUGH	REWARD
8	7	The Strand	£: 2200 XP: 500 Metal: 45 Leather: 45 Silk: 18
9	7	The Strand	£: 2200 XP: 500 Metal: 45 Leather: 45 Silk: 18
10	8	Westminster	£: 2900 XP: 560 Metal: 108 Chemical: 18
11	9	Westminster	£: 3200 XP: 650 Metal: 72 Leather: 72 Silk: 52
12	8	Westminster	£: 2900 XP: 560 Metal: 54 Leather: 54 Chemical: 18
13	2	Lambeth	£: 900 XP: 450 Metal: 27 Leather: 27

MAP	LVL	BOROUGH	REWARD
14	3	Lambeth	£: 1550 XP: 450 Metal: 45 Leather: 45 Chemical: 18
15	2	Lambeth	£: 900 XP: 450 Metal: 27 Leather: 27
16	5	Southwark	£: 2200 XP: 500 Leather: 90 Chemical: 18
17	4	Southwark	£: 1550 XP: 450 Leather: 45 Silk: 18
18	4	Southwark	£: 900 XP: 450 Leather: 27 Metal: 27
N/A	N/A	All of London	£: 700 XP: 350 22 Total Resources Mixed/Unmixed

BOAT RAIDS

Board the docked Blighter boat just before it leaves. You are only allowed three minutes to hunt down the manifest and mark the cargo for the Rooks. If you accomplish the objectives in time, you get a great amount of money and resources.

GETTING THE MANIFEST

Activate Eagle Vision to identify the leader of the Blighters, who is holding the manifest. You need to either pickpocket him, or kill him and loot his body.

Don't worry about kicking the manifest holder into the water during a fight; if he or she falls into the water you still acquire the manifest. With the manifest collected, your task changes to marking the payload for the Rooks.

MARKING THE CARGO

Once you have the manifest you are fighting against the clock and any remaining enemies. Marking the crates takes about four seconds so make sure that you've left yourself enough time to travel and mark each of the four crates. If you are struggling with enemies, use a smoke bomb and run to a different piece of cargo. Wasting too much time on one crate could use all of your time.

TAKE YOUR PRIZE

Both Boat Raids and Smuggler's Boat activities earn you varying rewards based on your level. We've marked possible locations for these on the map, but please note that not all of them will be available at the same time.

 # SMUGGLER'S BOAT

Smuggler's Boat activities only occur in The Thames River. You are tasked with sabotaging their cargo, with an added optional Challenge of killing the Lead Smuggler.

SABOTAGING THE GOODS

Each Smuggler's Boat activity requires you to destroy valuable cargo aboard the ships. These can only be destroyed with the TNT or Nitroglycerin crates that are scattered around the ships.

While there is plenty to use, make sure you don't use all of the explosives to clear out enemies.

If there are no explosives left on the ship containing the goods, use Eagle Vision to locate some on one of the other ships. If there is no bridge connecting them, toss some over by pressing **L2 / LT** to aim, then **R2 / RT** to throw the crate.

EXPLODE ON IMPACT

Unlike TNT, which has to be ignited, a box of Nitro bottles explodes on impact. This makes them a good option to take out goods on other ships. The nitro can also be easily used against the lead smuggler.

KILLING THE LEAD SMUGGLER

First things first! Identify the smuggler. The smuggler is outlined in yellow with the help of Eagle Vision.

Killing the lead smuggler is a pretty easy task due to the amount of explosives available. Assassinating the smuggler by jumping off of a nearby crate or using a cover assassination is also a good option.

Nitro bottles are the easiest to use against the lead smuggler, but you can also ignite TNT on the ground, then quickly pick it up and throw it at the smuggler. Depending on how close the lead smuggler is to the blast, you may need to use a ranged attack to finish them off. Use cover to give yourself time to line up some critical ranged attacks.

THE ESSENTIALS
WALKTHROUGH
SIDE QUESTS
COLLECTIBLES
REFERENCE & ANALYSIS
INDEX

ASSOCIATES & INCOME
LONDON STORIES
WORLDISE ANOMALY
TRAIN HIDEOUT
DREADFUL CRIMES

◈ CARGO ESCORT

Cargo Escorts occur randomly on the streets of London. They have no level requirement and reward £700, 350 XP, and 22 of mixed or unmixed resources. The type of resource awarded can be viewed by hovering over the icon on the large map.

ESCORT TIPS

Take the wheel! Kick out one of the initial Rooks who is driving the carriage. You want to be in charge of the drive, allowing you to hit top speed and ram other carriages out of the way.

Enemies begin to come flying out from around the corners. Use smoke bombs to throw them off your path.

The journey plays out much like the Cargo Hijacks after you initially hijack the cart. Once you're at the drop off point, kill off any Blighters to make yourself incognito and receive your reward.

◈ TRAIN ROBBERY

The Train is always visible on the map, though it may require some searching to locate its current location. Once you've found the icon on the map, place a marker on it to highlight its location. Each robbery rewards £3750, 563 XP, and 250 assorted materials, in addition to whatever loot you find aboard the train.

BOARDING THE TRAIN

Once you've deciphered the train's direction on the rails, head for the nearest train station in the direction it is heading. The train stops at the station, making boarding it as simple as walking up and hopping on.

Board the train from the front and immediately de-couple the engine from the rest of the train cars. You do this the same way as in Sequence 3, by pressing ◎ / Ⓑ then ⬜ / Ⓧ repeatedly. With the train cars uncoupled from the engine, you don't have to worry about catching back up to the train if you fall off.

FINDING THE TREASURE

Use your Eagle Vision to scan the carts. The treasure is in a small briefcase and is highlighted in yellow. If you've stopped the train, you can jump off the train and walk to the car, bypassing any enemies that may be between you and the treasure.

COMPLETING THE ROBBERY

Once you've collected the prize, leave the train in any direction. When you get far enough away from the train the activity completes.

London Stories is a series of memories accessed through allied contacts met during the Story such as Charles Dickens, Charles Darwin, and Karl Marx. Many of these memories unlock one-at-a-time upon completing a previous memory. Other times there can be multiple memories unlocked at once from one contact. In this section we have sorted the London Stories by unlocking order first and then by suggested player level.

Dickens missions are unlocked after you complete Sequence 3. Follow the "C" icon to find Dickens.

SPRING-HEELED JACK

MISSION OVERVIEW

Memory Type: Charles Dickens / London Stories	ASSASSIN	CHALLENGES	REWARDS
Suggested Level: 4	Jacob or Evie Frye	Kill a cultist with dynamite	£: 700 + 125 (Full Synch Bonus)
			XP: 600 + 125 (Full Synch Bonus)

LOCATION: PUBLIC HOUSE PUB, LAMBETH

The Twins meet Charles Dickens in the Public House pub **(1)** in Lambeth where the famous writer asks the twins about their belief in ghosts. He tells them he's joined the Ghost Club, an organization that investigates the paranormal and weeds out the charlatans faking ghost experiences. He asks the twins to join the club. Jacob reluctantly plays along, but Evie, being a believer, gladly accepts the invitation for both of them. Dickens immediately gives you your first case….

OBJECTIVE: LOCATE AND SPEAK TO THE POTENTIAL VICTIM

❖ Exit the pub and find Spring-Heeled Jack's first victim in a small yard **(2)**. Speak to her.

OBJECTIVE: INVESTIGATE SPRING-HEELED JACK'S TRACKS

❖ Inspect the first footprint in the nearby alley **(4).** Use Eagle Vision to spot a long trail of prints and claw marks that leads to another inspection print.
❖ The second print is a claw mark on the side of a house **(5).** Rope Launch to the rooftop, following the direction of the marks up the wall.

THE ESSENTIALS
WALKTHROUGH
SIDE QUESTS
COLLECTIBLES
REFERENCE & ANALYSIS
INDEX

ASSOCIATES & FOES
LONDON STORIES
WARTIME ANOMALY
TRAIN HIDEOUT
DREADFUL CRIMES

OBJECTIVE: LOCATE AND DEFEND ANOTHER POTENTIAL VICTIM

❖ Race to the second victim **(3)**. If you are fast enough you can set up an Air Assassinate on Spring-Heeled Jack. He does not die here and escapes in a flash of smoke.

❖ Follow the tracks across the rooftop to the end of a pole on the other side of the house **(6)**. You can see tracks leading across the yard to another two houses. Take a shortcut Rope Launch to the house with the Templar on the rooftop **(7)**. Kill him.

❖ Zipline to the house across the street **(8)**, and then again to the next house **(9)**, to inspect the footprints on the rooftop. Next, zipline to the Cultists'(Blighters') house **(10)** to the north.

OBJECTIVE: LOCATE A SECRET ENTRANCE

CHALLENGE: KILL A CULTIST WITH DYNAMITE

❖ To fulfill the Challenge before you enter the secret entrance in the well, use the dynamite on the ledge on the north side of the house to blow up some cultists on the ground around the house.

OBJECTIVE: REACH JACK'S LAIR

❖ Free Run Down into the well **(11)** on the east side of the house to find Spring-Heeled Jack's lair. Use smoke to help defeat his three Cultist guards in the underground hideout.

HELL'S BELLS

MISSION OVERVIEW

Memory Type: Charles Dickens / London Stories	ASSASSIN	CHALLENGES	REWARDS
Suggested Level: 4	Evie or Jacob Frye	Climb on the same bus as the thief	**£:** 800 + 125 (Full Synch Bonus)
		Tail the thief without getting spotted	**XP:** 700 + 150 (Full Synch Bonus)

LOCATION: CALLANT COMMODORE, THE STRAND

The Twins meet Charles Dickens in the Gallant Commodore restaurant **(1)** near Scotland Yard in The Strand. In this memory you must uncover the truth behind some paranormal thefts.

OBJECTIVE: SPEAK TO THE POLICEMAN AT THE POLICE STATION

❖ Run toward the green blip **(2)** at Scotland Yard. Enter the police station through a window close to the rooftop. Speak to the policeman near the jail cell and listen to the prisoner.

OBJECTIVE: SPEAK TO THE PAWN SHOP OWNER

A CLAMOR OF ROOKS

Recruit a full gang of Rooks on the way to the pawn shop. The lady you have to tackle runs out of the pawn shop and is often caught up in your gang of Rooks, making that objective extremely easy.

❖ Exit the police station and head to the green blip **(3)**. Speak to the Apothecary Pawn Shop owner inside the shop.

OBJECTIVE: TACKLE AND SPEAK TO THE THIEF

❖ The lady inside the pawn shop takes off running. If you have a Rooks gang, she may have difficulty getting out of the store. Chase her and tackle her.

OBJECTIVE: LOCATE THE LAST BUYER

❖ Hijack a carriage and head southwest to the green blip **(4)**. When you get close, the camera focuses on the buyer. Keep an undetectable distance away.

OBJECTIVE: TAIL THE THIEF

CHALLENGE: CLIMB ON THE SAME CART AS THE THIEF

CHALLENGE: TAIL THE THIEF WITHOUT GETTING SPOTTED

❖ The buyer walks through a building **(4)** and begins a long walk to the cart **(5)**. Use the Rope Launcher and rooftops to follow him without being spotted and to get ahead.

❖ You can get around 30 meters ahead of the target without receiving a warning. So stand behind his carriage in the street **(5)** and wait for him to enter it before you climb on top to satisfy the Challenge.

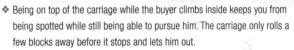

❖ Being on top of the carriage while the buyer climbs inside keeps you from being spotted while still being able to pursue him. The carriage only rolls a few blocks away before it stops and lets him out.

❖ You must get off the rooftop of the carriage before it stops or the target will see you when he exits.

❖ Once at Green Park **(6)** you can watch the buyer meet his contact **(7)** near a fork in the dirt path from a safe distance.

OBJECTIVE: SPEAK TO THE MYSTERIOUS MAN

❖ After their meeting, speak to the mysterious man he met to complete the memory. The man hypnotizes you and gets away. You wake up in the Scotland Yard jail **(2)**!

THE ESSENTIALS

WALKTHROUGH

SIDE QUESTS

WAR PROFITEERING

ASSASSIN'S CREED

INDEX

COLLECTIBLES & MINIGAMES

LONDON STORIES

STARTING ASSASSINS

TRAINING FIGHT

DREADFUL CRIMES

MISSION OVERVIEW

Memory Type: Charles Dickens / London Stories	ASSASSIN	REWARDS
Suggested Level: 5	Evie or Jacob Frye	£: 800
		XP: 700

LOCATION: LORD NELSON PUB, THE STRAND

The Twins meet Charles Dickens at the Lord Nelson pub **(1)** in The Strand. The Ghost Club investigates the circumstances that led to the arrest of the confused Assassin. Charles Dickens hypnotizes you to figure out how you ended up in jail without a memory of knowing how you ended up there.

OBJECTIVE: STEAL FROM 3 RICH CITIZENS

❖ After Dickens hypnotizes you, you are taken back to Green Park **(2)** where the mysterious man at the end of Hell's Bells hypnotized you.

❖ Hop the fence and walk behind the rich lady **(3)** and hold the Steal button while continuing to follow her until the Steal gauge fills. Avoid the policeman in this yard by not causing her any harm.

❖ Walk into the open courtyard from the street and Steal from the rich man **(4)** when the cop walks away. Cause him no harm as to not attract any unwanted attention.

❖ Steal from the rich man **(5)** in Green Park while avoiding the nearby policeman.

OBJECTIVE: SPEAK TO THE HYPNOTIST

❖ Find the hypnotist in one of the backyards **(6)** to the east. Talk to him and he hypnotizes you and tells you to turn yourself into the police and forget everything. That's how you ended up in jail.

OBJECTIVE: LOCATE THE HYPNOTIST

❖ You snap out of Dickens' hypnosis and are tasked with finding the mysterious man. Head back from the pub **(1)** to his last known position **(6)**.

OBJECTIVE: KIDNAP THE HYPNOTIST

❖ Try a rooftop approach to kidnapping the hypnotist. Drop a smoke bomb before you drop into the yard where the hypnotist and some Templars are located. If the hypnotist sees you, he hypnotizes you and sends you back to the street to try again.

OBJECTIVE: DELIVER THE HYPNOTIST TO THE POLICE

❖ Walk the hypnotist through the house he was near, carefully avoid the Templars inside, and place him in a nearby carriage parked out front. When you reach Scotland Yard **(7)** you must take him out of the carriage (tap the Kidnap button) and lead him into the police station and into the jail cell.

50 BERKELEY SQUARE

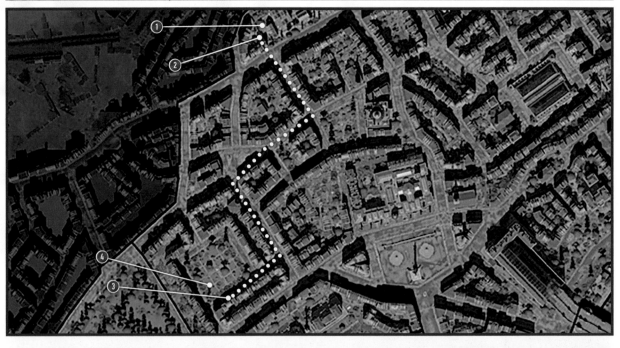

MISSION OVERVIEW

Memory Type: Charles Dickens / London Stories	ASSASSIN	REWARDS
Suggested Level: 4	Evie or Jacob Frye	£: 700
		XP: 600
		Cane-Sword: Charles Dicken's Cane-Sword

LOCATION: PUBLIC HOUSE PUB, THE STRAND

Meet Charles Dickens in the pub **(1)** in The Strand to start an investigation of the most haunted house in London.

OBJECTIVE: FOLLOW DICKENS

❖ Follow Dickens out of the pub and to the nearby carriage **(2)**. Enter the carriage and Charles boards.

OBJECTIVE: REACH THE HAUNTED HOUSE

❖ Drive Dickens to the haunted house **(3)** just north of the Royal Society Buildings.

OBJECTIVE: INVESTIGATE THE HAUNTED HOUSE

❖ You must find two clues inside the house: the piano on the second floor and the rocking crib on the third. Once you inspect both, a child can be head laughing in the hallway.

OBJECTIVE: FIND THE ORIGIN OF THE LAUGHTER

❖ Follow the little girl down the stairs to the second floor and inspect the piano.

❖ A little boy appears at the stairs. Chase him outside the house.

THE ESSENTIALS

WALKTHROUGH

SIDE QUESTS

COLLECTIBLES

REFERENCE & ANALYSIS

INDEX

ASSOCIATES & ALLIES

LONDON STORIES

WAR TIME ANOMALY

TRAIN HIDEOUT

DREADFUL CRIMES

❖ Outside, two more children join the run to confuse you. Only chase down and tackle one of them.

OBJECTIVE: SPEAK TO DICKENS AND OPEN SECRET DOOR

❖ Speak to Dickens who is now on the third floor of the haunted house. Use a key (that you have already) to unlock a secret passage. The lock is below the painting near Dickens. Use Eagle Vision to find it easily.

OBJECTIVE: INVESTIGATE THE HAUNTED HOUSE

❖ Head up the stairs through the secret door and pull both the levers (they glow yellow with Eagle Vision activated). These control the haunted piano and crib.

OBJECTIVE: KILL THE MADMAN AND SPEAK TO DICKENS

❖ The levers open another secret wall beside you on the fourth floor. Quickly rush into the room and catch the madman off guard. Kill him and then speak to Dickens outside in the backyard **(4)** to complete the memory.

DEAD LETTERS

MISSION OVERVIEW

| **Memory Type:** Charles Dickens / London Stories | **ASSASSIN** | **CHALLENGES** | **REWARDS** |
| **Suggested Level:** 4 | Jacob Frye | Hijack the carriage in less than 2 minutes | **£:** 700 + 100 (Full Synch Bonus)
 XP: 600 + 125 (Full Synch Bonus) |

LOCATION: JUNKYARD, WHITECHAPEL

Meet Charles Dickens **(1)** in the junkyard near the tracks in Whitechapel. Dickens wants you to investigate a haunted carriage.

OBJECTIVE: INVESTIGATE THE JUNKYARD: FIND 4 CLUES

❖ There are four clues to find in the junkyard. Inspect the dead letters **(2)** on the ground near where you found Dickens to start the memory.

❖ Investigate the wrecked mail carriage **(3)** and the mattress **(4)** beside the carriage. You take a nap on the mattress when you investigate it.

❖ When you wake up, the fourth clue, a love letter **(5)** to "My darling Frye" from Elizabeth, can be found on the ground near the carts.

OBJECTIVE: HIJACK THE KIDNAPPER'S CARRIAGE
CHALLENGE: HIJACK THE CARRIAGE IN LESS THAN 2 MINUTES

❖ A speeding carriage races by the junkyard. You have two minutes to hijack this carriage. Run out to the street and jack the nearest Growler **(6)**.

❖ Whip the horse for speed until you catch up with the kidnapper in the carriage (the orange blip on Mini-Map). Ride beside the kidnapper and go to the roof. Jump onto the fleeing carriage and hijack the driver out of the front seat.

OBJECTIVE: REACH THE LADY'S HOME

❖ With the carriage in your control, Elizabeth (the kidnap victim you saved in the carriage) wants you to take her home. Follow the green blip to the bridge **(7)**.

OBJECTIVE: DEFEND THE CARRIAGE

❖ With the carriage in your control, Blighter carriages appear on the end of the bridge behind you. To continue delivering Elizabeth home you must first get rid of the pursuing enemies.

❖ A quick way to get rid of the enemy is to just stop the carriage, quickshoot the enemies, and then jump out of the carriage and finish off the remaining Blighters if you run out of ammo. Stay close to the carriage if you exit the driver's seat.

OBJECTIVE: REACH THE LADY'S HOME

❖ Once the Blighters are dead, drive Elizabeth to her home in Lambeth **(8)**.

OBJECTIVE: SPEAK TO THE LADY

❖ Once you have delivered the lady to her home you must enter the house with her. Walk up to the door and "Hide" inside to complete the memory. Once inside you discover the carriage is empty and another letter is found inside. It's a suicide letter from her to her parents. Spooky!

THE ESSENTIALS
WALKTHROUGH
SIDE QUESTS
COLLECTIBLES
UPGRADES & ADVICE
INDEX

ASSOCIATES MENU
LONDON STORIES
WORLD WAR ONE MINI-MAP
TRAIN HIDEOUT
DREADFUL CRIMES

MISSION OVERVIEW

Memory Type: Charles Dickens / London Stories Suggested Level: 5	ASSASSIN Evie or Jacob Frye	CHALLENGES Do not touch the ground	REWARDS £: 1100 + 125 (Full Synch Bonus) XP: 850 + 150 (Full Synch Bonus) Belt: Spring-Heeled Jack Belt

LOCATION:

NEAR LAMBETH ASYLUM, LAMBETH

Meet Charles Dickens **(1)** standing on the side of the road near a tree on a corner near Lambeth Asylum. In this memory, Spring-Heeled Jack returns to bedevil the good people of London and he must finally be stopped.

OBJECTIVE: FOLLOW DICKENS

❖ Follow Charles as he runs north for Jack's last known position **(2)**.

OBJECTIVE: KILL JACK

❖ When you run to attack Jack, who is currently assaulting a female victim on a wet dirt road, he suddenly throws a smoke bomb and escapes heading north. Your objective changes.

OBJECTIVE: TACKLE JACK

❖ Follow him up to the rooftop of the nearest building to the right **(3)**. Once you reach the rooftop the Challenge kicks in: *Do not touch the ground*.

❖ There's no catching him until he reaches his predetermined destination, so just concentrate on Rope Launching from rooftop to rooftop without ever touching the ground until you reach the railroad bridge.

THE ESSENTIALS

WALKTHROUGH

SIDE QUESTS

COLLECTIBLES

REFERENCE & ANALYSIS

INDEX

ASSOCIATES & SHOPS

LONDON STORIES

WORLD TIME ANOMALY

TRAIN HIDEOUT

DREADFUL CRIMES

- Avoid ziplining the few times Spring-Heeled Jack stops to shoot at you. Press ⬤ / Ⓨ to dodge the bullet or get behind cover when this happens.
- See our map for help with a good Rope Launching path.
- After a few rooftop hops, Jack appears directly behind you **(4)** and you get a chance to attack him. Attack him but don't attempt to tackle him. After some damage he uses a smoke bomb to escape.
- When you reach the rooftop **(5)** near the tracks, Rope Launch to the signal truss **(6)** instead of getting on the tracks with Jack. A train wizzes by and could kill you if you get hit.
- Jump down to the tracks and attack Jack. The tracks are not the ground—so you won't fail the Challenge. He throws a smoke bomb again and appears again on the ground to the north **(7)**. Do not follow him to the ground.
- Zipline to the corner of the rooftop **(8)** to the north of the tracks and Jack.

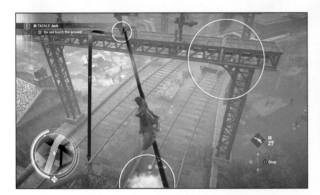

- Continue to follow the rooftops as Jack runs along the street below heading for the train station. Zipline to the train station rooftop as soon as it's within range.
- Run after Jack on the train station rooftop. Tackle him and he splits into three Jacks, so defeat them all. In the end, Spring-Heeled Jack disappears in smoke and can be seen leaping off the end of the train station's rooftop. The mystery remains unsolved.

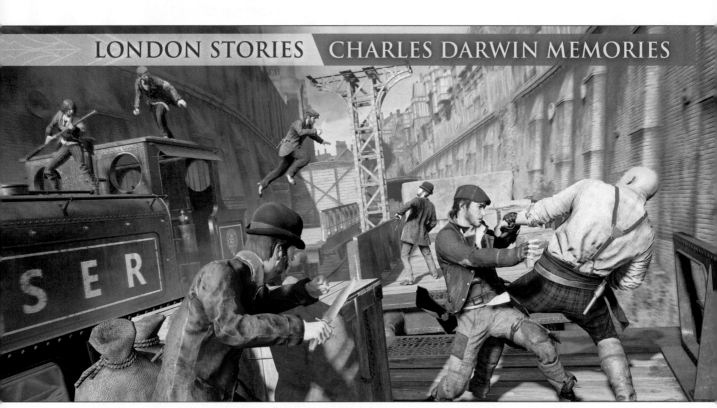

Darwin missions are unlocked after you complete Sequence 3. Follow the "D" icon to find Charles Darwin.

THE BERLIN SPECIMEN

MISSION OVERVIEW

Memory Type: Train Hideout / London Stories	ASSASSIN	CHALLENGES	REWARDS
Suggested Level: 5	Jacob or Evie Frye	Remain undetected	£: 800 + 150 (Full Synch Bonus)
			XP: 700 + 150 (Full Synch Bonus)

LOCATION: CHARING CROSS STATION, THE STRAND

Talk to Charles Darwin **(1)** to start this memory. He's located in a field next to the Charing Cross Station in The Strand. Darwin meets Evie for the first time in the opening cinematic. In this memory, you must protect Darwin's colleague and retrieve a valuable fossil that supports his theory.

THE ESSENTIALS

WALKTHROUGH

SIDE QUESTS

COLLECTIBLES

REFERENCE & ANALYSIS

INDEX

ASSOCIATES & ALLIES

LONDON STORIES

WORLD WAR ANOMALY

TRAIN HIDEOUT

HOMICIDE CRIMES

OBJECTIVE: LOCATE DR. SCHWARTZ

❖ From Darwin **(1)**, head west toward the green blip (70 meters away) that represents Dr. Schwartz' general location **(2)**. He's in the Charing Cross Station. We suggest a rooftop, skylight entry.

❖ Walk along the rafters heading for the northwest side of the train station. Use Eagle Vision to spot the glowing yellow Dr. Schwartz.

OBJECTIVE: KIDNAP DR. SCHWARTZ

CHALLENGE: REMAIN UNDETECTED

❖ Drop down from the highest level of framework to the lower rafters. This is done from one side of the station or the other; there's nothing to drop down to when you're in the middle top of the station.

❖ You can spend some time Air Assassinating the various Templars patrolling the people bridge below or you could just drop and kidnap the doctor. You have time if you want to capture the doctor when he himself is closer to the exit, making your getaway that much easier.

❖ Zipline to the rafters above the doctor and then drop down and capture him near the southwest exit stairwell. Activate Eagle Vision immediately to look for nearby Templars. Go down the stairs here **(3)**.

OBJECTIVE: DELIVER DR. SCHWARTZ

CHALLENGE: REMAIN UNDETECTED

❖ There are multiple locations where you can drop off Dr. Schwartz, but if you've been following our tips, there's one at the bottom of the stairwell tunnel **(3)**. You only need to walk slowly past one guard on a landing along the way to avoid detection.

OBJECTIVE: KILL THE IMPOSTER

❖ When you deliver the doctor at the Reach marker you discover you've kidnapped an imposter and he slugs you to get free. Now you must kill the fleeing imposter who has the real Dr. Schwartz' fossil.

❖ Get out of the fight that ensues when your hostage takes off. Throw a smoke bomb to make it easier to escape the gang of Templars around you.

❖ The imposter flees in a carriage. Get in one yourself and chase him. Shoot him with Quickshot or jump to his rooftop while riding beside him. Execute him.

OBJECTIVE: LOOT IMPOSTER

❖ Loot the imposter's body.

OBJECTIVE: SPEAK TO DARWIN

❖ Return with the fossil to talk to Darwin where you left him **(1)**. You break the news to Darwin that his colleague is most likely dead. He tells you that he was approached by some men that offered to purchase all his research as long as he worked only for them. He obviously refused—he's Darwin.

AN ABOMINABLE MYSTERY

MISSION OVERVIEW

Memory Type: Train Hideout / London Stories	ASSASSIN	CHALLENGES	REWARDS
Suggested Level: 5	Jacob or Evie Frye	Aim and shoot at a Templar inside the flower's pollen	£: 800 + 125 (Full Synch Bonus)
			XP: 700 + 150 (Full Synch Bonus)

LOCATION:

ST. JAMES'S PARK, WESTMINSTER

Talk to Charles Darwin **(1)** in St. James's Park in Westminster. He's near the pond along the north shore. He wants you to investigate a strange flower that has appeared in London.

OBJECTIVE: INVESTIGATE THE 3 TOXIC PLANTS

CHALLENGE: AIM AND SHOOT AT A TEMPLAR INSIDE THE FLOWER'S POLLEN

CHALLENGE: NEUTRALIZE A PURSUING CART WITH THE FLOWER EFFECT

❖ Look westward down the pond's shoreline and you see three colorful clouds in the distance. The closest one is through an opium cloud near a Gazebo **(2)**. Inspect the plant (it glows white through the cloud in Eagle Vision).

❖ The next closest cloud to check out is near the bridge to the west. Investigate the flower **(3)** on the shoreline beside the bridge.

❖ The final flower **(4)** is through a large crowd near a pathway intersection at the west end of the pond.

❖ This is where you finish the Challenge. Defeat a Templar in this cloud using a firearm before inspecting the flower.

OBJECTIVE: LOCATE THE SOURCE

❖ After investigating all three flowers you must now find out who put them there. Look south for the colorful cloud in the distance and the green blip that states, "60 m." You find a Blighter driving a wagon full of the flowers.

OBJECTIVE: STEAL THE CARRIAGE

❖ Take the wagon **(5)** next to where the flower wagon was parked and use it to chase the Blighter out the south exit and through the Royal Guard compound across the street.

❖ By the time the flower carriage **(6)** enters the narrow street across from the Royal compound you are able to catch up to it. Jumping to the rooftop is difficult in the slow motion effects of the toxic cloud. We suggest Quickshooting the driver to take over his carriage.

OBJECTIVE: REACH DARWIN

❖ Talk to Darwin who now stands near the road on the north tip exit out of St. James's Park **(7)**. He tells you the real deal with the hallucinogenic cloud you're carrying and directs you to a place to deposit the toxic material.

OBJECTIVE: REACH A SAFE PLACE

❖ Allow Darwin to enter the carriage and follow the route across the bridge to the area in Southwark **(8)** to dispose of the carriage.

OBJECTIVE: DEFEND THE CARRIAGE

❖ Three Blighter carriages attack from behind when you enter the bridge. Swerve back and forth so they cannot pass and ride for extended periods of time in your toxic cloud. This gets rid of them and fulfill the second challenge. Shoot them if they pass you.

OBJECTIVE: REACH A SAFE PLACE

❖ Once the enemy is dealt with, enter the Reach marker at the College Wharf **(8)**. Stop the wagon next to the dynamite crates.

OBJECTIVE: SABOTAGE THE CART

❖ Ignite the crates or shoot the crates from a safe distance to sabotage the cart and complete the memory.

DEFAMATION

MISSION OVERVIEW

Memory Type: Charles Darwin Memories / London Stories **Suggested Level:** 5	**ASSASSIN** Jacob or Evie Frye	**REWARDS** £: 1100 **XP:** 850

LOCATION: SOUTHWEST WHITECHAPEL

❖ Talk to Charles Darwin **(1)** on a corner near a flower saleswoman a block southwest from the Spitalfield Marker. In this memory you must fetch Darwin a newspaper.

OBJECTIVE: REACH THE STREET VENDOR

❖ Follow the green blip from Darwin to the street vendor **(2)** on the nearest street through the alleyway to the southeast. When you spot the vendor you also see a Blighter run by and steal the paper from him.

OBJECTIVE: TACKLE THE AGGRESSOR

❖ Chase after the Blighter. He runs south along the sidewalk and takes a right at the first corner.

❖ Follow the route indicated on our map to keep up with the fleeing Blighter. It's a long route that ends up on the railroad tracks **(3)**.

❖ When he stops on the tracks, you are given seven seconds to rush and tackle him off the tracks before he's splattered by a passing train.

❖ The Blighter is grateful for you saving him and tells you that he and his mates were paid to give leaflets to the paperboys to distribute with the papers. It shows a funny caricature of Darwin and makes fun of his theory of evolution.

261

CRUEL CARICATURE

MISSION OVERVIEW

Memory Type: Charles Darwin Memories / London Stories	**ASSASSIN**	**CHALLENGE**	**REWARDS**	
Suggested Level: 6	Jacob or Evie Frye	Sabotage all printers at once	**£:** 1100 + 150 (Full Synch Bonus)	
			XP: 850 + 150 (Full Synch Bonus)	

LOCATION: COVENT GARDEN, THE STRAND

❖ Talk to Charles Darwin **(1)** inside Covent Garden. He is standing beside one of his distasteful caricatures being distributed around town. He wants you to track down the source of the anti-Darwin propaganda.

OBJECTIVE:
FIND AND REMOVE 4 POSTERS
POSTER 1

❖ There are four Darwin propaganda posters to remove, starting with the one near Darwin at the beginning of the memory. There are three in The Strand and the furthest one is in City of London.

POSTER 2

❖ Recruit Rooks in the area as needed; you run into Templars guarding each poster location. Head to the second blip representing the next closest flier **(2)**. When you get near, a green search area appears on the map. From the framework at the top of the building, use Eagle Vision to spot the flyer on the southwestern wall on the first floor of the market.

❖You must be anonymous to rip the flyer off the wall, so defeat the three Templars in the area starting by Air Assassinating one of them to get to the lower floor. Use a smoke bomb to defeat the remaining two if needed.

POSTER 3

❖ Exit the market and grab a carriage. Drive it to the next nearest flier **(3)** to the east. Recruit Rooks along the way if needed.

❖ Send your Rooks into the alleyway **(3)** to fight the Templars. Eliminate the rooftop sniper yourself. You can hide inside the nearby house to stay anonymous afterward. Tear down the poster when the Templars are drawn away to fight your Rooks.

POSTER 4 - LOCATION: CITY OF LONDON

❖ Exit the alley and grab a carriage. Drive it to the next nearest flier **(4)** in the City of London. Recruit Rooks along the way if needed. When you reach the intersection marked on our map, you spot a horse-drawn bus moving in your direction. The poster is on the driver's side of this bus.

❖ Follow the bus and ride alongside of it. Get to your rooftop and leap to the bus. Hijack the bus, stop it, and tear the poster off.

OBJECTIVE: FIND POSTERS

❖ Now you need to find who is distributing the posters. Follow the green blip (or the route if you are in a carriage) on the map to the location **(5)** in Southwark under a bridge.

OBJECTIVE: TACKLE THE BILLPOSTER

❖ When you reach the location you can spot a man in a top hat running away. Chase him and tackle him. Follow our route on our map to head him off in the railyard. If you don't catch him he leads you directly to the sewer entrance. If you do catch him, he spills the beans revealing the sewer entrance.

OBJECTIVE: FIND THE SEWER'S ENTRANCE

❖ Follow the green blip to find the sewer entrance beside a warehouse **(6)** in the area. Enter the sewers.

OBJECTIVE: FIND THE PRINT SHOP
LOCATION: SOUTHWARK SEWERS

❖ Follow the sewer pathway, jumping down to the lower tunnels in the first clearing. There are a of couple Templars with their backs to you just beyond a Slide Under grate. Dual Assassinate them. Just beyond these two is the sewer print shop **(7)**.

THE ESSENTIALS

WALKTHROUGH

SIDE QUESTS

COLLECTIBLES

NARRATIVE & ANALYSIS

INDEX

ASSOCIATES & RIVALS

LONDON STORIES

WAR TIME ANOMALY

TRAIN HIDEOUT

DREADFUL CRIMES

OBJECTIVE: SABOTAGE 5 PRINTERS AND POSTERS
CHALLENGE: SABOTAGE ALL PRINTERS AT ONCE

❖ Use the high hanging pipes in the printing chamber to Air Assassinate the enemies inside. Avoid blowing up the dynamite crates.

❖ Use all of the dynamite crates from all over the room to complete the Challenge of blowing everything up at once. Spread the crates evenly between all the printers and the poster on the easel in the middle of the chamber.

❖ Get to the high platform near the entrance tunnel and shoot the dynamite crate in the middle of the crate trail. This completes the objective as all of the targets blow up at once.

OBJECTIVE: REACH THE SEWER EXIT

❖ Exit the printer chamber through the high exit tunnel to the north, on the opposite side of the entrance tunnel. Follow the tunnels to the exit near a shallow channel **(8)**.

A STRUGGLE FOR EXISTENCE

MISSION OVERVIEW

Memory Type: Charles Darwin Memories / London Stories
Suggested Level: 6

ASSASSIN	CHALLENGE	REWARDS
Jacob or Evie Frye	Kidnap the policeman without being detected	**£:** 1100 + 150 (Full Synch Bonus)
		XP: 850 + 150 (Full Synch Bonus)
		Unique Material: Dinosaur Talon

LOCATION: CITY OF LONDON

❖ Instead of meeting Darwin to start this memory, you will be meeting and following Florence Nightingale **(1)** who is waiting for you on a City of London sidewalk.

OBJECTIVE: FOLLOW NIGHTINGALE

❖ Follow Nightingale as she walks south along the sidewalk. Nightingale says the unspeakable has happened. Darwin has been arrested by a corrupt policeman and their last known position was at a funeral.

❖ You go your separate ways at the next corner. Nightingale waits for you on a stoop of the corner building **(2)**. The graveyard to the southwest is the area to locate the corrupt policeman.

OBJECTIVE: LOCATE THE CORRUPT POLICEMAN

CHALLENGE: KIDNAP THE POLICEMAN WITHOUT BEING DETECTED

❖Leave Nightingale and to avoid most of the patrolling policemen inside and outside of the graveyard before you can reach the corrupt cop, follow the street heading south and turn right into the alley beside the graveyard. Stop just short of the graveyard's southwest corner **(3)**.

OBJECTIVE: KIDNAP THE CORRUPT POLICEMAN

CHALLENGE: KIDNAP THE POLICEMAN WITHOUT BEING DETECTED

❖ You can spot the corrupt cop **(A)** patrolling westward toward you along a graveyard pathway **(4)**. While he is in the distance, hop the graveyard fence and hide behind a nearby grave until he walks by. Quickly leave your hiding spot and hop up a small ledge to the sidewalk. Come up behind him and kidnap him.

OBJECTIVE: DELIVER THE CORRUPT POLICEMAN

CHALLENGE: KIDNAP THE POLICEMAN WITHOUT BEING DETECTED

❖ Turn the corrupt policeman back the way he came and follow pathway to the northwest corner **(5)**. To avoid the policemen **(B)** & **(C)** standing at the northwest corner, walk your victim between the gravestones and the short wall in this corner.

❖ Continue to follow our route until you see two patrolling cops coming toward you on the same pathway. Go off-path and walk around the backside of two large stone columns **(6)**. When you reenter the pathway you are at the north exit **(7)**.

265

❖ Wait for the patrolling street cops to walk past the exit before you enter the street. Once in the street, head east to where you left Nightingale. Deliver the cop to her **(2)**.

OBJECTIVE: LOCATE DARWIN

❖ Threaten the cop with a gun or throwing knife (aim at him) and he tells you a man paid him to bring Darwin to his secret base. The area is now marked on your map.

❖ Knock the cop out and enter a carriage. Allow Nightingale to ride along. Follow the route marked on the street to the secret base **(9)**.

OBJECTIVE: EXAMINE DARWIN'S CONDITION

❖ When you reach the house to the northeast, activate Eagle Vision and look into the house to spot Darwin highlighted yellow with a few Templar guards around. He's on the second floor. There's an open second floor window and the front door is open as well.

❖ Enter the home and defeat the Templars to get to Darwin who is lying on a bed on the second floor.

OBJECTIVE: DEFEND NIGHTINGALE

❖ Darwin is very weak and Templars are on their way in the house. You must defend Nightingale while she tends to his wounds. Cover beside the stairs and Cover Assassinate the first to arrive and then slay the second quickly.

OBJECTIVE: PICK UP DARWIN

❖ Darwin has fallen out of the bed. Pick him up and carry him down the stairs.

OBJECTIVE: DELIVER DARWIN TO THE CART

❖ When you reach the first floor you see a Templar in the doorway. Place Darwin on the floor and defeat this Templar and any others that rush in

or are outside the house before you pick up Darwin again.

❖ When the coast is clear, pick up Darwin and carry him outside and place him in the carriage on the street. Nightingale will take him to safety.

THE ESSENTIALS
WALKTHROUGH
SIDE QUESTS
COLLECTIBLES
REFERENCE & ANALYSIS
INDEX

ASSOCIATES & INCOME
LONDON STORIES
WWI TIME ANOMALY
TRAIN HIDEOUT
DREADFUL CRIMES

LONDON STORIES ⟩ KARL MARX MEMORIES

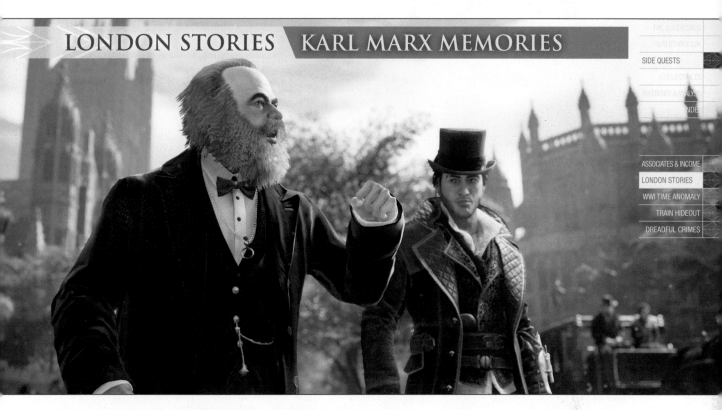

Marx missions are unlocked after you complete Sequence 4. Follow the "M" icon to find Marx.

CAT AND MOUSE

MISSION OVERVIEW

Memory Type: Karl Marx Memories / London Stories	**ASSASSIN**	**CHALLENGES**	**REWARDS**
	Jacob or Evie Frye	Create a faction fight outside the pub to attract the spy	**£:** 800 + 125 (Full Synch Bonus)
Suggested Level: 5		Kill 2 spies with hanging barrels	**XP:** 700 + 150 (Full Synch Bonus)

LOCATION: TRAIN STATION, WHITECHAPEL

Speak to Karl Marx (1) who is talking to a policeman inside the train station in Whitechapel. Marx needs to meet with sympathizers to his cause, without attracting the attention of the police. The policeman asks that Marx keeps his rallies off the streets and Marx argues that they need police assistance.

OBJECTIVE: FOLLOW MARX

❖ Follow Marx out of the train station and to a lot across the street (2).

OBJECTIVE: LOCATE AND KILL THE 4 SPIES

CHALLENGE: KILL 2 SPIES WITH HANGING BARRELS

❖ Get to the rooftop of the building to your left (3) as you enter the lot (2). Marx walks alone through the alleyway, walking past the spies. The first spy is at the mouth of the alley. Watch him from above and shoot the hanging crates (4) when he walks under them to pursue Marx.

❖ If you don't get into position fast enough, allow the spy to live as he follows Marx to the northeast. There's another set of hanging barrels near the alley clearing (5).

❖ Get to the corner rooftop (6) where Marx turns and heads more southward. Wait for the second spy (7) to walk under the nearby hanging barrels (8). Drop the barrels on this spy to complete the Challenge. If you miss, you have another opportunity nearby.

❖ Drop the barrels at the alley exit (9) on a spy if you have missed previous opportunities. This is above the short tunnel that leads to the street to the east.

OBJECTIVE: FOLLOW MARX

❖ Follow Marx across the street, taking out the remaining spies. Marx stops at the brewery (10) to talk with a fellow supporter about a meet tonight.

OBJECTIVE: LOCATE THE SPY

❖ Now you can take off and leave Marx behind. Rooftop travel west to the bar marked with the green blip (11), but do not enter.

THE ESSENTIALS

WALKTHROUGH

SIDE QUESTS

COLLECTIBLES

TROPHIES & AWARDS

INDEX

UNLOCKABLES & REWARDS

LONDON STORIES

HURTING ANIMALS

FRESH OFF THE

DREADFUL CRIMES

OBJECTIVE: KILL THE SPY

CHALLENGE: CREATE A FACTION FIGHT OUTSIDE THE PUB TO ATTRACT THE SPY

❖ Get to the street corner to the north and recruit the Rooks **(12)** standing there. Enter Eagle Vision and walk kitty-corner to the southwest and have the Rooks attack the Blighters **(13)** on this corner. When the cops come out of the bar **(11)** have the Rooks attack them next; this fulfills the second Challenge.

❖ Kill the spy, if your Rooks have not already done so.

OBJECTIVE: FOLLOW MARX TO THE MEETING

❖ After Karl Marx speaks with his contact inside the pub **(11)**, follow him as he runs south along the sidewalk and darts into the alleyways to the east **(14)**.

OBJECTIVE: KIDNAP THE TRAITOR

❖ The police have paid the traitor, who glows yellow with Eagle Vision activated, **(15)** to lead Karl into this ambush at the meeting location. The traitor and the police walk together heading northeast out of the alleyway.

❖ Throw a smoke bomb into the group of cops, take them out, and then kidnap the traitor.

OBJECTIVE: DELIVER THE TRAITOR

❖ Run the kidnapped traitor into the street heading southwest past the pub and **(16)** into the park on the next block.

OBJECTIVE: SPEAK TO MARX

❖ Marx and the traitor work out their grievances. Talk to Marx to complete the memory.

WHERE THERE IS SMOKE

MISSION OVERVIEW

Memory Type: Karl Marx Memories / London Stories	**ASSASSIN**	**CHALLENGES**	**REWARDS**
Suggested Level: 5	Jacob or Evie Frye	Air Assassinate a guard	**£:** 800 + 125 (Full Synch Bonus)
			XP: 700 + 150 (Full Synch Bonus)

LOCATION: WAREHOUSE C, SOUTHWARK

Meet Karl Marx **(1)** on a sidewalk in front of Warehouse C in Southwark. He needs you to find proof that a factory is abusing its work force.

OBJECTIVE: FIND AND IGNITE THE 3 COTTON BALES

CHALLENGE: AIR ASSASSINATE A GUARD

❖ Walk south away from Marx, cross the street and Rope Launch to the rooftop of the factory across the street **(2)**. Activate Eagle Vision to find the glowing yellow cotton bales.

❖ Defeat the guard on the rooftop and enter the factory through the open skylight.

- Walk along the rafters until you are above the guard on the top level (above the lowest level cotton bale). Air Assassinate this guy to complete the Challenge.
- You cannot ignite the cotton bales if you are not anonymous so defeat everyone in sight or use smoke bombs to cover your work. Each bale you ignite creates more smoke, which works to your advantage.

OBJECTIVE: SPEAK TO THE FOREMAN

- There's one bale **(2)** on the top floor and two on the bottom **(3)** & **(4)** level. Once all three have been ignited (ignite them the same way you ignite dynamite crates) the foreman runs out of the smoky factory. Talk to him **(5)**. He calls for a fire engine.

OBJECTIVE: HIJACK A FIRETRUCK

- Three fire trucks **(6)**, **(7)**, and **(8)** appear and are represented by orange blips on the map. Wait a little while and they come closer to the fire. Search for the closest one, hijack a carriage, and intercept the fire truck. Hijack the driver.

OBJECTIVE: REACH THE FACTORY

- Hijack and drive the fire truck to the front of the factory **(9)**.

OBJECTIVE: FOLLOW THE FOREMAN

- When you return, you ask the foreman about the reports and getting them out of the factory before the fire takes them. Follow the foreman up the stairs and into the office.

OBJECTIVE: STEAL FROM THE FOREMAN

- On your return trip out of the burning factory, walk closely to the foreman and press and hold ◎ / Ⓑ while the steal gauge fills to take the reports from him stealthily.

OBJECTIVE: ESCAPE THE AREA

- Rope Launch to the top of the factory before the cops can stop you and then zipline across the railroad tracks to the buildings in the distance to escape the restricted zone and complete the memory.

ANARCHIST INTERVENTION

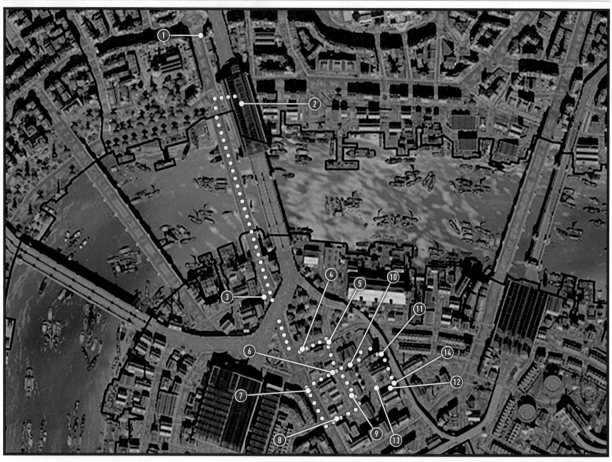

MISSION OVERVIEW

Memory Type: Karl Marx Memories / London Stories	**ASSASSIN**	**CHALLENGES**	**REWARDS**
Suggested Level: 5	Jacob or Evie Frye	Flip a pursuing carriage	**£:** 800 + 125 (Full Synch Bonus)
			XP: 700 + 150 (Full Synch Bonus)

LOCATION:

LUDGATE CIRCUS, CITY OF LONDON

Find Karl Marx **(1)** in Ludgate Circus intersection in the City of London. A grieving worker plots violent

revenge involving some Templar explosives. Stop him before someone gets hurt.

OBJECTIVE: LOCATE THE CARRIAGE

❖ Grab a carriage and follow the route marker to the street running through the train station to locate the explosive cart **(2)**.

PRESS ⬚ to activate EAGLE VISION and IDENTIFY your target

OBJECTIVE: HIJACK THE CARRIAGE

❖ Use Eagle Vision once in the train station tunnel to spot the carriage of explosives. Once spotted it takes off toward you. Hop onto the carriage as it rides by. If you miss it, ride alongside it in your carriage and rooftop jump to it.

OBJECTIVE: REACH THE DELIVERY LOCATION

CHALLENGE: FLIP A PURSUING CARRIAGE

❖ The driver is a disgruntled worker, a good guy, so don't kill him. Simply drive the explosive carriage with him as a passenger.

❖ Your carriage has a Nitroglycerin Stability Meter. It explodes if it drains completely. Don't let this happen. Do not run into things.

LOCATION: SOUTHWARK

❖ When you cross the bridge, a Templar carriage comes rushing at you from the right at the first intersection in Southwark.

❖ Swerve to miss the impact and ram his carriage in the first left corner to hit the first route checkpoint **(4)** in Southwark. You can flip him in this corner and complete the Challenge.

❖ Turn right into the compound to enter the second checkpoint **(5)**. Continue up the ramp to the south and use Quickshot to take out the Templars around the ramp.

❖ Take a right at the top of the ramp to hit the third checkpoint **(6)**. Now you circle around the building passing through checkpoints 4 thru 6 **(7 – 9)**. A Templar carriage tries to ram you when you return to the street. Shoot him or use this as another opportunity to flip him with a ramming move if you have not passed the Challenge yet.

❖ Circle the building and continue using Quickshot on any attacking Templars. Follow the route through remaining checkpoints **(10 – 12)** stopping in an alley near the tracks. There's a Templar roadblock **(13)** at the other end of the alley. You cannot pass. Get out of the carriage.

OBJECTIVE: DEFEND THE ANARCHIST

❖ Defend your passenger, the anarchist, by first tossing a smoke bomb at the group of attacking Templars and then slaughter all of them in the cloud of smoke. If you have no smoke, then unleash long combos and attempt dual finishing moves. Make sure to dodge the shots fired from the sniper **(14)** on the rail bridge above.

❖ Leave the sniper for last. Rope Launch to the top of the rail bridge and execute her.

OBJECTIVE: SPEAK TO THE ANARCHIST

❖ Speak to the anarchist in the alley after the battle is over. This completes the memory.

AN EXPLOSIVE END

MISSION OVERVIEW

Memory Type: Karl Marx Memories / London Stories	**ASSASSIN**	**CHALLENGES**	**REWARDS**
Suggested Level: 6	Jacob or Evie Frye	Kill 5 Templars using Nitroglycerin	**£:** 1100 + 150 (Full Synch Bonus)
			XP: 850 + 150 (Full Synch Bonus)

LOCATION: SOUTHWARK

Follow the "M" icon in Southwark to a man at the mouth of an alley near the Abbot's Cocoa Powder building. This is Frank Morris **(1)**; you just helped his son, the anarchist in the last Marx memory. He has found the Templar's stash of explosives and will stop at nothing to acquire it.

OBJECTIVE: HIDE IN THE TEMPLAR CARRIAGE

❖ Frank points to a carriage on the other end of the alley that you can hide in to get carried to the Templar explosive cache. You have 30 seconds to reach it. Run east through the alley.

❖ Ignore whatever Templars may be around and just run behind the carriage **(2)** and sneak up to the side door. Make sure to press and hold the Hide button. If you miss your chance and the carriage drives off, tail it.

OBJECTIVE: REACH THE TEMPLAR HIDEOUT

❖ Take the ride to the factory (3). Wait inside the carriage until the two Templars get out.

OBJECTIVE: DESTROY NITROGLYCERIN (5)

CHALLENGE: KILL 5 TEMPLARS USING NITROGLYCERIN

❖ Allow one Templar to walk away and then whistle while inside the cart. Cover Assassinate the Templar when she inspects the sound closely. Whistle for the Templar that walked away and execute him the same way.

❖ You do not need to remain undetected for any reason except easier survival, so move about the hideout seeking out the nitroglycerin crates (they glow yellow when Eagle Vision is activated). Red blips on the map represent the locations of the nitro.

❖ If you want to complete the Challenge, it's best to throw the crates at the Templars.

❖ Once you have fulfilled the Challenge of defeating five Templars with nitro, you can dispose of the remaining crates how you please.

❖ Shoot the nitro crates when Templars pass them on their patrol routes.

OBJECTIVE: SPEAK TO MARX

❖ Once all the nitro crates are destroyed you must find and speak with Marx (4) to complete the memory. Follow the green blip on the map. He is now located to the southwest about 120 meters away from the hideout.

MISSION OVERVIEW

Memory Type: Karl Marx Memories / London Stories	ASSASSIN	CHALLENGES	REWARDS
Suggested Level: 6	Jacob or Evie Frye	Hide a body in a hiding spot	£: 1100 + 125 (Full Synch Bonus)
		Don't kill any policemen	XP: 850 + 150 (Full Synch Bonus)
			Color: Wine

LOCATION: LONDON BRIDGE STATION, SOUTHWARK

Meet Karl Marx (1) on the corner in Southwark near London Bridge Station. In this memory you must protect Karl Marx while he gives a speech.

OBJECTIVE: FOLLOW MARX

❖ Follow Marx west along the sidewalk. He stops at the first alley entrance (2). Follow him through the alley and activate Eagle Vision.

OBJECTIVE: KIDNAP 4 TROUBLEMAKERS WITHOUT BEING SEEN

CHALLENGE: HIDE A BODY IN A HIDING SPOT

CHALLENGE: DON'T KILL ANY POLICEMEN

❖ When you round the corner (3) with Marx, spot the nearest patrolling policeman (A). This is the only one you need to be concerned with using our strategy. Your first kidnapping target (B) glows yellow and is in the crowd in the distance.

❖ When the policeman **(A)** is on his patrol route **(4)** behind the building, walk up behind the troublemaker **(B)** and kidnap him where he stands **(5)** facing the stage like the other troublemakers.

OBJECTIVE: EXTRACT TROUBLEMAKERS FROM THE AREA

❖ You must remove the troublemaker from the red restriction zone around the stage. Walk the vkidnapped troublemaker **(5)** back the way you came and when the cop **(A)** is behind the building, walk your victim up to the edge of the bulkhead **(6)** and slash his throat. If he does not drop into the water, then quickly pick him up and throw him in. This completes the first Challenge.

OBJECTIVE: KIDNAP 3 TROUBLEMAKERS WITHOUT BEING SEEN

❖ Getting rid of the three remaining troublemakers is easy after you have completed the Challenge. Simply crouch next to the stage stairs **(7)** and throw knives at the heads of the remaining three troublemakers. Do it quickly so that one does not see the body of the others. Otherwise, you fail the memory.

OBJECTIVE: DEFEND MARX

❖ Karl Marx moves down from the stage **(8)** to the floor area in front of the stage during this segment of the memory. Enemies attack from the street to the west and from the alleys behind you to the east. Use smoke bombs around Marx and annihilate anyone that gets near him, including cops (the Challenge for not killing any policemen is over now). Defend him until all enemies are dead to complete the memory.

Queen Victoria Memories become available after you complete the Story Memories. You can start these memories in Westminster by visiting the "V" icon **(1)** representing Victoria at Buckingham Palace.

OPERATION: DYNAMITE BOAT

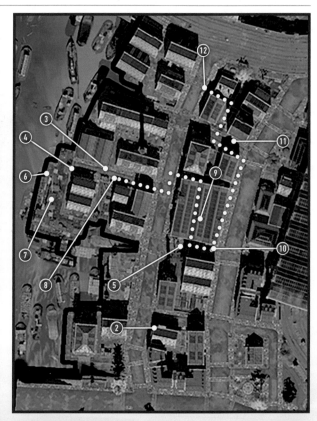

MISSION OVERVIEW

	ASSASSIN	CHALLENGES	REWARDS
Memory Type: Queen Victoria / London Stories	Jacob or Evie Frye	Air assassinate from a crane	**£:** 1500 + 350 (Full Synch Bonus)
Suggested Level: 10			**XP:** 1000 + 300 (Full Synch Bonus)

OBJECTIVE: SPEAK TO FLEMING

LOCATION: SOUTHWARK SHIPYARD

❖ You start this task on top of a rooftop **(2)** in Southwark near The Thames. Rope Launch and zipline to Fleming **(3)** standing in the shipyard.

❖ Alfred Fleming **(3)** runs her majesty's secret service. Before the Templar attack, he suggests you remove anything that would give you away.

OBJECTIVE: DRIVE THE POLICE CARRIAGE OUT OF THE AREA

❖ Start by moving a police carriage **(4)** out of the restricted zone. We suggest taking a right on the street then the first left **(5)**. Get out and recruit the Rooks standing on this corner.

OBJECTIVE: REACH FLEMING

LOCATION: SOUTHWARK SHIPYARD

❖ Now return to Flemming **(6)** who has moved near the docks at The Thames between the two cranes. He tells you to prepare for a fight with a boatload of Templars arriving shortly.

OBJECTIVE: DEFEND THE AREA

CHALLENGE: AIR ASSASSINATE FROM A CRANE

❖ You have 30 seconds to get ready before the enemy comes ashore at this dock. Climb the south crane and wait for the Templar boat.

❖ The crane swings out over the Templar boat as it pulls to shore. Throw a smoke bomb down onto the boat and perform an Air Assassination on one of the lucky Templars below. This completes the Challenge.

❖ Alternatively, you can utilize dynamite to set up traps and ignite the crates by tossing nitro from the roofs for a more explosive fight.

❖ Help the secret service and the Rooks defeat all the Templars.

OBJECTIVE: REACH FLEMING

LOCATION: SOUTHWARK SHIPYARD

❖ Now return to Flemming **(3)** who has moved near his first location in the shipyard. He points east to the Templar leader getting away and asks you to bring him back alive.

THE ESSENTIALS
WALKTHROUGH
SIDE QUESTS
COLLECTIBLES
ASSEMBLY RANKING
INDEX

ASSOCIATES & ALLIES
LONDON STORIES
WWI TIME ANOMALY
TRAIN HIDEOUT
DREADFUL CRIMES

OBJECTIVE: TACKLE THE TEMPLAR LEADER

❖ Chase the Templar **(8)** as he runs out into the street, turns left and runs through an alley and quickly ducks right into a warehouse (follow our route on our map).

❖ Keep your distance from him when he stops inside the warehouse. He's igniting a dynamite crate **(9)**. Avoid the explosion and continue chasing him.

❖ He ignites a second crate on the warehouse's southeast corner **(10)**. Avoid this explosion and continue to chase him.

❖ The Templar ignites a third crate **(11)** on the sidewalk where he darts into an alleyway.

❖ Tackle him after he gets to his feet from getting run down in the street **(12)** by a speeding carriage.

OBJECTIVE: DELIVER THE TEMPLAR LEADER

❖ Run the kidnapped Templar leader back to Fleming who is now in a carriage back at the shipyard **(8)**. Put the captive inside the carriage to complete the memory.

OPERATION: LOCOMOTIVE

MISSION OVERVIEW

Memory Type: Queen Victoria / London Stories **Suggested Level:** 10	**ASSASSIN** Jacob or Evie Frye	**REWARDS** **£:** 2000 + 350 (Full Synch Bonus) **XP:** 1200 + 400 (Full Synch Bonus)

OBJECTIVE: FIGHT THE TEMPLAR LEADER

LOCATION: BUCKINGHAM PALACE, WESTMINSTER

❖ This time you must enter Buckingham Palace and talk to the Queen who is now on the second floor just outside her study near a fireplace **(1)**. Talk to her to start the memory.

LOCATION: WESTMINSTER POLICE STATION

❖ A yellow blip representing the Templar leader appears on the map. The leader is in a Westminster jail cell in the police station **(2)** near the train station. Leave the palace and take a carriage or zipline to this building now.

❖ Enter the open top window on the north side of the police station to gain entry near the unlocked cell. Enter the cell and fight the Templar leader. Yes, in front of the watching policemen.

❖ When you rough up the leader enough, he gives in and tells you what you want to hear. There are explosives on a train leaving Westminster and it will explode before it reaches its destination.

OBJECTIVE: DEFUSE THE BOMB

❖ Follow the green blip representing the bomb **(3)** on the train. Exit the police station out the window near the cell and get to the rooftop. You have two minutes and 20 seconds to diffuse the bomb. Get to the rooftops and zipline the most direct route possible to the east exit out of the train station (see our route on our map).

❖ When you get a good view of the tracks you can see the train rigged with explosives leaving the station. Zipline to the rail bridge and run up alongside the train and latch onto it.

❖ Run along the rooftops of the train cars to get to the front of the train and to the explosives. Only deal with the Templars you run into if you have time to quickly eliminate them.

❖ You spot the bomb in the first car behind the engine. Free Run down on the third car, turn and face the second car and punch the connectors to detach the engine and explosives car from the rest of the train. You have saved everyone aboard and have completed this memory.

TOP EXPEDITIONS
WALKTHROUGH
SIDE QUESTS
COLLECTIBLES
REFERENCE & APPENDICES
INDEX
ASSOCIATES & ALLIES
LONDON STORIES
MAIN TIME ANOMALY
TRAIN HIDEOUT
RESOURCE GUIDES

OPERATION: DRIVE FOR LIVES

MISSION OVERVIEW

Memory Type: Queen Victoria / London Stories	ASSASSIN	CHALLENGE	REWARDS
Suggested Level: 10	Jacob or Evie Frye	Reach a safe place in less than 80 sec	£: 2000 + 350 (Full Synch Bonus)
			XP: 1200 + 400 (Full Synch Bonus)

LOCATION: BUCKINGHAM PALACE, WESTMINSTER

You can find Queen Victoria **(1)** out for a walk on the pathway behind Buckingham Palace in Westminster. She tells you that Mr. Fleming has found out from the Templar leader you captured in the last memory that an attack is imminent. He escaped custody and is thought to be hiding in Westminster.

OBJECTIVE: LOCATE THE TEMPLAR LEADER

❖ Follow the green blip two blocks to the south. When you near the corner **(2)** you spot a carriage with the Templar leader inside (still marked with a green blip).

OBJECTIVE: TAIL THE TEMPLAR LEADER

❖ Hijack a carriage and pursue the fleeing Templar. His route is marked on our map. If you lose sight of him a timer counts down from 15 seconds. If it reaches zero you fail the mission. If you get too close to the leader then you also fail the mission.

Follow the Templar leader to London Victoria Station. He pulls into the tunnel running through the station. Exit your carriage and watch the Templar exit his to interact with more Templars in the tunnel.

OBJECTIVE: HIJACK THE CARRIAGE

❖ Once the Templar Leader is out of the carriage you can rush into the tunnel staying to the far left side and rush to the driver's seat of the carriage and jack it without a fight. Drive off quickly.

OBJECTIVE: REACH A SAFE AREA
CHALLENGE: REACH A SAFE PLACE IN LESS THAN 80 SEC

❖ Before you could leave, a Templar ignites the explosive crates in your carriage. There is a "Time before explosion" meter at the top of the screen. If this drains, you blow up and fail the memory. Running into objects takes time away from the explosion meter so drive fast, but carefully.

❖ Speed eastward away from the train station and across the bridge following the route indicated on the street and your Mini-Map. You have to deal with an unusually high volume of traffic along the way as well as some carriage-driving Templar aggressors. Use Quickshots to fend them off while focusing on your driving. Just beyond the first right over the bridge you see the Reach marker. Quickly pull into it and get out of the carriage.

OBJECTIVE: ESCAPE THE AREA
BEFORE THE CARRIAGE EXPLODES

❖ After parking the carriage in the reach marker you can see a little red restricted zone around the carriage on the Mini-Map. Run away from this zone to avoid the explosion and to complete the memory.

OPERATION: WESTMINSTER

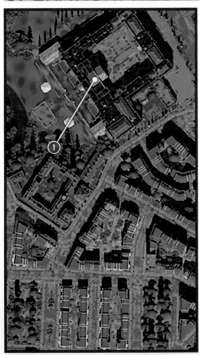

MISSION OVERVIEW

Memory Type: Queen Victoria / London Stories	**ASSASSIN**	**CHALLENGE**	**REWARDS**
	Jacob or Evie Frye	Make a Templar kill himself, but not innocents	£: 2000 + 350 (Full Synch Bonus)
Suggested Level: 10			XP: 1200 + 400 (Full Synch Bonus)

LOCATION: BUCKINGHAM PALACE, WESTMINSTER

Find Queen Victoria **(1)** on the second floor hallway outside her study. She says the final group of Templar upstarts are making their last desperate stand. They plan to detonate the last of their bombs at the Houses of Parliament. Stop the Templars from blowing up the Houses of Parliament

OBJECTIVE: FIND THE SECRET AGENT

❖ Exit Buckingham Palace and take a carriage to the House of Parliament **(2)**.

❖ Enter Buckingham Palace through the southwest corner doorway **(2)**. The door is locked. Pick it open and follow the green blip to find Fleming **(3)**.

OBJECTIVE: KILL THE ISOLATED TEMPLAR

❖ Fleming is hiding around the corner from a Templar **(4)** strapped with bombs standing in a crowd of people further down the adjoining hallway.

❖ The Challenge is not active yet, but we suggest you practice the Challenge with the first Templar bomber. You have to get him to kill himself without killing innocents. Walk up behind him in the crowd and kidnap him.

❖ Walk the kidnapped Templar through the crowd of people in the hallway heading east (the way he was facing) and turn right at the hallway intersection. Stop at the end of the next hallway **(5)** where there are no civilians and let him go. Run away. Moments later he detonates the bomb and blows himself up.

OBJECTIVE: LOCATE AND KILL THE 5 TEMPLARS

CHALLENGE: MAKE A TEMPLAR KILL HIMSELF, BUT NOT INNOCENTS

❖ Now that we've shown you how to beat the Challenge, head to the nearest Templar bomber **(6)** who is through the now-open door to the courtyard near where your first victim was taken **(4)**. Perform the same maneuver as before, kidnapping him and leaving him in the same location **(5)** to blow himself up.

❖ After completing the Challenge you can simply kill the remaining four Templars by running up behind them and silently executing them. Follow the red blips on the map to find and kill them all.

OBJECTIVE: SPEAK TO FLEMING

❖ Find and Speak to Fleming **(7)** who is now at the end of the main hall in the chapel-looking area.

OBJECTIVE: TACKLE THE TEMPLAR LEADER

❖ When you reach the area **(7)** where you were to meet Fleming you see the fleeing Templar leader. Chase him through Parliament, heading east down the nearest hallway.

❖ The Templar leader runs east until he reaches the end of the hallway (were your bomber kill zone is located) and turns left and stops **(8)**. He holds Fleming at gunpoint.

OBJECTIVE: KILL THE TEMPLAR LEADER

❖ Hold **L2** / **LT** to aim your gun. Aim for the Templar leader's head when it moves from behind Fleming's head. Take the shot with **R2** / **RT**. The sooner you can kill the leader, the more time you have to defuse the four bombs remaining in the building. You start with two minutes and 28 seconds.

THE ESSENTIALS
WALK THROUGH
SIDE QUESTS
COLLECTIBLES
DATABASE ENTRIES
REFERENCE

OBJECTIVE: DEFUSE 4 EXPLOSIVE CHARGES

❖ You have whatever time is left from the 2:28 given to kill the Templar leader and free Fleming from the gun pointed at his head to diffuse four bombs.

BOMB 1

❖ Rush to the bomb **(9)** in the room at the end of the hall heading north away from Fleming. Quickly pick the lock on the door and enter. Turn right in the room and find and defuse the bomb in the right corner.

BOMB 2

❖ Exit the room, turn right in the hallway, take a left at the end of the next hallway, and exit into the courtyard through the first open door

on the right. The bomb **(10)** is in the back right corner of the courtyard. Defuse it. You should have around 1:30 left on the timer.

BOMB 3

❖ Rope Launch to the rooftop from the second bomb location. Scale over the top of the building and drop down on the balcony on the west

side. Enter the building through open doorway balcony entrance. Drop down off the balcony inside and find the bomb **(11)** on the floor under the stairs.

BOMB 4

❖ The last bomb is in Big Ben. Run out the front door to the north and cross the yard heading directly for the Big Ben clock tower **(12)**. Following our directions, you should have almost a minute left to defuse the last bomb.

❖ Climb or Rope Launch up to the lower balcony around Big Ben. Walk directly under the tower until you achieve a Rope Launch lock-on that elevates you directly to the bell tower floor above the clock where the bomb **(12)** is located. Do not attempt to climb the tower; there is not enough time.

❖ Find the bomb on the bell tower level above the clock in the southeast corner. Defuse it to save the Houses of Parliament and everyone inside.

OBJECTIVE: SPEAK TO DISRAELI

❖ Drop down off of Big Ben and talk to Disraeli standing outside the main entrance **(13)** to be formally thanked by the Queen and to complete the memory.

UNIQUE ITEMS

Be sure to grab the unique items from Large Chests which can only be found during this time anomaly. Bouddica's Torque, a unique crafting component can be found on the first floor of the Tower of London, in the Armory Building. You can also grab the Reaper Belt from the right side of St. Katherine's Docks.

World War I Memories become available during Sequence 6. Follow the time rift icon on your map to locate the time rift. You can find the impressively large portal on a barge in the middle of The Thames and as far to the east as you can get on the river. Inspect the rift to begin "The Darkest Hour."

THE DARKEST HOUR

MISSION OVERVIEW

Memory Type: World War I / London Stories	**ASSASSIN**	**REWARDS**
Suggested Level: 6	Lydia Frye	£: 3532 + 150 (Full Synch Bonus)
		XP: 4000
	CHALLENGES	
	Use the generator to attract a spy	**Outfits:** Military Suit

OBJECTIVE: INVESTIGATE THE HOUSE

❖ You start **(1)** this memory on the first floor of a house where an unknown man—who you apparently just killed—is sliding off a dining table and onto the floor. You look like Evie, but you're not...you are Jacob's granddaughter, Lydia. It's World War I in London and the year is 1916.

OBJECTIVE: ELIMINATE THE 3 SPIES

CHALLENGE: USE THE GENERATOR TO ATTRACT A SPY

❖ Ascend the stairs and activate Eagle Vision. Spot the glowing yellow enemies on the floor below. These are the three spies you need to eliminate. Another generator sits in the next room. Activate it.

❖ Cover beside the stairs and two spies walk up the stairs to investigate the generator problem. Assassinate them both.

❖ Winston Churchill and his guards enter the room after you defeat the three spies. You did him a favor; he was after the same group. You agree to work together.

OBJECTIVE: FIND INFORMATION ABOUT THE RADIO

STEAL INFORMATION ABOUT THE RADIO

❖ You regain control of Lydia in a room **(2)** where half of the walls have been blown away, revealing a smoky London landscape and the sounds of war. Use Eagle Vision to identify who holds the radio information. Evie left Lydia the Rope Launcher; use it to reach the top of the house.

❖ There are three different locations green blipped on the map: one around a guarded crane **(3)** on the shoreline of The Thames; another on a barge **(4)** guarded by Templars in The Thames; and the last one is below the bridge's south tower **(5)** on the ground level.

❖ Zipline to the crane platform first **(3)**. Activate the generator to get the attention of the guard that holds the information. Cover Assassinate him to retrieve the radio info.

❖ Zipline to the Templar boat **(4)** and throw a smoke bomb on the boat before you jump to it from the adjacent boat. Defeat everyone and loot the radio info. Zipline out of the area heading for the bridge.

THE ESSENTIAL
WALKTHROUGH
SIDE QUESTS
COLLECTIBLES
APPENDIX & MINUTIAE

ASSOCIATES & INCOME
LONDON STORIES
WWI TIME ANOMALY
TRAIN HIDEOUT
DREADFUL CRIMES

❖ Blend into the crowd on the ground, next to the soldier speaking on top of the tank, and wait for the soldier to pass by to quietly steal the information from him.

OBJECTIVE: REACH THE NORTH TOWER

❖ Clamber up, Rope Launch, and zipline to scale the many different surfaces of the bridge to reach the north tower **(6)**. Keep out of the spotlights to avoid sniper fire.

OBJECTIVE: KILL THE 4 SPIES MANNING THE RADIO

❖ Drop down from the north side of the north tower **(6)** to find a series of open windows above a large window ledge. Cover behind the windows and shoot hallucinogenic darts or knives into the spies inside the communications base. Kill them all and enter the room.

OBJECTIVE: TALK TO CHURCHILL OVER THE RADIO

❖ Operate the radio on the table on the left side of the room.

OBJECTIVE: REACH THE ANTI-AIRCRAFT GUN

❖ Exit out the east window **(7)** and perform a Leap of Faith into a haystack below. A boat outfitted with an anti-aircraft gun pulls up directly below you **(8)**.

OBJECTIVE: DESTROY TWO WAVES OF PLANES

❖ Zipline to the boat and take control of the large anti-aircraft gun. Aim to the sky and shoot the attacking bi-plane down. Follow its flight path with the reticle and shoot when it turns red. Shoot using **R2 / RT**.

❖ There's only one plane in the first wave. If you allow it to live long enough that it performs a shooting dive, then cover behind the gun shield by pressing the ⊗ / Ⓐ button. Don't be a hero! Cover to live to shoot again.

❖ Pilots know they are the most vulnerable when flying out of a dive run. Use this to your advantage, as soon as the last bullet from the dive attack is fired, come up from cover and take aim on the aircraft(s) as they perform the slow climb out of the dive.

OBJECTIVE: KILL THE 3 BOARDERS

❖ The first wave of planes has one plane to destroy and the second wave has two. After destroying three planes, Templars board your ship. Leave the gun and defeat the three Templars.

OBJECTIVE: DESTROY TWO MORE WAVES OF PLANES

❖ After defeating the Templars, return to the anti-aircraft gun and blow up five more planes and watch as the zeppelin is taken down by allies.

ADDITIONAL COVERAGE OF THE WORLD WAR I ADVENTURES

The additional adventures of Lydia Frye in 1916 London are covered in our Associate Activities section of this guide. You will notice that these other adventures are categorized as such in the Progress Tracker—where you can replay the memories.

WWI ASSOCIATE AND INCOME ACTIVITIES

Although they are technically Associate and Income Activities given to you by Winston Churchill, we've placed these memories here, with your other adventures in WWI.

SPY HUNTS

Spy Hunts task you with identifying and eliminating enemy spies in the city. Speak to Winston Churchill to start each hunt.

⊙	Zeppelin Raid
●	Master Assassin
⊙	Spy Hunts
⊙	Spy Hideout

THE MAGPIE

Memory Type: Spy Hunt
Suggested Level: 6
Challenge: Have the guards kill the spy.
£: 400+150

INVESTIGATE THE DEAD GUARD

Climb down into the mote, then grapple up to the top of the outer wall. From there, grapple to the top of the square tower. Drop down to the north side of the tower, then drop off the flagpole and follow the path to the open window with the body of the guard inside

FIND AND KILL THE SPY

Head back out the window and stay to the south side, eventually putting yourself on the lower wall to the south of the courtyard containing the assassin. There will be one guard on this wall, kill him with a throwing knife quickly so you don't draw any unwanted attention.

Use Eagle Vision to locate the spy as he runs around the courtyard. Get your Hallucinogenic dart ready! Once the spy is in range, your crosshair turns red. Hit him with a dart

He pauses for a moment before running directly into the combat with the nearest set of guards. The spy is no match for the guards. As soon as they kill him, head south over the wall you are standing on, then out the front gate of the area to finish the mission.

SPY HUNTS

MAP	LVL	NAME	CHALLENGE	REWARD
1	6	The Magpie	Have the guards kill the spy.	£: 400
2	6	The Apothecary Twins	Bring the Nurse's body to the morgue.	£: 400

THE APOTHECARY TWINS

Memory Type: Spy Hunt
Suggested Level: 6
Challenge: Bring the Nurse's body to the Morgue
£: 400

LOCATE THE ASSOCIATE AND NURSE

Climb to the top of the roof to the northwest corner of this medical camp. The Associate is walking with three guards around the courtyard.

Wait for him to get close enough to be hit by a hallucinogenic dart, then hit him with it. The Associate is strong enough to kill all three guards before dying from the effect of the dart.

Move to the power pole within jumping distance of the roof. The nurse comes outside of the north tent and directly into range of an Air Assassination.

Jump down and kill her, pick up her body, and run it through the center of the courtyard. Go past the guard at the door of the south tent, and quickly toss the body of the nurse onto the marker.

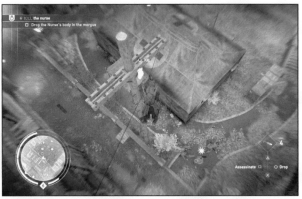

The enemies know of your presence now, but with both the Nurse and Associate dead, all you have to do is escape. Continue out the south door of the tent, then grapple up the building immediately in front of you. Jump down the other side of the building and run as far as you need to become unnoticed and complete the mission.

SPY HIDEOUTS

Stealing documents to gain intel is the main goal of spy hideouts.

CLARENCE STOCK HOUSE

Memory Type: Spy Hideout
Suggested Level: 6
Challenge: Destroy the spies' military equipment (3)
£: 400 + 150 (Full Synch Bonus)

STEAL DOCUMENTS (3)

Enter from the window facing the street to the north of the stock house. Wait on the small ledge until the Spy is close, then use a hallucinogenic dart to force a fight among the enemies inside. This fight should kill all of the

enemies on the top level making it easy for you to loot the body of the first spy.

Stay on the top floor and head east across a small bridge that connects the two buildings in the complex. In the room across the bridge, there is one spy and one other enemy. Throw a smoke bomb and run in to kill them quickly, loot the body of the spy, then head back to the bridge.

Jump down from the bridge and work your way to the east side of the dock. This can be done without alerting an enemy. Use throwing knives to clear a path if you don't want to take a full stealth approach.

Once you're on the docks, get behind the small building on the east side, then whistle to grab the attention of the last spy. If he is out of whistle range, stand out in the open to grab his attention. Move back into cover and assassinate him as he comes around the corner.

DESTROY THE SPIES' MILITARY EQUIPMENT (3)

In the first warehouse (the west building) that you entered, there are two pieces of military equipment, an emplaced gun and an armored car. On the top floor of this building there are plenty of ammo boxes that you can use to destroy the equipment. Ammo boxes function exactly like TNT boxes. They must be ignited to explode.

There are two enemies in the bottom floor of this building. Take them out before attempting to move ammo boxes as you cannot attack them while holding a box.

Move the boxes near each item, the gun in the northwest corner of the room, and the armored car parked in the center facing towards the open garage door.

Ignite them both then head back upstairs, grabbing another crate of ammo and heading to the bridge. Toss the ammo box off the bridge towards the armored car that is parked on the boardwalk. Jump down and make any adjustments needed to put the box within range to damage the armored car. Ignite the box and run to a safe distance.

HOPTON'S

Memory Type: Spy Hideout
Suggested Level: 6
Challenge: Plant false information **(1)**
£: 400 + 150 (Full Synch Bonus)

STEAL DOCUMENTS (3)

There is only one scout on all of the roofs in the area. Zipline to the roof with the scout and kill him. Continue to the west of the roof to the small room containing one enemy and the first spy. Do not ledge assassinate this spy as his body falls into the road below, putting the police on alert.

Use a hallucinogenic dart on the spy. Doing this causes him to kill the other enemy and then eventually drop dead from its effects. Loot the documents, then focus on the spy in the top floor of the center building.

Your target is in a room with three other enemies. Throw a smoke bomb in the room when they are all grouped up. Under the cover of smoke, run in and quickly kill all of the enemies.

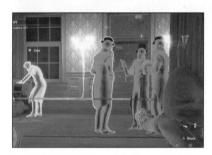

The third spy is on the bottom floor of the building. Continue down the stairs, then use a throwing knife to quickly kill the spy and any other enemies that may notice you when you go to loot the body.

PLANTING FALSE INFORMATION (1)

As you are working your way down from the top level of the house, stop off at the second level. In a room behind a door, one enemy guards a book on a desk. Open the door, kill the guard, and plant the information in the book. Eagle Vision shows the book as a white square on the table. This helps you locate the correct area as you descend towards the bottom floor of the house.

17 WALPOLE LANE

Memory Type: Spy Hideout
Suggested Level: 6
Challenge: Free allies **(2)**
£: 400+150 (Full Synch Bonus)

STEAL DOCUMENTS (3)

Enter the area from the north, killing the one scout that inhabits the roof. Work your way around the roof towards the east, following it as it curves to the south. Once you are lined up with the roof of the center building, zipline across. Two scouts are on the roof: one on the north side, one on the south. Kill the scouts before locating the spies.

Two spies roam the courtyard while the third is inside the center building. Police also walk the courtyard. Use your hallucinogenic darts on fuel sources to quickly turn some enemies against each other on the south side of the center building.

This pulls other nearby enemies, and at least one spy back behind the building. Once you see a spy come around, hit him with a dart, or go for a headshot with a throwing knife. The spies do not need to be alive for you to obtain the documents.

Keeping the fight behind the building lessens the chances of the enemies on the north side being alerted, making the fight much easier. Once you've grabbed the first file, hunt down the second spy that is in the courtyard if

they haven't already been pulled back behind the building by the fight. Use a throwing knife or dart to take them down then grab the documents from their corpse.

There is a small window with a post just below it on the south side of the center building that is home to the third spy. Simply climb to one of the sides of the window and whistle when the spy is closest to the window. Use a cover assassination to pull him out of the window, then loot the documents from the corpse below.

FREE ALLIES

If you have killed the scouts on the rooftops, all you need to do is get to the roof nearest your captive allies. Once you are above them, Air Assassinate the one target guarding either set of your allies, then free them.

Open the door for them before heading out of their small enclosure. If there are any enemies in the area, they begin to fight. Your allies do not need to stay alive after you have freed them, so don't worry about protecting them.

SPY HIDEOUTS

MAP	LVL	NAME	CHALLENGE	REWARD
1	6	Clarence Stock House	Destroy the spies' military equipment **(3)**.	£: 400
2	6	Hopton's	Plant false information **(1)**.	£: 400
3	6	17 Walpole Lane	Free allies **(2)**.	£: 400

THE MASTER SPY

Suggested Level: 6   **£:** 600

THE ESSENTIALS
WALKTHROUGH
SIDE QUESTS
COLLECTIBLES
REFERENCE & ANALYSIS
INDEX

ASSOCIATES & BOSSES
LONDON STORIES
WWI TIME ANOMALY
TRAIN HIDEOUT
DREADFUL CRIMES

INFILTRATE HQ

Head south away from Churchill's HQ toward the marker on your map. The entrance to the HQ building is on the bottom floor of the east side of the building.

Once inside, head upstairs and pick the lock of the door to the right. Using your Eagle Vision, follow the footsteps toward a suspicious bookcase. Examine the bookcase to reveal the entrance to the secret spy HQ.

KILL THE SPIES

After gaining entry, you need to kill four spies. Shoot one with a hallucinogenic dart, then pick off the rest with throwing knives while they attempt to fight the hallucinating spy.

KILL THE MASTER SPY

With four spies dead, your focus shifts to the Master Spy. You have a short fight with him in the room, however he uses a device to stun you and then escapes out the window.

LOCATE THE MASTER SPY

Chase the Master Spy through the streets. There is no need to stop and fight the enemies that you encounter along the way, just be ready to press ▲ / Ⓨ to counter their ranged attacks as you run. Keep your smoke bombs equipped to quickly get through the enemies that try to slow your chase on the target before eventually cornering him in a courtyard.

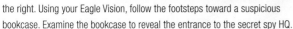

There are a large amount of enemies nearby. However, most of them will be fighting Rooks so they do not pose much of a threat. Focus your attacks on the Master Spy. Throw a smoke bomb down on the ground before attacking to disorient any enemies around you.

Once the Master Spy is dead, flee the area. You do not need to kill the remaining enemies for completion. If you flee to the north, you can climb up and over the building before jumping in the water and swimming to safety.

 # ZEPPELIN RAID

Memory Type: Zeppelin Raid / Income Activity   **£:** 500

SHIFTING LOCATION

The Zeppelin Raid shifts between locations 1 and 2 on the map. It is never in both at the same time.

Begin a Zeppelin Raid by using the Radio located underneath the bridge. Once you've used the radio, you need to head straight for the water, looking for the boat that has the Anti-Aircraft gun mounted on the front.

This plays out the same as the introductory mission to this chapter so it should be fairly easy to accomplish

SMOKE THEM OUT

Before hopping into the gunner seat, have your smoke grenades equipped. This makes the fight against the enemies who board your ship much easier.

Use the Anti-Aircraft gun to take out the first two planes using **R2 / RT** to fire the gun and ✕ / Ⓐ to take cover when the planes dive-bomb you. After destroying the two planes, the ship begins to relocate and a wave of enemies hops aboard.

If you have your smoke bomb equipped quickly throw one down. This stuns the enemies, making them easy targets to be quickly killed. One more wave of two planes awaits. Upon destroying them, the activity ends.

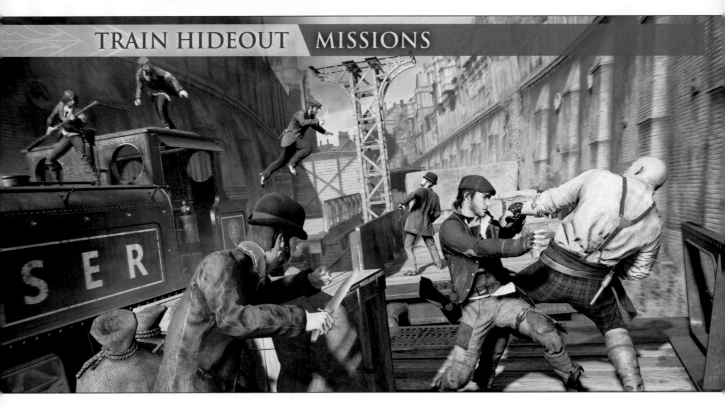

The Train Hideout missions become available after you unlock the Train Hideout during Sequence 3. Follow the Assassin icon to find the train. You can Fast Travel to the train by pressing and holding ⊙ / ⊗ when the train icon is selected on the world map. Agnes is your contact to start these memories.

STALK THE STALKER

MISSION OVERVIEW

Memory Type: Train Hideout / London Stories	ASSASSIN	CHALLENGES	REWARDS
Suggested Level: 3	Evie Frye	Air Assassinate all snipers	£: 75 + 100 (Full Synch Bonus)
			XP: 660 + 350 (Full Synch Bonus)

THE ESSENTIALS
WALKTHROUGH
SIDE QUESTS
COLLECTIBLES
REFERENCE & ANALYSIS
INDEX

ASSOCIATES & INCOME
LONDON STORIES
WWI TIMELINE
TRAIN HIDEOUT
DREADFUL CRIMES

LOCATION: TRAIN HIDEOUT

Talk to Agnes in the Train Hideout to start this memory. This is an Evie Frye only memory. Agnes says she's being followed, so Evie decides to follow her to stalk the stalker.

OBJECTIVE: REACH THE MEETING POINT

LOCATION: SOUTHWARK

❖ Leave the train and travel to the rooftop green blipped on the map in Southwark. Agnes starts her morning routine while Evie watches from above.

OBJECTIVE: TAIL AGNES' STALKER

❖ Use the rooftops to tail the stalker **(2)** who glows yellow when Eagle Vision is activated. He follows Agnes. If he leaves your sight, a 15 second timer starts and if it reaches zero before you can get him in sight again, you fail.

❖ Follow him as he walks around the building to the north and under a shelter across the street to the east **(3)**. Jump from the rooftop to a rope stretching to that shelter, then walk in the shelter's rafters to keep him in view.

❖ The stalker bumps into some gang members in the shelter and mentions Agnes is with a train gang. These guys organize rooftop snipers to take her out.

OBJECTIVE: DEFEND AGNES

CHALLENGE: AIR ASSASSINATE

ALL SNIPERS

❖ Leap from the rafters of the shelter to the flagpole on the building to the east and drop down to the catwalk rail and Air Assassinate the first sniper on the catwalk **(4)**.

- Rope Launch to the rooftop above the sniper's catwalk and then zipline to the edge **(5)** of the rooftop to the north. Leap off the north edge of this building to Air Assassinate the sniper **(6)** on the suspended platform between buildings.
- Rope Launch back to the previous rooftop and head to the peak of the rooftop on the north edge. Air Assassinate the sniper on the northeast edge **(7)**.

- Rope Launch to the chimney **(8)** on the building to the east. Leap to the rooftop toward the next sniper **(9)** on the west edge of this rooftop. Air Assassinate him from the roofline above the gabled windows.

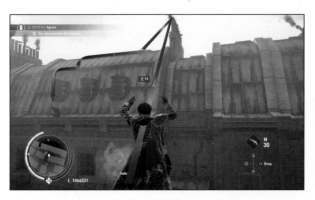

- Run north along the rooftop ledge from where the last sniper was and free run up the next building. Continue running north and Air Assassinate the last sniper on the next rooftop below you **(10)**.

OBJECTIVE: REACH THE TRAIN STATION

- Rope Launch and zipline to the top of the train station. Enter the station through any entry point and enter the Reach marker inside near stairs **(11)**.

OBJECTIVE: ELIMINATE 15 BLIGHTERS

Help the Rooks defeat the Blighters in the train station. Reinforcements arrive via a train. Defeat all 15 and then enter the Reach marker at the Train Hideout to complete the memory. Nigel, the stalker, wants to join the gang and Evie and Agnes accept his proposal.

AVOID REINFORCEMENTS

If you take down the enemies stealthily and remain undetected, the train bringing reinforcements doesn't arrive and you only have to kill seven guards.

NIGEL IN FOR THE CHOP

MISSION OVERVIEW

	ASSASSIN	CHALLENGES	REWARDS
Memory Type: Train Hideout / London Stories **Suggested Level:** 3	Evie Frye	Knock out 4 guards	**£:** 75 + 100 (Full Synch Bonus) **XP:** 660 + 350 (Full Synch Bonus)

LOCATION: TRAIN HIDEOUT

Talk to Agnes in the Train Hideout to start this memory. This is an Evie Frye only memory. In this memory you must free Nigel who has been captured by the police and charged for the murder of a Blighter. You must destroy the evidence they have on him.

OBJECTIVE: SPEAK TO NIGEL

LOCATION: THE STRAND

❖ Walk up to the police wagon **(1)** in The Strand where Nigel is incarcerated. Nigel says he got drunk and his things are scattered everywhere. He doesn't remember killing anyone. You must destroy the evidence.

OBJECTIVE: DESTROY THE EVIDENCE (3)

CHALLENGE: KNOCK OUT 4 POLICEMEN

❖ As soon as control returns to you, Rope Launch to the top of the nearby rooftop **(2)** from beside the police wagon.

❖ From the east edge of the rooftop **(3)**, Rope Launch to the building **(4)** to the east across the courtyard below so that your path intersects with the haystack **(5)** below. Leap of Faith into the hay from the zipline.

❖ There are six policemen in the area. Three of them patrol and the other three stand still facing away from the courtyard at the entrances while stopping the onlookers from entering the crime scene.

❖ Exit the haystack and knock out the policeman **(A)** when he walks away from the haystack.

❖ Head to the north exit **(6)** and knock out the policeman **(B)** at the gate when the other patrolling policeman **(C)** is not in the area. Hide his body away from the entrance so the body is not seen by patrolling policeman **(C)**.

❖ Stay behind the entrance wall **(6)** looking into the courtyard and wait for the patrolling policeman **(C)** to stop in the little area to the left of the entrance. Come up behind him and knock him out.

❖ Watching the patrol route of the distant policeman to the south, sneak up behind the policeman **(D)** at the west entrance and knock him out. That completes the Challenge of knocking out four policemen.

❖ Destroy the evidence **(7)** beside the gazebo when the patrolling policeman **(E)** is nowhere near. Hold the ◎ / Ⓑ button to burry Nigel's hat. Rope Launch to the rooftops to the east **(8)**.

❖ Jump from the east side of the rooftop **(8)** into the haystack **(9)** in the next courtyard below. Exit and knock out the policeman **(F)** near the haystack when his back is turned.

- Cover up the evidence **(10)** in the next yard near the square tree planter in the middle of the courtyard when the nearby cop is away on patrol. Evie tears up the paper. Rope Launch to the nearest rooftop to the north **(11)**.
- Zipline to the church rooftop to the south **(12)**. From the east edge **(13)** of the church, zipline across the patrolled garden area below to a ledge on the building to the east **(14)** above the hiding booth. Drop down to the ground and cover behind the concrete planters to hide from the patrolling cop **(G)**.
- Watch the patrol route of the cop **(G)** in the garden and the cop **(H)** patrolling the walkway outside the garden. When they are at the farthest point in their patrols from the evidence in the corner **(15)**, make your move from behind the planters to destroy the evidence. Evie steals the knife.

OBJECTIVE: HIDE THE BODY

- Quickly exit the garden through the north garden exit **(16)** and enter the nearby haystack **(17)**. Hide in the haystack to study the police patrols around you. When the coast is clear, exit the haystack heading north into the graveyard with the body and knock out the nearby patrolling guard **(I)**.
- Quickly head directly for the dead body **(18)** near the large middle mausoleum in the middle of the graveyard. Pick up the body and run south through the graveyard for the haystack in the southwest corner **(19)**.
- Dump the body in the haystack **(19)**. Walk up to it, face it, and press the ◎ / Ⓑ button to deposit the body in the hay to complete the objective.

OBJECTIVE: SPEAK TO THE CHIEF OF POLICE

- Return to the rooftop **(2)** above the police wagon where Nigel **(1)** is being held.
- Drop a smoke bomb around the police wagon and then drop down to the sidewalk to talk to the Chief of Police. There's no evidence and no body so they have to let Nigel go.

HULLO MR. GATLING

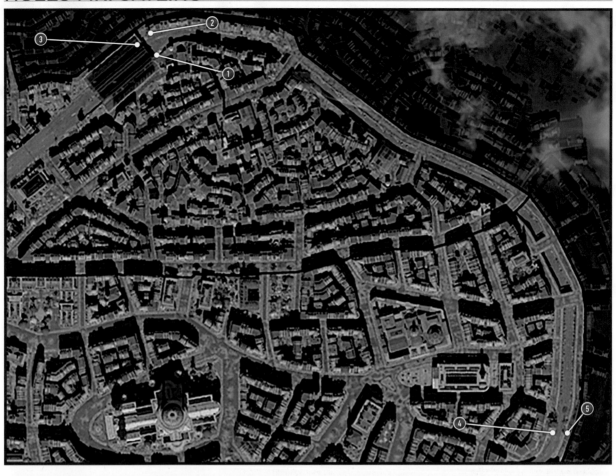

MISSION OVERVIEW

Memory Type: Train Hideout / London Stories	ASSASSIN	CHALLENGES	REWARDS
Suggested Level: 5	Jacob Frye	Don't take any damage	£: 660 + 100 (Full Synch Bonus)
		Detach 5 wagons	XP: 350 + 350 (Full Synch Bonus)

LOCATION: TRAIN HIDEOUT

Talk to Agnes in the Train Hideout to start this Jacob Frye only memory. In this memory you must hold off the rival gang who want their Gatling gun back. You begin this mission just outside the Whitechapel Train Station **(1)**.

OBJECTIVE: DEFEAT THE ATTACKERS

CHALLENGE: DON'T TAKE ANY DAMAGE

❖ After talking to Nigel about the jammed Gatling gun, tap ◎ / Ⓑ quickly and continuously to load the weapon. When the gauge is full the gun is ready to fire.

REMEMBER TO COVER

Use ✕ / Ⓐ to cover while enemies are shooting at you.

THE ESSENTIALS

WALKTHROUGH

SIDE QUESTS

COLLECTIBLES

OUTFITS & ABILITIES

INDEX

RESOURCES & MAP

LONDON ATLAS

WAR TIME ANOMALY

TRAIN HIDEOUT

DREADFUL CRIMES

❖ So that you don't have to reload at critical times, use the Gatling gun wisely. Take your time to make each shot count using only a couple of rounds at a time and aim for headshots.

❖ Activate Eagle Vision so you can see the enemy Blighters across the rails more easily. Use the Mini-Map to see where enemies are entering the area.

❖ If you take damage, it's usually from the rooftop snipers that arrive after a few waves of attacks. Make sure to take these enemies out first. They appear on the rooftop across the rails **(2)** and on top of the train station rooftop **(3)**.

❖ Save the explosive crates for when large groups of enemies appear near the end of the first stage of attacks (before the train starts to move).

OBJECTIVE: DESTROY THE COUPLING SYSTEM

CHALLENGE: DETACH 5 WAGONS

❖ When the train moves, the first Challenge has ended (it's okay if you take a little damage now). The second Challenge is to detach five train cars. Look toward the front of the train to anticipate the next wave of armed Blighters.

❖ Clear the enemies from the nearby cars on the enemy train rolling beside you and then concentrate your fire on the coupling between the last two cars. With enough firepower the coupling gives way and the last car detaches.

❖ Work quickly so you can detach the fifth car, the covered one with Blighters inside and on top of the car.

OBJECTIVE: DEFEAT THE ATTACKS

❖ Your train is stopped **(4)** by an obstruction placed on your tracks. Enemies appear on the street to the east **(5)**. Aim for the explosives on the street and then take out the two snipers on the balconies above.

❖ Lay waste to the four Blighters that roll up from the right in a carriage. Take them out and the train starts to move again.

OBJECTIVE: DESTROY THE DYNAMITE CRATE

❖ Your train catches up with the enemy train on the parallel tracks. Shoot the Blighters as the position of the trains moves them out of their cover.

❖ Counting five cars up from the back you spot the car that contains a large crate of explosives. Defeat the Blighters on the cars in-between then shoot through the window of the covered car with the explosives to hit the crate.

OBJECTIVE: DETACH THE FLATBED WAGON

❖ Jump onto the next train car ahead of yours and detach the wagon with the Gatling gun on it to complete the memory.

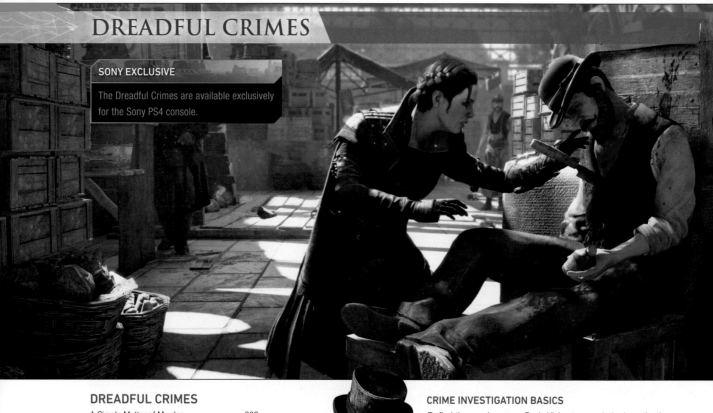

DREADFUL CRIMES

SONY EXCLUSIVE

The Dreadful Crimes are available exclusively for the Sony PS4 console.

DREADFUL CRIMES

Dreadful Crimes unlock after you complete Sequence 3. Follow the magnifying glass icon to the nearest murder scene to begin.

In this section, we have created the ultimate spoiler! All you need to know is "*who done it*" to solve these memories. We list all the clues in each area and tips to get through it, but we also reveal the name of the person to accuse of the crime. Every wrong guess costs you money and experience points when the reward is dished out at the end of the memory. One other point of interest: these replays disappear from the Progress Tracker after you play once. That means you only have one shot to get it right.

CRIME INVESTIGATION BASICS

To find the murderer, use Eagle Vision to search the investigation zones for clues. Clues glow yellow and, when you approach them, prompt an investigate button. Once clues are inspected, they glow white and descriptions appear near that person or object, but only while Eagle Vision is activated. In one case, Eagle Vision even allows you to see a bullet trajectory.

Interrogate every suspect. Unlocking more clues could add additional questions in a previously investigated suspect's conversation options. So question them more than once if applicable. The suspects have a red exclamation point icon near them when there are matters to be discussed. Sometimes talking to suspects actually opens a larger investigation zone with important clues that could point you in a new investigation direction—one that makes the new evidence undeniable.

Press *Options* to enter the Progression Log and access your collected evidence. This view option keeps you from running back and forth looking for the Eagle Vision text labels around the clues when you need to review the case.

Accuse the guilty suspect to solve the case and collect your reward. Be careful though, as every false accusation reduces the reward. Or, read on and see "who done it."

DISAPPEARING DREADFUL CRIMES

If you are accessing the Progress Tracker to replay previous memories (in an attempt to get 100% Synch Bonuses) you will notice that the Dreadful Crimes category completely vanishes once you've completed them. You earn 100% for completing these mysteries, even if you at first accuse the wrong person. It would be way too easy to complete them a second time if you already knew "who done it."

A SIMPLE MATTER OF MURDER!

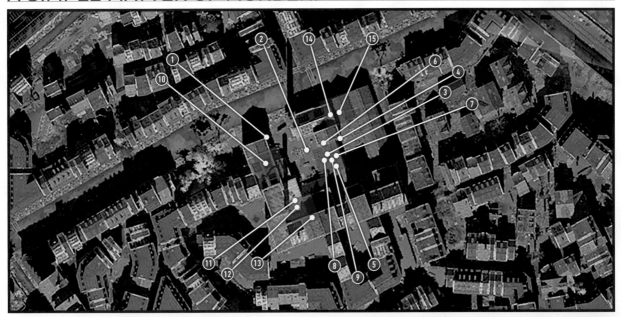

MISSION OVERVIEW

Memory Type: Dreadful Crimes / London Stories	ASSASSIN Jacob or Evie Frye	REWARDS **£:** 1000 (Max) **XP:** 800 (Max) **Cape:** Country Cloak

LOCATION: NORTH WHITECHAPEL

This is the mystery of the factory worker's death. You meet a young boy, Artie, and an author, Henry Raymond **(1)**. Doyle is fascinated by the crimes Raymond writes about. And Henry Raymond escorts his little fan to many of the crime scenes.

FIND ALL THE CLUES FIRST

It's best to approach an investigation with all the evidence possible. So look for all the clues available in an area before speaking to any suspects. This is an efficient way of doing the work but also keeps you from having to go back and talk to the same suspect multiple times as more clues are found.

OBJECTIVE: FOLLOW RAYMOND AND ARTIE

❖ Follow your two guides to Mr. Freems **(2)**, only a few yards away in the factory compound.

OBJECTIVE: SPEAK TO MR. FREEMS

❖ You have only two choices to talk about: Workers and Body. Talk about both.

OBJECTIVE: INSPECT WILKIN'S BODY
INVESTIGATION AREA: WAREHOUSE

CLUES: 3

❖ **Mr. Wilkins' Body:** Head to the left of Freems and find the factory worker's body **(3)** on the ground (it glows yellow in Eagle Vision). Stand over the body and inspect it. He has a deep stab wound to the chest and a bandana obscures the victim's face.

❖ **Warehouse - Letter**: This is located on the corner of the wall to Dooley's left, behind the barrel stack. The letter **(4)** states that workman, Mr. Coulton beats child laborers.

❖ **Warehouse - Knife**: This is located on the ground to Buck's left, the small knife **(5)** has the initial "D" crudely scratched in the handle possibly linking the knife to Dooley.

SUSPECTS: 3

- **Dooley:** Speak to Dooley **(6)** after you find the three clues. This is the little boy the evidence points to. He is Buck's brother and a child laborer. Talk to him about Buck and the Body. He tells you he grabbed a fallen knife in self-defense before he was knocked out and then woke up to see the crime scene.

- **Buck:** Speak to Buck **(7)**, Dooley's brother, after you find the three clues. Talk to him about Dooley, the Body, and the Knife. He confirms the knife is Dooley's and that he saved him from being beat up by a worker. He also arrived on the scene when Wilkins was already dead and Dooley was holding the knife.

- **Mr. Freems:** Mr. Freems is the first suspect and you spoke to him to start this investigation. If there are no red exclamation icons near any suspect's head and all clues have been found, you must then make an accusation.

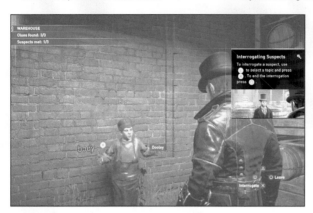

OBJECTIVE: ACCUSE A SUSPECT
INVESTIGATION AREA: WAREHOUSE

- Based on the knife and Buck's testimony, accuse Dooley to continue.
- This false accusation opens a larger investigation zone.

OBJECTIVE: CONTINUE YOUR INVESTIGATION
INVESTIGATION AREA: WAREHOUSE

CLUES: 5 (2 ADDITIONAL CLUES)

- **Warehouse - Large Footprint:** With Eagle Vision you can now spot labels around Wilkins' body. Investigate a large footprint **(9)** in front of Buck near the victim's head.

- **Warehouse – Medium Footprint:** Investigate a medium footprint **(8)** about a yard away from the victim's foot. Follow the footprints leading away into the Coal-Yard.

INVESTIGATION AREA: COAL-YARD

SUSPECTS: 1

- **Taylor:** Follow the footprints to Taylor **(10)**, a worker in the coal-yard. Talk to him about the Footprints and

Bandana. He said he and Wilkins heard screaming and only Wilkins went to investigate. He also says only men that work in the brewery wear bandanas. This leads you to determine the bandana was placed on the body.

INVESTIGATION AREA: BREWERY ENTRANCE

CLUES: 2

- **Brewery - Cigarettes:** Head to the brewery and find the cigarette **(11)** on the large porch. These are Joy's cigarette brand.

- **Brewery – Large Footprint:** Next to the cigarette butts is a large footprint **(12)** like the one near the body.

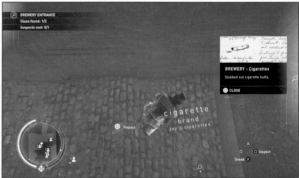

SUSPECTS: 1

- **Morris:** Morris **(13)** is standing at the brewery entrance. Talk to him about the Bandana and Cigarette.

- Make sure you have also talked to **Mr. Freems (2)** about the Bandana and to **Taylor** again **(10)** about cigarettes. This unlocks a new investigation zone, the Loading Area **(14)**.

SPOILER ALERT: SUSPECT ACCUSED

Read no further if you want to figure out "Who Done It" on your own.

INVESTIGATION AREA: LOADING AREA

CLUES: 1

- ❖ **Loading Area – Cigarettes**: Head north to the Loading Area to find the cigarette butts **(13)** on the ground not far from a new suspect.

SUSPECTS: 1
ACCUSE:

- ❖ **Coulton: (15)** is standing facing the cigarette clue in the Loading Area. Talk to him about the Bandana and Cigarette. After talking to him it's obvious this is the guy who did it. Accuse him to have the cops come haul him off, Artie congratulate you, and to complete the mystery and the memory. At the end you receive a very detailed overview of the events that occurred up to the murder that solidifies your case.

MOTIVE

The dead worker, one John Wilkins, heard screams and ran to offer assistance. Once there he found the boy unconscious and another workman, Tom Coulton, standing unharmed. But Coulton, long angry with Wilkins, thought fast and stabbed the man with the boy's knife. He then put his own bandana over Wilkins' face! Quick thinking, however, did not win out.

THE CASE OF THE CONFLICTED COURTSHIP

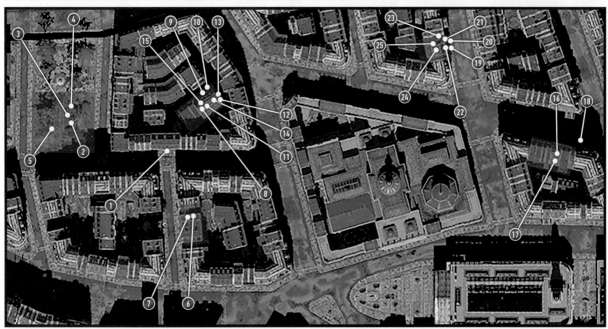

MISSION OVERVIEW

Memory Type: Dreadful Crimes / London Stories	**ASSASSIN** Jacob or Evie Frye	**REWARDS** £: 1500 (Max) XP: 850 (Max)

Dreadful Crimes
THE CASE OF THE CONFLICTED COURTSHIP

LOCATION: THE CITY OF LONDON

This is a perplexing murder of a woman in a public park. You meet Artie and Henry Raymond **(1)** outside the main entrance to the large hotel in City Of London. After starting the memory, walk to the nearby park **(2)** a block to the west.

OBJECTIVE: INSPECT PRUDENCE BROWNE'S CORPSE
INVESTIGATION AREA: THE PARK

CLUES: 4

- ❖ **The Park – Prudence Browne:** Prudence **(2)** lies on the ground (glowing yellow with Eagle Vision) by a tree in the southeast corner of the park, a young woman with identifying papers. She has been stabbed many times in a highly violent manner. Wounds indicate a left-handed attacker. These types of wounds usually indicate a crime of passion.

- ❖ **The Park – Packet:** This packet **(3)** can be found on the ground near Prudence's body. It contains powdered medication. Stamped "Dr. Trevor Alton" with an address.

- ❖ **The Park – Handbag:** This bag **(4)** can be found on the ground behind the tree that Prudence is propped up against. It contains an

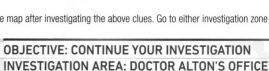

appointment diary "10 A.M.: Trevor, park. Noon: Gilbert, his house." Gilbert's address is on the back of the agenda.

- ❖ **The Park – Knife:** This standard kitchen knife **(5)** is on a curb near the park exit where a policeman is holding back a gathering crowd. It's the bloodied murder weapon.

- ❖ Doctor Alton's Office and Gilbert's House become new investigation zones on the map after investigating the above clues. Go to either investigation zone now.

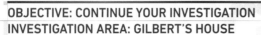

OBJECTIVE: CONTINUE YOUR INVESTIGATION
INVESTIGATION AREA: GILBERT'S HOUSE

CLUES: 1

- ❖ **Gilbert's House – Letter from Prudence:** This letter **(6)** is located on a bookcase on the second floor of Gilbert's house. In it, Prudence writes, "Dearest Gilbert, I have something of the utmost importance to tell you. I shall call tomorrow at noon…." And includes her address. This opens another investigation zone, Prudence's House.

SUSPECT: 1

- ❖ **Gilbert Higgins:** Speak to Gilbert **(7)** standing on the first floor of his house. Ask him about Prudence. His tells you that he and Prudence are engaged to be married. He acts like he does not know she is dead.

OBJECTIVE: CONTINUE YOUR INVESTIGATION
INVESTIGATION AREA: DOCTOR ALTON'S OFFICE

CLUES: 5

- ❖ **Dr. Alton's Office – Doctor's Note:** This note **(8)** says, "Drear Miss Knight, I would ask you to please suspend Mr. Shelby's prescription." This was written by a right-handed person. Further investigation is needed to find out why this prescription was stopped.

- ❖ **Dr. Alton's Office – Prudence's Medical File:** This file **(9)** is located on the desk to your left as soon as you enter the second floor office. The note says that Dr. Alton gave Prudence a sedative for grave anxiety over her recent engagement with Gilbert Higgins. It also says she was involved with an unnamed other and the doctor commented that this was "intolerable." This was right-handed writing.

❖ **Dr. Alton's Office – Mr. Shelby's Medical File:** This file **(10)** is located on the small table in the back of the same second floor office where you find Prudence's file. This one says that Mr. Shelby has overcome his paralyzing timidity with astonishing success. It goes on to say that he will terminate Shelby's use because of the adverse effects the same drug had on Mr. Baxter. This was right-handed writing. This points to the powder being a drug that turns introverts into uber-extroverts with possible negative side effects.

❖ **Dr. Alton's Office – Personal Note:** This note **(11)** is located on a small side table to the left as you enter the back office on the third floor. It's a personal note from Claire Knight to the doctor about a relationship that's going beyond doctor / patient association. This suggests the doctor is not always on his best professional behavior.

❖ **Dr. Alton's Office – Baxter's Medical File:** This file **(12)** is located in the same third floor office with the personal note. This note box is located on the desk on the north side of the room. It documents Baxter's overconsumption and addiction to his treatment drug. He's become alarmingly aggressive, has struck the doctor, and has seduced several women. This is why Shelby was taken off the medication.

SUSPECTS: 3

❖ **Doctor Trevor Alton:** Speak to Dr. Alton **(13)** in the third floor study about Medicine, Prudence, and Treatment. Notice he has a cut cheek. He seems shocked that Prudence is dead and denies he had a meeting with her scheduled today in the office or in the park. He also says Prudence's packet was not a drug subscription from him. Much evidence you've found contradicts the doctor's statements.

❖ **Mr. Shelby:** Speak to Shelby **(14)** on the first floor in a room off the lobby near the front desk. Speak to him about Prudence and Treatment. He's under the impression the Doctor has ended his prescription for no reason. He is unaware of the adverse side effects.

❖ **Claire Knight:** Claire **(15)** is also on the first floor of the doctor's office. Speak to her about Prudence, Alton's Cut, Baxter, and a Park Meeting. This is the lady the doctor is involved with according to the personal note. She is sorry to hear about the murder but says Prudence started stopping by more frequently socially. She said the doc could do better, in her opinion. Jealousy could be a motive but no other evidence points to Claire.

OBJECTIVE: CONTINUE YOUR INVESTIGATION
INVESTIGATION AREA: PRUDENCE'S HOUSE

CLUES: 2

❖ **Prudence's House – Unsent Letter to Dr. Alton:** This letter **(16)** is located on the third floor of Prudence's house. You can enter this room through an open 3rd-floor window on the north side of the house. Prudence writes to Dr. Alton about a woman that berated her after an afternoon meeting together in the park. It goes on to say that this lady shared shameful allegations involving Baxter. She ends the letter calling the doctor, "my love." This connects Prudence to an unprofessional relationship with Dr. Alton.

- **Prudence's House – Prudence's Diary:** This diary **(17)** is located in the hallway outside the room where you found Prudence's unsent letter. The gist of the diary is that she can't imagine being married to Gilbert. The doctor made a pass at her in the park, but he starts to become moody, even tormented (a side effect of his experimental drug. Maybe he's taking the drug himself?). This diary is the second source confirming a meeting between the doctor and Prudence in the park. She thinks he's going to propose marriage.

SUSPECT: 1

- **Lulu:** Speak to Lulu **(18)** outside in front of Prudence's house after you have collected all the clues. Talk to her about Prudence and Baxter. She is the crazy woman referred to in Prudence's unsent letter. She says she saw Prudence kissing her Baxter. She said she'd come visit her each day she can to catch her with Baxter again. If this lady is not crazy, then the doctor has introduced himself to her as Baxter.
- Talking to Lulu unlocks the final investigation zone, Baxter's house.

OBJECTIVE: CONTINUE YOUR INVESTIGATION
INVESTIGATION AREA: BAXTER'S HOUSE
CLUES: 7

- **Baxter's House – Scattered Papers:** Enter Baxter's house through the second-floor window **(19)** above his front door on the north side of his home. You enter his house into an office with five clues in it and two more out in the adjoining hallway. The first set of papers closest to the window is written by a left-handed man and is a death threat to a woman with a spot of blood on it. Remember, a left-handed attacker killed Prudence.

- **Baxter's House – Scattered Papers:** This second set of scattered papers **(20)** is in the corner near the window papers. Baxter learns Prudence is breaking her engagement with Gilbert.
- **Baxter's House – Scattered Papers:** The third set of scattered papers **(21)** is on the large desk in the middle of the office. "She means nothing to you! You are a monster of my own making!" A message from the doctor?
- **Baxter's House – Scattered Papers:** The fourth set of scattered papers **(22)** is on the floor in front of the desk. "I always got what I want. It is my due!"
- **Baxter's House – Scattered Papers:** The fifth set of scattered papers **(23)** is in the corner on the floor behind the desk in the office. "...you are a burden to me. A pathetic, sniveling burden! If only I could be rid of you!"
- **Baxter's House – Paper Packets:** These packets **(24)** are located on the hallway floor just outside the office. They have powder residue on them. Powder was found in a packet at the crime scene.
- **Baxter's House – Knives:** The knives **(25)** are located on a table in the hallway with the packets. They are indeed kitchen knives identical to the one found at the crime scene. There seems to be a lot of evidence pointing to Baxter. It's time to make an accusation.

SPOILER ALERT: SUSPECT ACCUSED

Read no further if you want to figure out "Who Done It" on your own.

INVESTIGATION AREA: DOCTOR ALTON'S OFFICE
ACCUSE:

- **Doctor Trevor Alton:** Return to Dr. Trevor Alton **(13)** and talk to him about his cut cheek. He says a patient attacked him. That means he lied about meeting Prudence in the park. Accuse the doctor. The police take him away and Doyle congratulates you.

MOTIVE

Doctor Trevor Alton's experimental medication seemed to be so successful on one of his patients that he tried it himself, and created a monster! Going under the name of Baxter, this second, drug-altered personality lived a wild, scandalous life, seducing women as he went. The unsuspecting Prudence Browne, believing him to be Dr. Alton, fell in love with the passionate Baxter. Meanwhile, Baxter continued his seductions, which included the possessive Lulu, who later followed Prudence, planning to threaten her. Horrified by Baxter's actions, Dr. Alton resolved to marry Prudence in order to save her reputation. Baxter, however, would not have his freedom curtailed in any way, and arranged to meet Miss Browne in the park, where he viciously murdered her. A crime for which Dr. Alton will pay the price!

DEATH STALKS THE COLONEL

MISSION OVERVIEW

Memory Type: Dreadful Crimes / London Stories	**ASSASSIN** Jacob or Evie Frye	**REWARDS** £: 1500 (Max) XP: 850 (Max)

LOCATION: ABBOT'S COCOA, SOUTHWARK

Find Artie and Henry Raymond **(1)** standing outside the Abbot's Cocoa factory in Southwark. In this case, you must determine which bullet struck and killed the former colonel.

OBJECTIVE: INSPECT COLONEL PRESCOTT'S BODY
INVESTIGATION AREA: MUNITIONS FACTORY

CLUES: 7

❖ **Munitions Factory – Prescott's Body:** Head to the east a block and find the colonel's body **(2)** near a fountain in a small, short-walled courtyard at the Munitions Factory. He was killed with high precision by a single bullet passing through his heart and exiting his back at 12 o'clock.

MUNITIONS FACTORY –
Prescott's body

Louis Prescott. Killed by a single bullet that entered his chest, passed directly through his heart, and exited from his back.

CLOSE

❖ **Munitions Factory – Dynamite Crates:** Find empty munitions crates **(3)** clearly marked "Prescott Munitions No. 408." These are located just outside the courtyard wall near the body.

❖ **Munitions Factory – Bloodstain:** This bloodstain **(4)** is near the colonel's head. The spread is consistent with the direction of the bullet.

❖ **Munitions Factory – Banner:** This banner **(5)** is located next to the blood spray and the body. The banner is for the 11th Regiment of Foot, marked "Gold Coast—Ashanti Campaign."

❖ **Munitions Factory – Feather:** This feather **(6)** is located at the base of the fountain. It's a single white feather, which in WWI was a symbol of cowardice in the British army.

- **Munitions Factory – Clock:** This clock **(7)** is leaning on the courtyard short wall in the trajectory of the bullet path. There's a hexagonal-shaped bullet lodged exactly below the numeral 12 and the clock is still running. With Eagle Vision you can see the bullet trajectory and where it originated.
- **Munitions Factory – Bullet Hole:** This hole **(8)** is located in the park bench next to the clock. The second bullet and trajectory further confuses the case. Each bullet's trajectory crosses the victim's body. You need to determine which one killed him and which one missed.

SUSPECTS: 2

- **Jonas Hassett:** Speak to Hassett **(9)** standing against the factory wall in the courtyard. He's the foreman and a veteran. Talk to him about Prescott, Banner, Shooting, and the Clock. He was proud to have served under the colonel. He heard two shots at the stroke of noon on his way to the factory. The banner was to honor those who fell under his command at an operation gone bad in the war. This story introduces motive to harm the commander. Possibly a disgruntled solder?
- **Frederick Abberline:** Speak to Abberline **(10)** standing near the north entrance of the courtyard. Talk to him about the Shooting,

Factory, the Clock, and the Suspect. He says some young lads were playing with a pistol they found across the street and a bullet went astray through the fence and possibly through the victim. He also says the factory was opened to give those soldiers that returned from the war a place to work.

OBJECTIVE: CONTINUE YOUR INVESTIGATION
INVESTIGATION AREA: SHOP
SUSPECTS: 1

- **Curtis:** Speak to Curtis **(11)**, the shop owner inside the shop across the street from the crime scene (where the bullet trails lead). Talk to him about Prescott and the Military. He said the colonel and he used to joke insult each other every morning. He was a lieutenant under the colonel's command in Africa. After you investigate the rifle in his attic, ask him about the Attic. He admits to selling stolen rifles. Talk to him about the Whitworth (the brand of rifle). He said he used that gun for Prescott's shooting challenge this morning.

OBJECTIVE: CONTINUE YOUR INVESTIGATION
INVESTIGATION AREA: COURTYARD
CLUES: 5

- **Courtyard – Beer:** The courtyard is the area between the shop and the factory including the alley beside the shop. The beer puddle **(12)** is in the street between the factory and the shop. Once you've investigated all the clues and suspects in this area, follow this beer trail to another investigation zone, the Barrel Depot.
- **Courtyard – Bullet Hole:** The bullet hole **(13)** can be found in the wooden fence blocking the alley next to the shop. It indicates that the bullet exited the courtyard behind the fence.

Courtyard – Target: The target dummy **(14)** is hanging on the backside of the wooden fence at the end of the alley next to the shop. Another indicator that the boys were actually performing target practice.

Courtyard – Mark: The mark **(15)** is on the ground behind the wooden fence with the bullet hole and the target dummy. It's the place where children stood when firing at the target.

Courtyard – Impact Mark: The impact mark **(16)** is on the ground behind the shop. It appears a small, heavy object may have fallen here, perhaps a revolver. Use Eagle Vision to display the "Fall" trail. Follow it to discover the attic.

SUSPECTS: 1

Earl: Speak to Earl **(17)** the young orphan boy who was shooting the target in the alley beside the shop. Talk to him about Shooting and the Gun. The boys found the revolver underneath the lumberyard window and shot at the target from the spot near the fence. The impact mark supports his explanation.

OBJECTIVE: CONTINUE YOUR INVESTIGATION
INVESTIGATION AREA: (SHOP) ATTIC

CLUES: 1

Attic – Whitworth Rifle: Enter the open windows at the top of the shop to access the attic. Find the rifle **(18)** on the floor near a gun case. It's the first sniper rifle with astonishing accuracy. It smells as if it's been fired in the past few hours. "11th Regiment of Foot—Gold Coast" is carved into the stock. Most importantly, it has a hexagonal barrel. This proves that Curtis shot the clock but, as the bullet hole is below the number 12, his shot didn't kill the victim.

OBJECTIVE: CONTINUE YOUR INVESTIGATION
INVESTIGATION AREA: BARREL DEPOT

CLUES: 4

Barrel Depot – Empty Barrel: Follow the beer trail to the Barrel Depot a couple of blocks west of the crime scene. Investigate the barrel **(19)** near the stack of barrels inside the depot yard. You find a round hole in the barrel and a spent revolver bullet inside matching the orphan's gun, thus proving the kid is innocent.

Barrel Depot – Backpack: to the west of the barrel with the bullet hole is a backpack **(20)** with a flap that bears the insignia of the 11th Regiment. This is near the stairs that lead to the bulkhead where you can find the goose. This proves that someone in the colonel's regiment was here and near the source of a white feather.

Barrel Depot – Goose: to the west of the backpack and down the stairs is a dead goose **(21)** on the bulkhead. The white goose was partially plucked (remember the feather at the crime scene).

Barrel Depot – Medicine: Find the medicine bottle **(22)** on top of a barrel near the alley between the barrel depot buildings. The drug is for the treatment of trypanosomiasis, a disease transmitted by tsetse flies in Africa. This is where the failed battle occurred.

SUSPECTS: 2

Bennett: Speak to Bennett **(23)**, the delivery cart driver and the first suspect you see when you enter the barrel depot yard. Talk to him about Prescott, Beer, and Samuel. He found the bullet hole in the barrel he was delivering. After talking to him about his helper, Samuel becomes a suspect you can interrogate.

SPOILER ALERT: SUSPECT ACCUSED

Read no further if you want to figure out "Who Done It" on your own.

INVESTIGATION AREA: BARREL DEPOT

ACCUSE:

Samuel: Speak to Samuel **(24)** standing near the bottle of medicine you found. He is Bennett's employee who helps with beer deliveries and was in the cart when the barrel got damaged. Talk to him about Prescott, Beer, and Disease. He says he doesn't know Prescott, doesn't know how the hole got in the barrel, and admits to having trypanosomiasis, which means he was in Africa. Curious, isn't it? Accuse this suspect. He is guilty.

MOTIVE

An army sharpshooter watches his friends die in a bungled military maneuver and vows revenge! Slowed by a tropical disease contracted on the Gold Coast, Private Samuel Frye spent years planning his vengeance on Louis Prescott, the colonel whose cowardice meant death for his companions. He taunted Prescott with the symbolic white feather and then, at the stroke of noon, took his final revenge. Many bullets flew that day: a bullet from the shop attic lodged in Prescott's factory clock; a bullet from the revolver found by some children lodged in a passing beer cart. And the bullet fired by Samuel from the back of that cart struck Prescott directly in the heart.

THE FIEND OF FLEET STREET

MISSION OVERVIEW

Memory Type: Dreadful Crimes / London Stories	**ASSASSIN** Jacob or Evie Frye	**REWARDS** **£:** 2000 (Max) **XP:** 1000 (Max)

LOCATION: THE WHITE HARE, WHITECHAPEL

Meet Artie and
Henry Raymond **(1)**
outside The White
Hare in southwest
Whitechapel. This is
the case of the missing
Detective Murphy.

OBJECTIVE: TALK TO FREDERICK ABBERLINE
INVESTIGATION AREA: FLEET STREET

SUSPECT: 1

❖ **Frederick Abberline:** Find Abberline **(2)** at the gated entrance to Fleet
Street one block to the east of where you talked to Doyle to pick up this
assignment. Talk to him about Det. Murphy. He says Murphy went missing
after investigating this area for other missing people. Ask him about
Missing People.

❖ Check your map, there are three other areas nearby that you can
investigate: Flower Shop, Bakery, and Leather Shop.

OBJECTIVE: CONTINUE YOUR INVESTIGATION
INVESTIGATION AREA: FLOWER SHOP

CLUES: 3

❖ **Flower Shop – Leather Bag:** Pass through the open gates behind
Abberline and head northeast in the courtyard to reach the flower shop.
Here you can find the leather bag **(3)** next to a cart. There's a fading green
image on the back of this leather bag, it appears to be a cross of some sort.

❖ **Flower Shop – Woman's Jacket:** This jacket is just a few feet away, up
a small set of stairs **(4)** near stacks of barrels. It is made of soft brushed
leather and decorated with diamond-shaped holes.

❖ **Flower Shop – Manure:** Just south of the jacket you can find this sack of
manure near a stack of crates **(5)** around the middle of the courtyard. This
is plant fertilizer but shows small bits of bone mixed in. One appears to be a
human knuckle.

SUSPECT: 1

❖ **Joanna:** Speak to the lady near the sack of manure. The assistant florist, Joanna **(6)** has plenty to say when you ask her about Detective Murphy and Missing People. She saw Murphy going into the barbershop on her way to work.

❖ **Stephen Bean:** The florist, Stephen Bean **(7)** is located near the sidewalk to the east. Talk to him about Det. Murphy, Missing People, and Manure. He says George delivers the amazing manure fertilizer. This opens a new topic: George. He says he's a sweet boy that gives his assistant gifts, including a handbag.

❖ Talk to Joanna about George after Stephen Bean mentions his name during interrogations. Ask Joanna about George. She calls him her sweetheart and believes he's going to propose marriage to her as soon as today.

OBJECTIVE: CONTINUE YOUR INVESTIGATION
INVESTIGATION AREA: BAKERY

CLUES: 2

❖ **Bakery – Bills:** Head north on the same block and find the bills **(8)** on the ground near a table full of baked goods. The bills are paid. There are several from George for meat delivery. This ties George to multiple types of deliveries (meat, fertilizer and handbags). Mrs. Moffat pays promptly and gets a good deal from George.

❖ **Bakery – Crate of Meat:** Walk past the suspect and find this crate **(9)** near the building and the playing boys. There's no label. The meat smells a little odd.

SUSPECT: 1

❖ **Mrs. Moffat:** Speak to the lady **(10)** near the table of baked goods. She is the baker of meat pies and those were her bills you found.

Talk to her about Det. Murphy, Missing People, and Meat. She says George delivers the meat for the pies she makes. He gets his meat from the butcher (this unlocks the butcher shop for investigation). She also says the detective bought a meat pie and then went to the barber. This makes two people connecting the Detective to the barber.

OBJECTIVE: CONTINUE YOUR INVESTIGATION
INVESTIGATION AREA: BUTCHER

SUSPECT: 1

❖ **John Tines:** Find the butcher **(11)** to the west of Mrs. Moffat's bakery in the same shopping center and talk to

him about Det. Murphy, Meat, and George. He says he only sells quality meat but someone is selling more cheaply because his sales have dropped. This coincides with the odd smelling meat found at the bakery. Mrs. Moffat thinks she's getting quality meat from George, but she is not. John Tines doesn't know George, which means he's not delivering his meat.

OBJECTIVE: CONTINUE YOUR INVESTIGATION
INVESTIGATION AREA: LEATHER SHOP

CLUES: 2

❖ **Leather Shop – Leatherworking Tools:** Go to the Leather Shop a block northeast from the other shops. Find the two clues on the second floor. The leatherworking tools **(12)** reveal awls, which would be used to punch distinctively shaped holes.

❖ **Leather Shop – Leather Scrap:** On the second floor of the leather shop is a leather scrap **(13)** that has a diamond shaped hole in it. This connects the Leather Shop to the Leather Jacket found at the Flower Shop.

SUSPECT: 1

❖ **Tobias Jeffers:** Speak to the leatherworker on the first floor. Tobias **(14)** talks about Det. Murphy, Missing People, and George.

He has very little love for George and defensively says he has very little to do with him except George buys his tanning leather. He also said the detective was in asking questions and that he answered them to his satisfaction.

OBJECTIVE: CONTINUE YOUR INVESTIGATION
INVESTIGATION AREA: BARBER SHOP

CLUES: 2

* **Barber Shop – Razors:** Find the razors **(15)** on the shelf in the corner of the back porch of this open barber shop.
* **Barber Shop – Blood:** Find the blood **(16)** on the ground near the stairs, not far from where you found the razors. Someone stepped in the blood, leaving a trail. Follow it after speaking to the Barber.

SUSPECT: 1

* **Feeney Sodd:** Speak to the barber, Sweeney Todd...we mean Feeney Sodd **(17)**, standing in the open barber shop. Talk to him about Det. Murphy, Missing People, Blood, and George. He noticed the detective had a green Celtic cross tattooed on his neck when he gave him a haircut. He also cut George's hair and George told him he's saved enough money to ask Joanna to marry him. He is also the first to admit knowing some of the missing people.
* Follow the blood trail from the barber shop to George's house.

OBJECTIVE: CONTINUE YOUR INVESTIGATION
INVESTIGATION AREA: GEORGE'S HOUSE

CLUES: 3

* **George's House – Ledger:** Find the ledger **(18)** on a desk by a window on the second floor of George's house. It's a list of pick-ups and deliveries. Pick-ups are mysterious. Drop offs are: Meat to bakery, Manure to florist, Leather to Tobias and to leather-worker. Totals show good business but the supplier is getting most of the money. You can come to the conclusion that something is up with the cheap meat, the manure has body parts in it, and the leather comes from a man who gets defensive when the name "George" is mentioned.

* **George's House – Diary:** Find the diary **(19)** on the third floor of George's house. You have seen George's dead body on the way to reaching this book. It says George has become increasingly suspicious concerning his deliveries. He had written to the detective about his suspicions regarding the true source of the products he delivers.

* **George's House – George's Body:** Find George **(20)** lying dead on the third floor of his house. His chest has a diamond-shaped puncture wound. The diamond-shaped cutter connects the scene to the leather shop.

SPOILER ALERT: SUSPECT ACCUSED

Read no further if you want to figure out "Who Done It" on your own.

INVESTIGATION AREA: BARREL DEPOT

ACCUSE:

* **Tobias Jeffers**: Speak to Jeffers **(14)**, the leather shop owner. Accuse him of the murders to complete the mystery and the memory. The story of why he did it will interest you but won't surprise this super sleuth, right?

MOTIVE

Even a detective can run adrift when a nefarious business is afoot! Was Detective Murphy getting too close to a secret source of "raw goods"? A leatherworker was in the habit of doing away with local folk, flaying them, and then chopping them up! He had the skin tanned for leather, the bones ground up to sell as manure, and the bloody flesh sold to supply pie-shops with cheap meat, all delivered by the unwitting carter, George. Thus did the fiend take macabre pleasure in seeing his victims happily consumed by the citizens of Fleet Street!

THE MYSTERY OF THE TWICE-DEAD PROFESSOR!

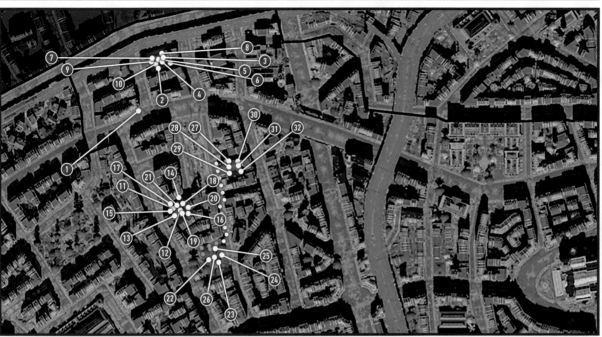

MISSION OVERVIEW

Memory Type: Dreadful Crimes / London Stories	**ASSASSIN** Jacob or Evie Frye	**REWARDS** **£:** 2000 (Max) **XP:** 1000 (Max)

LOCATION: SOLICITORS BLD, CITY OF LONDON

This is the mystery of the professor who, once buried, returned to die in his parlor! Meet Artie and Henry Raymond **(1)** in front of the Solicitors building in the City of London to start this memory.

OBJECTIVE: INSPECT PROFESSOR BYNG'S BODY
INVESTIGATION AREA: BYNG'S HOME

CLUES: 7

❖ **Byng's Home – Prof. Byng's Body:** Byng's house is to the northeast from where you started the memory. Byng's body **(2)** is on the floor at his open front door. His body shows evidence of having been in a violent struggle. There's a deep cut to the forehead that appears to be surgical—the cut goes into the skull. He also has a sting mark on his neck.

- ❖ **Byng's Home – Sculpture:** This sculpture **(3)** is on a small decorative table in the second floor hallway. The sculpture is of African origin and there's a small recess area where something, like a spider, could have been hidden.
- ❖ **Byng's Home – Dead Spider:** The spider **(4)** is on the floor at the top of the stairs on the third floor. It is a large, distinctive spider, curled up in death. Could it be venomous?
- ❖ **Byng's Home – Legal Letter:** This letter **(5)** is in the same hallway as the spider and sits on the edge of a half-circular table with a gas lamp glowing nearby. It's a letter to Byng from his attorney. He is agreeing to amend his will to discourage the marriage of his son to an unnamed lady. His son's allowance will be suspended if he marries her. Byng believes that this woman is only after his money.
- ❖ **Byng's Home – Crate:** The Crate **(6)** is in the corner on the third floor, not far from the dead spider. Shipped from London and marked: "To be opened only by Prof. Byng personally."
- ❖ **Byng's Home – Letter from Colleague:** The letter **(7)** is on a candlelit table in the back of the room on the third floor. This letter is from a humbled and traveling researcher and admirer of the professor's writings on unusual tribal customs, signed "Prof. Silas."
- ❖ **Byng's Home – Personal Letter:** This letter **(8)** is on a table in a nook on the opposite side of the first floor room from where Byng's body lies. This letter is to his son from his son's fiancée. She doesn't understand his father's antipathy towards her. And if she marries him or not, she wants to make sure he is rendered his due when the time comes.

SUSPECT: 2

- ❖ **Emmett Byng:** Speak to Byng's son Emmett **(9)** who stands on the first floor facing the fireplace and to Angela, the maid. Talk to Emmett about Byng, the Crate, and the Will. He feels his father's death is a great tragedy, reveals that his father was an anthropologist, and his colleagues often sent trinkets from abroad. He's agitated when you talk about the will. He swears his father and fiancée would have become friends given the chance.

- ❖ **Angela:** The maid, Angela **(10)** has all the answers. She explains that Professor Byng died of a heart attack a few days ago then showed up at the door and died again. She says a common statue was in the crate but doesn't know who sent it. When asked about Byng's last words she replies, "He kept repeating "Bagesu" over and over again."
- ❖ Head south to investigate the University.

THE ESSENTIALS
WALKTHROUGH
SIDE QUESTS
COLLECTIBLES
REFERENCE & ANALYSIS
INDEX

ASSOCIATES & VILLAINS
LONDON STORIES
WARTIME ANOMALY
✦ TRAIN HIDEOUT
DREADFUL CRIMES

OBJECTIVE: CONTINUE YOUR INVESTIGATION
INVESTIGATION AREA: UNIVERSITY

CLUES: 8

❖ **University – Handkerchief:** The handkerchief **(11)** is located on the first floor of the university. It's on a roll-top bookshelf next to the stairs. It is a lace handkerchief with red embroidery that matches the cemetery.

❖ **University – Receipt:** The receipt **(12)** is located on the first floor of the university. It's non-descript and is for seven pounds.

❖ **University – Treatise by Prof. Wilson:** This book **(13)** is located on a desk at the top of the stairs on the second floor. This treatise states that the Bolivian spider's venom produces a state resembling death and some Andean tribes use the venom during a rite of passage in which initiate boys experience a symbolic death lasting two or three days. It sounds like Byng was first "killed" by the spider and then by some other means.

❖ **University – Small Box:** This empty box **(14)** is located on the floor near the window on the second floor. It's labeled "Arachnid Harpadectus."

❖ **University – Pedestal:** The pedestal **(15)** is located on the third floor. There's nothing on it. A descriptive label reads: "Bagesu tribal mask: a jackal." Bagesu is the word the maid said Byng was repeating over and over just before he died a second time.

❖ **University – Spider Illustration:** The spider drawing **(16)** is on the east wall of the second floor, not far from the stairs. It resembles the dead spider found in the Byng home. A note describes it as a rare spider found in Bolivia whose venom is a strong tranquilizer.

❖ **University – Bookcase:** The bookcase **(17)** is located on the third floor near a window. It's well-stocked with anthropological books. Many are from Prof. Byng.

❖ **University – Book Written by Prof. Byng:** The book **(18)** is located on the floor of the third story. A chapter is torn from this book named: "The Intriguing Customs of Deepest Africa."

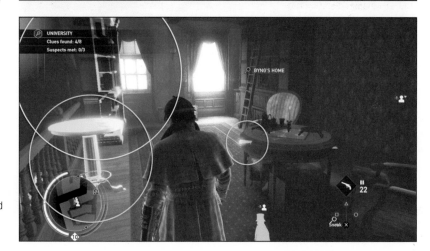

SUSPECT: 3

❖ **Professor Silas:** Speak to Prof. Silas **(19)** who stands on the third floor. Talk to him about Byng, Byng's Book, and Travels. He is fond of Byng's research and aspires to be as impactful. He tells you he's lost his glasses when asked about Byng's book. He's recently traveled to Africa to continue Byng's research.

❖ **Dr. Wilson:** Speak to the doctor **(20)** on the second floor about Byng, the Empty Box, and the Spider. He says Byng was an enamored colleague and he holds Byng in high regard. Wilson links the spider to the empty crate. He also links the spider to the Bolivian Andes and this information is stated in the *Treatise by Prof. Wilson.*

❖ **Virginia:** Speak to the assistant **(21)** who stands on the first floor. You see her when you enter the university. Talk to her about Byng and the Receipt. You can assume this is the fiancée. She plays dumb when asked about the will. The receipt question is the one that gets interesting results: several of the faculty purchased cadavers for research purposes.

OBJECTIVE: CONTINUE YOUR INVESTIGATION
INVESTIGATION AREA: CEMETERY

CLUES: 4

❖ **Cemetery – Gravedigger's Coat:** The coat **(22)** is on the ground beside the suspect. One pocket contains a crumpled note: "Here's the sum agreed upon for last night's transaction." This may be connected to the receipt you found for seven pounds at the University.

❖ **Cemetery – Money:** The money **(23)** can be found on the curb behind the suspect. Seven pounds sterling. Why would this university transaction amount be here? Was someone purchasing cadavers from the cemetery?

❖ **Cemetery – Byng Family Vault:** The vault **(24)** is not far from the suspect. It glows yellow with Eagle Vision on. You must interact with it from the north side. The lock is broken and the door is ajar. Prof. Byng's casket is empty.

❖ **Cemetery – Handkerchief:** A lace handkerchief **(25)** with red embroidery is located between the vault and the suspect. It matches the one at the university.

❖ **Muddy tracks:** Find the muddy tracks starting near the north entrance of the cemetery and follow them to the abandoned house to the north.

SUSPECT: 1

❖ **Beswick:** Speak to Beswick, the gravedigger, **(26)** about Byng, the Tomb, Grave Robbery, Body-Snatching Proven, and Money. He says he saw the son lock

the tomb himself. He also admits to grave robbing to sell a body or two for a little money. He said he broke the lock and left the body on a barrel behind his tomb. He said some fella came and picked him up and it was muddy so you can still see the tracks.

OBJECTIVE: CONTINUE YOUR INVESTIGATION
INVESTIGATION AREA: ABANDONED HOUSE

CLUES: 6

❖ **Abandoned House – Tools:** Tools **(27)** are located on the floor to the right as soon as you walk into the abandoned house. They include a bloody saw and a small hammer. This is getting interesting. Could this be how the professor was cut on the head?

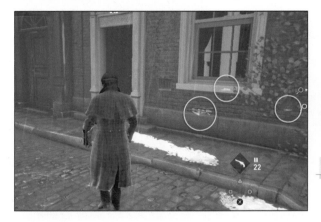

❖ **Abandoned House – Single Page:** The page **(28)** torn from a book sits on the floor near the tools. It describes the ceremonial rituals involving sacred masks, incense, and the chanting of the Bagesu tribe. This is the word that the Professor was mumbling over and over before he died.

❖ **Abandoned House – Ripped Chapter:** The ripped chapter **(29)** from Byng's book is on the floor on the other side of the table from the single page. It describes how the Bagesu tribes ceremonially ingest the living brains of respected elders in order to obtain the knowledge of that elder. Interesting.

❖ **Abandoned House – Mask:** The missing, wooden jackal mask **(30)** is on the floor in front of the ripped chapter.

❖ **Abandoned House – Ashes:** The small pile of perfumed ritual incense ashes **(31)** is on the ground next to the wall, near blood splatter.

❖ **Abandoned House – Spectacles:** There are broken eyeglasses **(32)** on the floor near the backdoor. You know someone who is missing some

glasses. This last clue is key to making the correct accusation.

> **SPOILER ALERT: SUSPECT ACCUSED**
>
> Read no further if you want to figure out "Who Done It" on your own.

INVESTIGATION AREA: UNIVERSITY

ACCUSE:

❖ While in the university you can talk to Virginia about the new evidence: handkerchief. She says she misplaced one at the funeral.

❖ **Professor Silas:** Speak to Professor Silas **(14)** who stands on the third floor. Accuse him of the murder and he confesses because he wanted to be the greatest anthropologist in the English Empire and he believed he could do that by eating his colleague's brain.

MOTIVE

The esteemed Professor Byng was the victim of a diabolical plot confected by his colleague and erstwhile acolyte, Professor Silas. Using a powerful spider venom, Silas put his mentor into a deep coma. He went so far as to attempt to eat Byng's brains in an effort to ingest his knowledge! All this was inspired by the very African tribe Professor Byng had himself discovered. No doubt Silas's mind was unbalanced, as he believed he would surpass all anthropologists by absorbing his mentor's cerebrum. Rest in peace, Professor Byng; The Royal Anthropological Society mourns your passing.

LOCKED IN...TO DIE!

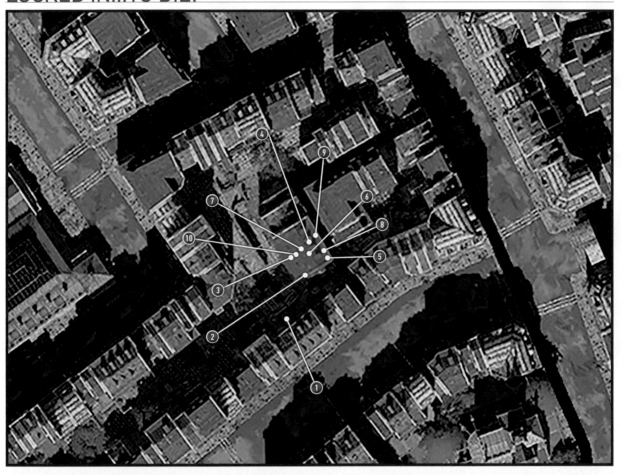

MISSION OVERVIEW

Memory Type: Dreadful Crimes / London Stories	ASSASSIN Jacob or Evie Frye	REWARDS £: 2000 (Max) XP: 1000 (Max) Brass Knuckles: Engraved Knuckles

LOCATION: NORTH WHITECHAPEL

During this crime scene investigation you must solve the perplexing locked-room murder. Artie and Henry Raymond (1) stand in a backyard in The Strand. This is where you start the mystery.

OBJECTIVE: INSPECT BYRON CASHAN'S BODY
INVESTIGATION AREA: CASHAN'S ROOM

CLUES: 10

❖ **Cashan's Room – Cashan's Body:** Byron Cashan's body (2) is located on a bed in his room on the third floor of the apartment building. Pivot northeast from Doyle and Raymond with Eagle Vision on and you see his glowing body in the building beside you. Climb the window and enter the third floor window. Inspect the body to find no signs of a struggle and no wounds.

- ❖ **Cashan's Room – Editor's Letter:** This letter is on the desk beside Cashan's bed. It's a congratulatory letter from his editor about how much readers love his music reviews and how the ensembles in town live in fear of his harsh criticism.
- ❖ **Cashan's Room – Candles:** The yellow candle on the bedpost at the foot of the bed is burned down to the nub. The gas lamps in the building went out last night and everyone used candles for light.
- ❖ **Cashan's Room – Gas Lamp:** The gas lamp is on the wall beside the desk with the letter. It's a common fixture but the light won't turn on. This is a common clue found throughout the apartment building.
- ❖ **Cashan's Room – Air Vent:** the vent is on the wall below the chair rail. This could allow communication between neighboring apartments.
- ❖ **Cashan's Room – Review:** Bryon's review is on the desk behind the open door in the room. It's a crushing review to the Aldwych Chamber Orchestra with a focus on the first violin solo, which he said was a disaster.
- ❖ **Cashan's Room – Window:** The window in Byron's room is shut and locked from the inside. No sign of a break-in.
- ❖ **Cashan's Room – Anonymous Letter:** The letter is on the desk near the window. It's written with a feminine hand. A lady is asking for another adventure with Byron and it is signed, "Florence."
- ❖ **Cashan's Room – Concert Program:** The program is stuck on the filing cabinet near the doorway. It's a ticket for a chamber orchestra that performed a series of Mendelssohn pieces a few nights ago.
- ❖ **Cashan's Room – Door:** The door into Byron's room is a standard door with lock and hinges in a normal state.

SUSPECT: 1

- ❖ **Mrs. Henman:** Speak to Mrs. Henman **(3)** the housekeeper who stands out in the hallway outside of Byron Cashan's room. Talk to her about Cashan, Last Night, and the Concert Program. She says he was a dear friend and each morning she brings him coffee. His door was locked shut this morning. Her husband is the caretaker; they live upstairs. They have the keys to all the apartments. She let herself in and found Byron dead. The lights weren't working last night and she and her husband retired early as not to waste anymore candles. She confirms Cashan was a music critic.

OBJECTIVE: CONTINUE YOUR INVESTIGATION
INVESTIGATION AREA: BLOOMFIELD'S ROOM

CLUES: 6

- ❖ **Bloomfield's Room – Key:** This key **(4)** is located on the edge of the desk just inside the Bloomfield's room, which is adjacent to Cashan's apartment. The key is labeled "Basement."
- ❖ **Bloomfield's Room – Gas Lamp:** The gas lamp is on the wall beside the desk with the key. It's a common fixture but the light won't turn on. Mrs. Henman confirmed that, starting last night, the lights were not working.
- ❖ **Bloomfield's Room – Air Vent:** the vent is on the wall below the chair rail between the chalkboard and the gas lamp on the wall. Allows communication with Cashan's flat.
- ❖ **Bloomfield's Room – Sheet Music:** The sheet music is on the edge of the mail-sorting desk in the back of the room near the chalkboard. It's Andante for Violin and piano in D minor by Felix Mendelssohn. Could the violinist who plays this be the same one Byron crushed in his review?
- ❖ **Bloomfield's Room – Newspaper:** The newspaper is on the mail sorter in the back of the room. One of the three articles in it is about the Aldwych Chamber Orchestra, which has disbanded for lack of funds. Byron's reviews crushed all hope of attracting an audience. If someone were involved with that orchestra, they would have a motive to kill.
- ❖ **Bloomfield's Room – Candelabra:** The candelabra between the windows on the east wall has partially burned candles.

SUSPECT: 2

- ❖ **Mrs. Bloomfield:** Speak to Mrs. Bloomfield **(5)** in the back of her apartment. She is Cashan's neighbor. Talk to her about Cashan, Last Night, and Candles. She's

surprised he's dead, stating he was in the peak of health yesterday but paid too much attention to the caretaker's wife, Mrs. Henman, seeing her nearly every day. Mrs. Bloomfield was knitting last night and started feeling sickly so she opened the window. When the lights went out Mr. Golden handed out candles to everyone.

- **Mr. Bloomfield:** Speak to Mr. Bloomfield **(6)** in the middle of his apartment. Talk to him about Cashan, Bon Vivant, Last Night, and Sheet Music. He said Byron would come home late from his concerts drunk and singing at the top of his lungs—drove

his wife nearly crazy. Mr. Bloomfield says he's an amateur chemist and was fiddling with his experiments in the cellar last night. The sheet music is Mr. Golden's, he rehearses in their apartment during the day while they are out. This connects Golden to playing violin and to the sheet music by Felix Mendelssohn for the violin, which received a bad review by Byron.
- Speak to Mrs. Henman **(3)** the housekeeper after talking to Mrs. Bloomfield. She admits that she and Byron were having an affair.

OBJECTIVE: CONTINUE YOUR INVESTIGATION
INVESTIGATION AREA: GOLDEN'S ROOM
CLUES: 7

- **Golden's Room – Sheet Music:** The sheet music **(7)** is on the edge of the desk to the left as you enter Golden's Room on the second floor. Written on it are a couple of pieces for Violin.
- **Golden's Room – Clothing:** This clothing is on the coat stand to your right as you enter Golden's room. Men's clothes, dirty with soot, are hanging on it.
- **Golden's Room – Gas Lamp:** The gas lamp is on the wall behind the coat rack. It's a common fixture but the light won't turn on.
- **Golden's Room – Candle:** The candle is above the fireplace mantel. This candle is white and comes from the nearby box.
- **Golden's Room – Shavings:** The shavings are on the desk in the back of the room. They appear to be white candle wax shavings. Looks like someone was carving a candle.
- **Golden's Room – Box of candles:** The box of candles is on the floor below the open window. Almost all are gone.
- **Golden's Room – Violin string box:** The box of violin strings are on the mail-sorting desk behind the suspect. There are also some string trimming tools inside.

SUSPECT: 2
- **David Golden:**

  The musician, David Golden **(8)** is standing in his room on the second floor. Speak to him about Cashan, Last Night, and the Box

  of Candles. He claims he works late like Cashan so only met him a couple times over the two years he's lived there. Last night he was out late giving a benefit recital for unemployed musicians. And the candles are for ambience during private recitals, he says.

OBJECTIVE: CONTINUE YOUR INVESTIGATION
INVESTIGATION AREA: BASEMENT
CLUES: 3

- **Basement – Gas Tank:** This gas tank **(9)** is on the first floor near the open north doorway. It's a coal gas tank that supplies gas to all the rooms in the building. It is covered in dirt and soot—like the men's clothing on the coat rack in Golden's room.
- **Basement – Chemical:** A small beaker of yellow liquid, half full, sits on a table near the chemist worktable. It could be poison used inside a candle that is activated when burned.
- **Basement – Chemistry Experiment:** Beakers, funnels, a mortar and pestle, and various chemical compounds are scattered around a worktable in the basement.

OBJECTIVE: CONTINUE YOUR INVESTIGATION
INVESTIGATION AREA: HENMAN'S ROOM
CLUES: 4

- **Henman's Room – Gas Lamp:** The gas lamp is on the wall to the right as you enter Henman's room on the first floor. It's a common fixture but the light won't turn on.
- **Henman's Room – Key Holder:** The key holder is on the opposite side of the entrance from the gas lamp. Keys to all the apartments, as well as the basement, are located here.
- **Henman's Room – Screwdriver:** A screwdriver is on the right side of the long desk in Henman's room. It's just a standard screwdriver. It could have been used to tamper with the gas supply to the apartment lamps.
- **Henman's Room – Candles:** Unused white candles are on the left side of Henman's desk.

SPOILER ALERT: SUSPECT ACCUSED

Read no further if you want to figure out "Who Done It" on your own.

❖ **Mr. Henman:**

Mr. Henman is the caretaker; he is located in his room on the first floor behind his desk **(10)**. Ask him about Cashan, Clothes, and the Screwdriver. He says he didn't know Cashan died. Says he's a lonely man and that his wife helped him as much as she could. He says the screwdriver wasn't put away after he fixed Mr. Golden's music stand the other morning. He left it there and he came to get it back. This means Golden could have used the screwdriver. Talk to him about Gasoline after the screwdriver. He says the gas quit working yesterday and he doesn't know enough about it to fix it himself. He says his clothes were dirty from working in the basement.

INVESTIGATION AREA: GOLDEN'S ROOM

ACCUSE:

❖ **David Golden:** The musician, David Golden **(8)** is the murderer. Accuse him. Cashan destroyed his career with his music reviews. He was the violinist for the Aldwych Chamber Orchestra. He poisoned the candle given to Cashan and made it so the gaslights would not come on to force the use of candles for light.

MOTIVE

So wicked was the pen of Byron Cashan that it brought down an entire orchestra! Scathing review upon scathing review eventually led to the demise of the Aldwych Chamber Orchestra. Perhaps Mr. Cashan was distracted by his irregular friendship with his caretaker's wife, and did not realize that one of his neighbors was the first violinist with the ensemble that his reviews had destroyed. That very same Mr. Golden constructed his revenge with care. Taking advantage of his access to a screwdriver and a key, Golden fashioned a poisoned candle using an unusual chemical found in the basement. He turned off the gas at the mains and handed candles to his neighbors, insuring that his enemy Mr. Cashan received the Candle of Death! Critics beware!

THE MOST HATED MAN IN LONDON

MISSION OVERVIEW

Memory Type: Dreadful Crimes / London Stories	ASSASSIN Jacob or Evie Frye	REWARDS £: 2500 (Max) XP: 1000 (Max)

LOCATION: CITY OF LONDON

In this murder mystery you must deduce which of all the potential murderers actually killed Ashton. You meet Artie and Henry Raymond **(1)** outside an open industrial yard in southeast City of London. They discuss how a crate just crushed the most hated man in London. Raymond says something almost so off key that it had to be damning…but quickly changes the subject.

OBJECTIVE: INSPECT JOHN ASHTON'S BODY
INVESTIGATION AREA: STREET
CLUES: 5

❖ **Street – Mr. Wilkins' Body:** Find Mr. Wilkins' body **(2)** on the sidewalk a block east from your starting position. Upon inspection you find the body is definitely crushed under a crate. But there's also a puncture wound in the back and the victim's skin has an odd, green pallor along with yellowing around the eyes. Inspection of the bullet wound indicates that such a wound would have caused death in 12 minutes. This one will test your math skills.

❖ **Street – Ashton's Agenda:** The agenda **(3)** on the sidewalk beside Mr. Wilkins' body lists his daily activities: Pharmacy 1:00pm; Pub 1:05pm; Apple 1:09pm; Household acct: 1:10pm.

❖ **Street – Watch:** The pocket watch **(4)** on the sidewalk beside the agenda is broken. It's inscribed: "John Ashton." It stopped at 1:17 precisely (when the crate hit it).

❖ **Street – Crate:** The crate **(2)** on the sidewalk on top of Mr. Wilkins' body appears to have fallen from the overhead crane.

❖ **Street – Tracks:** The tracks **(5)** on the sidewalk near the victim's feet appear to be the victim's own footprints. The track can be followed into multiple investigation zones.

THE ESSENTIALS
WALKTHROUGH
SIDE QUESTS
COLLECTIBLES
REWARDS & UNLOCKS
INDEX

ASSOCIATES & ALLIES
LONDON STORIES
WARTIME ARCHIVES
TRAIN HIDEOUT
DREADFUL CRIMES

SUSPECT: 1

❖ **Dr. Chester:** Talk to the concerned doctor **(6)** who was just walking by. He's on the corner near the footprints. Talk to him about Ashton, the Puncture, and his Pallor. Chester says he was stabbed with some kind of spike or something, but six minutes would pass before he died from the wound. He also says there's at least one deadly toxin in his system.

OBJECTIVE: CONTINUE YOUR INVESTIGATION
INVESTIGATION AREA: APPLESTAND
CLUES: 1

❖ **Applestand – Apple:** Find this apple **(7)** on the sidewalk while following Ashton's footprints toward the applestand. It has a single bite out of it. The inside of the apple is oddly pink. Looking at the time on his footprints here with Eagle Vision, he took a bite and dropped it at 1:12pm.

SUSPECT: 2

❖ **Mrs. Ashton:** Mrs. Ashton, **(8)** wife of the victim, is on the street around 1:10pm in the footprints. She had an argument with her husband, which is why she is still standing here apparently. Her hair is held by a knitting needle. Talk to her about Ashton and Hair. Each day she brings him the household expenses just after he eats his apple. She also brought him his invitation to the knighthood ceremony—the one with the special scepter. She's convinced he was not taking her along. She says she often ties her hair with a knitting needle.

❖ **Apple Seller:** This lady **(9)** sells apples daily in this street. Ask her about Ashton. She says he stopped to buy an apple every day at the exact same time. He tries to cheat her out of tuppence.

323

OBJECTIVE: CONTINUE YOUR INVESTIGATION
INVESTIGATION AREA: PUB

CLUES: 2

❖ On your way north to the pub following Ashton's footprints from the applestand you can see that the footprints lead into a pub. The footprint time of entry is 1:05pm and the exit time is 1:07pm.

❖ **Pub - Newspaper:** Find the paper **(10)** on a table on the left as you enter the pub.

❖ **Pub - Revolver:** Find a Webley Boxer revolver **(11)** in a wastebasket on the floor, just past the newspaper on the left near a piano. One chamber is empty. Mr. Hendricks admits to being a gun owner.

SUSPECT: 1

❖ **Mr. Hendricks:** Mr. Hendricks **(12)** stands facing the door at the pub—a prime target for questioning. Ask him about Ashton, Sabotage, and the Gun. He said Ashton stopped in every day to check on business rumors. Hendricks tells you Ashton had "a little jam on the side." Interpret that how you wish. The wife didn't know about it but now the jam wants out of the relationship and he won't let her. When asked about Sabotage, he says Ashton paid workers to wreck his machines. "As long as Ashton was around I'd never prosper," he ends with. He also admits to carrying a revolver with him at all times when pressed about the gun.

OBJECTIVE: CONTINUE YOUR INVESTIGATION
INVESTIGATION AREA: PHARMACY

CLUES: 3

❖ **Pharmacy – Medicine Box:** While following Ashton's footprint path from the pub to the pharmacy, you can find this medicine box **(13)** on the sidewalk just before you reach the entrance to the pharmacy. There's proof by prescription that these are Ashton's blue pills. There's only a few left in the bottle when it was dropped at 1:03pm.

❖ **Pharmacy – Pharmaceutical Cabinet:** Enter the pharmacy and turn left as you enter and look back out the window. There's a cabinet **(14)** there. Search it. It contains chemicals labeled "Warning! Not to be ingested!" One of the drugs is bluish in color, causes erratic movement after 10 minutes, and death after an additional 16 minutes. It also causes jaundice about the eyes and has an extreme anesthetic effect. The second chemical is pinkish in color (like the apple) and is listed as causing erratic movement after two minutes and death after nine. It yields a green tint to the skin.

❖ **Pharmacy – Letter:** This letter **(15)** is located in the back right corner beside the drug counter. It's addressed to the pharmacist from his brother. It says John Ashton was responsible for the foreclosure on their family farm. This gives Mr. Reese motive to kill the victim.

SUSPECT: 2

❖ **Mr. Reese:** Mr. Reese **(16)** is the neighborhood pharmacist standing behind the drug counter. Talk to him about Ashton, Mary, and the Letter. He doesn't want to talk about the letter and says John Ashton came for his blue medication. This medication bottle was found on the sidewalk outside the pharmacy.

❖ **Mary:** Mary is the pharmacist's assistant **(17)** and she stands to his right behind the drug counter. Talk to her about Ashton and she says he seems a bit unpleasant but doesn't really know him. But after talking to the apple seller about Mary, talk to Mary about the Apple. She admits to buying the apple for him but that's all she says… nothing about poisoning him.

❖ It's important you go back and talk to people as more evidence comes to light. Talk to the apple seller **(9)** about Ashton's Pallor. She says,

"He did look strange like, eye's all yellow then he turned pale green when he bit into the apple." And now ask about Mary, the girl that works at the pharmacy. She says Mary bought the apple intended for Mr. Ashton that day. Talk to her after you've talked to Frank (the worker at the construction site). She confirms he was there when they heard the crate hit the ground.

OBJECTIVE: CONTINUE YOUR INVESTIGATION
INVESTIGATION AREA: CONSTRUCTION SITE
CLUES: 2

❖ **Construction Site – Crane:** Find the crane **(18)** in the construction site on the other side of the wall from where the victim lies. The crane did not malfunction. It requires a skilled operator.

❖ **Construction Site – Handbill:** There is a small handbill **(19)** on the ground behind a shack. It reads: "Please contribute to the benefit fund

for the man who had his arm crushed. Any help will be much appreciated."

SUSPECT: 2

❖ **Edie:** Talk to Eddie **(20)** the construction worker farthest from the crane. Talk to him about Ashton, Crane, and the Crushed Arm handbill. He calls Ashton a bastard. His best chum has been maimed for life and Ashton didn't care a bit. He also says he's not a crane operator.

❖ **Frank:** Talk to Frank **(21)** the crane operator standing next to the crane. Ask him about Ashton and 1:17pm, and the Crane. He owns the site and pays the workers but always tried to find ways to cheat them out of their wages. Around 1:17 is when he is given time to eat something. Says about that time he'd be buying an apple at the stand. The apple seller **(9)** will confirm that he was there then.

SPOILER ALERT: SUSPECT ACCUSED

Read no further if you want to figure out "Who Done It" on your own.

INVESTIGATION AREA: APPLE STAND
ACCUSE:

❖ **Mrs. Ashton:** Always look at relatives first, they say. Accuse John Ashton's wife **(8)** for his murder. The time adds up that the puncture wound from Mrs. Ashton's knitting needle killed her husband. She found out about his affair with the pharmacy assistant, Mary. At the end, Doyle seems to think the bit about the Knighthood ceremony was odd.

MOTIVE

Wealthy business owner, John Ashton, was murdered not once, but five times! So hated was he that his business rival, his employee, his wife, his mistress, and his pharmacist all made attempts on his life! Poisoned, shot, stabbed, and finally crushed, Ashton came to a very gruesome end indeed!

NEXT STOP: MURDER!

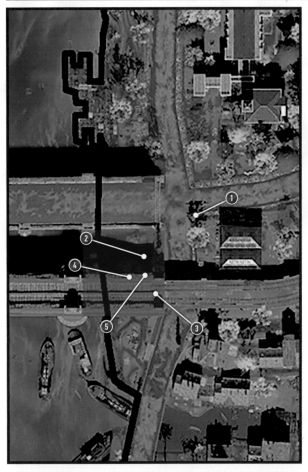

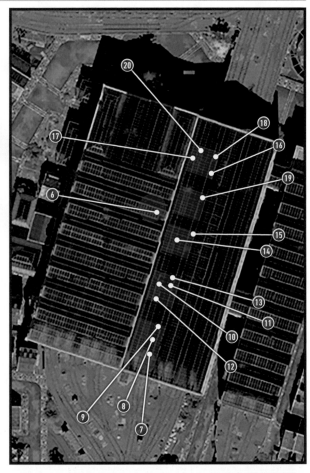

MISSION OVERVIEW

Memory Type: Dreadful Crimes / London Stories	ASSASSIN	REWARDS
	Jacob or Evie Frye	£: 2500 (Max)
		XP: 1000 (Max)

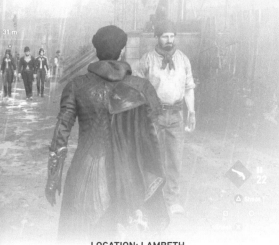

LOCATION: LAMBETH

Solve the mystery of the body found on the banks of The Thames. This time, Artie and Henry Raymond are nowhere to be found; you're on your own. Meet the worker on the corner **(1)** in Lambeth near The Thames. He screams for help and something about foul play and then walks off.

OBJECTIVE: INSPECT THE UNIDENTIFIED BODY
INVESTIGATION AREA: RIVERBANK

CLUES: 3

❖ **Riverbank – Body:** Find the dead body **(2)** to the southwest from where you start the mystery. Jump down off the road wall to the riverbank below. You can find the body in the mud near a small dock. It's a male body dressed in the manner of a wealthy businessman. He is wearing one shoe. He has sustained multiple fractures indicating a fall from a great height. There's nothing on the body that can identify him.

- Near the dead body are drag marks that lead toward the water but stop at an impact mark. If you look up with Eagle Vision from the impact mark you can see a "fall" trail from the rail bridge above.

- **Riverbank – Coat:** Directly under the rail bridge, near the road wall and a small campfire is the discarded coat **(3)**. It is a rich man's coat with a name sewed in the lining: Matthew Killian. You can assume this is the victim's coat and name.
- **Riverbank – Pocket Watch:** Climb to the top of the rail bridge and find this silver watch **(4)** on the north edge from where the body possibly fell. With Eagle Vision, you see a clue that says the edge of the rail bridge was too low for the impact mark made. So the body had to be higher, which means it came from a passing train. The watch is broken and the hands have stopped just after midnight, marking time of death.

SUSPECT: 2

- **Vagrant:** Talk to the vagrant **(5)** under the bridge standing near a tree. Talk to him about the Body, Shelter, and Midnight. He heard a splash so he pulled the body out of the shallow water. He was dead. After asking him about Shelter, ask him about the Coat. He admits to stealing it since the dead man no longer needed it. He says the midnight train is the 616 and stops in the station down the road. Hurry and it might still be there.

OBJECTIVE: CONTINUE YOUR INVESTIGATION
INVESTIGATION AREA: VICTORIA TRAIN STATION

SUSPECT: 1

- **Trainmaster:** Talk to the trainmaster **(6)** inside Victoria Train Station near the north stairs. Talk to him about train 616. He tells you to hurry; the train is leaving now. Check out your Mini-Map and you see five more investigation areas (the train cars) become available to the east.

OBJECTIVE: CONTINUE YOUR INVESTIGATION
INVESTIGATION AREA: SLEEPER 2

CLUES: 2

- **Sleeper 2 – Handbag:** Race to the train to the east before it leaves the station. Once on the train, make your way to the southernmost car, Sleeper 2 and begin your investigation with the Handbag **(7)** on the floor next to the suspect. It contains a letter from Viv's sister. She talks about a nice scheme Viv is pulling off and is interested in pulling off a similar scheme.
- **Sleeper 2 – Note:** The note **(8)** is located on the other side of the suspect from the handbag and near a door. It's a handwritten note, "Come to the restaurant carriage quickly." This note becomes key to the investigation so keep this in the front of your mind as you continue.

SUSPECT: 1

- **Vivian:** Talk to the lady **(9)** on Sleeper 2 about Last Evening, Killian, Letter from Sister, and the Note. She says last night she had some drinks with some gents and then retired to her suite and someone slipped that note under her door a few minutes before midnight. Only Ryan and Wolf were there and both were drunk. She said she did talk to the rich fellow and wonders if something happened to him. When asked about the letter, she admits to flirting with rich folks and that the barman colludes by sliping them a mickey. She takes them back to her room and they nod off before she has to do anything shameful.

OBJECTIVE: CONTINUE YOUR INVESTIGATION
INVESTIGATION AREA: SLEEPER 1
CLUES: 2

❖ **Sleeper 1 – Derringer:** This gun **(10)** is located on the floor on the left side of the train under a seat. It's a small Derringer, ivory-plated with a chamber for two bullets, one is missing.

❖ **Sleeper 1 – Letter:** This letter **(11)** is located on a seat on the right side of the train in Sleeper 1. "Killian will be on the 616 train to Cardiff to sign the papers. You must prevent him from signing them at all costs or we shall be ruined." This looks like good motive to kill someone.

SUSPECT: 2

❖ **Sam:** The valet, Sam **(12)** stands in a corner on the left on Sleeper 2. Ask him about Last Evening and Killian. He says that Mr. Wolf had a few to drink with Mr. Killian then Vivian invited herself over to have a glass with them. Mr. Wolf was buying many drinks for Killian and they started to argue but Killian ended up leaving with Vivian around 11:30pm. Mr. Wolf became very tired but only had one drink and retired well before midnight. Sam stayed in the dining car for a few drinks with the barman.

❖ **Angus Wolf:** Mr. Wolf **(13)** stands in a corner on the right, not far past the letter on Sleeper 2. Ask him about Last Evening, Valet, and Killian. He said it was a surprise to see Killian on the train; they've had previous business

dealings. He confirms they had a few drinks together and they argued a bit over business and money. He confirms that Killian and Vivian hit it off famously. He also raises the point that Sam, the valet, is very strong, making him useful in many situations. However, do not jump to conclusions, there are several men strong enough to lift a man to the top of a train.

OBJECTIVE: CONTINUE YOUR INVESTIGATION
INVESTIGATION AREA: PASSENGER CARRIAGE
CLUES: 1

❖ **Passenger Car – Shoe:** Climb to the top of the Passenger Carriage to find this Shoe **(14)** on the rooftop. Be careful; the train is moving now. The shoe is caught on a bolt and it matches the one found on the victim. The body was obviously thrown from atop this car.

SUSPECT: 1

❖ **Luke:** Luke **(15)** stands in the far right corner on the Passenger Carriage. Noises on the roof woke him up at night (referencing

the shoe clue above). He points out that you'd have to be a strong fellow to drag someone up on the roof to push them off. He acts like he didn't know Killian is on the train, but he used to work for Killian at the foundry and that none of the workers have ever seen what he looks like. He confirms that Vivian has a scam going on with the bartender. Talk to him about Midnight and he says Vivian had another one of her visitors in her compartment then.

OBJECTIVE: CONTINUE YOUR INVESTIGATION
INVESTIGATION AREA: RESTAURANT CARRIAGE
CLUES: 3

❖ **Restaurant Car – Sleeping Pills:** The restaurant carriage is actually two connected carriages. The first car you enter has no clues, but one suspect. Continue to the second car to find the pills **(16)** on a corner shelf on your right next to the entry door. The bottle is half empty.

❖ **Restaurant Car – Newspaper:** On the second restaurant car you can find this newspaper **(17)** on a chair at a dining table. It's an article about Matthew Killian's efforts to close an enormous business deal. Killian is well known for replacing workers with machinery. There's a likeness of Killian that matches the victim.

❖ **Restaurant Car – Pamphlets:** This pamphlet **(18)** is in the second restaurant car on a table on the right. It's an anti-industrialist pamphlet.

SUSPECT: 2

❖ **Ryan:** Ryan **(19)** is the bartender and stands near the exit on the first restaurant car. Talk to him about Pills, and the Scheme. He says he

keeps the sedatives at the bar for passengers that need to sleep regardless of the noise from the train. He admits to slipping the pills in each Killian's and Wolf's drinks last night and then Vivian would pick the richest one.

❖ **Peter:** Peter **(20)**, the train steward, is standing at the end of the second restaurant car. Talk to him about Last Evening, Killian, and Vivian. He said nothing was unusual until you arrived with the story of a murder. He was tiding up in the passenger cart when Vivian ran by him at midnight. She thought someone was looking for her, prompted by the letter she received.

SPOILER ALERT: SUSPECT ACCUSED

Read no further if you want to figure out "Who Done It" on your own.

SIDE QUESTS

ASSOCIATE WELCOME

LONDON STORIES

WWW TIME ANOMALY

TRAIN HIDEOUT

DREADFUL CRIMES

INVESTIGATION AREA: RESTAURANT CAR 2

ACCUSE:

❖ **Peter:** Peter **(20)** is big enough to have lifted Killian to the rooftop. Peter was a former employee of Matthew Killian, put out of work by Killian's mechanization. It was a last minute crime as he didn't know he was going to be on the train but recognized him from the photo in the newspaper.

MOTIVE

Industrialist Matthew Killian was drugged and thrown from the top of a moving train by his former employee, Peter Jespers! Put out of work by the mechanization of Killian's factory, Peter found employment as a humble train steward. However, one evening Peter realized that Killian was on his very train (prior to this journey Peter had never seen Killian, but now recognized him from a recent newspaper article). Peter, knowing that frequent passenger Vivian often swindled wealthy fellow passengers, waited until she lured Killian to her compartment. He cunningly arranged for her to be called away by means of an anonymous note. Peter then used his considerable strength to lift the drugged magnate and drag him to the top of the train, whence he threw him to his death at midnight! Killian's rival, Angus Wolf, had hoped to get Killian so inebriated as to prevent him from participating in a business meeting on the following day, but Wolf himself fell afoul of the drugged brandy and slept through the entire episode! As for Peter the murderer…perhaps he meted out justice, in turn he will now meet justice himself!

CONJURING UP A KILLING!

MISSION OVERVIEW

Memory Type: Dreadful Crimes / London Stories	**ASSASSIN** Jacob or Evie Frye	**REWARDS** £: 2500 (Max)
		XP: 1000 (Max)

LOCATION: SOUTHWEST WESTMINSTER

In this mystery you must solve the murder of spiritualist Thaddeus the Amazing. Meet Charles Dickens **(1)** near the park and train station in southwest Westminster.

OBJECTIVE: REACH THE SÉANCE

❖ When you reach the Psychic's House southwest from where you meet Charles Dickens, you walk in on a séance in progress. The lights flicker out, a "bang" is heard and the Psychic is found dead when they flicker back on a second later.

OBJECTIVE: INSPECT THADDEUS THE AMAZING'S BODY
INVESTIGATION AREA: PSYCHIC'S HOUSE

CLUES: 7

❖ **Psychic's House – Thaddeus' Body:** Find Thaddeus Smith's body **(2)** slumped over in a chair at the séance table on the first floor of his house. His hair and clothing have been slightly scorched from the "explosion." A bloody knife is stuck in his torso. There are five suspects (the séance attendees) about the room.

❖ **Psychic's House – Timer and Flashpot:** This item is found on the floor to the right of the body. It is a rudimentary timer with the charred remains of a fuse. The fuse leads to the empty plaster cylinder of what contained a non-lethal amount of gunpowder to produce a flash and smoke. This is evidence that the Psychic may not be legit and used props to enhance his show.

❖ **Psychic's House – Client List:** The list is found on a desk in the hallway at the top of the stairs on the second floor. All that is important is that Dr. Wilburn is missing from this list of clients, their addresses and a money amount per séances. It is unclear what a second column of money refers to. Why is the doctor not on the list?

❖ **Psychic's House – Threatening Note:** This item is found on the floor on the other side of the doorway near the desk and client list. "For

the love of God, get his signature at the next session, or I swear I'll expose you! —A. R." Keep these initials in mind as you meet new suspects.

❖ **Psychic's House – Old Note:** The Old Note is found on the floor at the foot of the bed in the room on the second floor. It looks to be a week old. "I've found a tramp who lives on the street near one of the pigeons. The fellow smokes like a chimney and for the price of a few cigarettes he supplies me with all the information we need." Sounds like the Psychic's source for finding details on his clients, fooling them into thinking his information comes from beyond.

❖ **Psychic's House – Receipt:** Find this item on the second floor in the northeast corner under a small table near the fireplace. Theatrical Supply: Flash pot, 8 shillings. Proof that the flashpot was purchased by the "Psychic."

❖ **Psychic's House – Legal Papers:** The Legal Papers are found on the second floor on a table near the windows, along the north wall. It's an unsigned paper, which would enable Thaddeus Smith to act as Howard Roberts' legal representative. Was the Psychic in cahoots with someone to swindle one of his clients?

SUSPECT: 5

❖ **Douglas:** Speak to Douglas **(3)** standing closest to the entryway on the first floor of the house. Talk to him about Thaddeus and the Séance. He thinks Thaddeus is nothing more than a showman saying the more people at a séance the more dramatic it becomes. He doesn't believe in the afterworld, but if it comforts his lady, Ursula, he sees no harm. Douglas is Lady Ursula's butler.

❖ **Lady Ursula:** Speak to Ursula **(4)** standing near the windows in the living room. She comes to séances after the death of her cat, Mittens. She wants to reach out to her dead cat and also has accepted her own fate as she is not well and does not have long to live. She wants her dead cat to decide to whom she should leave her inheritance.

❖ **Howard Roberts:** Speak to Roberts **(5)** also standing in the living room but closer to the séance table than Ursula. Talk to him about Thaddeus and the Legal Paper. He's been coming to séance after séance getting a number each time but never receiving the full multi-digit bank account number he needs. The psychic had promised today he would get the full number. If he had signed the legal paper it would prove to his father that he had absolute trust in Thaddeus.

❖ **Dr. Wilburn:** Speak to the doctor **(6)** standing in the séance room to the left of the victim. Talk to him about Thaddeus and the Séance. He calls Thaddeus an incredible psychic but stumbles on his words and says he "…came to clarify his son's…err ah… his personal financial matters." He also says that Thaddeus predicted his own death.

❖ **Janice Asquith:** Speak to Janice **(7)** standing in the séance room to the right of the body near the fireplace about Thaddeus and the séance. She's convinced Thaddeus was genuine. He had all sorts of personal details of her comings and goings that she believes he could have not otherwise known had he not been a psychic. She said he was going to put her in contact with her sister. Now ask her about her dead Sister. She was hoping that her dead sister would help her decide if she should get married to a certain fellow or not. She's referring to Mr. Everett Boyd.

❖ Now there are three new investigation areas available on the map: Lady Ursula's House, Asquiths' House, and Robert's House.

OBJECTIVE: CONTINUE YOUR INVESTIGATION
INVESTIGATION AREA: ROBERTS' HOUSE

CLUES: 3

❖ **Roberts' House – Sydney Newspaper Clipping:** Find this clipping **(8)** on a corner table on the first floor of the Roberts' House. This is in the back right corner near a window. The article describes another story exactly like your mystery unfolding only it happened a year ago. A Psychic (Felix Magnus) predicts his own death at his next séance and reveals to his clients that their family members were using him to swindle them. There was also a doctor present at this event attending as a client.

❖ **Roberts' House – Paper:** Find this paper **(9)** on a small table with drawers at the top of the stairs on the second floor. There are three incomplete bank account numbers crossed out: "Bentland bank? A7?; Bank of Kent? 270?; York Bank? A72?" These are signs of someone trying multiple, incomplete account numbers at multiple banks.

❖ **Roberts' House – Note Added to Father's Will:** Find this note **(10)** on a small table next to a bookcase in the bedroom on the second floor. It's an amendment to add to the father's will specifying, "the bulk of my fortune is safely secured in an account, the particulars of which will be communicated by word-of-mouth to my son."

SUSPECT: 1

❖ **Anne Roberts:** Speak to Anne **(11)** standing in the middle of the room on the first floor. She is Howard Robert's sister. Talk to her about Howard Roberts, the Séance, and the Legal Papers. She feels the séances are a waste of her brother's time. She thinks that him giving the psychic power of attorney is very unusual. She also says that her brother inherited a large amount of their father's money but some was hidden in a secret account and her brother is obsessed with getting to it. She feels it can't be a significant amount of money there. Her initials match those on the threatening letter found at the Psychic's house.

OBJECTIVE: CONTINUE YOUR INVESTIGATION
INVESTIGATION AREA: LADY URSULA'S HOUSE
CLUES: 3

❖ **Lady Ursula's House – Boston Newspaper Clipping:** When you walk into Ursula's front door you can find this clipping **(18)** to your right near the fireplace. It's yet another story of a Psychic foretelling his own death dated seven months ago. Roberto Magnifico. It's the exact story as the last and what seems to be the story you are in now. The family traduced the victim with the psychic's help and death by explosion. What are the odds?

❖ **Lady Ursula's House – Letter:** Under the bed on the second floor is the letter **(19)** to Douglas from an accomplice, someone who found yet another story on a psychic predicting his death at a séance. The writer is convinced that they will be exposed at the next séance just the way the others were. The writer demands a way out.

❖ **Lady Ursula's House – Lady Ursula's Will:** On the third floor, on top of a bedside desk is Ursula's will **(20)**. It reads, "To Miriam, my maid, and to Douglas, my butler, I leave my Belshingham china…I leave my dear cat Mittens all my remaining worldly goods, in the hope that they bring him even a small portion of the joy he has brought me." Scrawled in a margin is: "Whatever will I do now that my dear Mittens is no more?" How do you think this makes the maid and butler feel? All that money to a cat!

SUSPECT: 1

❖ **Miriam:** Speak to Miriam, **(21)** the maid on the first floor. Speak to her about Lady Ursula, Douglas, and Mittens. Mariam and the butler, Douglas, are to be married. She says he's waiting for a little nest egg; he says he'll have some money soon. She says since Mittens has passed on, Lady Ursula has been going to the psychic to find out what to do with that money she left to the cat.

OBJECTIVE: CONTINUE YOUR INVESTIGATION
INVESTIGATION AREA: ASQUITHS' HOUSE
CLUES: 4

❖ **Asquiths' House – Diary:** There's an open, third-story window on the south side of the home. Find Janice's diary **(12)** under the head of the bed on the third floor of the Asquiths' house. Diary entry: "I have some affections for Everett, but I don't think my sister would approve of him. She always bade me to strive for more than that which merely appears directly in front of my nose. If only father weren't urging me otherwise!" This is Janice's diary and she writes about her dead sister.

Asquiths' House – Business Letter: Find this business letter **(13)** on the floor on the second level of the house. It's among scattered books below a bookshelf in the study. The very interesting letter reads, "Mr. Everett Boyd's business plans appear to be sound. As long as he has no other pressing obligations, I believe that—if your daughter accepts his proposal—the money you settle on the happy couple would mean the success of Mr. Boyd's venture and your daughter, Janice, would live a comfortable life." It's important to note that her father is a suspect in this room.

Asquiths' House – Coat: This Coat **(14)** is on a coatrack at the front door. There's a letter in a pocket, "Boyd, dear lad, if you don't get me the money by the end of the month, you will be in a heap of trouble. The kind of trouble that hurts. Need I say more?" Boyd needs money quickly. Could this be why he wants to marry Janice?

Asquiths' House – Cigarette Butts: Exit the house through the front door, turn right and find the cigarette butts **(15)** on the ground near the alley. They seem to have been left by a vagrant. You can still smell the tobacco smoke. The tobacco scent is a trail that leads to another investigation zone, the street corner. Do not follow it yet, instead, interrogate the nearby suspects.

SUSPECT: 2

Colonel Asquith: Speak to Janice's father, Colonel Asquith **(16)**, on the second floor of the house. Talk to him about Thaddeus and Sister (his daughter).

He's furious with the psychic for taking advantage of his daughter's love for her departed sister. "With Thaddeus gone, things can get back to normal" is what he says. And continues, "Janice's engagement to Everett Boyd can be announced at last!" Talk to him about Engagement and he talks about Boyd's success, not his daughter's happiness.

Everett Boyd: Speak to Janice's betrothed, Everett Boyd **(17)** on the first floor near a bookshelf. Talk about Thaddeus, the Engagement, and business. He calls Thaddeus a swindler and is upset he is causing a delay to his marriage to Janice. When asked about business, he mentions an investment he can make in a local brewery. He'll use the family's money to invest and make a fortune, he says.

OBJECTIVE: CONTINUE YOUR INVESTIGATION
INVESTIGATION AREA: STREET CORNER
SUSPECT: 1

Billy: Follow the cigarette scent from the Asquith House to Billy **(22)**, the vagrant (heavy smoker) on the street corner to the north. Ask him about Tramp and he admits that's him. He says some bloke comes about so often and gives him a silver sixpence to tell him everything about the people in that house. Ask him Who. He said a regular looking fellow that he's seen go into the office down the street. This opens the last investigation zone.

OBJECTIVE: CONTINUE YOUR INVESTIGATION
INVESTIGATION AREA: OFFICE
CLUES: 4

Office – Note: All of the clues are on the top floor of the office. The note **(23)** is on the floor below the window on the right as you enter the only room on the top floor. "She says the account number is A72 at Kentish Bank."

Office – Business Cards: Several business cards **(24)** are on a piano stool beside the piano. They're for a medical doctor. All are identical except each is printed with a different name. Sounds like the doctor is suspect.

Office – Thaddeus' Note: This note **(25)** is on the floor under the window on the southeast corner of the room. It reads: "W. Arrive after the others as usual. It will deflect suspicion. Also, make certain that we get a big flash this time—they must be convinced it's enough to kill me! —T. the Amazing." Sounds like the doctor was in cahoots with the Psychic, which could explain how his death was declared at other séances, but the Psychic continues onto the next town to pull another scam.

Office – Client Files: The damning files **(26)** are on the table on the west wall of the only room on the top floor. They contain details regarding Thaddeus' clients. For example: —"Wants cat to tell he should inherit." —"Janice's sister called her 'Sissy.'" —"The cat loved to play with Lady U's teaspoons." —"Wants you to tell her that her sister approves of the marriage." —"Knows acct number. Needs his signature to access." Information, no doubt, obtained by the paid spy, the Vagrant.

SPOILER ALERT: SUSPECT ACCUSED

Read no further if you want to figure out "Who Done It" on your own.

INVESTIGATION AREA: PSYCHIC'S HOUSE

ACCUSE:

❖ **Douglas:** You can get more information from the suspects in the Psychic's House now, but it's apparent now who done it. Accuse Douglas of the murder.

MOTIVE

Spiritualist Thaddeus Smith routinely swindled not just his clients, but his clients' friends and families! In city after city, Thaddeus and his confederate, "Dr." Wilburn, lured in those desperate to speak to the departed in the after-world. But the swindlers were doubly paid, first by their clients, then by those close to them, who wished to manipulate them! In such a fashion, Miss Anne Roberts hoped to gain legal authority for her brother in order to remove funds from a secret bank account; Mr. Everett Boyd wished to ensure his marriage to Janice Asquith would take place in order to gain a lucrative settlement; and Lady Ursula's butler, Douglas, wished to have her dead cat counsel her to leave her fortune to[md]Douglas himself!

But none of these accounted for Thaddeus' odd quirk of enjoying giving a good lesson to his fellow swindlers once he'd emptied the coffers of his clients. Thaddeus then habitually exposed these manipulators before escaping by feigning his own death! This was corroborated by the supposed Dr. Wilburn, purporting to be simply one more client. But on this occasion, Anne realized the coming exposure, and enticed the butler Douglas (the only swindler present at the crime scene) to murder Thaddeus in the dark! Farewell Thaddeus! You may now speak to those in the after-world at your leisure!

MURDER AT THE PALACE!

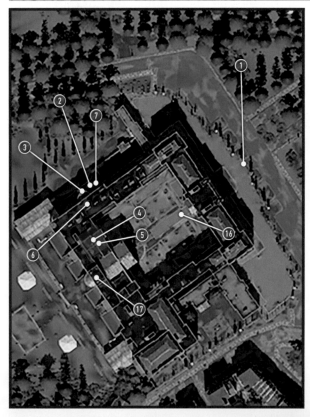

MISSION OVERVIEW

Memory Type: Dreadful Crimes / London Stories	**ASSASSIN** Jacob or Evie Frye	**REWARDS** £: 2750 (Max) XP: 1500 (Max) Cane-Sword: Dove Cane-Sword

LOCATION: BUCKINGHAM PALACE, WESTMINSTER

Solve the perplexing murder of a palace guard. Meet Frederick Abberline outside the palace **(1)** to start the investigation. He says there's been a murder at the palace and tensions are high. The Queen is very nervous about security.

OBJECTIVE: FOLLOW ABBERLINE

❖ Follow Abberline from the front of the palace **(1)** to the Queen's Study **(2)** on the second floor of the palace.

OBJECTIVE: INSPECT THE PALACE GUARDSMAN
INVESTIGATION AREA: QUEEN'S STUDY

CLUES: 6

❖ **Queen's Study – Guardsman's Body:** Find the guardsman's body **(2)** on the floor propped up against the screen near the wall safe. His eyes and mouth are wide open. There are no signs of violence.

❖ **Queen's Study – Guest List:** Find this on top of the roll-top desk **(3)** near the body. It's a list of invites to the investiture this evening. The Queen will knight several industrialists who oppose child labor.

❖ **Queen's Study – Vase:** A broken vase **(4)** is on the floor beside the guardsman's body. This is a sign of struggle.
❖ **Queen's Study – Letter from Scotland Yard:** This letter **(5)** is on a small table near the chairs in front of the fireplace. It's a letter to Her Majesty's Private Secretary, Sir Henry Ponsonby. He warns the secretary of a young boy (Artie!) being abducted and they think there's a connection to disrupt tonight's ceremony at the palace.

❖ **Queen's Study – Window:** Discover the broken window shards **(6)** on the floor below the west-facing windows. The broken area is large enough to allow access to someone.
❖ **Queen's Study – Vault:** Find the vault **(7)** on the wall next to the dead guardsman's body. It's marked by deep gashes as if someone attempted to break in. The Queen enters the room after you search the vault.

OBJECTIVE: REACH OUTSIDE THE STUDY

❖ When you have inspected the vault in the Queen's Study, the Queen enters the room and requests some time to be alone in the room while she looks in the safe.

OBJECTIVE: WAIT FOR THE QUEEN

❖ You can hear the Queen talking to herself while opening the safe if you activate Eagle Vision while out in the hallway waiting. She's concerned someone is after the scepter and has to see it with her own eyes to know it's safe. She says it's "untouched" so all is well.

SUSPECT: 1
❖ **Queen Victoria:** When the Queen opens the door to her Study, reenter the room and interrogate her. She becomes the first suspect. Ask her about the Body, the Vault, and the Event. She said the guardsman was dead when she arrived. She is the only one with the vault combination and knowledge that it contains the dove scepter to be used in tonight's knighthood ceremony. All of tonight's luminaries are invited to the ceremonies.

THE ESSENTIALS
WALKTHROUGH
SIDE QUESTS
COLLECTIBLES
REFERENCE & INDEX
INDEX

ASSOCIATES & ALLIES
LONDON STORIES
REAL-TIME ANTWERP
STRONG HUNTING
DREADFUL CRIMES

- ❖ **Artie's Yard – Evidence Wall:** Your little buddy, Artie has been abducted. His backyard is your investigation zone. Get a carriage and make the long haul northward. In his backyard you find two suspects and an evidence wall **(8)**. Here you find that Doyle made clue connections from all the mysteries you've solved together, links from one murder to the other. And the final scrawl is unfinished: "Leading to… Raymond—".
- ❖ **Artie's Yard – Blank Paper:** Pivot around from the evidence wall and find this apparently blank notepaper **(9)** on the opposite wall.

SUSPECT: 2

- ❖ **Buck:** Talk to the little boy **(10)** closest to the evidence wall. Ask him about Artie, and the Evidence Wall. He thinks there's a master criminal on the loose by how Artie was acting. He said Artie went missing in the morning. He said he was going on about the Queen for the last day or two…thinks she's in some sort of trouble.
- ❖ **Dooley:** Ask the second boy **(11)**, Dooley, about Artie, the Evidence Wall, and Henry Raymond. He said Raymond had come by on the way from his publisher with his latest penny dreadful and was pretty excited about it. Dooley never liked him much. The most important thing is to ask him about the evidence wall. He tells you he writes the important stuff with invisible ink. Ask about the Blank Paper next. He tells you if you have smoke, you can see what it says.
- ❖ Return to the Blank Paper **(9)** on the wall facing the evidence wall. Throw a smoke bomb at the ground and re-examine the blank paper. This is written in invisible ink: "Purlock Publishing…Henry Raymond… It's all connected…Follow the clues!" This opens a new area of investigation.

- ❖ **Purlock Publishing – Dynamite crates:** Head southwest a block to Purlock Publishing. The front door is open. There are no clues on the first floor. Dynamite crates **(12)** can be found on the second floor hallway. They are empty but marked "Prescott Munitions No. 408."

- ❖ **Purlock Publishing – Map:** This map of Buckingham Palace is on a wall **(13)** on the third floor. The Queen's study is circled in black.

❖ **Purlock Publishing – Galley Proof:** This proof **(14)** is on a shelf on the top floor.

❖ **Purlock Publishing – Anti-royalist Pamphlets:** Find these pamphlets **(15)** in the same room with the galley proof, on a table near the south corner window. It reads: "Down with the Monarchy!" "An End to our Suffering under Victoria!" "The Queen must pay for her Sins!"

OBJECTIVE: SPEAK TO A PALACE GUARDSMAN
INVESTIGATION AREA: BUCKINGHAM PALACE, WESTMINSTER

❖ Return to Buckingham Palace and talk to the guardsman **(16)** in the middle of the long walkway to the palace entrance.

THE ESSENTIAL

WALKTHROUGH

SIDE QUESTS

COLLECTIBLES

REFERENCE & ANALYSIS

INDEX

ASSOCIATES & INCOME

LONDON STORIES

WWI TIME ANOMALY

TRAIN HIDEOUT

DREADFUL CRIMES

73

OBJECTIVE: EVACUATE THE 3 PARTY GUESTS
OBJECTIVE: LOCATE THE QUEEN

❖ You have one minute to evacuate three party guests. Stop talking to the guard if he's still yappin' and rush into the palace towards the green blips representing the party guests. Run into the palace and turn right to Warn the crowd standing near the stairs. Press and hold the ⊙ / Ⓑ button.

❖ Turn and run up the opposite stairs (to the left as you enter the palace). Stop to Warn the group at the top of the first set of stairs.

❖ Continue up the stairs and run in the direction of the Queen's Study to Warn the crowd standing in the hallway outside the Study.

LOCATION: MEMORY PALACE

❖ After freeing the guests you discover Henry Raymond has tricked you. There's no explosion. You enter the Animus white room with Henry Raymond. Labels surround him: "*Kidnapped Artie? Mad Bomber? Penny Dreadfuls, Who is he?* and *He is the key!*" At this point you revisit the key areas of all the murder mysteries you worked on but this time they appear in the white room.

LOCATION: MEMORY PALACE; A SIMPLE MATTER OF MURDER!

❖ Enter the Whitechapel G.A. gate and speak to Artie about "why evacuate?" He responds, "look beyond the obvious."

LOCATION: MEMORY PALACE;
CONJURING UP A KILLING!

❖ Move away from the Whitechapel murder scene to the psychic's séance table and interrogate Douglas—the accused. He says, "nothing more than a showman….

LOCATION: MEMORY PALACE;
PURLOCK PUBLISHING

❖ Move away from the séance scene and Purlock Publishing appears nearby. Inspect the dynamite crates clearly marked, "Prescott Munitions No. 408." Look away and another past crime scene appears. Walk to it.

LOCATION: MEMORY PALACE;
DEATH STALKS THE COLONEL

❖ When you enter the new scene you recognize it from your earlier crime scene, Death Stalks The Colonel. Prescott's body lies at the Munitions Factory. Inspect the dynamite crates, empty munitions crates clearly marked, "Prescott Munitions No. 408."

LOCATION: MEMORY PALACE;
THREE HENRYS

❖ Walk out of the crime scene, heading toward the three Henry Raymonds standing back, to back, to back. You must choose which Henry is the Henry that did the crimes. Which one is telling the truth? You must choose between the Diversion, Save Lives, or the Terrorist Henry. Talk to them all or just go straight to Diversion and "Accuse" him. This unlocks another, old crime scene…

LOCATION: MEMORY PALACE;
THE CASE OF THE CONFLICTED COURTSHIP.

❖ After accusing Diversion Henry, walk into the next crime scene simulation. It's Prudence Brown from the Conflicted Courtship. She is not the focus here; continue past her to the picnic table. Inspect the scattered papers on the table. They read: "I always got what I want." Written by a left-handed man.

LOCATION: MEMORY PALACE;
THE MOST HATED MAN IN LONDON

❖ Now walk to the corner where the crate has crushed Mr. Ashton. Walk past him and talk to his wife you accused. Talk to Mrs. Ashton about "Diversion from what?" She says she brought him the invitation to the knighthood ceremony, the one with the special scepter.

LOCATION: MEMORY PALACE;
LOCKED IN…TO DIE

❖ Now go into the Locked In…To Die set and inspect the newspaper next to Cashan's bed. There are several articles, one about the coming ceremony wherein the queen will use the storied Scepter with the Dove to knight an industrialist.

LOCATION: MEMORY PALACE;
CONJURING UP A KILLING!

❖ Head back into the psychic's set and interrogate Colonel Asquith who is now standing near a china cabinet. Talk to him about "diversion from what?" and he responds, "Never trust a man who tells you what you want to hear. He's after something."

LOCATION: MEMORY PALACE;
THREE HENRYS

❖ Confront the three Henrys again. This time there are: Kidnapper, Murderer, and Master Thief Henrys. Talk to them all, or just get to it and "Accuse" Master Thief Henry. He says he got the scepter with your help.

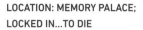

LOCATION: MEMORY PALACE; DEATH STALKS THE COLONEL

❖ Now return to the Death Stalks The Colonel set. Curtis is there now. Talk to him about "how was it stolen?" "No one questions you when you wear a uniform," he responds.

LOCATION: MEMORY PALACE; THE MYSTERY OF THE TWICE-DEAD PROFESSOR!

❖ Enter the professor's house and inspect the spider on the edge of the table by the professor's dead body near the front door. It is a large distinctive spider, curled up in death. If you walk up the stairs here and drop off the end of the set you find Artie in the street. Talk to him.

LOCATION: MEMORY PALACE; STREET BLOCKADE

❖ Talk to Artie in the blocked-off street set next to the Death Stalks the Colonel set. Ask, "How was it stolen?" He suspects the solution will turn on geometry.

THE ESSENTIALS
WALKTHROUGH
SIDE QUESTS
COLLECTIBLES
REFERENCE & ANALYSIS
INDEX

ASSOCIATES & INCOME
LONDON STORIES
WWI TIME ANOMALY
TRAIN HIDEOUT
DREADFUL CRIMES

LOCATION: MEMORY PALACE; BUCKINGHAM PALACE, QUEEN'S STUDY

❖ You must again accuse one of three Henrys. Accuse Observe Henry. Safe Cracker and Coerce Henrys are incorrect. He says "quite right." And he explains, the dead guardsman was him; he used the poisonous spider to fake death. He had a perfect view of the safe when the queen opened it to check on the contents. He has stolen the scepter. He says he left clues for you at every turning point. He feels accomplished that he has outwitted you.

LOCATION: BUCKINGHAM PALACE; ENTRYWAY

❖ You exit the Animus white room and you spawn with Frederick Abberline screaming at you to wake up. He says Raymond has taken Artie hostage, they're on the roof, and your twin is here to help you. You see a green blip coming from the palace's rooftop. Rope Launch there now.

❖ Enter the Reach marker **(17)** on top of the palace. Here you see Raymond holding the scepter with Artie as his hostage at the edge of a rooftop. You hold a gun on Raymond and then control switches to the other twin assassin.

❖ As the other Frye twin, get to the rooftops but come up behind Raymond from the backyard side of the palace and silently execute Raymond, who now has a "Kill" icon over his head.

❖ You killed Henry Raymond and saved Artie. That completes the Dreadful Crime memories. Unfortunately, they are no longer repayable in the Progress Tracker, because now you know who done it. Enjoy the happy ending and enjoy the reward: the Dove Cane-Sword.

MOTIVE

Little Artie Doyle helped his friends solve several murders, all under the eye of Penny Dreadful author Henry Raymond. But Raymond was mad! All along, Raymond was plotting a final crime to demonstrate to the world his fiendish cleverness. Taking a uniform and some venom from the sites of previous murders, he entered the palace and feigned death in order to gain access to the precious Sceptre with the Dove! But all came to naught, and Raymond himself was slain!

339

COLLECTIBLES

Within *Assassin's Creed Syndicate* there are hundreds of things to collect. While some of the collectibles lead to item unlocks and resources, others are purely for collecting. Maps can be purchased from the various merchants in the city to mark all of the collectibles on the map. When you are close to the item, use Eagle Vision to hunt it down. This is made much easier if you have the upgrade that allows you to see and mark through walls with Eagle Vision.

 CHESTS

Chests are found everywhere throughout the cities. Each Chest grants you an amount of money and valuable crafting materials used to upgrade your equipment. Buying the map to mark the Chests is always a good idea. If you collect the Chests marked, you will definitely turn a profit. Hold the action button near the Chest to loot it.

 PRESSED FLOWERS

Pressed flowers are located inside of books that are usually left on a park bench or near a tombstone. Collecting them unlocks different dyes for your clothing.

 POSTER ADS

While many Poster Ads litter the streets of London, only a few are collectible. These Ads are normally located at the front of the alleys branching off of the main road, or in heavily trafficked walkways in between and under buildings in the city.

 BEER BOTTLES

Beer Bottles can be found in and around the various bars on the map. Purchasing the drinking guide from the merchant marks all of them on the map, making it easy to find the ones you are missing. Press the action button when you are near the Beer.

PRESSED FLOWER UNLOCKS

	NAME	DESCRIPTION		NAME	DESCRIPTION
5	Violet	Violet, woody brown, and grass green.	20	Black	Black, pink, and purple
10	Fuchsia	Fuchsia, muted green, and turquoise.	25	Steel Gray	Steel gray, pink, and dark gray
15	Midnight Blue	Midnight blue, warm gray, and terra cotta.	30	Crimson	Deep crimson, salmon, and gray.

LARGE CHESTS

Large Chests require lock picking and a little bit more searching to find them. They do not contain resources, but rather blue prints and unique crafting materials.

HELIX GLITCHES

Helix Glitches are found around the city, usually near high points or hanging over the middle of streets. Once you have the Rope Launcher, collecting these becomes much easier. Simply move through the Glitch to collect it. Helix Glitches unlock Audio Logs, which you can find in the Encyclopedia under Present Day Assassin Intel.

HELIX CREDITS

Earn Helix Credits by collecting Helix Glitches, Letters from the Front, Beer Bottles, and Historical Poster Ads. For more information on Helix Credits, please see The Essentials section of the guide.

SECRETS OF LONDON

Keep your ears tuned in while walking the streets of London, listening for the faint sound of a music box. These music boxes are the Secrets of London, collecting all of them grants you access to a treasure map leading you into Michael Reuge's Vault, a secret vault hidden beneath the city where you find the Precursor Armor.

ROYAL CORRESPONDENCE

Royal Correspondences are misplaced letters from London's elite. Unlike other collectibles, Royal Correspondences are only found in the Borough of Westminster. They appear as a letter with a red wax seal. Picking up one of the letters grants you immediate XP, collecting all of them grants you access to Lady Anne Greenwood's Cape as well as an Achievement/Trophy for your effort.

LETTERS FROM THE FRONT

These Letters are only found in the WWI Time Anomaly. Be sure to collect them all when exploring London during the Great War.

CITY OF LONDON

 CHESTS

	DESCRIPTION
1	On the roof of the small brick church next to the bell tower.
2	On the balcony of the brick building that is connected to the back of the small church via rope.
3	In the back alley on top of a balcony with a sign for Godfrey & Cook Ltd. next to it.
4	On a metal framed balcony underneath an attic window.
5	Through the window with the small wooden overhang next to the A Shuffre Ltd. sign.
6	Inside the small office inside Warehouse C.
7	Off the main road next to a restaurant.
8	On the lowest roof of the Abbot's Cocoa building.
9	Behind some dying bushes against a wall in the alley.
10	In the top floor of a broken down house only accessible via the windows.
11	On the top floor of a decrepit house on the north side of the block. Enter from the bottom floor or use the top windows to gain access.
12	On a balcony behind the red brick building that has a Deacon's Soap sign.
13	Head in through the front doors of the Bank of England, working your way all the way to the back right room.
14	Jump through the window to the left of the Tea Importer Sign off the main road. The Chest is just behind the bed.
15	On the back balcony of Betteley, Linders & Co.
16	Behind the Insurance building on the balcony.

	DESCRIPTION
17	Next to a broken headstone on the ground behind the small church.
18	Underneath the small wooden walkway in the construction site.
19	Across from the church on the roof of the building between two chimneys.
20	On the roof directly behind Abbiss Wilbur & Co.
21	On the first floor in the brick building with the small addition built onto it.
22	Top floor of the red brick building nearest to the water on the docks.
23	On a lower roof between two buildings with a line of rope hanging over the street.
24	On the backside of the solicitors' building on the lower balcony.
25	On the east roof of the building with two national flags facing the main street.
26	On top of a dock behind a load of cargo.
27	On the second floor of Warehouse C.
28	On the first floor on the west side of Warehouse C.
29	Inside the courtyard of a few buildings on the scaffolding to the west.
30	On the top floor of the building neighboring Bookbinder to the north.
31	At the northeast corner of the Temple Church roof.
32	On the roof of the south side entrance to the Temple Church.
33	In the dead end of the alley on a balcony, on the other side of a large wooden beam holding a platform.
34	Behind Linders & Co on the ground in the large alley.
35	On the second floor of the building next to Morton & Co bakery.

342

	DESCRIPTION
36	Sitting on the balcony behind a Godfrey & Cook LTD building.
37	In the construction site behind a carpenter's work bench.
38	On the second floor of a Herbington's Teas building.
39	Using the roof entrance to the factory, the Chest is in the office straight ahead.
40	On the first floor of the factory near the loading door on the north side.
41	On the roof of the factory near the base of its only smokestack.
42	In a small park near a cart of hay.
43	North of the Holborn Viaduct on some wooden scaffolding.
44	Inside the top floor of the stone brick building with the window washer cart attached to it.
45	Next to a tombstone that is propped up against a wall near a tall stone fence.
46	On the top floor of the brick building with a clothesline strung up on the inside.
47	Inside of the buildings' courtyard, on a balcony that is barely big enough to fit the Chest.
48	Underneath the railway, next to many wooden crates.
49	In the tunnel underneath the railway on an upper level, placed above the stacked crate.
50	On the backside of a building labeled Arnett. Bowditch & Co
51	On a balcony across from the Fight Club entrance. A large sign for Maslin & Healy's matches leads from the ground up to the small balcony containing the Chest.

	DESCRIPTION
52	Drop down into the construction area, finding the chest at the dead end before the sewer begins.
53	Underneath the arches of a large stone brick building facing the main street.
54	On the balcony above the wooden post behind the Merchants building.
55	On the backside of the roof behind the Offices Brokers and Traders building.
56	At the top of the north bell shaped tower at St. Paul's Cathedral.
57	On the balcony behind the Locksmith's building.
58	On a ledge half way up the rounded east side of St. Paul's Cathedral.
59	On the south side underneath the arches around the base of the large dome of St Paul's Cathedral.
60	In a walled off area with no roof on the north side of St Paul's Cathedral. Drop into it from the main roof.
61	On the building to the west of Kenway Mansion, behind the chimneys.
62	Lockpicking II is required to get to this chest. Pick the lock on the front door of the mansion then, head into the back of the Kenway mansion and pick the lock on the blue door. The Chest is at the foot of the bed inside the room.
63	Between a small yellow brick building and a stack of barrels on the upper level of the dock.
64	Outside on the southwest side of the Cannon Street Station, in a small cutout at the end of the path.
65	Behind the small mausoleum hiding in some bushes and small trees.

CITY OF LONDON

POSTER ADS

	DESCRIPTION
1	Through the half-opened gate next to the Chadwick Jones & Lancaster Trading Merchant.
2	Underneath the brick building with the Tea Importer sign and clock.
3	On the wall of the alley underneath the warehouse sign, near the Auction House.
4	When looking at the gate that prevents you from walking into the alley to the Ad, head right (away from the bar) and follow the path around back to get into the alley.
5	Between Whitehead and J Mailings in the brick alley.
6	In the alley at the end of the Stockbrokers sign where the brick building begins.
7	Off the main road between the Locksmith and Bakery, in the shadows of the alley.
8	Look for the vertical sign "Hatter" off the main road, the poster is in the alley underneath it.
9	In the alley leading underneath the brick Bank building from the main road.
10	In the alley to the left of the blue shop named Abbiss Wilbur & CO.

BEER BOTTLES

	DESCRIPTION
1	In the Public House behind the bar on the back counter.
2	On the top right of the fireplace mantle in the Seven Bells.
3	Inside George and the Dragon, in the far corner behind the bar.
4	Underneath the hanging flag at the far end of the bar in the Horse and Groom.
5	On the table closest to the fireplace inside the Prince of Wales.

PRESSED FLOWERS

	DESCRIPTION
1	Near the fountain in a small park, on a park bench.
2	On the west side of the building directly to the east of the Kenway Mansion, on a bench.
3	On the south side of St. Paul's Cathedral, underneath a bench.
4	In front of a small lantern on the ground in the cemetery.
5	On the floor of the gazebo in the southwest corner of the courtyard behind Temple Church.

LARGE CHESTS

	DESCRIPTION	CONTENTS
1	On the southeast side of the Royal Exchange's roof.	Golden Lion Cane-Sword
2	From the south entrance into the Bank of England head in and then take the door to the east, entering into a circular room. Take the door to the left heading north into a larger room, then in the northeast corner of the room behind a changing screen you find the Chest. Through the Golden doors in the back of the Royal Exchange, after heading into the vault slide underneath two brick walls to end up in the room with the Chest and an elevator that provides a fast way out.	Chimera Gauntlet Schematic
3	At the top platform on the top of the dome where it begins to turn into a tower.	Baron Jordan's Finery
4	Between the chimneys on the northwest rooftop of St. Bartholomew's Hospital.	Hallucinogenic Dart Upgrade II Schematic
5	On the bridge over the tracks at the south side of the Cannon Street Station.	Jaw Tenderizer

SECRETS

	DESCRIPTION
1	Given to player during cutscene upon entering Reuge's Vault.
2	Southeast corner of the red brick building's roof.
3	Behind the Cockham Merchants building on the roof near the railroad.
4	In the park east of the Kenway mansion, on a bench to the right of the gazebo entrance.
5	On a stool outside the entrance to the Herbington's Tea store.

HELIX GLITCHES

	DESCRIPTION
1	Use your Rope Launcher to get to the top of the tower of Temple Church.
2	Free Run up to the branch containing the Glitch.
3	Jump off the wooden crane onto the boardwalk below.
4	Climb up the wooden crates and over the metal ledge onto the balcony containing the Glitch.
5	Leap from the set of chimneys from the east building, down into the hay below.
6	From the top of the factory smokestack, take a Leap of Faith into the hay below.
7	Zipline to the top of the golden spire on the bell tower.
8	On the small walkway containing railway signals, climb atop one of the signals, then jump across to the other signal.

COLLECTIBLES

REFERENCE

CITY OF LONDON

THE STRAND

THAMES

WESTMINSTER

WHITECHAPEL

WWI LONDON

HELIX GLITCHES

	DESCRIPTION
9	From the upper level of wooden support beams, drop down to the beam containing the Glitch.
10	Jump from the head of one of the statues to the head of the statue next to it, collecting the Glitch in the middle. Located above the east wing of St Bartholomew's Hospital.
11	On the "&" of the Curtis & Harvey building. From the road below, use the Rope Launcher to grapple the top of the "&".
12	From the top of one of the bell towers in St. Paul's Cathedral, Rope Launch to the top of the bell tower opposite of it.
13	Take a Leap of Faith into the hay below from the building with the two sets of chimneys lining the edge closest the hay.
14	Free Run up to the branch of the tree containing the Helix Glitch.
15	Leap from the top of the bell tower connected to the Stockbrokers building, down to the hay in the courtyard below.
16	Tightrope walk across the rope connecting a small wooden platform to the roof of the building across from it.
17	From the top of the spire above the Bank of England, Rope Launch across to the top of the spire of the circular building to the east.
18	From the top of this red bell tower, jump into the hay located in the small alley below.
19	From the corner of the Solicitors building, get to the roof of the red building directly across from it, then zipline across the railway and towards a desynch area, picking up the Glitch above the railroad.

	DESCRIPTION
20	From the roof of the Royal Exchange, line up with the Glitch and then zipline across to pick it up.
21	Cross the rope connecting two rooftops.
22	From the corner of the yellow brick building closest to the track, aim your Rope Launcher for the farthest corner of the building across the way, then zipline to pick up the Glitch.
23	Take a leap from the Monument to the Great Fire of London down into the hay below.
24	From the highest point of the building's roof, aim for the same point on the identical building across the way. Work your way across the line to grab the Glitch.
25	Zipline to the top of the Mansion House, then climb down to the top of the large oval glass window. Let your feet hang down to grab the Glitch.
26	Zipline to the top of this small church's bell tower to grab the Glitch.
27	On the edge of the metal support beam at the very top of this building's roof.
28	Standing between the pair of chimneys, zipline to the same point of the roof across the road.
29	Climb to the very top of the northernmost tower of the Cannon Street Station, using your Rope Launcher when available to make the climb much faster.
30	Jump from the flagpole on the dock onto the street below.

LAMBETH

CHESTS

	DESCRIPTION
1	On top of the storage silo.
2	A little over halfway up the silo on the wooden scaffolding.
3	Behind the shed at the small farm.
4	In the top story of a house, enter through the window or head up the stairs inside.
5	Next to a broken cart in the alley.
6	Upper floor of the building, underneath a clothesline.
7	On the small wooden balcony branching off the building.
8	Top floor at the foot of one of the beds.
9	Back side of the building with the London World News signs.
10	Beside a pile of lumber.
11	Behind a mossy stone fence.
12	Climb on top of the Lambeth Asylum. Head away from the clock in the direction of the hay bale on the roof. At the end, look to your right and jump down to the small balcony. The Chest is located in the room it leads to.
13	Near the edge of the map, tucked away between two graves.
14	Hidden in a dying bush.
15	On the roof between a few chimneys.
16	On the south side of the market near the end of the wall.
17	Behind a bundle of rope with a large wooden spool behind it.
18	Underneath the railway, tucked into the brick wall.
19	On the east balcony of the roof with the metalwork on the peak in the Lambeth Palace.
20	On the lowest tier of the brick building with the rusted green roof in the Lambeth Palace.
21	Next to a pitchfork propped up against the wall.
22	In the sewers on the floor in a large open area that contains crates and a wooden walkway. Enter from the construction site next to Chest 23. Follow the path north, into the sewers and into the room containing the Chest.
23	On the small porch of the building tucked in the dark corner, near the construction walkways.
24	To the left of a wooden ramp leading over an alley.
25	Underneath the wooden overhang against the brick wall.
26	On the lower level of the roofs of the chapel.
27	Go to the South side of the Lambeth Asylum. Closer to the east half you see a window with a light on in the main floor. Climb up to the open window above to find the room with the Chest.
28	In the top floor of the house with the lift on the roof.
29	Next to the window in the bottom floor of the house. Enter through the main door.
30	Inside the wooden fenced area.
31	Near the backdoor of the building, underneath the lantern.
32	Inside the main floor of the building, underneath the Knife Polish poster.
33	Against the brick wall separating two porches.
34	Behind the table in the corner of the building.
35	On top of the roof near the bell tower.
36	Next to the fire, along the wooden fence.
37	In the northern corner of the factory.
38	On top of the office in the upper level of the factory.
39	Inside of the office in the west corner of the factory.
40	Behind the wooden fence with the Deacon's Soap ad on it.

HELIX GLITCHES

	DESCRIPTION
1	Take a Leap of Faith off the tower south of Lambeth Palace and into the leaf pile in front of the steps, just before the road.
2	Use the Rope Launcher to get to the top of the tallest wooden pole, then look south and jump to the smaller wooden post below.
3	Hop on the chimney to the north side of the building, then use the Rope Launcher to connect to the other row of chimneys that is also located on the north side.
4	Walk across the wooden support beam over that gap between the two houses. Use the Rope Launcher from below the beam to quickly get to it.
5	Take a standard jump from the upper roof to the lower level roof below, no Leap of Faith needed.
6	Climb to the very top of the church bell tower. Standing on top of the cross, aim across the road at the tallest chimney located in the center of the buildings and zipline across the road.
7	From the top of the cross above the clock tower of the Lambeth Asylum, take a leap into the pile of leaves on the lower roof near the door into the tower.
8	From the top of the roof of the house to the east, grapple the chimney in the center of the building to the west.
9	Take a leap from off the row of 6 chimneys on this roof into the hay below.
10	Launch from roof to roof grabbing the Glitch floating above the road.
11	Take a leap off the wooden platform sticking out of the roof, aiming for the hay down below.
12	Jump from the metal cranes hanging off the west side of the building, grabbing the Glitch between two of them.
13	From the covered single chimney on the taller building, aim between the windows of the factory roof and zipline across.
14	Launch to the top of one of the smokestacks, then cross the gap to the other smokestack.
15	Jump from the wooden platform sticking off the roof and into the cart of hay below.
16	Free run jump across the gap, starting from the wooden building with the green shingles, toward the building with the brick chimneys.
17	From the rooftop closest to the tree, take a leap towards the center of the tree, aiming for the low branch sticking up into the air.
18	Jump from the wooden post hanging off the east side of the building and onto the branch extending off the tree directly across from it.
19	From the east chimney of the two on this roof, jump across to the other roof, aiming for the wooden post extending from it.
20	Underneath the Railroad, Rope Launch to the center beam with the Glitch on it.

POSTER ADS

	DESCRIPTION
1	Behind the Black Bull bar on the south wall.
2	In the alley between Hebbington's Teas and A Shuffre Ltd.
3	In the alley across the street from the P. James and Sons building.
4	In the path leading underneath the buildings.
5	On the side of the A Shuffre Ltd building in the alley.
6	Underneath the railway overpass.

PRESSED FLOWERS

	DESCRIPTION
1	On top of the planter to the left of the main entrance to the building.
2	On top of a grave inside of the graveyard.
3	On top of a grave inside of the graveyard in the church.
4	On top of a small grave pressed up against the brick wall with a dog standing nearby.

LARGE CHESTS

	DESCRIPTION	CONTENTS
1	Enter from the roof into the backside of the clocktower of the Asylum. Drop down one level, ending up next to the chest.	Unique Material - Tanjore Poison
2	On the lower roof in the rear of the church building.	Light and Dark Cloak
3	To the right of the door leading into the north building of the Lambeth Palace	Unique Material - Bluestone

BEER BOTTLES

	DESCRIPTION
1	Behind the bar, on top of a small counter.
2	Inside the Public House to the right of the bar, on top of a few barrels.

SECRETS

	DESCRIPTION
1	At the very top of the smokestack, next to a Synchronization point.
2	On the rooftop of the red brick building with the bell tower.
3	Located on a pile of rope near the end of the docks.
4	On a tree stump along the dirt path in the small park.

SOUTHWARK

CHESTS

	DESCRIPTION
1	Fenced in a small brick area next to a blue door.
2	At the bottom of a crane next to the boiler.
3	On the upper level of the factory, just before the bridge leading into the other building.
4	Inside the room with the iron bars surrounding it.
5	In a fenced-in brick area with a blue tool chest next to it.
6	In between two of the shaping machines on the upper level of the factory.
7	Next to a red door lit by a lantern.
8	Off the road on the wooden boardwalk next to the red door lit by a lantern.
9	Enter the sewers from 100m east of the Chest. Follow the path down using the waypoint to guide you in the direction of the Chest, finding it at the dead end.
10	Next to a stack of sacks.
11	Enter into the top floor window from the street. Next to a stack of baskets near the window.
12	Inside the factory in the east corner office.
13	Underneath a crane next to a stack of sacks.
14	Next to a pot of food at a small food stand.
15	Between a crane and a stack of lumber.
16	On the Top of the A. Shuffrey LTD building next to the smoke stack.
17	Next to a hay cart behind a wooden fence.
18	Jump into the water next to the south-side crane. Then head north into the sewers and follow the path to the Chest.
19	In the office of Warehouse C on the west side of the Building.
20	In the alley located behind the food stands.
21	Outside of the Office facing the water, next to a red door with the word "Private" on it.
22	On the upper floor of Waterloo Station, behind the counter in the north corner.
23	Behind the counter on the upper floor in the northeast corner of Waterloo Station.
24	Hidden behind a fallen tree and a group of bushes. On the north side of the rails.
25	Drop to the lower area in the eastern point of the construction site.
26	On top of the wooden scaffolding near the entrance to an alley.
27	On the main floor of the house, near the back window facing the railway.
28	Inside the storage room in the top of the south side of the factory.
29	Head into the sewers from the west side of the main road; follow the path to find the chest.
30	Next to some stacked barrels in the market area.
31	On the tallest roof of the Starrick Factory, next to the small smokestack.
32	Along the rail in the small railway station.
33	On the outer balcony of the factory next to a rolling crane.
34	In the office on the southeast corner of the factory.
35	In a fenced off brick area with a red door, right next to an animal carcass.
36	In the center of a large alley next to a pile of cargo.
37	Next to a stack of planks on the west side of the railway.
38	Inside the London Bridge Station behind the counter.
39	At the bottom of the wooden scaffolding that is being built.
40	Behind a wooden fence next to a tree and fire pit.

PRESSED FLOWERS

	DESCRIPTION
1	On the ground beside the walkway through the park.
2	Underneath the national flag on the small table in the fenced in brick area.
3	On the small table underneath the P. James and Sons sign.
4	On top of the table next to the Hats and Umbrellas stand.

HELIX GLITCHES

	DESCRIPTION
1	Jump from the the metal crane onto the railroad tracks below.
2	Climb the small wooden post on the upper walkway and jump to the tops of the wooden fences below.
3	From the railway platform, jump through the window of the building across the way.
4	Use the Rope Launcher to pull yourself up onto the metal support beam with the Gltich on it.
5	Jump across from one wooden crane to the other in the harbor.
6	Vault off of the wall of one building across to the other.
7	Launch to the top of the building, then jump down to the large pipe below.
8	Take a Leap of Faith from one of the surrounding buildings closest to the pile of hay.
9	Leap from the top of the highest metal beam in the small construction site, down into the hay below.
10	Jump from the wooden beam to the boardwalk across the way.
11	From below the Glitch, fire your Rope Launcher up toward the roof, the Glitch is collected along the way.
12	Climb to the top of one of the smokestacks that goes all the way to the ground, then zipline across to the same style smokestack across the street.
13	Rope Launch to the top of the roof, then drop down onto the metal support beam in the center beneath the roof.
14	Hop onto the wooden platform sticking off of the building, then cross over to the metal support beams of the small shelter across from it.
15	Run across the rope connecting the tall tree to the building across the alley.
16	Underneath the Railroad, Rope Launch up to the center beam with the Glitch on it.
17	From the upper level metal crane, Rope Launch to the roof of the building across the water.
18	From the metal flagpole in the alley leading to the water, face toward the buildings and aim your Rope Launcher at the lower roof, ziplining to grab the Glitch.
19	Launch to the top of the metal roof, then drop to the support beam below it.
20	Climb up onto the pipe to the left or right of the Glitch and then walk over to it.
21	Climb one of the pipe's supports then run towards the Glitch, partially climbing the wall to collect it.
22	Rope Launch to the top of the London Bridge Station, then across to the roof's windows across the way, picking the one that best lines up with the Glitch floating in the air.
23	Jump from one wooden balcony to the other.
24	Climb the trunk of the tree, gaining the Glitch at the first split in the tree.

POSTER ADS

	DESCRIPTION
1	In the alley next to the London World News building.
2	On the west side of the bridge leading out of Southwark.
3	On the wall leading into the alley beside Dolman Gasfitter.
4	Between the two blue buildings in the archway.
5	In the alley between the Deacon's Soap Sign and the Godfrey & Cook Sign.
6	At the front of the alley next to a Deacon's Soap shop.
7	Across the alley from the northeast corner of Waterloo Station.

BEER BOTTLES

	DESCRIPTION
1	In the Duke of York bar, underneath the table located directly in front of the entrance.
2	Inside the George bar on the table slightly left of the entrance.

THE ESSENTIALS
WALKTHROUGH
SIDE QUESTS
COLLECTIBLES
REFERENCE & ANALYSIS
INDEX

CITY OF LONDON
LAMBETH
SOUTHWARK
THE STRAND
THAMES
WESTMINSTER
WHITECHAPEL
WWI LONDON

LARGE CHESTS

	DESCRIPTION	CONTENTS
1	In the office on the top floor of the Attaway Transport factory building.	Eagle Dive Cape
2	On the upper level in the center of the factory.	Darbe's Bear Paw
3	In the back of the offices near the window facing the street behind the Train Ticketing booth.	Lord Pearson's Cane
4	In the metalworking factory office on the upper level.	Unique Material-Rhodium

SECRETS

	DESCRIPTION
1	On the north side of the northern-most storage tank.
2	On the wooden platform parallel to the railway sticking out of the yellow brick building.
3	Located on the flat roof of the small brick workshop nearest the road.
4	Behind a motorized crane on a barrel near a sign that says "Danger."

THE STRAND

CHESTS

	DESCRIPTION
1	On the top floor of the house next to several stacked barrels.
2	Next to a broken down brick fence.
3	On the top floor of the Solicitors building.
4	Behind the Offices building.
5	On the bottom floor of the building with the broken down barrel cart outside the window.
6	On the west lower roof of the large church building.
7	South of the Bank building on top of the roof.
8	On the balcony facing a park to the south of the building.
9	On the roof of the building east of St. Mary le Strand.
10	Enter the sewer entrance on the west corner of St. Paul's Church. The sewer leads you directly to the Chest.
11	On the northeast balcony facing the main road away from the Covent Garden.
12	Behind the bank building on the balcony in the alley.
13	Next to an overturned cart at the north entrance to the small park.
14	Inside a small construction site behind a large spool of rope.
15	On the cobblestone walkway behind some tarp-covered boxes.
16	Behind the carpenters' workbench in St. Pancras Station.
17	Top floor of the Printers, enter through the window above the side stating "Rooms to Let."
18	On the roof behind Deacon's Soap.
19	On the balcony next to a blue door.
20	In a small square area fenced off on the roof of St. Pancras Station.
21	Behind the tables next to the window in the outside meeting area.
22	Behind an ivy covered stone wall.
23	On the balcony behind Arnett. Bowditch & Co.
24	Just before the top of the walkway next to the stairs.
25	On the ground behind the Pale Ale & Stout building.
26	Located on the west lower roof of the Alhambra Music Hall.
27	Enter through the top floor window to the left of the national flag hanging into the side street.

	DESCRIPTION
28	Inside the upper level of the factory in the northwest corner.
29	On the balcony behind the red brick Traders building.
30	Behind the Stationer building on the ground, up next to an ivy colored brick wall.
31	On the balcony behind the Hatter/Cloakmaker building.
32	On the roof of a P. James and Sons building near its chimneys.
33	Next to some barrels on the ground against a stone brick wall.
34	Use the stairs or climb in through the top window to reach the Chest on the floor of this brick abode.
35	Behind the Bankers and Hotel buildings on an upper balcony.
36	On the top floor of the Warehouse building with the yellow bricks.
37	On the second floor in the changing room of the building with the Herbington's Teas sign.
38	Between the two rows of chimneys on the border of Westminster.
39	On the first floor of this housing unit. Enter through the window or take the stairs up from below.
40	On the top floor of the rickety building next to the armoire.
41	Underneath a bunch of poster ads against a brick building.
42	On the top floor in this decrepit building.
43	On the balcony of the brick building opposite of the side with the national flag.
44	Near one of the archways exiting from the National Gallery.
45	Behind the red brick "Room" building on the roof.
46	On the second floor of the building behind a desk.
47	Next to the small staircase leading towards the doors of the building.
48	Near a large group of chimneys closest to the main street on top of the Charing Cross Station.
49	West across the street of St. Mary Le Strand on a building.
50	Grapple to the top floor of the tallest yellow brick building on the west side of the road, then enter the window. The Chest is located inside the top floor room, there is no entrance from the ground.

THE ESSENTIALS
WALKTHROUGH
SIDE QUESTS
COLLECTIBLES
REFERENCE & ANALYSIS
INDEX

CITY OF LONDON
LAMBETH
SOUTHWARK
THE STRAND
THAMES
WESTMINSTER
WHITECHAPEL
WAR ANOMALIES

THE STRAND

POSTER ADS

	DESCRIPTION
1	Leading into a brick paved road next to a Green Luncheons and Teas.
2	In the alley beside a yellow office building branching off of the main road.
3	Underneath a Chamber's Sewing Machines sign on a brick wall.
4	On the wall in a brick alley, leading off the main street.
5	In the archway leading into a small courtyard.
6	Alley between the Locksmith and Wholesale Insurance.
7	On the side of the Pale Ale & Stout, in the alley next to a tree.
8	Below the tall vertical sign that says "Trader" in the alley.

BEER BOTTLES

	DESCRIPTION
1	Inside a Public House, to the left of the sink on the bar counter.
2	Inside the Crow bar, behind the counter in the north corner of the building.
3	In a Public House, to the left of the sink on the bar counter.
4	On the counter inside the Lord Nelson Bar.

PRESSED FLOWERS

	DESCRIPTION
1	Northeast of the Lincoln's Inn Fields on a green bench in the park.
2	In the stone circle in the south side of the courtyard on a bench.
3	South of the gazebo on a green bench against a small stone wall.
4	On a green bench in the pathway next to a small gazebo that leads towards a main street.
5	In the north corner of the large square park on a green bench under a tree.

LARGE CHESTS

	DESCRIPTION	CONTENTS
1	Next to a boarded up window in a decrepit shack.	Large Bullet Pouch Schematic
2	Inside the Charing Cross Station. Enter underneath the railway heading into the Station.	Unique Material- Wabar Pearl
3	Underneath the National Gallery. Hop over a fence containing a stand up hiding spot in the east side of the Gallery's courtyard. Follow the path down into the sewers and take a left, leading into the dead end containing the locked Chest.	Unique Material - Golden Spider Silk
4	Enter through the door leading into the Fight Club. Once inside head to the northwest corner of the bottom floor. It is up against a wall with a small lantern next to it.	Lord Johnathan's Retribution (Knuckles)

SECRETS

	DESCRIPTION
1	Around the backside of the Gazebo in this small park, placed on top of a piece of luggage.
2	Underneath the steps leading out of the lower south corner of the Covent Garden.
3	Inside the square tower above the National Gallery.
4	On the ledge of the ivy covered balcony protruding from the back side of the yellow brick building.

HELIX GLITCHES

	DESCRIPTION
1	Climb above the open window with the red drapes, then perform a back eject onto the fence below.
2	Jump from the metal flag pole to the rope with banners hanging from it.
3	From the lower rope, get underneath the Glitch and then fire your Rope Launcher across to the chimneys on top of the building behind the tree.
4	Drop down onto the wall connected to the row of chimneys nearest the rope, then Back Eject on to the rope below.
5	Climb to the top of the wooden scaffolding connected to the building, then zipline to the chimney to the east.
6	From the flat part of the smaller building's roof, aim across the alley to the north, ziplining to the lowest roof on the other side of the alley.
7	Climb the tree and then jump across to the metal post expanding out of the roof of the building to the east.
8	Climb to the top of either tree branching over the small walkway, then take a leap from one to the other.
9	Climb to the top of the metal structure in the park, then jump to the peak of the side directly across from it.
10	Climb onto the wooden overhang below a window of the yellow brick building, then jump across to the open window of the broken down wooden building across the way.
11	Rope Launch up to the row of chimneys directly above the hay, then take a Leap of Faith off the chimney back down into the hay.
12	Launch up to the small ledge of the metal roofed building facing the alley side. Once on the ledge, leap toward the small metal roof on the opposite side, grabbing the floating Glitch mid-jump.
13	Climb to the top of the southwest corner of the Covent Garden, look for the open window, jump through, and swing your way into the Glitch.
14	From the top of the chimney on the west side of the street, aim your Rope Launcher for the top of the stone building's upper balcony.
15	From the corner near the "s" in the Curtis sign on this building's roof, aim for the chimney of the building directly across the way.
16	Between the two sets of chimneys on the taller building of the two connected by the wooden support. Launch to the identical chimneys on the smaller building on the other side of the support beam.
17	Rope Launch to the top of the tower in St. Martin-in-the-Fields. Then take a Leap of Faith into the pile of leaves to the north of the tower's top.
18	From the upper level chimneys of the building on the north side of the courtyard entrance, zipline across to the top of the roof of the building with no windows to the south.
19	Zipline from the second level of chimneys on the building closest to the tree to the building directly across from it, barely visible through the tree.
20	Climb the tree to the west side of the courtyard, then jump across to the east tree.
21	Jump from the wooden platform hanging off the side of the yellow building toward the flag pole of the red brick building.
22	Take a Leap of Faith off the longer post of the two on the north side of the "L" shaped building into the pile of leaves below.
23	From one of the popped out windows on the mossy roof, aim across to the top roof of the yellow building with the red roof.

THE ESSENTIALS

WALKTHROUGH

SIDE QUESTS

COLLECTIBLES

REFERENCE & ANALYSIS

INDEX

CITY OF LONDON

LAMBETH

SOUTHWARK

THE STRAND

THAMES

WESTMINSTER

WHITECHAPEL

WWI ANOMALY

THAMES

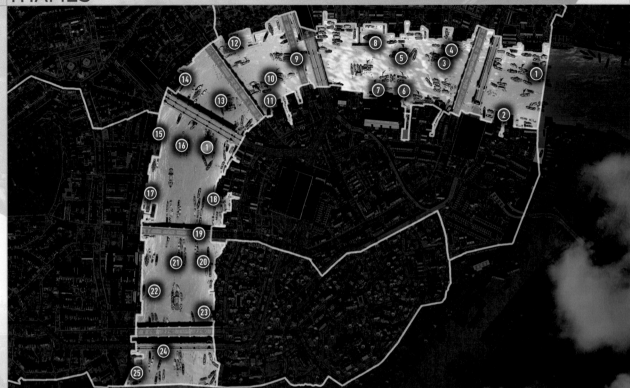

354

CHESTS

	DESCRIPTION
1	On the deck of the sail boat between the two barges.
2	Underneath the wooden bridge on the lower level of the dock.
3	On the deck of the sail boat with the small row boat anchored next to it.
4	Next to a stack of barrels near a motorized crane.
5	On the deck of the ship near a pile of hay below the Synch point.
6	On the dock against the wall, near the barge full of coal.
7	On the dock behind the stationary metal crane, next to barrels of coal.
8	Underneath the overhang in the south walkway of the Hutton.
9	On the small path beneath the bridge against the wall.
10	Against the mast of this sail ship.
11	Next to a few sacks and a fire pit on the bottom level of the dock.
12	Hidden behind the upper shielding on the bow of the ship.
13	Between some stacked crates and a pile of lumber on this barge.
14	Underneath the roofing of the café at the storefront.
15	Behind the Whitehall Stairs building, next to a tree in the corner of the wall.
16	Between some crates on the barge south of the barge with a crate of hay.
17	On the main deck of the London Hutton ship, between the two staircases leading to the top deck.
18	On the dock next to some lumber underneath the Receiving and Shipping sign.
19	Between the doors on the bow of the red boat parked underneath the bridge.
20	Hidden by some crates on this barge, near a gap that can be slid under.
21	Against a pile of lumber on the barge east of the one with the green tarp.
22	On the deck of the stationary sail ship.
23	Next to a few luggage crates on the loading dock for the ferry.
24	Under the bridge on the deck of the sail ship that has its masts taken down.
25	On the top deck of the parked ferry near the west smokestack.

POSTER ADS

	DESCRIPTION
1	On the side opposite the water of the wooden office for Chamber's.
2	On the stone wall behind the larger building in the area before the stairs leading into the City of London.
3	On the wall facing the water on the north set of steps heading up away from the dock.
4	Next to a bench on the south wall of the small Godfrey & Cook LTD building.

PRESSED FLOWERS

	DESCRIPTION
1	On the bench of the wooden bridge connecting the two stone docks.
2	In front of the Whitehall Stairs building to the south on a bench facing the water.
3	On a backless bench next to a small booth facing the water.

LARGE CHESTS

	DESCRIPTION	CONTENTS
1	Directly below the Synch point on the deck of the ship.	Unique Material- Sea Silk

SECRETS

	DESCRIPTION
1	On the roof of the smaller boat next to the large boat with the flag of England at the top of its mast.
2	In front of a metal door on the small walkway above the water connected to one of the bridge supports.
3	Above the shop at the edge of the docks on the roof.
4	In a small cut out on the top east of the bridge on a bench.

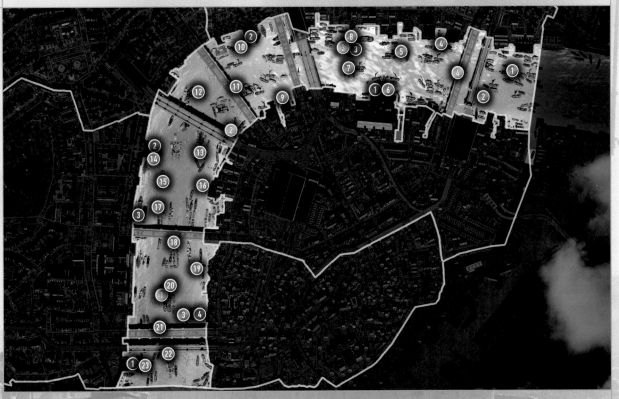

HELIX GLITCHES

	DESCRIPTION
1	At the top of the Ship's sail.
2	From one of the wooden boats below, use the Rope Launcher to quickly get to the top of the wooden pole.
3	Rope Launch to the top of the wooden post from one of the ships below.
4	A motorized crane moves back and forth into the area with the Glitch. Climb to the tip of the Crane and wait for it to move back into the Glitch.
5	From the top of the sail from the stationary ship farthest from the Synch point in this group of ships, zipline all the way across to the Synch Point collecting the Glitch on the way.
6	The tip of a motorized crane moving a bunch of barrels grants you access. Get to the tip of the crane and wait for it to move into the Glitch.
7	Rope Launch to the top of the wooden post.
8	From the top of the flag post at the loading dock for the ferry, zipline southeast across to the wooden post in the water then zipline to the Glitch.
9	Get to the tip of the motorized crane that is a little bit closer inland than the other crane near it, and wait for it to move through the Glitch.
10	From the flag post on the dock, aim for the mast of the stationary sailing ship across the way.
11	Hop over the edge of the bridge and slowly drop down to the level of the Glitch, ending up holding on with just your hands above one of the lion faces.

	DESCRIPTION
12	From one of the wooden posts in the water, aim diagonally across for another identical post, ziplining into the Glitch.
13	From the flag at the top of the massive sailing ship, jump into the hay pile of one of the barges below.
14	Get on top of the flag post at the ferry dock, then grapple across to the wooden post in the water.
15	Walk on the ropes between both of this ship's exhausts.
16	From the tip of this motorized crane hauling barrels, wait for it to move you through the Glitch.
17	Climb to the top of the stationary ship's sails, then zipline to the wooden post on the other side of a stationary ship in the Thames.
18	From the bridge, jump onto the ledge and then zipline to the top of the ship's mast.
19	Take a Leap of Faith off the docked sailing ship's mast and into the hay on the barge below.
20	Jump from the top of the Synchronization point on this ship's tallest mast and into the hay on the barge below.
21	From the ledge of the bridge, drop down, leaving yourself hanging by just your hands, then shuffle into the Glitch.
22	Get onto the Railroad, look for the spot inhabited by some pigeons, and then take a Leap of Faith into the hay on a barge below.
23	From a ship below, use the Rope Launcher to get to the top of the post sticking out of the water.

WESTMINSTER

CHESTS

	DESCRIPTION
1	On the main floor of the Accountants building, just before the rear exit.
2	On the south corner of the roof above the Chapel Royal.
3	Underneath the small overhang in the north area of the Horse Guards.
4	East balcony of the Montagu House.
5	On the balcony facing east to the main street above the Dover House.
6	In the back of the Dover house next to some barrels against an ivy covered stone brick wall.
7	On the tallest roof of The Foreign Office.
8	On the southeast corner of the roofs in the Richmond Terrace.
9	In the highest accessible floor in the building with the Deacon's Soap sign hanging off of it. Enter through the top window or take the stairs up from the main floor.
10	In the western courtyard of Big Ben, almost underneath the clock itself.
11	Just off the walking path in the courtyard of the Houses of Parliament.
12	At the bottom of a collection of stained glass windows inside the Houses of Parliament.
13	On the west balcony of St. Margaret's, Westminster.
14	Next to a cart of hay in the Westminster Abbey courtyard.
15	First floor of the stone brick building with the yellow accents next to a window.
16	Behind the fenced off area closest to the small gazebo.
17	Backed up to the railway next to a pile of chopped wood.
18	On the upper floor of the factory next to two steaming pots.
19	Tucked in the corner near a small horse stable.
20	Underneath the roofed area of the wooden walkway built above the rest of the area.
21	On the back end of a broken down carriage.
22	In a beat down shack with a drinking man using it as a chair.
23	Underneath a large tree near some steps leading into a house.
24	Enter into the window next to the lantern on the brick building. At the foot of the bed inside.
25	On a balcony above some woven baskets next to a blue door.
26	In a well-guarded gazebo to the West of Buckingham Palace.
27	Across the street to the north of Chest 61, near a building on the west side of the fenced in area.
28	Head to either stairway on the north side of Victoria Station then use your Rope Launcher to pull yourself up to the top of the large wall opposite the staircase.
29	On the top floor of the house with red curtains that are visible in the windows from the street, use the stairs or enter through the top window.
30	This house has a poster ad for Fitch's Fire Wheels. Enter through either the top window or main floor, heading for the top floor to find the Chest.
31	Hop the small fence or over the door to access this Chest in the alley.
32	In a fenced off area behind Storr & Mortimer.

	DESCRIPTION
33	On the highest balcony facing the small courtyard behind the row of buildings.
34	On the first floor of the building, next to a small table with a lit candle.
35	Next to a small fire pit and a door.
36	Below some hanging coats in the second floor of the building.
37	East side of the factory's main floor.
38	The highest floor of the west factory building near the windows facing east.
39	Next to some empty horse carts underneath a small roofed area.
40	Right next to the window with the flag pole that faces the main street.
41	Just inside the window up and to the left from the Dentist sign on the neighboring building.
42	Inside the top floor of the building with two national flags framing the open window. The Chest is to the right once inside.
43	Behind an armored cart in the Wellington Barracks.
44	Top floor of the building next to another building labeled Underground Railway.
45	Next to a cart of flowers in Green Park.
46	On a balcony facing south toward Green Park from the Royal Society Buildings.
47	Top floor of the Northern Royal Society Building close to the Boroughs edge.
48	On the north facing balcony of the Royal Society Buildings.
49	On the northwest side of the roof above The Admiralty building.
50	In the construction site behind a bunch of boxes covered in tarp.
51	West side of the roof above the Horse Guards.
52	On the south side of the small peninsula that leads into the lake, sitting next to a cart.
53	On the south side of the Wellington Barracks between two staircases leading in. Gain easy access to the restricted area by using the roof to the south, then jump to the tree that is in line with the Chest before jumping off the branch and landing right in front of the Chest.
54	Inside a small fruit stand that faces the water from the east side of the Houses of Parliament
55	Near the railway backed up to an ivy covered brick wall and building.
56	On the top floor of one of the decrepit houses to the west; a tree leads into one of the windows.
57	Southside of the courtyard inside of The Royal Mews. Zipline across the gap, dropping down on the Chest to avoid attention, watch out for Royal Guards on the rooftops.
58	Northside of the courtyard inside of The Royal Mews. Zipline across the gap dropping down on the chest to avoid attention; watch out for Royal Guards on the rooftops.
59	Outside a small building to the east of The Royal Mews. Horseshoes decorate the wall above it.
60	On the rooftops of the northeast corner of Buckingham Palace.

COLLECTIBLES

CITY OF LONDON

SOUTHWARK

THE STRAND

THAMES

WESTMINSTER

POSTER ADS

	DESCRIPTION
1	In the Alley of the Whitehead store.
2	On the side of the Dolman Hop & Seeds building.
3	Behind the China Glass Warehouse.
4	Look for the nation's flag on the main road; the Ad is located in the smaller road just under it.
5	A clock on the main road is just above the alley containing the Ad.
6	On the side of a large brick house on the main road.
7	Behind the metal fence next to the Barber Shop.
8	On the brick building east of Herbington's Teas.
9	Next to the Gun Market on a stone wall facing the main street.
10	On a brick path between two large houses below an ad for "Electric Power."

SECRETS

	DESCRIPTION
1	Outside the row of buildings on the north corner of Victoria Station on a wooden table near a cooking fire.
2	On the roof of the red and white brick building, next to a small lantern and a suitcase.
3	In the west side of Green Park on a tree stump.
4	In the southeast corner of St. James's Park, on small crate with a lantern on top.
5	Outside a small shack on a bench in the north corner of St. James's Park.
6	On the ledge of the balcony in Richmond Terrace, facing the street to the east.
7	In the south courtyard of the Houses of Parliament, on a bench near the exit leading towards the water.

ROYAL CORRESPONDENCE

	DESCRIPTION
1	On a bench near the fountain in a small fenced in park.
2	Underneath a tree on the north side shore of the small pond.
3	On the ledge at the top of a small stone staircase.
4	Under a tree on a chair, next to a man in a top hat.
5	On top of a small wooden case next to a small fountain.
6	Behind Buckingham Palace on a stack of books, on top of a bench facing the water.
7	Partially buried next to a shovel sticking out of the ground on the island in the pond behind Buckingham Palace.
8	On a small table in front of a door of one of the outlying buildings near the Royal Mews.
9	Hidden behind a parked carriage. Grab it quickly as Royal Guards may be close by.
10	On the ground just inside the entrance to Buckingham Palace. Consider kidnapping a guard to help sneak past the other guards and into the palace.
11	In the room just to the north of the White Room. The easiest way in is through the window to the left of the large balcony. Make sure to look through the window before jumping right in as the place has a ton of guards.
12	This letter is located on the first level balcony. Hop up on the fence from the outside nearest the large balcony that extends from the rear of Buckingham palace. Follow it up to the balcony to gain access without alerting the guards.

HELIX GLITCHES

	DESCRIPTION
1	Take a Leap of Faith off the statue and into the hay cart on the roof.
2	Climb up the tree, following the branches out towards the Glitch, and then take a leap off the end branch and into the water to collect this Glitch.
3	In the center of the tree, climb up either side of the branches, collecting the Glitch on the way up.
4	Jump off the back end of the Dover House and into the hay cart. The Glitch is floating just above the cart.
5	Between the two chimneys on the Montagu House. Climb either one and then jump to the other to grab it.
6	On the north balconies of The Foreign Office. Climb up to one of the balconies before transferring to the other.
7	Floating in the courtyard of The Foreign Office. Get up to the first floor of the building, and then line up with the Glitch and use your Rope Launcher to zipline to the other side, grabbing the Glitch along the way.
8	On the west side of the Richmond Terrace. From the roof, use your Rope Launcher to zipline across to the other roof, grabbing the Glitch in the middle.
9	From the tower south of Big Ben, use the zipline to cross to the gold-topped spire. The Helix Glitch is floating between the tower and spire.
10	Zipline from the House of Parliament to Westminster Abbey to grab the Glitch.
11	Zipline from one chimney to the other at the top of the factory.
12	Take a Leap of Faith east off of the cross at the top of the church tower into the hay cart.
13	Zipline from the top of the chimneys on the north buildings of the Devils Acre. Aim for the upper roof across the way.
14	Take a Leap of Faith off of the small wooden structure built off the side of the rooftop and into the hay cart.
15	Between two trees above a small walkway near a tent for the Liberal Party Rally. Jump from one branch to the other.
16	Take a Leap of Faith off the roof into the leaf pile below.
17	Climb to the top of the one of the tallest towers in Westminster Abbey. Once on top, use the Rope Launcher to hook one of the points diagonal from you.
18	Jump from tree to tree via the extended branches to grab this Glitch.
19	From the lower corner of the tall brick building with the small wooden posts hanging off of it, aim for the very top of the triangle roof across the way.
20	Take a Leap of Faith off the cargo winch and into the Hay Cart.
21	Jump from the bridge to the wooden support beam between the two factories.
22	Stand between the two sets of chimneys on either side of the gap, then aim for the same spot on the roof opposite you.
23	Leap off the corner of the top balcony of this cathedral, landing in the large pile of leaves below.
24	From the top of the yellow brick building, aim for the top window of the red restaurant across the street and fire your Rope Launcher. Aiming too low causes you to miss the Glitch. (There is also a Beer Bottle inside this restaurant.)
25	Head to the waiting area between both pairs of rails. Use your Rope Launcher to pull yourself up onto the support beam. Line up with the Glitch and launch again to the higher support beam, grabbing the Glitch just before reaching the beam.
26	Hop on top of the chimney parallel to the Glitch, then aim for the chimney opposite of you, ending up higher or lower depending on which side you started from.
27	Take a short leap off the tree branch facing the pile of leaves below.
28	This Glitch is in a Restricted Area. Once inside the small courtyard, quickly jump from lamppost to lamppost over the walkway to grab the Glitch. Then keep free running through the trees to hopefully get away from the guards.

COLLECTIBLES

CITY OF LONDON

LAMBETH

SOUTHWARK

THE STRAND

THAMES

WESTMINSTER

LARGE CHESTS

	DESCRIPTION	CONTENTS
1	This building has no ground floor access, so use your Rope Launcher to enter through any of the top windows or the hole in the wall at the top of the beat down wooden building. The chest is in between the only two windows that are still intact.	Master Assassin's Belt
2	At the northern-most point on the Westminster Abbey roof.	Death Knuckles
3	Jump through any of the windows in the middle or to the right of the middle of the back side of the Palace. Head to the south room. There are guards along the way so lure them away or assassinate them. When the area is clear, pick up the Chest just below a painting in front of a few royal purple urns.	Eagle Splendor Belt
4	Enter through the first balcony on the left side of the round center of the building. This room is sealed so you shouldn't be troubled by any guards once inside.	Unique Material - Lignum Vitae
5	Jump in through the northeast balcony facing the water and the Chest is to the right.	Ulfberht Blade

BEER BOTTLES

	DESCRIPTION
1	Inside the Queen's Arms atop the closest round table through the door.
2	In the King's Arms bar at the closest table to the entrance.
3	Through the entrance of the Prince Albert, behind the bar on the back counter.
4	Inside the Prince Regent on the main bar.

PRESSED FLOWERS

	DESCRIPTION
1	On a carriage parked on the east side of Richmond Terrace.
2	On the ground near the statue in the courtyard of Westminster Abbey.
3	In the outer boundary of the map, on top of a tree stump behind Victoria Station.
4	On a green bench near the fountain in the small park.
5	Next to a stack of books on the back side of a wooden shack.
6	At the east edge of the pond, sitting on a green bench.
7*	(extra flower) On a bench in the north end of Green Park.

WHITECHAPEL

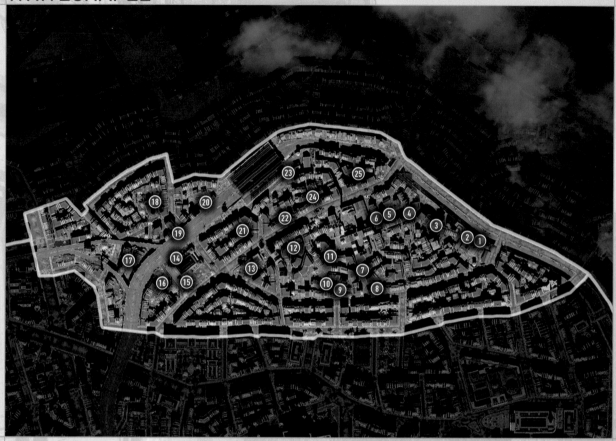

CHESTS

	DESCRIPTION
1	Top floor of the Whitechapel Sawmill.
2	Second Floor of the Whitechapel Sawmill.
3	On the wooden scaffolding connected to the northeast side of W. Packer & Son Building.
4	In the alley next to stacked cargo crates, sacks, and barrels.
5	Inside the derelict house, on the east side, between the windows.
6	Between the steps and tarp covered cargo.
7	In the lower alley across from the cart full of hay.
8	On the roof of the wooden blue building with the red roof, next to the chimney.
9	Tucked away in the cut out of a building; may be guarded by a pair of Blighters.
10	To the left of the Fruit and Vegetable stand that is propped up against the wall.
11	In the alley next to a pile of rubble.
12	Against the wall in the alley below some advertisements.

	DESCRIPTION
13	On the roof of the St. Mary Matfelon, on the west side of the tower's base.
14	Next to some woven baskets on the north side of the Spitalfields Market.
15	Near a row of barrels on the south side of the Spitalfields Market.
16	West across the street from the Spitalfields Market, next to some cargo.
17	Behind a broken wooden fence, next to a large tree.
18	On the lower north corner of the church rooftop.
19	On the ground in the dead-end of an alley, against a wall to the west of the train tracks. A crane holds a pallet that hangs off a building, just above the Chest itself.
20	East corner of the construction site, on the wooden walkway.
21	On the balcony with the metal bars covering the windows.
22	On the porch of a house next to a wooden fence, under a steam pipe.
23	In the east corner of the Bishopsgate railway station.
24	In the alley next to the water pump.
25	Tucked away in a small alley next to two clotheslines.

THE ESSENTIALS
WALKTHROUGH
SIDE QUESTS
COLLECTIBLES
REFERENCE & ANALYSIS
INDEX

CITY OF LONDON
LAMBETH
SOUTHWARK
THE STRAND
THAMES
WESTMINSTER
WHITECHAPEL
WWI ANOMALY

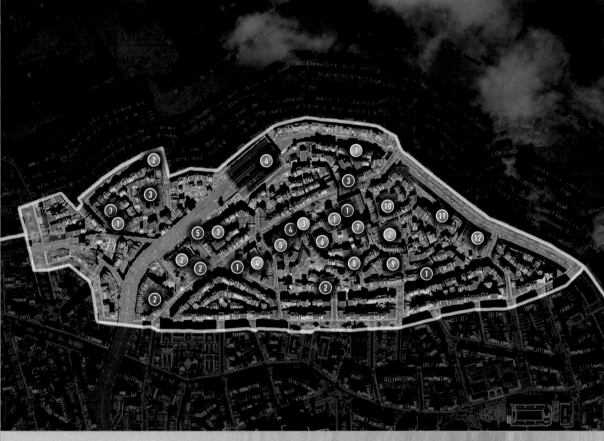

POSTER ADS

	DESCRIPTION
1	Next to J. Mailings Brush Maker in the alley.
2	At the entrance to the alleys next to Todd's Pies.
3	Across from Whitechapel Goose Ale in the alley entrance.
4	At the entrance to the alleys from the main road.
5	Underneath the rail overpass next to Woodge & Sons Pawnbrokers.

BEER BOTTLES

	DESCRIPTION
1	Behind the Whitechapel Goose Ale building in the corner next to a red door.
2	West across the street from Bashing's Buttons LTD, next to a large cart of bottles.
3	Through the entrance of The Cauldron and Stewpot on the small round table to the left of the bar.

PRESSED FLOWERS

	DESCRIPTION
1	In the small park on the top of a bench next to the monument.
2	On the ground to the right of the stairs leading up to the gazeebo.
3	Balanced on the top of a small tombstone.

LARGE CHESTS

	DESCRIPTION	REWARD
1	On the highest roof of the brewing company. Easily seen from the Synch point to the north of it.	Rough and Tumble Belt
2	On the ground level of the Spitalfields Market next to some baskets of food behind a wall of stacked crates full of food.	Green color shader

HELIX GLITCHES

	DESCRIPTION
1	From the roofs on either side of the trees, look for the Rope Launch prompt for the roof across the way and then zipline through the Glitch.
2	Launch to the roof on the other side of the street, don't zipline all the way across as the north side of the street begins to desynchronize you.
3	Zipline from roof to roof on the lower roofs to grab the Glitch.
4	Rope Launch up onto the metal support beam above the rails. Once on the beam, line up with the Glitch and jump down below.
5	Jump from the red shingle roof to the rope that is farthest from it.
6	Climb the wall above the trough full of water, collecting the Glitch about half way up the wall.
7	Climb to the top of the brick columns then perform a Back Eject onto the exhausts sticking out of the roof.
8	Take a Leap of Faith off the eastern roof into the hay below.
9	Rope Launch to the top of the cross above the church's bell tower. The Glitch is at the very top.
10	Jump from the east roof down to the small shack below, aiming for the small chimney on the roof.
11	From the roof with a flat top of wooden planks, aim for the west row of chimneys on the roof with the gray shingles.
12	Inside the top level of the Whitechapel sawmill, jump across the gap in the middle of the room, grabbing the floating Glitch on the way through.

SECRETS

	DESCRIPTION
1	On the ground next to the tracks at the bottom of the small wooden shack built into the bricks.
2	Under the window next to the small wooden shed built into the side of the yellow brick building.
3	On the east stone ledge of the tallest roof in the row of connected buildings.
4	Set on the grave nearest the tree in the small cemetary of St. Mary Matfelon.

WWI TIME ANOMALY

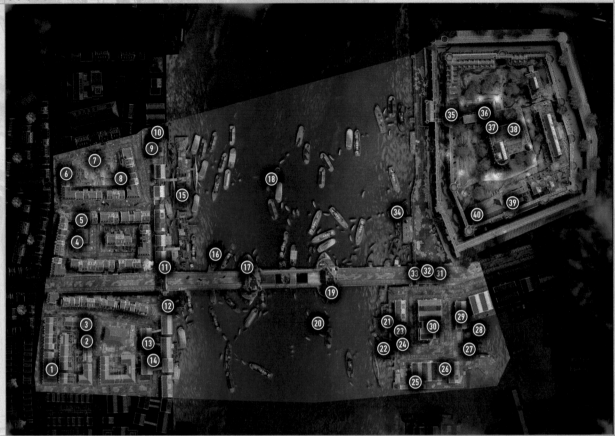

CHESTS

	DESCRIPTION
1	In a small fenced in area on the front side of a house, a Deacon's Soap sign is just to the left of the entrance.
2	On the northeast side of the block, inside a small fenced-in area on the side of the building not facing the street.
3	On a small wooden platform built onto the top of the roof.
4	Located on the top floor of the Hopton's building.
5	Enter through the open windows facing the east side of the Hopton's building.
6	On top of the Bankers building.
7	East of the Gazebo on the small walkway.
8	North of the medical camps on the balcony looking back towards them.
9	Underneath the outer roof just through the entrance to the Dolman & Co building.
10	On the east side of the Dolman & Co building, underneath a lamp.
11	On the roof of the building that straddles the south start of the bridge.
12	Below the upper level of the dock to the west of the stairs leading up to the streets.
13	In a small restricted alley next to a stack of lumber.
14	On a bridge between two buildings. Use Eagle Vision to spot the Chest from the ground below, then Rope Launch to the top of the bridge.
15	At the base of one of the cranes near the water's edge.
16	On a boat to the east of the bridge near the docks.
17	On the top of the tall south tower of the bridge.
18	Near the rift back to 1868 London, on a sailboat next to a barge full of hay.
19	On the east side of the north bridge tower base.
20	At the back of the sailboat to the west of the north bridge tower.

	DESCRIPTION
21	Hidden on the dock behind a stack of crates.
22	Near the mast of the docked sailing ship.
23	On the small top floor of the Pier 13 Warehouse.
24	At the top of the wooden scaffolding near the road.
25	Next to a small fire in the restricted area guarded by a group of Templars. (There is a Large Chest in the same area.)
26	On the highest bridge above the road connecting the two buildings.
27	Near a burning pile of cargo on a barge in a small restricted area, jump into the water and then climb up on the side of the Chest to stay undetected.
28	On the barge docked next to the barge with the flaming cargo.
29	On the short bridge connecting the two buildings.
30	In a small area guarded by Templars. Jump the fence to the north of it, using cover and the crate of hay to kill the Templars before grabbing the Chest.
31	Underneath the northernmost part of the bridge before the stairs.
32	In the restricted area underneath the north side of the bridge in the upstairs portion of the room.
33	In the lower half of the restricted area on the north side of the bridge.
34	Up the stairs on the upper level of the small boat.
35	On the roof of the round building connected to the walls on the south side of the fort.
36	Drop down from the roofs and go into stealth mode. Moving slowly, you should be able to get through the guards near the Chest without alerting them.
37	At the base of the tower on the roof of the southeast side of the main building in the fort.
38	Atop the roof on the north side of the main building in the fort.
39	On the high wall to the east near the center of it, on the circular part of the wall.
40	Inside the storage building on the east side of the fort. A Large Chest is found in the same building.

THE ESSENTIALS
WALKTHROUGH
SIDE QUESTS
COLLECTIBLES
REFERENCE & ANALYSIS
INDEX

CITY OF LONDON
LAMBETH
SOUTHWARK
THE STRAND
THAMES
WESTMINSTER
WHITECHAPEL
WWI ANOMALY

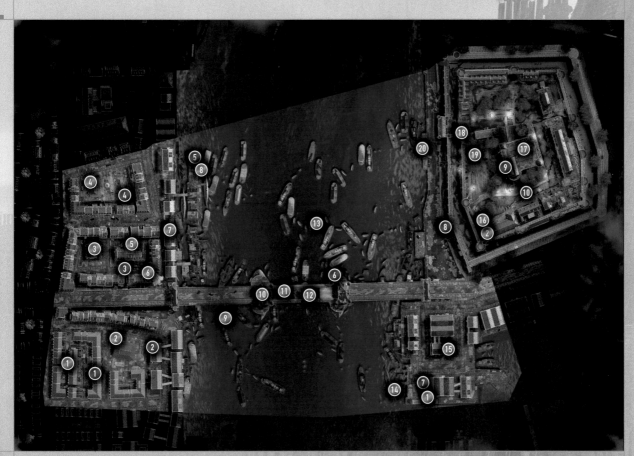

LARGE CHESTS

	DESCRIPTION	REWARD
1	On some wooden planks next to a stack of crates in a small restricted area guarded by Templars.	Eagle Dive Belt
2	Inside the building on the southwest side of the fort, use your Eagle Vision to slip into the area undetected. Once inside the building, find the Chest between some shelves and some crates on the south side of the room.	Unique Material - Boudicaa's Torque

LETTERS FROM THE FRONT

	DESCRIPTION
1	Jump over the wooden fence into the small area with a cart. The Letter is on top of a small table next to a teapot.
2	In the north side of the market on a table with flowers.
3	Beside a red mailbox on a bench, beneath a lantern.
4	Inside the northern medical tent, placed on a wheelchair.
5	On the wooden dock on some crates, just past the last metal crane to the east.
6	On the west side of the northern bridge tower's base, on the ledge near a few steps.
7	On the other side of the fence in front of the Pier 12 building, to the left of the small red door on a stool.
8	On a crate next to some medical supplies and a lantern, underneath a small tent decorated with recruitment posters.
9	At the bottom of the steps on a stack of green crates on the south side of the main building in the center of the fort. Make sure to avoid the searchlight that scans the courtyard.
10	Across the road to the east of the main fort building on a bench.

HELIX GLITCHES

	DESCRIPTION
1	When standing underneath the Glitch, Rope Launch to the edge of the roof above to collect it.
2	Take a Leap of Faith off of the power line and into the hay below.
3	Rope Launch to the top of the roof from underneath the Glitch.
4	Get to the top of the power line east of the Glitch, then zipline all the way across the medical camp, aiming for the chimney on top of the roof in the direction of the Glitch.
5	Take a Leap of Faith from the top of the highest chimneys south of the cart of hay.
6	Line up underneath the Glitch, then Rope Launch to the top of the roof.
7	From the top of the Hopton's sign, aim your Rope Launcher at the top of the roof to the east.
8	From the top of the crane farthest to the west, wait for the crane beside it to move towards you, then jump across.
9	Jump onto the mast of the ship nearest the bridge. Once on top, aim northwest to the mast of the ship and zipline across to grab the Glitch.
10	Rope Launch to the top of the south bridge tower, finding the Glitch at the highest point.
11	Zipline from one side of the bridge to the other.
12	Get to the top of the drawbridge, then begin to zipline across to the other bridge. Once above the Glitch, drop down into the hay on the ship below.
13	From the top of the mast on the ship to the north of the Glitch, aim south for the wooden pole coming out of the water, then zipline across.
14	Climb to the top of the parked submarine.
15	Take a Leap of Faith from the plank protruding from the top of the north end of the building near the Glitch, down into the hay below.
16	Jump from the end of the flagpole onto the roof, toward the Glitch.
17	From the lower flat part of the towers in the corner of the building, zipline to the tower diagonal from it.
18	Climb to the top of the chimney with the Glitch directly above it.
19	Climb to the top of the tree, then jump across to the upper walkway to the south.
20	From the top of the metal post near the water, jump across to the cargo floating in the water.

REFERENCE
AND ANALYSIS

SKILLS AND LEVELS

Whether you're playing as Jacob or Evie Frye, your skill set and level play a huge part in your survivability, as well as your offensive dominance, in the different areas of London.

LEVELING

Leveling is accomplished by investing certain amounts of Skill Points into Jacob or Evie's Skill Trees. They both start at level one, maxing out at level 10. Each level unlocks new skills, as well as new equipment and available upgrades to older equipment.

Skill Points are gained by acquiring experience. Your progression to the next skill point is seen as a small blue meter on the right side of your mini-map, on the lower left hand corner of the screen. Experience is shared between Jacob and Evie so swapping between the two does not cause a drop on the meter.

Experience can be gained by completing sequences, participating in public events, or completing various activities in the Boroughs.

LEVEL	SKILL POINTS FOR UPGRADE
1->2	4
2->3	4
3->4	8
4->5	10
5->6	10
6->7	10
7->8	15
8->9	15
9->10	18

SKILLS

Each character has a separate skill tree that must be trained and leveled. This means that you can really focus on making each character a specialist, with Evie being more stealth oriented and Jacob taking a more aggressive stance with enemies.

Skill points are distributed evenly between the Frye twins. For example, if Jacob is awarded skill points, Evie is automatically awarded the same amount of skill points, regardless of her participation in the event.

Evie and Jacob each have three unique abilities in the tree that can only be unlocked by that character.

EVIE'S SKILLS

ICON	NAME	EFFECT	REQUIREMENT	SKILL POINT COST
	Chameleon	In Sneak Mode Evie perfectly blends with her environment, which allows her to become nearly invisible. Only enemies in close proximity are able to detect her.	Level 5 and Assassin Steps	4
	Knife Master II	Evie can carry twice as many throwing knives. Her knives also inflict significantly more damage.	Level 6 and Knife Master I	6
	Stealth III	Evie's Stealth stat increases by an additional 11. She is less likely to be detected and her assassinations make very little noise.	Level 5 and Stealth II	4

JACOB'S SKILLS

ICON	NAME	EFFECT	REQUIREMENT	SKILL POINT COST
	Defense III	Jacob takes less damage overall.	Level 5 and Defense II	4
	Gunslinger II	Jacob's Countershots are automatic Headshots.	Level 6 and Gunslinger I	6
	Mutilate II	Jacob's successful attacks bring enemies to Near Death much more rapidly.	Level 5 and Mutilate I	4

THE ESSENTIALS

WALKTHROUGH

SIDE QUESTS

COLLECTIBLES

REFERENCE & ANALYSIS

INDEX

SKILLS

PERKS

GANG UPGRADES

CRAFTING

EQUIPMENT

ALLIES & ENEMIES

ACHIEVEMENTS

MISSION PROGRESSION

SHARED SKILLS

The shared skills are broken down into three different groups with very different benefits.

COMBAT

The Combat skill tree benefits Jacob more than Evie, giving bonuses to health, regeneration, damage dealt, and combat combos.

COMBAT SKILL TREE

ICON	NAME	EFFECT	REQUIREMENT	SKILL POINT COST
	Multi-Finisher	When close to multiple enemies that are near death, press ▢ / ✕ to execute up to 4 enemies at a time to gain extra XP.	Acquired during Sequence 1	0
	Stun Attack	Press ✕ / Ⓐ to break an enemy's defensive stance or to briefly stun them. Stunned enemies are taken out of the fight for a short while.	Acquired during Sequence 1	0
	Counter	Press ◯ / Ⓑ to Counter enemies' attacks in combat.	Acquired during Sequence 1	0
	Tool Combo	Press △ / Ⓨ to use your Tools (e.g. revolver, throwing knives) in combat without breaking your combo. Useful for quickly bringing a single enemy to Near Death or attacking multiple enemies at once.	Acquired during Sequence 1	0
	Health Boost I	Increase your Health by 1 segment.	Complete Sequence 1	1
	Health Boost II	Increase your Health by 1 additional segment.	Level 2 and Health Boost	2
	Health Boost III	Increase your Health by 1 additional segment.	Level 3 and Health Boost II	2
	Unstoppable I	Increase the time before you lose your combo streak due to inaction.	Complete Sequence 1	1
	Unstoppable II	The first hit you take during a combo doesn't end your combo.	Level 2 and Unstoppable I	2
	Slayer I	When your combo reaches x10, your next attack automatically puts the target in a near death state.	Complete Sequence 1	1
	Slayer II	When you bring an enemy to near death, your next attack against a different opponent automatically puts them in a near death state. Very useful to set up Multi-Finishers and other moves.	Level 3 and Slayer I	2
	Counter Boost	Counter attacks have a larger window of opportunity and do increased damage.	Level 2	2
	Execute I	Stun an enemy with ✕ / Ⓐ, then perform a Tool Combo with △ / Ⓨ to execute them, inflicting massive damage.	Level 3.	2
	Execute II	Enemies who see you perform an execution are frightened, causing them to break their defensive stance.	Level 5 and Execute I	4
	Mutilate I	Successful attacks bring enemies to near death more rapidly.	Level 3	2
	Adrenaline	Increase the Rate at which your Health regenerates.	Level 5	4
	Combat Stamina	Performing Multi-Kills now regenerates health based on the number of enemies killed.	Level 6	6

STEALTH

The Stealth tree increases Jacob's and Evie's ability to stay hidden. While multiple skills in the tree help with confrontations benefiting Jacob, the higher level areas of the tree contain all of Evie's special skills, making it worth investing the points when playing as her.

ICON	NAME	EFFECT	REQUIREMENT	SKILL POINT COST
	Whistle	Press ✚ to attract your target's attention and lure them to your position for a stealth assassination.	Acquired during first sequence	0
	Knockout	Hold ◎ / Ⓑ to knock an unsuspecting or kidnapped enemy unconscious.	Acquired during first sequence	0
	Stealth Navigation	Press ⓧ / Ⓐ to enter/exit Sneak Mode. In Sneak Mode your movement is faster, you are harder to detect, and you can stealthily move, Aim **L2/LT**, snap to cover, and Throw/Shoot **R2/RT** over low cover and around corners.	Acquired during first sequence	0
	Air Assassination	Press ◎ / ⓧ to perform a high-profile assassination from above the target.	Acquired during first sequence	0
	Lockpicking I	Open locked chests to find money, resources, and rewards.	Available after 1st sequence	1
	Lockpicking II	Open most doors in London—Except doors requiring a master key.	Level 2 and Lockpicking I	2
	Kidnap	Press ◎ / Ⓑ to kidnap an unsuspecting enemy and force them to walk with you. This can allow you to access restricted areas in plain sight.	Acquired in Second sequence for a mission	0
	Intimidation	Kidnapped enemies will not try to escape.	Level 2 and Kidnap	2
	Loot Takedown	Automatically loot enemies when you assassinate them, knock them out, kidnap them or perform Multi-Kills.	Complete first sequence	1
	Double Assassination	Press ◎ / ⓧ to stealthily kill two nearby unaware targets at the same time.	Acquired during second sequence	0
	Stealth I	Your Stealth stat increases by 7. You are less likely to be detected and your assassinations will make less noise.	Level 2	2
	Stealth II	Your Stealth stat increases by an additional 7. You are less likely to be detected and your assassinations will make less noise.	Level 3 and Stealth I	2
	First Strike I	Attack an enemy just before they enter conflict to inflict significant damage.	Level 2.	2
	First Strike II	Your First Strike attacks inflict even more damage. Possibly killing the enemy outright.	Level 6 and First Strike I	6
	Assassin Steps	You suffer significantly reduced damage from falls and make no noise when you land. Your movement also makes significantly less noise.	Level 3	2
	Knife Master I	Throwing knives stun enemies for a short time. You automatically recover throwing knives when performing Multi-Kills.	Level 3	2

ECOSYSTEM

The Ecosystem skill tree greatly increases the benefits you can gain from your surroundings. Investing points in the tree really pays off for the player who likes to recruit Rooks, use carriages, and hunt down and open chests. If you're looking to open chests early on, pick up Scavenger I and II. This greatly helps you later in the game when you begin to craft and upgrade equipment. Spend a point on Eagle Vision II ASAP, this allows you to see enemies and Collectibles through walls, making planning your attacks a breeze.

ECOSYSTEM SKILL TREE

ICON	NAME	EFFECT	REQUIREMENTS	SKILL POINT COST
	Countershot	While in combat, press ▲ / Y when prompted to shoot an enemy that's about to shoot you, preempting their attack.	Acquired during first sequence	0
	Eagle Vision I	Press L3 / LS to activate Eagle Vision. In Eagle Vision, enemies are highlighted in the world and on the Mini-Map. Look at enemies briefly to Tag them; this displays their level and allows them to be seen through walls.	Acquired during first sequence	0
	Fast Driver	Press ✕ / A to gain a significant short term speed boost while driving carriages.	Acquired during second sequence	0
	Leadership I	Press R1 / RT to recruit Rooks to follow you. Hold R1 / RT to bring up advanced commands. You may have up to two Rooks following you at a time	Level 2	0
	Leadership II	Press R1 / RT to recruit Rooks to follow you. Hold R1 / RT to bring up advanced commands. You may have up to three Rooks following you at a time	Level 3 and Leadership I	0
	Leadership III	Press R1 / RT to recruit Rooks to follow you. Hold R1 / RT to bring up advanced commands. You may have up to five Rooks following you at a time	Level 5 and Leadership II	0
	Eagle Vision II	Your Eagle Vision L3 / LS now allows you to see through walls to watch and tag enemies.	Complete first sequence	1
	Eagle Vision III	Your Eagle Vision L3 / LS shows enemies' facing on the Mini-Map. Also increases the range.	Level 2 and Eagle Vision III	2
	Scavenger I	You find more common crafting resources from every source.	Complete first sequence	1
	Scavenger II	You find more rare crafting resources from every source.	Level 2 and Scavenger I	2
	Defense I	Reduces all Melee damage suffered.	Level 2	2
	Defense II	Reduces all Ranged damage suffered.	Level 3 and Defense I	2
	Gunslinger I	When attempting to shoot an empty gun mid-combo, the gun will reload automatically.	Level3	2
	Driver I	Collisions inflict less damage and don't slow you down as much while driving.	Level 3	2
	Driver II	Carriages you drive accelerate significantly faster.	Level 5 and Driver I	4
	Demolition Derby	Carriages you drive inflict more damage and take less damage.	Level 6	6

PERKS

Perks are bonuses added to different general skills, and are achieved by completing a certain number of tasks in a related field. For example, getting 25, two-enemy, multi-finishers results in an increase to the lethality of the player. Perks are accrued cumulatively between Jacob and Evie.

Most of these Perks are completed through normal play, however, it is possible to focus on each perk individually to gain their benefits faster.

NAME	REQUIREMENT	BONUS
Absolutely Stunning	Break an enemy's guard 75 times.	Increase Stun Duration by 25%.
Assassination	Assassinate 120 enemies.	Knockouts will now be performed faster.
Brace For Impact	Destroy 25 carriages by ramming them.	Slightly increased damage when ramming another vehicle.
Combat Mastery	Kill 4 enemies in less than 12 seconds 25 times.	Slight overall damage increase.
Countershot	Countershot 2 ranged attacks in under 10 seconds.	Increased Countershot damage.
Cover Assassinate	Assassinate an enemy from Cover 75 times.	Slightly decreases the noise made by moving.
Death by Rook	Have Rooks kill 50 enemies.	This Perk slightly increases allies' hit points.
Double Air Assassinate	Double Air Assassinate 2 enemies 25 times.	Slightly decreases the noise caused by assassinations.
Double Kill	Perform a multi-finisher on 2 enemies 25 times.	Lethality increased by 2.
Electrifying	Stun 4 enemies with a single Voltaic Bomb 50 times.	Increased Voltaic Bomb damage.
Fancy Moves	Perform a combo using a gun or throwing knife 75 times.	Increased Gun or Knife damage when they are being used in a combo.
Flawless Fighter	Kill 4 or more enemies in the same conflict without being harmed 50 times.	Increases the time allowed to perform a Counter Attack.
Gone Lawing	Hijack 50 Police Carriages.	Increased acceleration of Police vehicles.
Headshot	Perform a headshot while using free aim 50 times.	Increased Critical Hit damage.
Knife Hill	Use Throwing Knives to kill an enemy from cover 75 times.	Increased Throwing Knife damage.
Ledge Kill	Kill an enemy with a contextual ledge finisher 25 times.	Slightly increased damage caused by contextual attacks.
London Drift	Turn 10 corners while drifting by using the break 75 times.	Increases vehicle control during boosts.
Multi-Counter Kill	Perform a Multi-Counter kill 50 times.	Increased Counter Attack damage.
Near Death Recovery	Survive a fight after entering a critical state 50 times.	Increased health regeneration.
No Touchbacks	Hit enemies 20 times in a row during the same conflict without being struck 25 times.	Slight overall damage increase.
Quadra Kill	Perform a multi-finisher on 4 enemies 25 times.	Lethality increased by 2.
Riding Shotgun	Kill an enemy with your gun while on top of a moving carriage 50 times.	Increased damage caused by guns while you are driving.
Road Rage	Kill 3 enemies with your carriage in less than 25 seconds 25 times.	Enemies receive more damage when hit by your carriage.
Shoot the Messenger	Kill a Lookout before they trigger the alarm 15 times.	Lookouts take longer to detect you.
Triple Kill	Perform a multi-finisher on 3 enemies 25 times.	Lethality increased by 2.
Vanish	Become anonymous after entering combat 25 times	Become anonymous faster after conflict.
Vanish in Smoke	Use a Smoke Bomb to end combat and Vanish 25 times.	Smoke Bombs now last longer.
Wanton Destruction	Destroy 4 destructible objects in less than 15 seconds 75 times.	Increased Ram damage when hitting another vehicle.
Zipline Assassin	Assassinate an enemy from a zipline 25 times.	Slightly decreased noise caused by assassinations.

GANG UPGRADES

Gang Upgrades affect the world around you in various ways. The upgrades are paired into three different groups: Ringleader, Insider, and Swindler.

RINGLEADER

The Ringleader upgrade path provides options to upgrade the Rooks and weaken the Blighters. If you like taking friendlies into combat, or if you find that you're too low of a level to fight the enemies in the area you are trying to explore, upgrade the level of the Rooks and let them do the work for you!

ICON	NAME	DESCRIPTION	COST	PREREQ.
	Rook Training I	Rooks receive basic combat training. They are now Level 5.	£1000 50 Leather	None
	Allies in Arms	When you order your Rooks to fight, they open conflict with a volley fire.	£2500 50 Metal 25 Chemical	Rook Training I
	Training Rooks II	Rooks receive advanced combat training. They are now Level 7.	£1000 100 Metal 50 Silk	Allies in Arms
	Enhanced Firepower	Your Rook's volley fire is more effective.	£6000 100 Metal 75 Chemical	Training Rooks II
	Training Rooks III	Rooks receive expert combat training. They are now Level 9.	£20000 100 Metal 50 Silk	Enhanced Firepower
	Rook Riders I	Rooks now appear in carriages too, instead of exclusively on foot.	£1500 50 Leather 100 Metal	None
	Rook Riders II	Even more Rooks now appear in carriages too, instead of exclusively on foot.	£3000 100 Metal 50 Leather	Rook Riders I
	Rook Carriage	Rook Growlers are made from sturdier material.	£5000 100 Leather 100 Silk	Rook Riders II
	Cavalry Call	Summon a carriage full of Rooks to your aid. Hold **R1 / RB** to open the Rooks Menu and press ⊗ / Ⓐ to call the carriage.	£8000 100 Leather 150 Metal	Rook Carriage
	Rook Watchers	Your gang now includes the Watcher Archetype. Watchers use their firearms more often than other Archetypes.	£2000 50 Leather	None
	Rook Brutes	Your gang now includes the Brute Archetype. Brutes are as tough as their name implies.	£5000 50 Leather	Rook Watchers
	Rook Enforcers	Your gang now includes the Enforcer Archetype. Enforcers favor long range weapons.	£8000 100 Metal 50 Silk	Rook Brutes
	Carriage Sabotage	The Blighter's repairman seems to have left the country. Blighter carriages are less resilient.	£4500 50 Metal 50 Chemical	None
	Poison the Well	Reduces the initial health of all Blighters.	£5000 50 Chemical	Carriage Sabotage
	Dull Blades	The Blighter's blades are in dire need of sharpening and deal less melee damage.	£3500 50 Leather 25 Silk	Poison the Well
	Bad Powder I	Low quality gunpowder causes the Blighters to occasionally misfire, or even causes the weapon to explode.	£4000 100 Metal 50 Chemical	Dull Blades
	Bad Powder II	Low quality gunpowder causes the Templars to occasionally misfire, or even causes the weapon to explode.	£6000 100 Metal 80 Chemical	Bad Powder I

THE ESSENTIALS
WALKTHROUGH
SIDE QUESTS
COLLECTIBLES
REFERENCE & ANALYSIS
INDEX

SKILLS
PERKS
GANG UPGRADES
CRAFTING
EQUIPMENT
ALLIES & ENEMIES
ACHIEVEMENTS
MISSION PROGRESSION

INSIDER

The Insider path makes life in London easier. The first thing you should research is Medicine Market. This enables you to buy medicine from the shops. The Insider path also increases the amount of objects available for you to wreak havoc on your enemies with, such as more Growler carriages running through the streets or more crates of explosives sitting about the city.

ICON	NAME	DESCRIPTION	COST	PREREQ.
	Police Bribes	Police will turn a blind eye to some of your illegal actions.	£5000 25 Silk	None
	Notoriety	The name of "Frye" inspires fear in the hearts of your enemies. The Blighters won't initiate conflict with you in the streets.	£7500	Police Bribes
	Little Rooks	Children are the best thieves in London. When using **R1 / RT** to interact with them, they'll give you better loot items.	£1500 100 Metal 50 Chemical	None
	Delivery Service	More hanging crates will appear around the city. Shoot the crates to have them fall on your unsuspecting enemies.	£1000 50 Leather 5250 Silk	Little Rooks
	Explosive Delivery	You'll see more explosives around the city. Press ◎ / ⑧ to carry the crate or hold ◎ / ⑧ to ignite it.	£2000 50 Metal 50 Chemical	Delivery Service
	Growler Boom	Increase the popularity of the Growler. Look for more of the gang favorite on the streets of London.	£1500 25 Metal	None
	Dispatcher	Nimbler, faster, and more reliable: fire trucks can reach the poorer boroughs of London.	£1500	Growler boom
	Medicine Market	You can now buy medicine in shops. Use medicine ✚ during combat to quickly recover health.		None
	Mad Science	Unlock the first Voltaic Bomb upgrade. Visit the crafting menu to use the new plan.	£2500 50 Metal 25 Chemical	Medicine Market

SWINDLER

The Swindler path is focused on saving you as much money as possible. Consider saving up and working your way up to the City Takeover option before researching the rest of Gang upgrades, this saves you more than the £10,000 that you spend on the upgrade, netting you a profit in the end. The earlier you research City Takeover, the larger the eventual profit.

ICON	NAME	DESCRIPTION	COST	PREREQ.
	City-Wide Craze	50% discount on Hallucinogenic Darts.	£500 50 Metal 50 Chemical	None
	Bomb Discount	A certain fireworks vendor likes it when things boom. He will reduce the price of all bombs by 50%.	£4500 100 Metal 25 Chemical	City-Wide Craze
	Black Market Affiliation	Ammunition comes cheaper when you know the right person. Save 25% on gun and throwing knife ammunition at any shop.	£3000 50 Metal 50 Chemical	None
	Black Market Ties	Having a hand in the black market dealings comes with its own benefits. Buy new weapons and other gear from the inventory at a discount of 20%.	£4000 50 Chemical	Black Market Affiliation
	City Takeover	Learn the not-so-subtle art of bribery. All other Gang Upgrades will cost less to purchase.	£10000 50 Chemical 50 Silk	Black Market Ties
	Ale Heist	Carts containing ale shipments run throughout the city. Hijack or Escort them for a cash reward.	£1500 50 Chemical	None
	Shell Company	Place your money in various accounts to increase the payout of all Income Activities.	£5000 25 Silk 25 Chemical	Ale Heist
	Rate of Income	Pass Bills that reduce business taxes. Increase the amount of money deposited in your hideout vault by 50%.	£8000 25 Silk 25 Chemical	Shell Company
	Pub Investor	Buy pubs in the city to increase the train hideout income by £500 every 30 minutes and your maximum safe capacity by £500.	£6000 150 Leather 50 Chemical	None
	Pub Games	Sponsor street-football games around pubs and increase pub clientele. This increases the train hideout income by £500 every 30 minutes and your maximum safe capacity by £500.	£10000 100 Leather	Pub Investor
	Bookmaker	Hire professional bookies to make money at the races. This increases the train hideout income by £500 every 30 minutes and your maximum safe capacity by £500.	£12000 100 Leather 50 Silk	Pub Games
	Tea Magnate	Invest in London tea businesses and increase the train hideout income by £500 every 30 minutes and your maximum safe capacity by £500.	£15000 50 Metal 50 Chemical	Book Maker
	Shop Investor	Buy shops in the city to increase the train hideout income by £1000 every 30 minutes and your maximum safe capacity by £1000.	£20000 100 Metal 100 Silk	Tea Magnate

CRAFTING

Crafting is essential in *Assassin's Creed Syndicate*. To craft an item you must first meet the minimum requirements for it, this can be a blueprint, unique and regular resources as well as some in-game currency, or £. Consumables cannot be crafted, however upgrades to increase the amount you can hold or their over all effectiveness can be crafted.

THE ESSENTIALS
WALKTHROUGH
SIDE QUESTS
COLLECTIBLES
REFERENCE & ANALYSIS
INDEX

SKILLS
PERKS
GANG UPGRADES
CRAFTING
EQUIPMENT
ALLIES & ENEMIES
ACHIEVEMENTS
MISSION PROGRESSION

CRAFTING MATERIALS

BASIC CRAFTING MATERIALS

Money (£) can be acquired by completing sequences, participating in crowd events, opening chests, as well as from the safe in the Train hideout. Silk, Leather, Chemicals, and Metal can be acquired from the Chests scattered around the city (check out the Collectibles section for all the Chest locations). Crafting Resources can also be purchased with real world currency in varying amounts by pressing (△ / Ⓨ) in the crafting menu. While not necessary, purchasing resources can save you some time, allowing you to focus more on the story and less on searching for resources.

UNIQUE CRAFTING MATERIALS

Unique crafting materials are given as rewards from the Large Chests (see the Collectibles section to learn which Chest holds each specific material). Unique materials are also earned by completing Memory Sequences.

BLUEPRINTS

Much like unique crafting materials, blueprints are given as rewards from Large Chests, as well as from different Memory Sequences. Blueprints can also be acquired by gaining levels with your Associates. Each blueprint is tied to a specific item, whether it be a new cloak or an upgrade for a piece of equipment.

EQUIPMENT

There are six different types of Equipment found in the Inventory of Jacob and Evie: Weapons, Assassin Gauntlets, Firearms, Belts or Capes, Outfits, and Colors. Each piece of Equipment, with the exception of Colors, can be upgraded one time.

WEAPONS

Assassin's Creed Syndicate grants you the choice of over 50 weapons separated into three different weapon classes, all with very distinct differences.

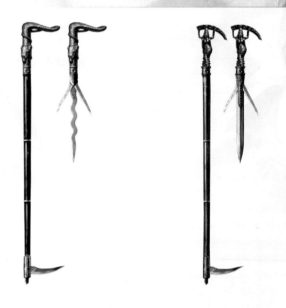

CANE-SWORD

Cane-Swords have the highest Impact, but are less lethal when compared to other weapon types.

LEVEL	NAME		
	INITIATE'S CANE SWORD		
	ATTACK	IMPACT	LETHALITY
1	2	4	0
	ADDITIONAL REQUIREMENTS		
	Evie's Starting Weapon		
	NOBLE CANE-SWORD		
	ATTACK	IMPACT	LETHALITY
2	2/3	3/4	1
	ADDITIONAL REQUIREMENTS		
	Purchase for £2500		
	ARBAAZ MIR'S CANE-SWORD		
	ATTACK	IMPACT	LETHALITY
3	3/5	4/5	2/3
	ADDITIONAL REQUIREMENTS		
	Uplay Reward		
	ADEPT CANE-SWORD		
	ATTACK	IMPACT	LETHALITY
3	3/4	4/5	2
	ADDITIONAL REQUIREMENTS		
	Conquer the borough of Whitechapel		
	OCEAN CANE-SWORD		
	ATTACK	IMPACT	LETHALITY
3	3/5	4/5	2/3
	ADDITIONAL REQUIRMENTS		
	Redeem with a promo code		

LEVEL	NAME		
	MAYAN CANE-SWORD		
	ATTACK	IMPACT	LETHALITY
4	4/5	5/6	3
	ADDITIONAL REQUIREMENTS		
	Complete the Whitechapel Gangwar, then craft for £1250 and 60 Metal		
	GODDESS CANE-SWORD		
	ATTACK	IMPACT	LETHALITY
4	4/5	5/6	3
	ADDITIONAL REQUIREMENTS		
	Reach Loyalty Level 1 with Robert Topping		
	SIR LEMAY'S CANE		
	ATTACK	IMPACT	LETHALITY
5	5/6	6/7	4
	ADDITIONAL REQUIREMENTS		
	Complete Sequence 5, Research and Development		
	CHARLES DICKEN'S CANE-SWORD		
	ATTACK	IMPACT	LETHALITY
5	5/6	6/7	4/5
	ADDITIONAL REQUIREMENTS		
	Complete the Charles Dickens Memories		
	GOLDEN LION CANE-SWORD		
	ATTACK	IMPACT	LETHALITY
6	6/8	7/8	4
	ADDITIONAL REQUIREMENTS		
	Complete Sequence 6, A Case of Identity then purchase for £3500		

LEVEL	NAME		
6	**LORD PEARSON'S CANE-SWORD**		
	ATTACK	IMPACT	LETHALITY
	6/8	7/8	4/5
	ADDITIONAL REQUIRMENTS		
	Waterloo Station Chest		
6	**OBSIDIAN LION CANE-SWORD**		
	ATTACK	IMPACT	LETHALITY
	6/8	7/8	4/5
	ADDITIONAL REQUIRMENTS		
	Craft for £3000 and 120 Metal		
7	**JADE DRAGON CANE-SWORD**		
	ATTACK	IMPACT	LETHALITY
	7/9	8/9	5
	ADDITIONAL REQUIRMENTS		
	Reach Loyalty Level 2 with Robert Topping		
7	**RUNIC MAYAN CANE-SWORD**		
	ATTACK	IMPACT	LETHALITY
	7/9	8/9	5
	ADDITIONAL REQUIRMENTS		
	Complete WWI Time Anomaly, The Darkest Hour		
8	**IVORY AND JADE CANE-SWORD**		
	ATTACK	IMPACT	LETHALITY
	8/9	8/9	5
	ADDITIONAL REQUIRMENTS		
	Craft with £4500, 120 Leather, and 40 Chemical		

LEVEL	NAME		
8	**LIGHT AND DARK CANE-SWORD**		
	ATTACK	IMPACT	LETHALITY
	8/10	8/9	5
	ADDITIONAL REQUIRMENTS		
	Reach Loyalty Level 3 with Robert Topping		
9	**FLAME DRAGON CANE-SWORD**		
	ATTACK	IMPACT	LETHALITY
	9/11	9/10	6
	ADDITIONAL REQUIRMENTS		
	Reach Loyalty Level 4 with Robert Topping		
9	**NIGHT TERROR CANE-SWORD**		
	ATTACK	IMPACT	LETHALITY
	9/11	9/10	6
	ADDITIONAL REQUIRMENTS		
	Craft with £6000, 160 Leather, and 250 Chemical		
10	**DOVE CANE-SWORD**		
	ATTACK	IMPACT	LETHALITY
	10/13	10/12	7
	ADDITIONAL REQUIRMENTS		
	Complete the Dreadful Crimes (Sony Exclusive)		
10	**WORLD'S GREATEST CANE-SWORD**		
	ATTACK	IMPACT	LETHALITY
	10/13	10/12	7
	ADDITIONAL REQUIRMENTS		
	Reach Loyalty Level 5 with Robert Topping		

KNUCKLES

Knuckles are well-balanced between impact and lethality.

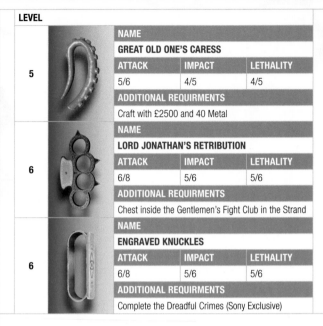

LEVEL	NAME		
1	**INITIATE KNUCKLES**		
	ATTACK	IMPACT	LETHALITY
	1/2	1/2	1/2
	ADDITIONAL REQUIRMENTS		
	Jacob's Starting Weapon		
2	**IRON MANACLES**		
	ATTACK	IMPACT	LETHALITY
	2/3	2/3	2/3
	ADDITIONAL REQUIRMENTS		
	Purchase for £2500		
3	**CROWS STRENGTH**		
	ATTACK	IMPACT	LETHALITY
	3/4	2/3	2/3
	ADDITIONAL REQUIRMENTS		
	Complete Sequence 4, A Spoonful of Syrup		
3	**DIRTY KNUCKLES**		
	ATTACK	IMPACT	LETHALITY
	3/5	2/4	2/4
	ADDITIONAL REQUIRMENTS		
	Redeem with promo code		
3	**ANGEL'S KNUCKLES**		
	ATTACK	IMPACT	LETHALITY
	3/5	2/4	2/4
	ADDITIONAL REQUIRMENTS		
	Redeem with promo code		
3	**PIRATE KNUCKLES**		
	ATTACK	IMPACT	LETHALITY
	3/5	2/4	2/4
	ADDITIONAL REQUIRMENTS		
	Redeem with promo code		
3	**SLYNKY'S FIST**		
	ATTACK	IMPACT	LETHALITY
	3/4	2/3	2/3
	ADDITIONAL REQUIRMENTS		
	Purchase for £3000		
4	**STEEL KNUCKLES**		
	ATTACK	IMPACT	LETHALITY
	4/5	3/4	3/4
	ADDITIONAL REQUIRMENTS		
	Reach Loyalty Level 2 with Frederick Abberline		
5	**DARBE'S BEAR PAW**		
	ATTACK	IMPACT	LETHALITY
	5/6	4/5	4/5
	ADDITIONAL REQUIRMENTS		
	Chest inside the Gas Work Factory of Southwark		

LEVEL	NAME		
5	**GREAT OLD ONE'S CARESS**		
	ATTACK	IMPACT	LETHALITY
	5/6	4/5	4/5
	ADDITIONAL REQUIRMENTS		
	Craft with £2500 and 40 Metal		
6	**LORD JONATHAN'S RETRIBUTION**		
	ATTACK	IMPACT	LETHALITY
	6/8	5/6	5/6
	ADDITIONAL REQUIRMENTS		
	Chest inside the Gentlemen's Fight Club in the Strand		
6	**ENGRAVED KNUCKLES**		
	ATTACK	IMPACT	LETHALITY
	6/8	5/6	5/6
	ADDITIONAL REQUIRMENTS		
	Complete the Dreadful Crimes (Sony Exclusive)		

THE ESSENTIALS

WALKTHROUGH

SIDE QUESTS

COLLECTIBLES

REFERENCE & ANALYSIS

INDEX

SKILLS

PERKS

GANG UPGRADES

CRAFTING

EQUIPMENT

ALLIES & ENEMIES

ACHIEVEMENTS

MISSION PROGRESSION

LEVEL	NAME		
7	**LION CLAWS**		
	ATTACK	IMPACT	LETHALITY
	7/9	6/7	6/7
	ADDITIONAL REQUIRMENTS		
	Craft with £3750 and 140 Metal		

LEVEL	NAME		
7	**JAW TENDERIZER**		
	ATTACK	IMPACT	LETHALITY
	7/9	6/7	6/7
	ADDITIONAL REQUIRMENTS		
	Chest Inside the Cannon Street Station		

LEVEL	NAME		
8	**DEATH KNUCKLES**		
	ATTACK	IMPACT	LETHALITY
	8/10	6/7	6/7
	ADDITIONAL REQUIRMENTS		
	Chest on the Westminster Abbey rooftop		

LEVEL	NAME		
8	**COPPER LOVE**		
	ATTACK	IMPACT	LETHALITY
	8/10	6/7	6/7
	ADDITIONAL REQUIRMENTS		
	Complete Sequence 8, Fun and Games		

LEVEL	NAME		
9	**MASTER ASSASSIN'S KNUCKLES**		
	ATTACK	IMPACT	LETHALITY
	9/11	7/8	7/8
	ADDITIONAL REQUIRMENTS		
	Crafted with £6000, 160 Metal, and 50 Silk		

LEVEL	NAME		
10	**EAGLE'S SPLENDOR KNUCKLES**		
	ATTACK	IMPACT	LETHALITY
	10/13	8/9	8/9
	ADDITIONAL REQUIRMENTS		
	Conquer the borough of Westminster		

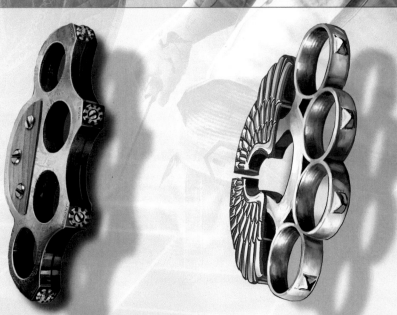

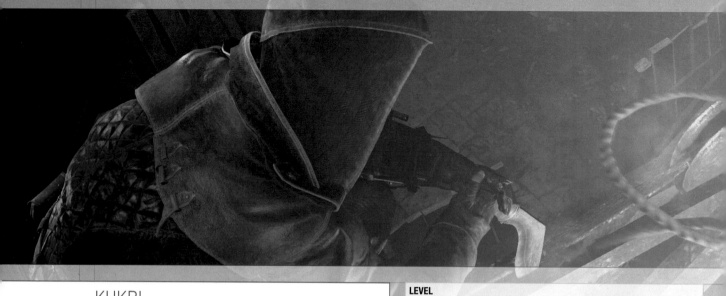

KUKRI

Kukris are the most lethal weapon in the game, but their impact stat is generally lower.

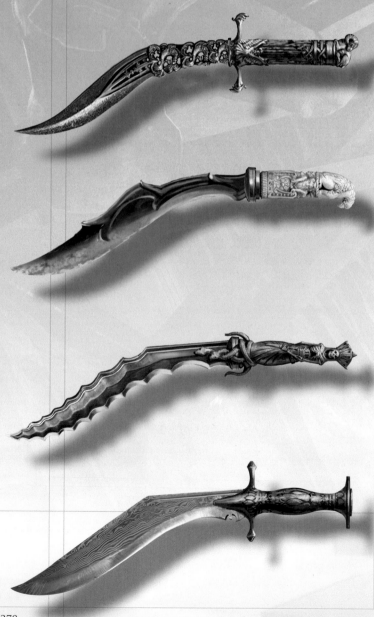

LEVEL		NAME		
2		**IVORY KUKRI**		
		ATTACK	IMPACT	LETHALITY
		2/3	0	3/4
		ADDITIONAL REQUIRMENTS		
		Complete Sequence 3, Somewhere That's Green		
3		**ADEPT KUKRI**		
		ATTACK	IMPACT	LETHALITY
		3/4	1/2	3/4
		ADDITIONAL REQUIRMENTS		
		Purchase for £3000		
3		**CEREMONIAL KUKRI**		
		ATTACK	IMPACT	LETHALITY
		3/5	1/3	3/4
		ADDITIONAL REQUIRMENTS		
		Redeem with promo code		
3		**GOLDEN KUKRI**		
		ATTACK	IMPACT	LETHALITY
		3/5	1/3	3/4
		ADDITIONAL REQUIRMENTS		
		Redeem with promo code		
3		**RAM'S KUKRI**		
		ATTACK	IMPACT	LETHALITY
		3/5	1/3	3/4
		ADDITIONAL REQUIRMENTS		
		Redeem with promo code		
4		**RUBY KUKRI**		
		ATTACK	IMPACT	LETHALITY
		4/5	1/2	4/5
		ADDITIONAL REQUIRMENTS		
		Reach Loyalty Level 1 with Henry Green		
4		**IRON KUKRI**		
		ATTACK	IMPACT	LETHALITY
		4/5	1/2	4/5
		ADDITIONAL REQUIRMENTS		
		Craft with £2000 and 80 Metal		

THE ESSENTIALS
WALKTHROUGH
SIDE-QUESTS
COLLECTIBLES
REFERENCE & ANALYSIS
INDEX

SKILLS
PERKS
GANG UPGRADES
CRAFTING
EQUIPMENT
ALLIES & ENEMIES
ACHIEVEMENTS
MISSION PROGRESSION

LEVEL		NAME		
		BOLD EAGLE KUKRI		
5		ATTACK	IMPACT	LETHALITY
		5/6	2	5/6
		ADDITIONAL REQUIRMENTS		
		Complete Sequence 5, Friendly Competition		
		NAME		
		GUARD KUKRI		
5		ATTACK	IMPACT	LETHALITY
		5/6	2	5/6
		ADDITIONAL REQUIRMENTS		
		Purchase for £5000		
		NAME		
		JADE KUKRI		
6		ATTACK	IMPACT	LETHALITY
		6/8	3	6/7
		ADDITIONAL REQUIRMENTS		
		Complete Sequence 6, A Case of Identity		
		NAME		
		MASTER RUBY KUKRI		
6		ATTACK	IMPACT	LETHALITY
		6/8	3	6/7
		ADDITIONAL REQUIRMENTS		
		Reach Loyalty Level 2 with Henry Green		
		NAME		
		HENRY'S KUKRI		
6		ATTACK	IMPACT	LETHALITY
		6/8	3	6/7
		ADDITIONAL REQUIRMENTS		
		Craft for £3000 and 120 Metal		
		NAME		
		ASSASSIN KUKRI		
7		ATTACK	IMPACT	LETHALITY
		7/9	3	7/8
		ADDITIONAL REQUIRMENTS		
		Crafted for £3750 and 140 Metal		

LEVEL		NAME		
		GOLD BLESSING KUKRI		
7		ATTACK	IMPACT	LETHALITY
		7/9	3	7/8
		ADDITIONAL REQUIRMENTS		
		Conquer the borough of The Thames		
		NAME		
		ANCIENT KUKRI		
7		ATTACK	IMPACT	LETHALITY
		7/9	4	7/8
		ADDITIONAL REQUIRMENTS		
		Purchase for £10000		
		NAME		
		MASTER ASSASSIN'S KUKRI		
8		ATTACK	IMPACT	LETHALITY
		8/10	4	8/9
		ADDITIONAL REQUIRMENTS		
		Reach Loyalty Level 4 with Henry Green		
		NAME		
		SERRATED DEATH		
9		ATTACK	IMPACT	LETHALITY
		9/11	4/5	9/10
		ADDITIONAL REQUIRMENTS		
		Reach Loyalty Level 4 with Ned Wynert		
		NAME		
		EAGLE'S SPLENDOR KUKRI		
9		ATTACK	IMPACT	LETHALITY
		9/11	4/5	9/10
		ADDITIONAL REQUIRMENTS		
		Craft with £6000, 160 Metal, and 50 Chemical		
		NAME		
		LEGENDARY ASSASSIN KUKRI		
10		ATTACK	IMPACT	LETHALITY
		10/13	5/6	10/12
		ADDITIONAL REQUIRMENTS		
		Reach Loyalty Level 5 with Henry Green		

FIREARMS

Firearms become available after Sequence 3. They make countering ranged enemies much easier and, in most cases, more lethal than combating them with throwing knives. This increased lethality comes at a cost however. These firearms are incredibly loud, making stealth assassinations with them nearly impossible.

LEVEL

	NAME			
3	**DERRINGER PISTOL**			
	DAMAGE	SPEED	ACCURACY	CLIP SIZE
	2	1	4/6	1
	ADDITIONAL REQUIRMENTS			
	Complete Sequence 3			

	NAME			
3	**POCKET PISTOL**			
	DAMAGE	SPEED	ACCURACY	CLIP SIZE
	2	2	5/7	4
	ADDITIONAL REQUIRMENTS			
	Purchase for £3000			

	NAME			
3	**MODEL 1 REVOLVER**			
	DAMAGE	SPEED	ACCURACY	CLIP SIZE
	3	4	6/8	5
	ADDITIONAL REQUIRMENTS			
	Complete Sequence 4			

	NAME			
4	**(54 BORE) 1856 REVOLVER**			
	DAMAGE	SPEED	ACCURACY	CLIP SIZE
	3	3	8/10	6
	ADDITIONAL REQUIRMENTS			
	Reach Loyalty Level 1 with Frederick Abberline			

	NAME			
4	**SINGLE ACTION ARMY**			
	DAMAGE	SPEED	ACCURACY	CLIP SIZE
	4	4	7/9	6
	ADDITIONAL REQUIRMENTS			
	Purchase for £4000			

	NAME			
4	**LANCASTER 4-BARRELS**			
	DAMAGE	SPEED	ACCURACY	CLIP SIZE
	7	2	3/5	4
	ADDITIONAL REQUIRMENTS			
	Complete Sequence 6, A Case of Identity			

LEVEL

	NAME			
4	**BULLSEYE REVOLVER**			
	DAMAGE	SPEED	ACCURACY	CLIP SIZE
	4/6	4/6	8/10	6
	ADDITIONAL REQUIREMENTS			
	Unlock with Uplay			

	NAME			
4	**DEMONIC REVOLVER**			
	DAMAGE	SPEED	ACCURACY	CLIP SIZE
	4/6	4/6	8/10	6
	ADDITIONAL REQUIREMENTS			
	Redeem with a promo code			

	NAME			
4	**STEALTH REVOLVER**			
	DAMAGE	SPEED	ACCURACY	CLIP SIZE
	4/6	4/6	8/10	6
	ADDITIONAL REQUIREMENTS			
	Redeem with a promo code			

THE ESSENTIALS
WALKTHROUGH
SIDE QUESTS
COLLECTIBLES
REFERENCE & ANALYSIS

SKILLS
PERKS
UPGRADES
CRAFTING
EQUIPMENT
GANGS & ENEMIES
THE ANIMUS
MAPS & APPENDICES

LEVEL		NAME			
		.38 DOUBLE ACTION			
5		DAMAGE	SPEED	ACCURACY	CLIP SIZE
		5	6	7/9	6
		ADDITIONAL REQUIRMENTS			
		Reach Loyalty Level 3 with Frederick Abberline			
		NAME			
		M1877 "LIGHTNING"			
6		DAMAGE	SPEED	ACCURACY	CLIP SIZE
		5	6	8/9	6
		ADDITIONAL REQUIRMENTS			
		Complete Sequence 7, Unbreaking the Bank			
		NAME			
		M1877 "THUNDERER"			
7		DAMAGE	SPEED	ACCURACY	CLIP SIZE
		6	8	9/10	6
		ADDITIONAL REQUIRMENTS			
		Conquer the borough of City of London			

LEVEL		NAME			
		MODEL 3 REVOLVER			
7		DAMAGE	SPEED	ACCURACY	CLIP SIZE
		8	7	8/9	6
		ADDITIONAL REQUIRMENTS			
		Reach Loyalty Level 4 with Frederick Abberline			
		NAME			
		SELF-LOADING PISTOL MODEL 1868			
9		DAMAGE	SPEED	ACCURACY	CLIP SIZE
		9	9	8/10	8
		ADDITIONAL REQUIRMENTS			
		Reach Loyalty Level 5 with Frederick Abberline			
		NAME			
		THE MARS			
10		DAMAGE	SPEED	ACCURACY	CLIP SIZE
		10	10	9	12
		ADDITIONAL REQUIREMENTS			
		Reach Loyalty Level 5 with Ned Wynert for the Crafting Plan, £10000, 150 Metal, and 100 Chemical			

ASSASSIN GAUNTLETS

Assassin Gauntlets are different than weapons in the fact that they only provide an Attack bonus with no values for Impact or Lethality.

LEVEL			
1		**NAME**	LEATHER GAUNTLET
		ATTACK	1/2
		ADDITIONAL REQUIRMENTS	Game Start
2		**NAME**	HARDENED LEATHER GAUNTLET
		ATTACK	2/3
		ADDITIONAL REQUIRMENTS	Plan found in Sequence 3
3		**NAME**	REINFORCED GAUNTLET
		ATTACK	3/4
		ADDITIONAL REQUIRMENTS	Plan found in Sequence 04, On the Origin of Syrup, £2500 and 100 Metal
3		**NAME**	REDBACK GAUNTLET
		ATTACK	4/5
		ADDITIONAL REQUIRMENTS	Unlock with Uplay
3		**NAME**	INDUSTRIAL GAUNTLET
		ATTACK	4/5
		ADDITIONAL REQUIRMENTS	Unlock with Uplay
3		**NAME**	ROYAL GAUNTLET
		ATTACK	4/5
		ADDITIONAL REQUIRMENTS	Unlock with Uplay
4		**NAME**	BLACK LEATHER GAUNTLET
		ATTACK	4/5
		ADDITIONAL REQUIRMENTS	Plan found in Sequence 5, Survival of the Fittest
5		**NAME**	MIRAGE GAUNTLET
		ATTACK	5/6
		ADDITIONAL REQUIRMENTS	Plan Found in Sequence 6, One Good Deed, £4500 and 100 Metal
6		**NAME**	IRON DEATH GAUNTLET
		ATTACK	6/8
		ADDITIONAL REQUIRMENTS	Plan found in Sequence 7, Driving Mrs. Disraeli, £5500, 120 Leather, and 50 Silk

CORE ESSENTIALS

WALKTHROUGH

100% QUEST

CHECKLIST

REFERENCE & ANALYSIS

INDEX

SKILLS

PERKS

GANG UPGRADES

CRAFTING

EQUIPMENT

ALLIES & ENEMIES

ACHIEVEMENTS

MISSION PROGRESSION

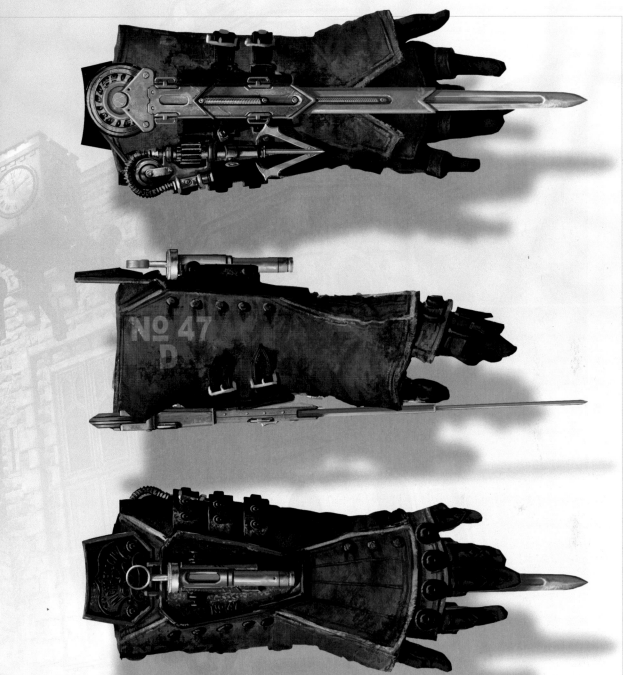

LEVEL		NAME
7		**ASSASSIN GAUNTLET**
		ATTACK
		7/9
		ADDITIONAL REQUIRMENTS
		Plan found in Sequence 8, Triple Threat, £200, 120 Iron, and 50 Silk
8		**NAME**
		THE DEVIL'S HANDSHAKE
		ATTACK
		8/10
		ADDITIONAL REQUIRMENTS
		Plan found in Sequence 9, Double Trouble, £8500,140 Leather, and 60 Silk

LEVEL		NAME
9		**THE CHIMERA**
		ATTACK
		9/11
		ADDITIONAL REQUIRMENTS
		Plan found in Chest inside the Bank Vault, £9000,140 Metal, and 60 Silk
10		**NAME**
		LEGENDARY ASSASSIN GAUNTLET
		ATTACK
		10/12
		ADDITIONAL REQUIRMENTS
		Reach Loyalty Level 5 with Clara O'Dea

BELTS & CAPES

Belts and Capes affect Jacob's and Evie's defense and stealth, with Jacob using Belts and Evie preferring to use Capes.

BELTS

LEVEL		NAME	DEFENSE	STEALTH	ADDITIONAL REQUIREMENTS
1		LEATHER BELT	1/3	0/1	Unlock after Sequence 1
2		INITIATE BELT	2/4	1/2	Unlock after Sequence 3, A Spanner in the Works
3		ROUGH AND TUMBLE BELT	3/5	2/3	Chest on the Factory Rooftop in Whitechapel
3		DARK LEATHER BELT	3/5	2/3	Unlock after completing Sequence 4, Unnatural Selection
3		IRON BELT	3/6	2/5	Unlock with Uplay
3		SUAVE BELT	3/6	2/5	Unlock with Uplay
3		NOBLE ASSASSIN BELT	3/6	2/5	Uplay Reward
3		ADEPT BELT	3/5	2/3	Purchase for £3000
4		THIEF BELT	4/6	3/4	Reach Loyalty Level 1 with Clara O'Dea
4		SASSY ASSASSIN BELT	4/6	3/4	Craft with £2000 and 80 Leather
5		GREENWOOD BELT	5/7	4/5	Craft with £2500 and 100 Leather
5		CROSSROAD BELT	5/7	4/5	Purchase from the Shops
6		SANGUINE BELT	6/8	5/6	Craft with £3000 and 120 Leather
6		METAL WEB BELT	6/8	5/6	Complete Sequence 6, A Spot of Tea
7		REAPER BELT	7/9	6/7	WWI Time Anomaly, St. Katherine's Docks
7		EAGLE SPLENDOR BELT	7/9	6/7	Inside the Chest outside the Royal Horse Guard Building in the Buckingham Palace Complex
7		IRON SCALE BELT	7/9	6/7	Complete Sequence 7, Playing Politics
8		BLACK DEATH BELT	8/10	7/8	Conquer The Strand
8		EAGLE DIVE BELT	8/10	7/8	Inside a Chest found in the interior courtyard of the Tower of London
9		SPRING-HEELED JACK BELT	10/12	8/9	Complete Charles Dickens Memories
9		MASTER ASSASSIN'S BELT	10/12	8/9	Complete Sequence 9, Dress to Impress
10		BEER COLLECTOR BELT	12/15	9/10	Complete the Beer Bottle Collection
10		LEGENDARY ASSASSIN BELT	12/15	9/10	Crafting Plan found as reward for completing Sequence 9, Dinosaur Talon, £10000, 150 Leather, and 100 Silk

CAPES

THE ESSENTIALS
WALKTHROUGH
SIDE QUESTS
COLLECTIBLES
REFERENCE & ANALYSIS
INDEX

SKILLS
PERKS
GANG UPGRADES
CRAFTING
EQUIPMENT
ALLIES & ENEMIES
ALMANAC

LEVEL		NAME	DEF	ST	ADD REQS
1		RED CLOAK	0/1	1/3	Complete Sequence 2
2		THRIFTY CLOAK	1/2	2/4	Purchase for £2500
3		HUNTER'S MANTLE	2/3	3/5	Complete Sequence 4, The Create Escape
3		BLACK JACK CLOAK	2/3	3/5	Purchase for £3000
3		ORANGE SILK CLOAK	2/3	3/5	Purchase for £3000
3		OUT OF THE BLUE CLOAK	2/5	3/6	Redeem with a promo code
3		KILLER'S LACE CLOAK	2/5	3/6	Uplay Reward
3		CRIMSON WING CLOAK	2/5	3/6	Unlock with Uplay
4		PATCHWORK CLOAK	3/4	4/6	Reach Loyalty Level 2 with Clara O'Dea
4		EAGLE DIVE CAPE	3/4	4/6	Complete Sequence 6, One Good Deed
5		LADY VIGNOLA'S CLOAK	4/5	5/7	Craft with £2500, 40 Leather, and 25 Silk
5		STORMY NIGHT CLOAK	4/5	5/7	Purchase for £5000

LEVEL		NAME	DEF	ST	ADD REQS
5		COUNTRY CLOAK	4/5	5/7	Complete the Dreadful Crimes (Sony Exclusive)
6		CLOAK OF THE PEOPLE	5/6	6/8	Craft with £3000, 50 Leather, and 25 Silk
6		LIGHT AND DARK CLOAK	5/6	6/8	Inside a Chest located in the Lambeth Cemetery
7		GOLDRED CLOAK	6/7	7/9	Complete Sequence 7, The Bodyguard
7		FLAME SILK CLOAK	6/7	7/9	Purchase for £7500
7		EMERALD ISLE CAPE	6/7	7/9	Collect all Royal Letters, Purchase in Shop for £6000
8		LADY CYRIELLE'S SHAWL	7/8	8/10	Complete Sequence 8, Strange Bedfellows
9		LEGENDARY ASSASSIN CAPE	8/9	10/12	Craft with £6000, 180 Leather and 50 Silk
9		CLOAK OF VICTORY	8/9	10/12	Complete Sequence 9, Family Politics
10		ROYAL CLOAK	9/10	12	Complete Queen Victoria's Memories
10		AEGIS CLOAK	9/10	12/15	Crafting Plan found in the Sequence 9, £10000, 150 Leather, 100 Silk

OUTFITS

Jacob and Evie each possess separate outfits that grant a wide range of different buffs.

EVIE'S OUTFITS

NAME	EFFECTS	ADDITIONAL REQUIREMENTS
SIMPLY EVIE	Increase Cane-Sword damage by 10%/20%	Game Start
NIGHTSHADE CLOAK	Increase Kukri damage by 10%/20%	Crafting Plan from Sequence 7, £10000, 150 Leather, and 100 Silk
DEFENDER'S GARB	Decrease melee damage received by 10%/15%	Complete Sequence 4, Playing It By Ear
MILITARY SUIT	Increase Firearms damage by 10%/20%	Complete WWI Time Anomaly, The Darkest Hour
LADY MELYNE'S GOWN	Increase Throwing Knife capacity by 2/3, Increase Hallucinogenic Dart capacity by 2/3, Increase Smoke Bomb capacity by 2/3, Increase Voltaic Bomb Capacity by 2/3	Complete Sequence 5, A Room With A View
MASTER ASSASSIN	Decrease detection speed by 15%/20%	Complete Sequence 6, A Throne in the Side
THE AEGIS	Decrease all damage received by 10%/20%, Increase Cane-Sword damage by 10%/20%	Collect all of the Secrets of London, then place them in Reuge's vault to unlock The Aegis
ELISE	Increase Kukri damage by 10%/20%	Unlock with Uplay
AVELINE	Increase Throwing Knife capacity by 2/3, Increase Hallucinogenic Dart capacity by 2/3, Increase Smoke Bomb capacity by 2/3, Increase Voltaic Bomb Capacity by 2/3	Unlock with Uplay
SHAO JUN	Increase Throwing Knife damage by 20%/30%	Unlock with Uplay
NIGHTHAWK OUTFIT	Decrease Detection Speed by 15%/25%	Redeem with a promo code

JACOB'S OUTFITS

NAME	EFFECTS	ADDITIONAL REQUIREMENTS
SIMPLY JACOB	Increase Brass Knuckles damage by 10%/20%	Game Start
GUNSLINGER COAT	Increase Firearms damage by 10%/20%	Reach Loyalty Level 2 with Frederick Abberline
OUTDOORSMAN OUTFIT	Decrease detection speed by 15%/25%	Complete Sequence 5
MASTER ASSASSIN	Increase Kukri damage by 10%/20%	Complete Sequence 6
BLACKGUARD'S SUIT	Decrease melee damage received by 10%/15%	Complete Sequence 7
MAXIMUM DRACULA	Decrease All Damage Received by 10%/20%, Increase Brass Knuckles Damage by 10%/20%	Crafting Plan from completing Sequence 8, £10000, 150 Leather, and 100 Silk
BARON JORDANE'S FINERY	Increase Throwing Knife capacity by 2/3, Increase Hallucinogenic Dart capacity by 2/3, Increase Smoke Bomb capacity by 2/3, Increase Voltaic Bomb Capacity by 2/3	Crafting Plan found in the Chest on the Rooftop of St. Paul in the City of London
EZIO	Increase Throwing Knife capacity by 2, Increase Hallucinogenic Dart capacity by 2, Increase Smoke Bomb capacity by 2, Increase Voltaic Bomb Capacity by 2	Unlock with Uplay
EDWARD	Increase Kukri damage by 10%	Unlock with Uplay
HUNTSMAN'S OUTFIT	Increase Eagle Vision range by 10%	Unlock with Uplay
SUAVE OUTFIT	Increase Cane-Sword damage by 10%/20%	Redeem with a promo code

COLORS

Colors change the shading of Jacob's or Evie's clothing.

NAME	DESCRIPTION	REQUIREMENTS
NO COLOR	The natural color of your clothing	Game Start
VIOLET	Violet, woody brown, and grass green	Collect 5 Pressed Flowers
FUCHSIA	Fuchsia, muted green, and turquoise	Collect 10 Pressed Flowers
MIDNIGHT BLUE	Midnight blue, warm gray, and terra cotta	Collect 15 Pressed Flowers
BLACK	Black, pink, and purple	Collect 20 Pressed Flowers
STEEL GRAY	Steel gray, pink, and dark gray	Collect 25 Pressed Flowers
CRIMSON	Deep crimson, salmon, and gray	Collect 30 Pressed Flowers
WINE	Wind, gold, and muted green	Complete the Karl Marx Memories
GREEN	Green, violet, and gray	Found in the Chest in Spitalfield Market
GOLD	Gold, turquoise gray, and terra cotta	Purchase for £500
FOREST GREEN	Forest green, violet, and terra cotta	Purchase for £1000
TAUPE	Taupe, salmon, and gray blue	Purchase for £1000
BEIGE	Beige, violet, and gray blue	Purchase for £1000
BEIGE AND BLUE	Beige, gray blue, and salmon	Purchase for £1000
UBISOFT BLUE	Ubisoft blue, gray blue, and violet	Uplay Reward
TEAL	Teal, violet, and mustard yellow	Uplay Reward

THE ESSENTIALS
WALKTHROUGH
SIDE QUESTS
COLLECTIBLES
REFERENCE & ANALYSIS
INTEL

SKILLS
PERKS
GANG UPGRADES
CRAFTING
EQUIPMENT
ALLIES & ENEMIES
ACHIEVEMENTS
MODERN PROGRESSION

ALLIES AND ENEMIES

The London of *Assassin's Creed Syndicate* is a living, breathing city, populated with a wide array of friends and foes. These are divided into six Archetypes and three Factions.

AGGRESSORS

Aggressors include members of the rival Blighter gang and the Templars. They are shown in Red in Eagle Vision and on the Mini-Map.

Templars attack you on sight. Blighters attack you, and also attack Rooks.

Use Protectors to your advantage by drawing them closer to Aggressors. Protectors attack Aggressors if they commit crimes.

ALLIES

Allies include members of the Rooks and other Assassins. Depending on the memory, they follow you and help you in combat.

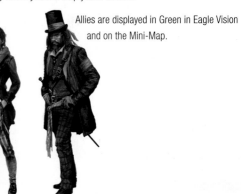

Allies are displayed in Green in Eagle Vision and on the Mini-Map.

PROTECTORS

Police, Royals, and Security Guards are protectors who maintain law and order in the city. They appear as Blue in Eagle Vision and on the Mini-Map

Protectors only become hostile towards those who commit violent acts.

Protectors are powerful enemies. If you try to fight too many at once, you will likely be overwhelmed. Escape and vanish when necessary. If you need to commit a violent act, try to do it out of their view.

ARCHETYPES

Archetypes appear in the Rooks, Blighters, and even the Templars. Each enemy Archetype responds differently upon spotting you or entering combat. When infiltrating an area, look out for the Watchers and Lookouts since alerting them causes them to quickly call for backup. The damage you take and deal to Archetypes is determined by player level and the quality of your current equipment. The level of the enemy can be seen above their heads, once you've marked them, ranging from 1-10. This gives you a good idea of the challenge that enemy will bring to the fight.

BRUTE

Brutes are lumbering giants. They hit hard and have a lot of health. However, they are very predictable in combat, and can be easily defeated by running away and performing an assassination from above.

ENEMY LEVEL	1	2	3	4	5	6	7	8	9	10
BASE DAMAGE	460	540	640	760	840	940	1020	1100	1220	1320
ARMOR	44	54	74	94	114	134	154	174	194	214

ENFORCER

Enforcers are a mix of the Brute and Soldier Archetypes. If you attempt to retreat, Enforcers answer with Flash Bombs, blinding you while you try to run. When fighting a group of enemies, Enforcers always try to gain a tactical advantage.

ENEMY LEVEL	1	2	3	4	5	6	7	8	9	10
BASE DAMAGE	410	490	590	710	790	890	970	1070	1170	1270
ARMOR	40	50	65	85	105	125	145	170	190	210

PROTECTOR

Protectors are the strongest of the Archetypes, however contact with them is easily avoidable. Enemy factions do not have the Protector Archetype; only Police and Royal Guards have Protectors. At lower levels, taking on a Protector in combat is almost a certain death sentence. Once you've reached a higher level you begin to gain a small advantage over them, but they are still formidable foes.

ENEMY LEVEL	1	2	3	4	5	6	7	8	9	10
BASE DAMAGE	540	620	720	840	920	1020	1100	1180	1300	1400
ARMOR	64	84	104	124	144	164	184	204	224	244

SOLDIER

Soldiers are the most common Archetype you encounter. They rely on numbers to pose a threat. Using melee attacks and basic combos they are easily defeated with counter attacks when you fight them in groups. Be wary when they are matched with a Brute or Enforcer as things can quickly get complicated by the stronger enemy's attacks.

ENEMY LEVEL	1	2	3	4	5	6	7	8	9	10
BASE DAMAGE	360	440	540	660	740	840	920	1000	1120	1220
ARMOR	0	20	40	60	80	100	120	140	160	200

WATCHER

Watchers are always ready to call their allies to their side with a quick whistle whenever they encounter trouble. Whenever possible, eliminate these threats with a sneak attack, or from afar, before they are even aware of your presence. If you give them time they'll call their friends for backup and you may have more trouble than you bargained for. Watchers have a high rate of counter attack, so be ready if you directly engage these foes.

ENEMY LEVEL	1	2	3	4	5	6	7	8	9	10
BASE DAMAGE	360	440	540	660	740	840	920	1000	1120	1220
ARMOR	-20	0	20	40	60	80	100	120	140	160

TROPHIES AND ACHIEVEMENTS

ICON	TITLE	REQUIREMENTS	TIPS	GAMERSCORE	TROPHY
I	A SPANNER IN THE WORKS	Complete Memory Sequence 1	Check out the Walkthrough for Sequence 1 for a full explanation.	20	Bronze
II	A SIMPLE PLAN	Complete Memory Sequence 2	Check out the Walkthrough for Sequence 2 for a full explanation.	20	Bronze
III	A MODERN BABYLON	Complete Memory Sequence 3	Check out the Walkthrough for Sequence 3 for a full explanation.	20	Bronze
IV	A QUICK AND RELIABLE REMEDY	Complete Memory Sequence 4	Check out the Walkthrough for Sequence 4 for a full explanation.	20	Bronze
V	THE PERILS OF BUSINESS	Complete Memory Sequence 5	Check out the Walkthrough for Sequence 5 for a full explanation.	20	Bronze
VI	A RUN ON THE BANK	Complete Memory Sequence 6	Check out the Walkthrough for Sequence 6 for a full explanation.	20	Bronze
VII	ALL IS FAIR IN POLITICS	Complete Memory Sequence 7	Check out the Walkthrough for Sequence 7 for a full explanation.	20	Bronze
VIII	THE JOYS OF FREEDOM	Complete Memory Sequence 8	Check out the Walkthrough for Sequence 8 for a full explanation.	20	Bronze
IX	SHALL WE DANCE	Complete Memory Sequence 9	Check out the Walkthrough for Sequence 9 for a full explanation.	50	Gold
	FRIENDS AT MY BACK	Recruit a gang of 5 allies	Have five Rooks recruited at the same time. This does not mean they all must be recruited in one button press. They can easily be found at a conquered outpost. Visit different groups until you have five following you. You must have Leadership III researched; this comes as a free upgrade when reaching Level 5.	20	Bronze
	THE WAR AT HOME	Complete the WWI simulation	Check out the WWI entry in the Side Missions section for all of the walkthroughs needed to complete the rift.	30	Bronze
	CEREVISAPHILE	Sample every beer brand in London	Consult the Collectibles section of this guide to find all of the Beer Bottles.	10	Bronze
	NO TICKET	Kick 50 enemies off of trains	Follow the railroad tracks looking for trains to raid. If push comes to shove, consider running through Sequence 1 and defeating the enemies Jacob faces on the train a few times.	50	Bronze

THE ESSENTIALS
WALKTHROUGH
SIDE QUESTS
COLLECTIBLES
REFERENCE & ANALYSIS
INDEX

SKILLS
PERKS
GANG UPGRADES
CRAFTING
EQUIPMENT
ALLIES & ENEMIES
ACHIEVEMENTS
MISSION PROGRESSION

ICON	TITLE	REQUIREMENTS	TIPS	GAMERSCORE	TROPHY
	FLAWLESS CONQUEROR	Secure 3 Gang Strongholds and complete their optional constraints	Use stealth mode and Eagle Vision to sneak around. Throwing knives can be used to quickly take out enemies inside of windows without raising the alarm of the enemies near you. For more tips check out the Gang Stronghold Section in Side Missions.	20	Bronze
	BARE-KNUCKLE CHAMPION	Win three different Fight Clubs	If you're struggling to make it to round 10 in Fight Club, consider thumbing through the Essentials section and studying the break downs of how to react in different combat situations.	20	Bronze
	A QUARTER-FURLONG AT A TIME	Finish 1st in 3 different Street Races	Keep your turns tight to the corners and boost out of them, ramming anybody who gets in your way. Do whatever it takes to get 1st place. Keep in mind, this is London—stay to the left!	20	Bronze
	TREASURE HUNTER	Complete 10 Raids of any type with Jacob or Evie	Raids are more common in The Thames, so practice your ziplining skills from end to end while looking for cargo ships to raid.	20	Bronze
	THIEFTAKER	Bring back 3 Bounty targets alive	Be extra stealthy and wait for the opportune time to sneak in and kidnap the target, and then slowly walk them out to the cart. Having points invested in the Intimidation skill can help you escape with the kidnapped target.	20	Bronze
	UNQUALIFIED SUCCESS	Complete 3 Templar Hunts and their Challenges	Consult the Templar Hunt information in Side Missions to help you complete their secondary objectives.	20	Bronze
	CHILDREN'S AID SOCIETY	Complete 5 Child Liberation memories	See the Child Liberation portion of the Side Missions if you are struggling to complete any of them.	20	Bronze
	GUARDIAN ANGEL	Successfully escort 10 friendly cargo shipments	Keep an eye out for Cargo Escorts while roaming the streets of London. Keeping some Rooks at your side may make the escort easier.	20	Bronze
	GODLIKE	Unlock all of the Secrets of London	Use the Secrets of London portion of each map in the Collectibles section to grab all of the music boxes. Gain entrance into Michael Reuge's Vault and place all of their discs.	30	Silver
	A BROAD BASE	Reach Loyalty level 1 with all Associates	Check out the Associates section to learn what activities grant you Loyalty with each individual associate.	20	Bronze
	BEDFELLOWS, STRANGE OR OTHERWISE	Reach maximum Loyalty with any Associate	Complete the activities necessary to gain the maximum amount of loyalty with a chosen Associate. The Associate section can show you which activities to focus on to accomplish this quickly.	20	Silver
	NEEDLE IN A HAYSTACK	Kill 5 enemies while in the same haystack	Killing enemies in a haystack is easy, killing them all in the same one presents some challenge. Your best bet is to get enemies to chase you towards a haystack that is near a wall. This allows you to quickly jump over the wall, breaking their line of sight and granting you the chance to pull them into the hay when they come around. Don't forget to whistle to lure enemies over.	10	Bronze

ICON	TITLE	REQUIREMENTS	TIPS	GAMERSCORE	TROPHY
	STREET SWEEPING	Conquer all the boroughs in London	To unlock the chance to fight the Crime bosses of London, you first need to conquer all of the Conquest Activities in their borough.	30	Gold
	MULTITALENTED	Acquire 10 Perks	Check out the Perks section to easily see the different Perks. The Perk menu in the pause screen shows you your overall progress towards the different Perks, allowing you to see how close you are to completing 10.	10	Bronze
	KEYS TO THE CITY	Acquire all Gang Upgrades	You need a lot of resources to acquire all of the gang upgrades. Use the Chest map to gather a vast amount of resources quickly.	20	Silver
	ARTISAN	Craft a Level 10 Item	Rank 10 Items generally require Unique Materials. These, as well as the necessary blueprints, can be found in the Large Chests. Consult the Collectibles section to see what each Large Chest rewards.	20	Bronze
	BARTITSU	Learn every Fight Skill as Jacob.	Focus points into the Fight Skill Tree with Jacob. Rushing for this tree may not be the best idea, depending on your play style.	20	Silver
	PHANTOM	Learn every Stealth Skill as Evie	Focus putting skill points into the Stealth tree with Evie. This can be done early on, however you achieve this upon completing the "Wonder of the Age" Achievement as well.	20	Silver
	WONDER OF THE AGE	Reach Level 10	Complete Sequences, Conquest Activities, Income Activities, and Crowd Events, pick up Collectibles, and even engage in random bits of combat to grind your XP up. Level 10 requires the research of all skills.	20	Silver
	ORDINARY CRIMINAL	Complete 20 Crowd Events	Listen for people calling for help and keep a watchful eye on the streets around you to make sure you don't miss an opportunity to complete a crowd event.	15	Bronze
	LANGUAGE OF FLOWERS	Collect all the Pressed Flowers	Use the Collectibles section of this guide to locate all of the Pressed Flowers.	20	Bronze
	STUDENT OF HISTORY	Collect All of the Historical Posters	Use the Collectibles section to find all of the Historical Posters in London.	20	Bronze
	A LIFE IN LETTERS	Collect all of the Royal Letters	Use the Collectibles Sections to quickly hunt down the Royal Correspondence.	20	Bronze
	CHIMNEY SWEEP	Synchronize every Viewpoint in London	Synchronize all high points in London, including the points in the Time Rift.	20	Bronze
	MENTOR	Reach 100% Synch in the Main Memories	Complete each Sequence and Memory to 100%, as well as gather all of the Collectibles, to achieve 100% Synchronization.	40	Gold

ICON	TITLE	REQUIREMENTS	TIPS	GAMERSCORE	TROPHY
	FURIOUS	Destroy 20 Vehicles by ramming them	Ram enemy vehicles off the road. Try to do this earlier in the game while the Blighters and Templars control more territory. This shortens the amount of time you spend going between zones looking for enemies.	15	Bronze
	WHAT IS WRONG WITH YOU	Flip 5 vehicles by shooting their horses	Take out the horses drawing the vehicles to flip vehicles. Most are much more vulnerable to flipping when taking a sharp turn.	15	Bronze
	LOOK OUT BELOW	Kill 3 enemies with a single stack of hanging barrels	There are multiple groups of enemies in Sequence 2 that can be found standing under the hanging barrels.	15	Bronze
	YOU WOULDN'T STEAL A POLICEMAN'S HELMET	Hijack 20 Police vehicles	Police vehicles are not very common on the streets of London, so seize every possible opportunity to steal them!	15	Bronze
	QUEENSBURY RULES	Reach combo level 40	A combo level of 40 is easily reached when facing multiple enemies. If they are dying too quickly, move to a higher level area and take on one or two enemies, moving between the two and countering when necessary to keep the timer up. Use your Quickshot to keep your combo going if you are a short distance from an enemy during a fight.	15	Bronze
	WHIRLWIND OF DEATH	Perform 50 Multi-Finishers	Leave enemies in a crippled state when fighting multiple enemies. Once you have more than one enemy that is crippled, attack either one to trigger a multi-kill finisher.	15	Bronze
	BLADE IN THE CROWD	Assassinate 50 enemies	Use any method of assassination to kill 50 enemies, check out The Essentials section to learn all of the different types.	15	Bronze
	OPIUM SCOURGE	Affect at least 4 Enemies simultaneously with the Hallucinogenic Dart	Conquest Activities, and even some restricted areas in the Rift, make this Achievement easy. Look for a group of enemies close together then quickly hit them with the darts. You have a little bit of time to infect each enemy, allowing you to focus on a different group of enemies if need be.	15	Bronze
	BLADE FROM ABOVE	Air Assassinate 20 enemies from a zipline	Survey the scene when completing Conquest Activities, looking for enemies that are between buildings. When hanging from the zipline, line up above the enemy and press ▣ / ✕ to perform the assassination.	15	Bronze
	MOST UNSPORTING	Shoot 50 enemies before they shoot at you	When you see the △ / Ⓨ button appear above your character's head, quickly press it to attack them before they attack you.	15	Bronze
	WITHOUT GRUDGE	Destroy 5000 destructibles with your carriage.	Use all the explosives you find scattered around the map. Blowing up some enemies likely destroys some objects around them. When driving, knock over lampposts and other small items that line the sidewalk. Be careful to not kill civilians as that desynchronizes you.	15	Bronze
	MASTER ASSASSIN	Win every Trophy	Complete all of the Trophies listed.	—	Platinum

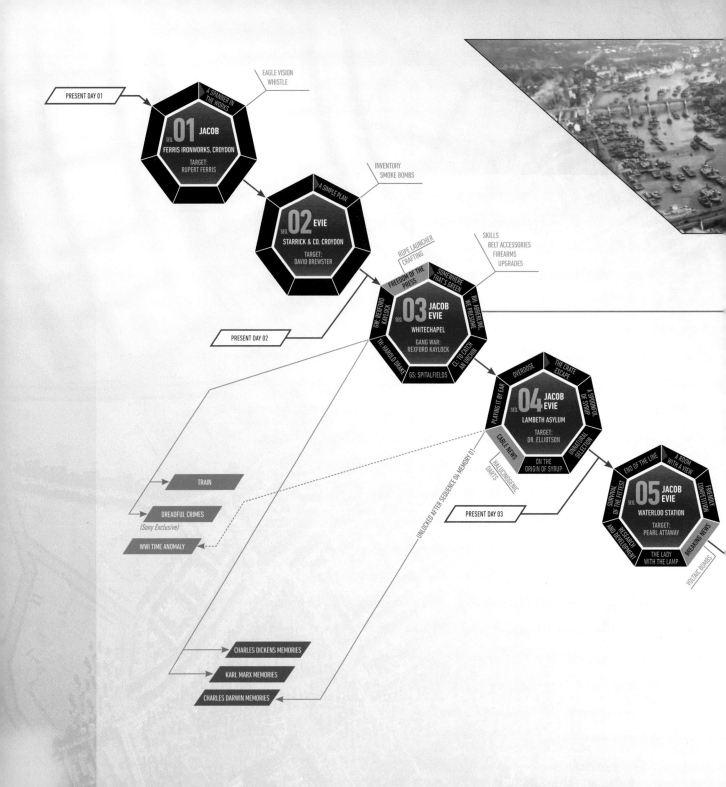

PRESENT DAY 01

EAGLE VISION
WHISTLE

A SPANNER IN
THE WORKS

01 JACOB
SEQ.

FERRIS IRONWORKS, CROYDON

TARGET:
RUPERT FERRIS

INVENTORY
SMOKE BOMBS

A SIMPLE PLAN

02 EVIE
SEQ.

STARRICK & CO. CROYDON

TARGET:
DAVID BREWSTER

ROPE LAUNCHER
CRAFTING

SKILLS
BELT ACCESSORIES
FIREARMS
UPGRADES

FREEDOM OF THE
PRESS

SOMEWHERE
THAT'S GREEN

GW: REXFORD
KAYLOCK

BH: ABBERLINE,
WE PRESUME

03 JACOB
EVIE
SEQ.

WHITECHAPEL

GANG WAR:
REXFORD KAYLOCK

THE HAROLD DRAKE

C1: TO CATCH
AN URCHIN

GS: SPITALFIELDS

PRESENT DAY 02

PLAYING IT BY EAR

OVERDOSE

THE CRATE
ESCAPE

04 JACOB
EVIE
SEQ.

LAMBETH ASYLUM

TARGET:
DR. ELLIOTSON

A SPOONFUL
OF SYRUP

CABLE NEWS

HALLUCINOGENIC
DARTS

ON THE
ORIGIN OF SYRUP

UNNATURAL
SELECTION

UNLOCKED AFTER SEQUENCE 04, MEMORY 01

TRAIN

DREADFUL CRIMES
(Sony Exclusive)

WWI TIME ANOMALY

PRESENT DAY 03

END OF THE LINE

A ROOM
WITH A VIEW

SURVIVAL
OF THE FITTEST

05 JACOB
EVIE
SEQ.

WATERLOO STATION

TARGET:
PEARL ATTAWAY

FRIENDLY
COMPETITION

RESEARCH
AND DEVELOPMENT

BREAKING NEWS

THE LADY
WITH THE LAMP

VOLTAIC BOMBS

CHARLES DICKENS MEMORIES

KARL MARX MEMORIES

CHARLES DARWIN MEMORIES

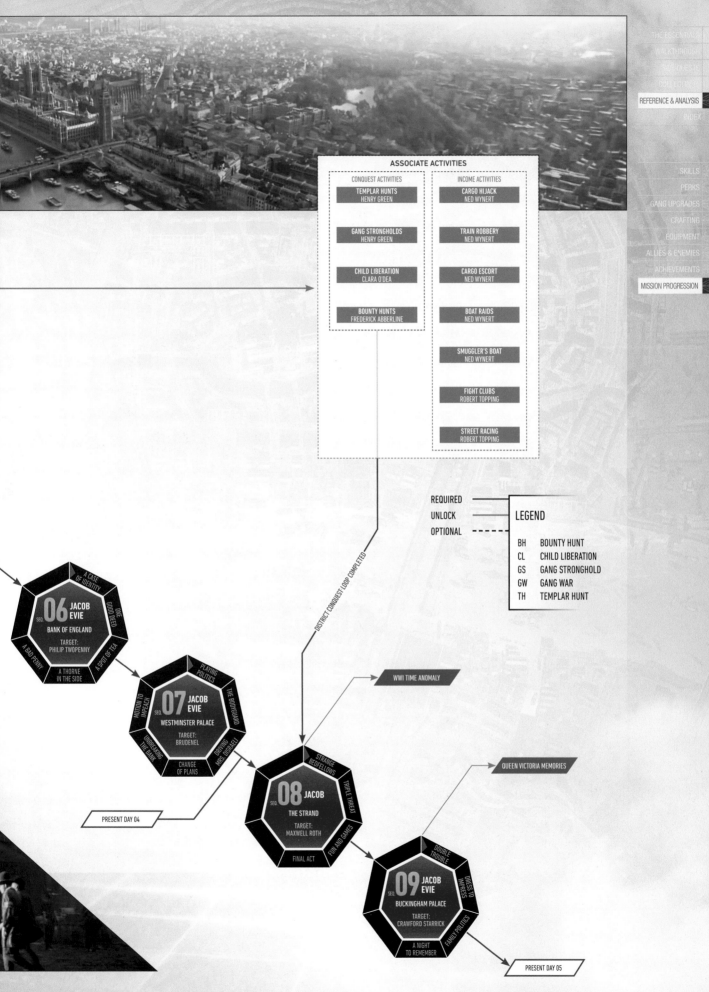

THE ESSENTIALS
WALKTHROUGH
SIDE QUESTS
COLLECTIBLES
REFERENCE & ANALYSIS
INDEX

SKILLS
PERKS
GANG UPGRADES
CRAFTING
EQUIPMENT
ALLIES & ENEMIES
ACHIEVEMENTS
MISSION PROGRESSION

ASSOCIATE ACTIVITIES

CONQUEST ACTIVITIES

TEMPLAR HUNTS
HENRY GREEN

GANG STRONGHOLDS
HENRY GREEN

CHILD LIBERATION
CLARA O'DEA

BOUNTY HUNTS
FREDERICK ABBERLINE

INCOME ACTIVITIES

CARGO HIJACK
NED WYNERT

TRAIN ROBBERY
NED WYNERT

CARGO ESCORT
NED WYNERT

BOAT RAIDS
NED WYNERT

SMUGGLER'S BOAT
NED WYNERT

FIGHT CLUBS
ROBERT TOPPING

STREET RACING
ROBERT TOPPING

REQUIRED
UNLOCK
OPTIONAL

LEGEND

BH	BOUNTY HUNT
CL	CHILD LIBERATION
GS	GANG STRONGHOLD
GW	GANG WAR
TH	TEMPLAR HUNT

DISTRICT CONQUEST LOOP COMPLETED

SEQ. 06 JACOB EVIE
BANK OF ENGLAND
TARGET:
PHILIP TWOPENNY

A CASE OF IDENTITY
ONE GOOD DEED
A SPOT OF TEA
A THORNE IN THE SIDE
A BAD PENNY

SEQ. 07 JACOB EVIE
WESTMINSTER PALACE
TARGET:
BRUDENEL

PLAYING POLITICS
THE BODYGUARD
DRIVING MRS. DISRAELI
CHANGE OF PLANS
UNBRAKING THE BANK
MOTION TO IMPEACH

WWI TIME ANOMALY

SEQ. 08 JACOB
THE STRAND
TARGET:
MAXWELL ROTH

STRANGE BEDFELLOWS
TRIPLE THREAT
FUN AND GAMES
FINAL ACT

PRESENT DAY 04

QUEEN VICTORIA MEMORIES

SEQ. 09 JACOB EVIE
BUCKINGHAM PALACE
TARGET:
CRAWFORD STARRICK

DOUBLE TROUBLE
DRESS TO IMPRESS
FAMILY POLITICS
A NIGHT TO REMEMBER

PRESENT DAY 05

395

ART GALLERY

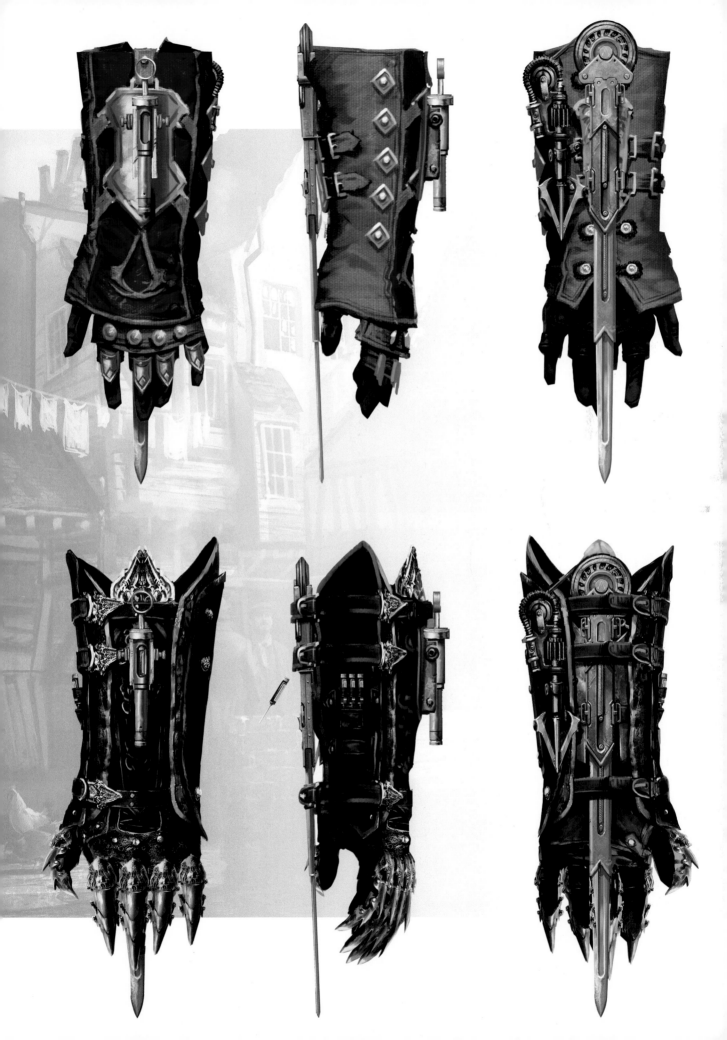

INDEX

THE SCENARIOS
WALKTHROUGH
SIDE QUESTS
COLLECTIBLES
DATABASE (GAMEPLAY)

INDEX

SKILLS
PERKS
GANG UPGRADES
CRAFTING
EQUIPMENT
ALLIES & ENEMIES
ACHIEVEMENTS
MEDIA PROGRESSION

CREDITS

Aaron Bridgett, Abby Carter, Abdo Hakim, Abdulmalik Shalabi, Abedenour Azzedine, Abraham Vega, Adam Axbey, Adam Novickas, Adam R. Csorba, Adam Silverman, Adam Steeves, Adam-Pier Turgeon, Adeline Aubame, Adeline Chétail, Adhemar Augusto, Aditi Sen, Adolfo Pastor, Adrian Barbosu, Adrian Bursumac, Adrian Buzatoaia, Adrian Cristian Ionescu, Adrian Danalache, Adrian Ghetu Bejan, Adrián Kovács, Adrian Lacey, Adrián Mier, Adrian Mitra, Adrian Neo, Adrian Ogrezeanu, Adrian Rosca, Adrian Simpetru, Adrian Tila, Adrián Viador, Adriano Dezulian, Adriano Pellegrini, Adrian-Valentin Simion, Adrien Anger, Adrien Cortes, Adrien Honvault, Adrien Tielmans, Agnès Letourneur, Ahmed Ghoneim, Aiden Glenn, Aiko Nogami, Aina Yasukuni, Aizuddin Zainal, Akihiko Ishizumi, Akim Gagnon, Akino Watanabe, Akira Harada, Akira Kawasaki, Alain Abbyad, Alain Bedel, Alain Chanoine, Alain Chenier, Alain Cormier, Alain Corre, Alain Gurniki, Alain Huynh, Alain Labédie, Alain Lafleur, Alain Matte, Alain Métivier, Alan Bravo, Alan Theron, Alberto Angrisano, Alberto Olivero, Alberto Tosi, Alberto Ziello, Aldis Bilalic, Alec Cannon, Alec Newman, Alejandro Nuez, Aleksandar Valkov, Aleksandr Hoshabaev, Aleksandr Hotchenkov, Aleksandr Kovrizhnyh, Aleksandr Novikov, Aleksandr Taranzhin, Aleksandr Voronov, Aleksey Aptovcev, Aleksey Mikhailov, Aleksey Voityuk, Alessandro Conte, Alessandro Degortes, Alessandro Messina, Alessandro Zurla, Alex Andrist, Alex Benavides, Alex Cadieux, Alex Dallas, Alex Dandurand, Alex Friend, Alex Gilbert, Alex Gingras, Alex Ivanovici, Alex Kelly, Alex Lim, Alex Lima, Alex Weiner, Alexander Katourgi, Alexander Khoo, Alexander Luke Chong, Alexander Selwood, Alexander Strandberg, Alexandra Serafim, Alexandra-Maria Marculetiu, Alexandre Bastien Riboni, Alexandre Beaumont, Alexandre Begnoche, Alexandre Benat, Alexandre Biron, Alexandre Bourlon, Alexandre Carlotti, Alexandre Carrier-Fortunato, Alexandre Chavanel, Alexandre De Lamberterie, Alexandre Drummond, Alexandre Fortier, Alexandre Fortin, Alexandre Fournier, Alexandre Gillet, Alexandre Gosselin, Alexandre Gouveia, Alexandre Grierson, Alexandre Lapointe, Alexandre Larouche, Alexandre Letendre, Alexandre Lussie, Alexandre Macé, Alexandre Messier, Alexandre Paquette, Alexandre Parizeau, Alexandre Pelletier, Alexandre Piché, Alexandre Pichette, Alexandre Pion, Alexandre Solopov, Alexandre Wooley, Alexandru Aconstantinesei, Alexandru Alexandrescu, Alexandru Bitulescu, Alexandru Bontu, Alexandru Carp, Alexandru Clontea, Alexandru Cosmin Niculae, Alexandru Dorin Bica, Alexandru Gasler, Alexandru Ghermanescu, Alexandru Grama, Alexandru Ionut Rosu, Alexandru Ispăşescu, Alexandru Ivana, Alexandru Macovei, Alexandru Narcis Stoica, Alexandru Neamu, Alexandru Negruţ, Alexandru Petru Sultanoiu, Alexandru Podeanu, Alexandru Teodor, Alexandru-Florin Timocel, Alexandru-Mihai Stan, Alexcendre Gosselin, Alexia Alderson, Alexis Belley-Dufault, Alexis Beverly, Alexis Dumas, Alexis Farand, Alexis Meunier, Alexis Vaisse, Alexis Van De Kerkhove, Alfonso Obregón, Alfonso Ramírez, Alfredo Cristinziano, Alfredo Martínez, Ali El Zein, Alicia Barragán, Alicia Gimenez Ruiz, Alina Galindo, Alina-Diana Milasan, Alina-Mihaela Lonescu , Aline Desruisseaux, Aline Domeau, Aline Piner, Alin-Florinel Văleanu, Alin-Marian Iuga, Alin-Nicolae Cojocaru, Alison Brown, Alison Rossi, Alizée Mialane, Alla Litvinenko, Allan Asiriah, Allan Cooke, Allan Murphy, Allen Keng, Allie Smith, Almut Zydra, Also Sampaio, Álvaro Navarro, Alvin Lim, Amanda Pimenta, Amariah Faulkner, Amber Goldfarb, Ambra Ravaglia, Amélie Jarry, Amélie Nolin, Amine Tarari, Amir Boutrous, Amit Karim, Ana Ángeles García, Ana Constantinof, Ana Fuentes, Ana Isabel Rodríguez, Ana Jiménez, Ana María Marí, Ana Raphael, Ana Sanmillán, Ana Sheppard, Analiz Sánchez, Ana-Maria Badita, Anamaria Musca, Ana-Maria Sofroni, Anastasia Sycheva, Anastasia Zharkova, Anatole De Bodinat, Anders Lejczak, Anders Månsson, Anderson Wu, Andon Nedev, András Gáspár, András Péterfi, André Caron, André Gosselin, André Machado, André Michaud, André Minotti, André Quirion, Andrea Aust, Andrea Bolognini, Andrea Cedillo, Andrea De Nisco, Andrea Patrone, Andrea Peruzzotti, Andrea Rudge, Andrea Suhett, Andréanne Milette, Andreas Avancini, Andreas Hosang, Andreas Lundgren, Andreas Müller, Andreas Nantke, Andreas Pajarinen, Andreas Tawn, Andre-Blue Felie, Andrée Cossette, Andreea Matei, Andreea Postolache, Andreea Stignei, Andreea Vatau-Bostan, Andreea-Cristina Zamfir, Andrée-Anne Boisvert, Andrée-Anne Leblanc, Andrei Alin Stoica, Andrei Begu, Andrei Bogdan Sandru, Andrei Bran, Andrei Costin Alexe, Andrei George Dobrin, Andrei Lange, Andrei Mihai, Andrei Moldovan, Andrei Niculae, Andrei Nicuşor Popa, Andrei Pavel, Andrei Strambei, Andrei Verzea, Andrei Vladimir Georgescu, Andrei Voicu, Andrei-Gabriel Florescu, Andrei-Ionut Ristea, Andrei-Marius Caravan, Andrei-Motaz Addas, Andrei-Vlad Stanescu, Andrei-Vlăduţ Cuteanu, Andres Chirino, Andrés Palancar, Andrew Chown, Andrew Evans, Andrew Farrier, Andrew Gillies, Andrew Gonzalez, Andrew Gray, Andrew Heitz, Andrew Kyrzyk, Andrew Marre, Andrew McKeon, Andrew Millmoor, Andrey Vakaev, Andrien Gbinigie, Andrii Nikolaev, Andrii Shafétov, Andrii Velychko, Andrik Vaimiti Kuhnen, Andy Kevin Servant Caron, Ang Jyh Yang, Ángel Amorós, Angela Magri, Ángela Villanueva, Angelica Borges, Angélica Villa, Anh Bang Bui, Anh-Xuan Desoutter, Anis Boujaouane, Anja Nitsche, Anke Reitzenstein, Ann Vielhaben, Anna Davis, Anna Dramski, Anna Gamburg, Anna van Tetterode, Annabelle Roux, Anne Blondel Jouin, Anne Day Jones, Anne Dûe, Anne Farmer, Anne Lewis, Anne Mounier, Anne-Laure Condamine, Anne-Lynn Sottas, Annemieke Boelen, Annie Bernard, Annie Dumais, Annie Nazoyan, Annie-Claude Gagnon, Annifride Alexander, Annora Schoorl, Anouk Bachman, Ant Hales, Anthony Guebels, Anthony Létourneau, Anthony Marcantonio, Anthony Robinow, Antoine Ceszynski, Antoine Corbin, Antoine Fortier-Auclair, Antoine Grivot, Antoine Guertin, Antoine Guilbaud, Antoine Merveille, Antoine Pecatikov, Antoine Rol, Antoine Serre, Antoine Tomé, Antoine Tous, Anton Degtiar, Anton Degtyaryov, Anton Kolesnikov,

Anton Litvinenko, Anton Marinov, Anton Mykhailenko, Anton Savenkov, Anton Sherstnev, Antonela Chiru, Antonio Abenójar, Antonio Alonso, Antonio Gálvez, Antonio Ramírez, Anurag Banerjee, Araceli Romero, Arantxa Franco de Sarabia, Arianne Borbach, Arin Murphy-Hiscock, Armelle Gallaud, Arnaud Clermonté, Arnaud Hubert, Arnaud Libeyre, Arnaud Mametz, Arnaud Ragot, Arnaud Vergne, Arne Stephan, Arturo López, Arturo Mercado Leonel, Asemta Bhattad, Ashin Ashroff, Assana Gueye, Assmahan Bitar, Atanas Karakolev, Aude de Rotalier, Audrey Laurent-André, Audrey Le Roy, Audrey St-Pierre, Aurélie Lepachelet, Aurélien Baguerre, Austin Wintory, Avin Shah, Axel Déau, Axel Lutter, Aymar Azaizia, Ayumi Ito, Bailey McAndrews, Barbara Allsopp, Bartlomiej Waszak, Bartosz Klofik, Bazz O'Reilly, Beatrice Revol, Beatriz Berciano, Beatriz Romilly, Behrang Khoshnood, Ben Bishop, Ben Merrick, Ben Spiller, Ben White, Benedicte Germain, Benjamin Ang, Benjamin Basso-Bert, Benjamin Clost, Benjamin Courantin, Benjamin Goldman, Benjamin Hall, Benjamin Huet, Benjamin Lassort, Benjamin Manigold, Benjamin Ortiz, Benjamin Plich, Benjamin Pommeraud, Benjamin Rigot, Benjamin Schimpke, Benjamin Teissier, Benjamin Zarka, Benoit Allemane, Benoit Baron, Benoit Batlle, Benoit Boulanger, Benoit Brière, Benoit Devost, Benoit Lambert, Benoit Lapalme, Benoît Larivière, Benoit Lasserre, Benoit Leduc, Benoit Lefort, Benoit Rivard, Bernard Alane, Bernard Bollet, Bernard Desmons, Bernard Fluet, Bernd Vollbrecht, Bertrand Bergougnoux, Bertrand Jouin, Bethynia Cardenas, Beto Vandesteen, Bhasker Patel, Bi Liang Hui, Bia Barros, Bianca Salgueiro, Bili Keogh, Bill Mahar, Blain Kramer, Blanca Hualde, Blanche Ravalec, Blandine Viegas, Bogdan Adrian Pantazi, Bogdan Chisamera, Bogdan Gabriel Avram, Bogdan Meca, Bogdan Popa, Bogdan Speriatu, Bogdan-Alexandru Mincu, Bogdan-Augustin Stroe, Bogdan-Costin Vajeiac, Boris Bauer, Boris Fersing, Boris Maniora, Boris Tokarev-Khrunov, Braden Bahen, Brady Watkins, Brandon Chua, Brandon Lising, Brell Li, Brenda Panagrossi, Brenda Puebla, Brendon Kelly, Brent Ashe, Brian Bowles, Brian Collins, Brian Fillion, Brian Gallant, Brian Mckinnon, Brice Paquier, Bridgette Smith, Brigitte Guedj, Brigitte Lecordier, Briony Glassco, Britney Kennedy, Brittney Schaeffer, Brock Starkweather, Bruce Beaton, Bruce Dinsmore, Bruce Godfree, Bruno Alborini, Bruno Beaudoin, Bruno Bouchard, Bruno Champoux, Bruno Choel, Bruno Gaugain, Bruno Meyere, Bruno Morin, Bryan Yeo, Cai Jing Yu, Caio Cesar, Călin-Mihai Oană, Calista, Calvin Kwan, Cameron Goodwin, Camille Vitroly, Cammy Goh, Carina Eiras, Carl Bouchard, Carl Descoteaux, Carl Dionne, Carl Dumont, Carl Thibeault, Carl Venne, Carla Castañeda, Carlo Mestroni, Carlo Scipioni, Carlo Vázquez, Carlos Del Campo, Carlos Ernesto Abrego, Carlos Gesteira, Carlos Hidalgo, Carlos López Benedí, Carlos Seidl, Carlos Torres, Carlos Torres-Cros, Carlos Vega, Carly Solven, Carol Crespo, Caroleen Beatty, Caroline Bergeron Lyonnais, Caroline Boulay, Caroline Combes, Caroline Lacrouts, Caroline Lafleur, Caroline Lamache, Caroline Pascal, Caroline Pineau, Caroline Soucy, Carolyn Vezina, Carsten Myhill, Cassandre Beaumier, Catalin Borangic, Cătălin Cimpoeru, Catalin Daniel Balan, Catalin Marian Ion, Catalin Marius Constantin, Cătălin-Mihăiţă Raşcov, Cătălin-Nicolae Pruteanu, Cătălin-Nicusor Neamţu, Catherine Auger, Catherine Blouin, Catherine Grenier, Catherine Paire, Catherine Simard, Catherine Vachon, Cecilia Santiago, Cédric Altes, Cédric Barthez, Cedric Orvoine, Cédric Tsang Chun Sze, Celina Choueiri, Céline Chapelain, Celine Dardel, Celine Lau, Celine Martinico, Céline Paiva, Ceri Young, César Beltrán, Cesare Rasini, Chad Acers, Chadi Chamas, Chadi El Zibaoui, Chadi Lebbos, Chae Dickie-Clark, Chang Hsiang Huang, Chantal Oury, Chantale St-Louis, Charbel Semaan, Charlee-Lou Borthwick, Charles Beauchemin, Charles Benoit, Charles Bérubé, Charles Emmanuel, Charles James Kershner, Charles Lefebvre, Charles Lelièvre, Charles Mathieu, Charles-Étienne Théberge, Charles-Simon Viau, Chen Mei, Chen Ming Jian, Chen Xi, Chen Xin, Cheng Si Min, Cherrie Chiu, Chiara Santilli, Chieko Miyazaki, Chloé Bauquier, Chloé Charbonneau, Chris Blackburn, Chris Early, Chris Jenner, Chris Mark, Chris Norris, Christelle Cotting, Christian Gaul, Christian Monfette, Christian Mulot, Christian Pacaud, Christian Pomerleau, Christian Talbot, Christina Nilsson, Christina Pemberton, Christine Bellier, Christine Burgess-Quémard, Christine Landry, Christof Putz, Christoph Banken, Christoph Drobig, Christoph Geissler, Christophe Beaudet, Christophe Derennes, Christophe Nadeau Grandmont, Christophe Remy, Christophe Rossignol, Christophe Zerathe, Christopher Dormoy, Christopher Grey, Christopher Lee, Christopher Nonis, Christopher Racine, Christopher Smith, Christrian Sirois, Chrys Piva, Cindy Shih, Cinzia Massironi, Ciprian Pitorac, Ciprian-Iulian Tudose, Claire Hong, Claire Morgan, Claude Esmein, Claude Gosselin, Claude Marais, Claudia Boisseau, Claudia Gahrke, Claudia Promegger, Claudine Bourget, Claudine Cezac, Claudine Lussier, Claudio Beccari, Claudio Colombo, Claudio Marricco, Claudio Ridolfo, Claudiu Robert Vasile, Claudiu-Adrian-Emanuel Rusu, Clément Lescalet, Clément Prevosto, Clementine Dombtail, Cleon Wong, Clifford Lasana, Clifford Roche, Clive Walton, Clodéric Marquis, Codrin-Ionuţ Ciobaniţa, Codrut Catargiu, Codrut Cosmescu, Cole Cheng, Colette Stevenson, Colin Ho, Colin Ward, Constantin Fotea, Constantin Ionita, Constantin Luca, Constantin Pappas, Constantin Petrisor, Constantin Vilceanu, Coralie Sevin Dupoux, Corentin François, Corey May, Corey Wardrop, Corinne Le Roy, Cory McMackin, Cory Sherman, Cosmin Barbălată, Cosmin Ionut Popa, Cosmin Lăzărescu, Cosmin-Florian Dobre, Cosmin-Gabriel Dobra, Costin-Alexandru Călăraşu, Costin-Bogdan Echert, Courtney Johns, Craig Lawson, Craig Pearn, Craig Pilkington, Craig Warnock, Cristi Arama, Cristian Berciu, Cristian Bogdan Albu, Cristian Iancu, Cristian Muresanu, Cristian Nidelea, Cristian Pascu, Cristian Santayana, Cristian Tache, Cristian-Alexandru Coteţ,

Cristian-Mihai Monoran, Cristin Ghihanis, Cristina Arion, Cristina Gheorghe, Cristina Herráiz, Cristina Paraschiv, Cristina Poccardi, Cristina-Mihaela Aldea, Cynthia Turcotte, Cyril Bordat, Cyril Cosenza, Cyril Lucaiano Tovena, Cyril Meynier, Cyril Solans, Cyril Vergne, Cyrille Artaux, Cyrille Gauclin, Cyrille Karmann, Dabe Chang, Dafnis Fernández, Dai Di Zi, Daisuke Hirakawa, Dallas Boyes, Damian Valdes, Damien Bastian, Damien Doute, Damien Gleizes, Damien Glorieux, Damien Goodwin, Damien Hartmann, Damon Redfern, Dan Black, Dan Dragomir, Dan Griffis, Dan Ruiz, Dan Vargas, Dan Yap Yeau Choong, Dania Cericola, Daniel Adrian Petrov, Daniel Agorander, Daniel Avila, Daniel Fleury, Daniel Gagné, Daniel Giverin, Daniel Jennings, Daniel Lacy, Daniel Luca, Daniel Lucchesi, Daniel Natapov, Daniel Pablo Hernandez, Daniel Palix, Daniel Roger, Daniel Sarrazin, Daniel Siu, Daniel Staton, Daniel Stewart, Daniel Tjondropuro, Daniel Vanasse, Daniel Vasilescu, Daniel Walta, Daniel Watchorn, Daniel Welbat, Daniela Fava, Daniela Miron, Daniela Schmitz, Daniele Demma, Daniel-Olivier Simard, Daniil Eldarov, Danil Shcheblanov, Danny Couture, Danny Hung, Danny Ruiz, Danny Wallace, Dan-Stelian Butiri, Danuta Psuty, Dănuţ-Alexandru Aruştei, Dany Arcand, Dany Boustani, Dany Lepage, Dany Paquet, Dany St-Laurent, Darek Zabrocki, Daria Bobyleva, Dario Bertollini, Dario Vangelista, Darius Copilau, Darya Frolova, Dave Bélanger, Dave Coleman, Dave Simard, Dave Tremblay, David Allende, David Alvarez, David Antell, David Barsam, David Blanco, David Bridet, David Clark, David Colin-Doiron, David Cook, David Daigle-Carignan, David Ferry, David Flores, David Forget, David Fournier, David Garcia, David Genest, David González, David Gossage, David Greig, David Harvey, David Jansen, David Kamal, David Kaufman, David Kennedy, David Knott, David Kruger, David Kunze, David Lee, David Legrand, David Levesque, David L'Heureux, David Lightbown, David Macachor, David Martínez, David Michaud-Cromp, David Noel, David Paquette, David Racine, David Rancourt, David Raposo, David Riedel-Brederlow, David Robinson, David Teo DDT, David Therrien, David Wilkinson, Davide Marzi, Deborah Silva, Debra Trotz, Decebal-Adrian Dragomir, Delia Condrea, Deng Hong Yi, Deng Xue Mei, Denis Bespalyj, Denis Boileau, Denis Capdeferro, Denis Lessard, Denis-Patrick Tremblay, Dennis Lafond, Denys Vorobyov, Derek Fortin, Des McAleer, Detlef Giess, Dhani Wiryawan Susilo, Diana Elena Chivu, Diana Vázquez, Diane Dassigny, Didier Gagnon, Didier Lord, Diego Sabre, Digital Dimension, Dilip Priyanath, Dilyana Dinkova, Dimitri Karakassides, Dindo Lin, DK Liao, Dmitri Polyanovskiy, Dmitriy Kurta, Dmytro Beznos, Dominic Chamberland-Mongrain, Dominic Desjardins, Dominic Gladu-Despatis, Dominic Jutras, Dominic Paquet, Dominic Spada, Dominique Lachance, Dominique Mac Avoy, Donat Bihr, Donny Wong, Dragoş Dogariu, Dragos Florin Sandru, Dragos Octavian Dumitru, Du Bo, Duck Chiang, Dudu Drummond, Dugal Nahuel Sampayo-Jaime, Dustin Boyce, EA Schepmann, Eamon Stocks, Ed Casey, Edgar Ernesto Hernandez, Edgar-Paul Catană, Edi-Cristian Ionel, Edoardo Nordio, Edouard D'Alnois, Edouard Vacher, Edson Matus, Eduardo Bastos, Eduardo Borgerth, Eduardo Gutiérrez, Eduardo Navarro, Eduardo Simioni, Edward Lyon, Edward Trallongo, Edwige Lemoine, Edwin Gellner, Eileen Cislak, Ekaterina Kalegina, Ekaterina Vinogradova, Elcio Romar, Eleanor Noble, Elena Balzano, Elena Chebaturkina, Elena Kharitonova, Elena Kischik, Elena Ruíz de Velasco, Elena Shulman, Elena-Cristina Boca, Eleni Molos, Eli Brown, Eli Martyr, Eli Roberton, Elias Riad, Elin Larsson, Eliot Canepa, Elisabeth Pellen, Elisabeth Torre-Vincent, Elisabetta Cesone, Elise Giffard, Elizaveta Uchiteleva, Ellen David, Ellen Wieser, Ellie O'Brien, Elliot Miville Deschênes, Elliot Smith, Elliott Walton, Elmar Gutmann, Elodie Anthony, Élodie Ceselli, Elodie Sok, Elson Soh, Emanuela Damasio, Emerald O'hanrahan, Emi Takeshita, Emil Drozda, Emil Gheorghe, Emil Sergiev, Emil Uddestrand, Emiliano Ragno, Emiliano Ugarte, Emilie Delsescaux, Emilie Doucet, Emilie Dugene, Emilio Gallardo, Emilio Rabat, Emilio Trevino, Emily Munster, Emma Campbell, Emma Fielding, Emma Stevens, Emmanuel Grondin, Emmanuel Oujoud, Emmanuelle Bondeville, Emmanuelle Carré, Emmanuelle Charles, Emmanuelle Faucher, Emmanuelle Novero, Enrique López, Enrique Suárez, Eri Goda, Eric Armstrong, Eric Aubrahn, Eric Bibeau, Éric Cinq-Mars, Eric Daniel, Éric Germain, Éric Girard, Éric Lamontagne, Éric Landry, Eric Le, Eric Lee, Éric Legault, Eric Lemay, Éric Martel, Eric Nabor, Éric Parayre, Éric Pelletier, Eric Pepin, Éric Tremblay, Erica Edwards, Eric-Jon Evangelista, Erick Bougleaux, Erick Jamel, Erick Salinas, Ernst Meincke, Erwin Lay, Estrella Karla Briones, Étienne Allonier, Étienne Borel, Etienne Capacchione, Etienne Cournoyer, Etienne Michon, Étienne Michon, Etienne Pouliot, Eugen Ganea, Eugen Knippel, Eugen Popescu, Eugene Chen, Eugene Ivanov, Eugene Kuczerepa, Eugenia Jiménez, Eugen-Ionuţ Neacşu, Eva-Maria Werth, Evan Davies, Evan Lai, Eve Berthelette, Eve Parent, Eytan Weigensberg, Fabian Kubicki, Fabien Bole-Feysot, Fabien Briche, Fabien Houédé, Fabien Simon, Fabien Troncal, Fabien Yorgandjian, Fabienne Laurède, Fábio A. Ludwig, Fabio Pantano, Fahd Filali, Fan Yin Jia, Fang Hong Jun, Fang Zhuo Bin, Fanny Campagnie, Fanny Desjardins, Faustine Jourdan, Federico Decotto, Federico Viola, Fedor Chinarev, Felipe Cardoso Gonçalves, Felipe Drummond, Felipe Soares Queiroga, Félix Belisle-Renouf, Felix Marlo Flor, Félix Norton-Barsalou, Felix Spieß, Felix Tievant, Felix Würgler, Ferelith Young, Fernando Acosta, Fernando G. Urquiza, Fernando Hernandez, Filip Lagerlöv, Fily Keita, Florence, Florent Devillechabrol, Florent Goy, Florent Guillaume, Florent Parage, Florent Perrin, Florian Alungulesa, Florian Glesser, Florian Köhler, Florian Leroy, Florian Mihai, Floriane Charles, Florin Catalin Gafton, Florin Cristea, Florin Iordache, Florin Nicolae Dita, Florin Vasile, Florin-Emilian Buse, Floris Sprokkreef, Floris-Lucian Costea Ştefănescu, FO Schenk, Foehn Gallet, Ford Dye,

Fran Jiménez, Francesco Meoni, Francesco Rizzi, Francesco Rossigno, Francine Baudelot, Françis Bacon-Desrosiers, Francis Baillet, Francis Beauchesne, Francis Charrette, Francis Coldeboeuf, Francis Dallaire, Francis Lefort, Francis Limoges, Francis Nadeau, Francis Pagé, Francis Quintal, Franco Perez, Francois Baillarge, Francois Bouchard, François Chartrand, François Cloutier-Tanguay, François Côté-Dulude, Francois Cournoyer, François Dallaire, François Daubet, François De Billy, François Dumas, François Emery, François Guertin, François Harvey, François Laperrière, François Lehoux, François Lévesque, Francois Luong, François Martel, Francois Moisan, Francois Nadeau, François Navarro, François Paquette, François Paradis, François Pelland, François Pelletier, Francois Poirier, François Raison, Francois Renouf, François Royer, François Schelling, Francois Tetreault, François Tremblay, François Vaillancourt, François-Philippe Lamirande-Gauvin, Frank Aiello, Frank Grimaldi, Frank Haut, Frank Haut, Frank Kitson, Frank Quercioli, Frank Schlusemann, Frankie Chan, Freddy Tu, Frederic Bernard, Frédéric Brochu, Frédéric Cerdal, Frederic Ferland, Frédéric Gagné, Frédéric Gaudet, Frédéric Guay, Frédéric Jean, Frederic Matz, Frédéric Mauxion, Frédéric Ostiguy, Frédéric Pichette, Frédéric Popovic, Frédéric Rambaud, Frederic Saclier, Frédéric St-Laurent B., Frederic St-Onge, Frédéric St-Pierre, Frederic Vekeman-Julien, Frédérick Boudreault, Frederick Champoux, Frederick Taylor, Frédérick Verreault, Frederik Audet, Frédérique, Fredrik Allansson, Fredrik Gunerius Fevang, Friedel Morgenstern, Fritz Rott, Fu Chong Bing, Fu Xiang, Fu Zhong Xiong, Gabi Costa, Gábor Novák, Gábor Tamás, Gabriel Bismuth, Gabriel Buhai-Volintiru, Gabriel Costin Nartea, Gabriel Espinoza Lahore, Gabriel Federico Reyes Baldó, Gabriel Gendron, Gabriel Graziani, Gabriel Le, Gabriel Ledoze, Gabriel Matthews, Gabriel Morisseau, Gabriel Olteanu, Gabriel Parent, Gabriel Salmi, Gabriel Tay, Gabriel Thivierge Robitaille, Gabriel Valois, Gabriela Gucho-Oliva, Gabriela Middlebrook, Gabriela Ramona Hera, Gabriela Servin, Gabriel-Daniel Ciobanu, Gabriele Calindri, Gabrielle Farias, Gabrielle Shrager, Gabriel-Sorin Preda, Gaëlle Dandoi, Gaetano Lizzio, Gao Kun, Gar Jun Lam, Gareth Richards, Gareth Taylor, Gary Beattie, Gary Hsu, Gary Keith, Gavin Fowler, Geanini-Ionuţ Grădineanu, Gema Carballedo, Genaro Contreras, Genevieve Dufour, Geneviève Perron, Geng Jun, Geoffrey Côté, Geoffrey Harding, Geoffroy Sardin, George Abou Salbi, George Alin Moroiu, George Cosmin Hanta, George Cosmin Radu, George Eduard Tărcavu, George Hong, George Oulton, George Stercu, George Valentin Pane, George Vourdoulas, George-Alexandru Popa, George-Catalin Iosif, George-Iulian Muntianu, George-Marian Badiu, Georges Caudron, Georgi Gavanozov, Georgiana Voicu, Georgii Kapralov, Gerald Paradies, Geraldine Asselin, Germán Rosado Martel, Gheorghe-Armando Gavrilă, Ghina El-Chemali, Giancarlo Rodrigues, Giancarlo Varanini, Gianni Quillico, Gigi Rosa, Gil Grandjean, Gilbert Lévy, Gilles Beloeil, Gilles Clavel, Gilles Vanwalleghem, Gilles Youssef, Gina-Lavinia Benedic, Giorgio Bonino, Gioseppe Ippoliti, Giovanni Battezzato, Giovanni Marcon, Giovanni Masin, Gisella Ramírez, Giselle Stewart, Giulia Monjardim, Giuliana Atepi, Giuliana Jakobeit, Giuseppe-Ion Andrei, Gladys Perez, Gong Jia Gen, Goulven Corouge, Graciela Gamez, Graham J. Cuthbertson, Graham Qually, Grant Hiller, Greg Forte, Greg Gale, Gregoire Badin, Grégoire Lucas Monteil, Gregory Garcia, Gregory Hermittant, Gregory Palvadeau, Greig Newby, Greta Bortolotti, Grover and Peggy Looter, Grzegorz Szabla, Gu Kun, Gu Wei Qi, Gualtiero Scola, Guilherme Vian, Guillaume Béland, Guillaume Blais, Guillaume Borgia, Guillaume Boucher, Guillaume Brunier, Guillaume Carmona, Guillaume Cessot, Guillaume Chiron, Guillaume Corbeil, Guillaume Croteau, Guillaume Descend, Guillaume Descent, Guillaume Dorme, Guillaume Fenollar, Guillaume Forest, Guillaume Gardin, Guillaume Gauthier, Guillaume Lévesque, Guillaume Louvel, Guillaume Lupien, Guillaume Mammi, Guillaume Moya, Guillaume Ouellet, Guillaume Renaudin, Guillaume Riby, Guillaume Ruest, Guillaume Thoreau, Guillaume Urbejtel, Guillermo Rojas, Gundi Eberhard, Gunnar Helm, Guo Jun Hua, Gus Díaz, Gus Rodríguez, Gustaf Ekberg, Gustavo Ottoni, Guy Parent, Guy Sprung, Guylaine Rheaume, Hadrian Santos, Hadrien Grandy, Hakim Abbas, Hakim Idjouadiene, Hamid Shahrestani Mehr, Hammeed Jailani, Han Jun Hong, Hana Takeda, Hani Barakat, Hanna Lai, Hannah Buttel, HardeepKumar Kumaravelu, Harry Liu, Harry Scott, Harry Standjofski, Hassan Al Masri, Hassan Hamdan, He Xiao Juan, He Xue Yuan, Heather Bamford, Heather Bartfield, Heather Golder, Heather Holmes, Heather Maclaren, Heather Steele, Hector Salazar, Heidi Etcheverry, Heidi Kwang, Helder Teixeira, Helen Johns, Hélène Raguin, Hendrik Vandecruys, Hendry Proni, Henrike von Kuick, Hensley Edwin, Hervé Caradec, Hervé Faynel, Hervé Grosdemanche, Heungshik Park, Hideaki Tezuka, Hiroaki Ichinowatari, Hiroki Eto, Hiroko Kiso, Hiroshi Iwasaki, Hiroshi Karasuda, Hiroto Kazuki, Hjörtur Stefánsson, Holly Gauthier, Holly Rawlinson, Holly Sedillos, Hong Hai Peng, Hong Meng Nai, Horatiu Bradeanu, Hou Rui, Howard Billerman, Hu Xing Yu, Huang You Gong, Hubert Chevillard, Hubert Drac, Hugo Daigle, Hugo Deschamps, Hugo Giacherio, Hugo Giard, Hugo Lemay-Proulx, Hugo Puzzuoli, Hugo Vezina, Hugo Wifredo Serrano Ruiz, Hugues Richer, Hugues Ricour, Hugues Rousseau, Hugues Thibodeau, Hyun Cho, Iain Farrington, Ian Burfield, Ian D Clark, Ian Danahay, Ian Deakin, Ian Golder, Ian St-Louis, Ievgen Shalimov, Igor Khlepitko, Igor Rudnyk, Igor Staroseltsev, Igor Tomilov, Igor Yalovetski, Ikuko Tani, Ilaria Egitto, Ileana-Georgiana Tănase, Ilie Muntean, Ilinca Marchis, Iliya Dimitrov, Ilja Zaitsev, Iikka Falck, Imad Feghali, Iman El-Gamati, Imane Annan, Imane Bitar, Imtiaz ul-Haque, Inma Gallego, Inouchka Kreuning, Ioan Turcanu, Ioana-Madalina Carapcea, Ioana-Mihaela Badea, Ioan-Dionisie Ciuciu, Ion-Dumitru Vornicescu, Ionuţ Adrian Dachin, Ionuţ Alexandru Fulger, Ionut Alexandru Grigore, Ionut Alin Hristea,

Ionut Catalin Petrache-Baluta, Ionuţ Iulian Tudorache, Ionuţ Manole, Ionuţ Milea, Ionuţ Petre-Diţei, Ionut Uceanu, Ionut Valentin Barbu, Ionuţ-Alexandru Niţă, Ionuţ-Petrişor Hărcău, Irene Hjorth, Irene Jiménez, Irene Osprey, Irina Gabriela Popa, Irina Kassina, Irina-Mariana Săndulache, Iris Choi, Iris Tee, Irvin Thomas, Isabel Martinez, Isabelle Belley-Ferris, Isabelle Fortin, Isabelle Gagnon, Isabelle Lafon, Isabelle Michaud, Isacha Mengíbar, Ismaël Auray, Ismael Castro, Isobel Griffiths, Isto Aitokari, Itzel Mendoza, Iulia Alexandra Anghel, Iulia Firescu, Iulia-Gabriela Popa, Iulian Baraghin, Ivan Andreani, Iván Bastidas, Ivan Litvinov, Ivan Sherry, Ivan Tan Lei, Ivana Coppola, Ivaylo Chipriyanov, Ivet Jordanova, Izaline, J. Adam Brown, Jack IP, Jackie Shave, Jacky Lin, Jaclyn Smith, Jacqueline Corley, Jade Kraus, Jade Lamarche-Levert, Jade Whitney, Jahel Morga, Jaime Alberto Carrillo, Jaime Gonzalez, Jake Jackson, Jakob Thiesen, James Arthur, James Barriscale, James Carnahan, James Giles, James Loye, James Nadiger, James Therien, James Wells, James Womack, Jan Degans, Jan Kurbjuweit, Jane Armstrong, Jane Chan, Janice Ang, Janice Ng, Janine Thériault, Janus, Jared Coliadis, Jared Pearson, Jared Schincariol, Jarom Giles, Jaskarn Grewal, Jasmine Hood, Jason Arsenault, Jason Clark, Jason Gosling, Jason Hsu, Jason Hunter, Jason Sekieta, Jason Tavares, Jason Tremblay, Javier Fernández, Javier Lorca, Jaz Deol, Jean Boucher, Jean Gauvin, Jean Guerin, Jean Guesdon, Jean Luc Tin Sive, Jean Raymond, Jean-Baptiste Dupuy, Jean-Baptiste Tremouiller, Jean-Benoit Chasles, Jean-Brice Dugait, Jean-Charles Fontaine, Jean-Christophe Authier, Jean-Christophe Boulle, Jean-Christophe Gagnon, Jean-claude Sachot, Jean-David Jacquemin, Jean-François Adolphe, Jean-François Allard, Jean-françois Aupied, Jean-François Bérubé, Jean-François Dupuis, Jean-François Durand, Jean-François Duval, Jean-François Gagné, Jean-Francois Gallant, Jean-François Gauthier, Jean-François Gosselin, Jean-François Guay, Jean-François Lavoie, Jean-Francois Leduc, Jean-François Lemay, Jean-François Lessard, Jean-François Martin, Jean-Francois Morin, Jean-François Renaud, Jean-Francois Richard, Jean-Francois Tremblay, Jean-Francois Vallee, Jean-Francois Viau, Jean-françois Viérick, Jean-Luc Blanchette, Jean-Luc Pedneault, Jean-Marc Goulet, Jean-Marc Prud'Homme, Jean-marco Montalto, Jean-Marie Mogentale, Jean-Marie Santoni-Costantini, Jean-Mathieu Bégin, Jean-Michel Gilbert, Jean-Michel Veilleux, Jean-Paul Mageren, Jean-Philippe Belliard, Jean-Philippe Durand, Jean-Philippe Duval, Jean-Philippe Huard, Jean-Philippe Saucier, Jean-Philippe Sirois, Jean-Philippe Turcot, Jean-Philippe Welsh, Jean-Pierre Lajoie, Jean-Sebastien Campagna, Jean-Sébastien Côté, Jean-Sébastien Duberger, Jean-Sébastien Guay, Jean-Sébastien Morin, Jean-Sebastien Pelletier, Jean-Sebastien Savard, Jean-Vincent Roy, Jean-Yves Chilot, Jeff Caron, Jeff Dandurand, Jeff Gartenbaum, Jeff Pilo, Jeff Preshing, Jeff Simpson, Jeff Skalski, Jeff Styga, Jeffery Bertrand, Jeffery Kaldma, Jeffrey Yohalem, Jelle de Vaal, Jennifer Birch, Jenny De Cesarei, Jeongki Hong, Jérémie Boisclair-Vandal, Jérémie Poidevin, Jeremy Blechet, Jeremy Mistry, Jérémy Tene, Jérome Hector, Jérôme Leclerc-Couture, Jérome Lescane, Jérôme Viens-Brie, Jesica Brucart, Jesper Kyd, Jesse Henderson, Jessica Barrier, Jessica Brard, Jesús Fernández López, Jesús Javier Sáiz, Jey Hicks, Jhony Siddík, Ji Xiao Chen, Ji Xiao Feng, Ji Yi Jin, Jianhui Li, Jie Hui Ho, Jihane Malla, Jill Frappier, Jill Murray, Jill Steinberg, Jill Streater, Jillián Soon, Jim Stadelman, Jim Stone, Jim Watson, Jimmy Boulianne, Jimmy Poujade, Jin Hai, Jin Yu, Jing Vern Lew, Jit Quan Tan, Jo Changer, Jo Worrall, Joakim Duchesne, Joanna Gail, Joanna Goldman, Joannie Hamelin, João Curzio, João Oliveira, Joao-Paulo Domingos Silva, Joaquin De Prado, Jocelyn Bastien, Jocelyn Daoust, Jocelyn Hotte, Jocelyn Veilleux-Nolin, Jodi Bland, Joe Bouchard, Joe Waters, Joël Engalenc, Joel Geulin, Joel Plourde, Joel Tremblay, Joel Walsh, Johan Durand, Johan Pfannenstill, Johan Sorăng, John Bigorgne, John Blake, John Carey, John E Nelles, John Fleming, John Hopkins, John McKenna, John Paul Tan, John Roney, John Santoso, John Serri, John Teymoorian, Johnathon Palmer, Johnny Lo Chun Pun, Johnstone Baumgartner, Jon Bursey, Jon Lilja, Jon Wild, Jonah Teoh, Jonas Axelsson, Jonathan Barbeau, Jonathan Bédard, Jonathan Brousseau, Jonathan Chin, Jonathan Coulon, Jonathan Dankoff, Jonathan Debray, Jonathan Drolet, Jonathan Dumas, Jonathan Dumont, Jonathan Gendron, Jonathan Hardy, Jonathan Huot, Jonathan Kydd, Jonathan Magnan, Jonathan Maurice, Jonathan Ouellet, Jonathan Pilon, Jonathan Pratte, Jonathan Rigg, Jonathan Rooney, Jonathan Simeone, Jonathan Toti-Buttin, Jonathan Veillette, Jong-Hyung Jung-Boix, Joni Maybury, Jordan Long, Jordan Mellado, Jordane Thiboust, Jorge Palafox, Jorge Roig Jr, Jori Lacroix, Joris Adrover, Jose Carlos Castellano Marrero, José Luis Rivera, José Manuel Ruiz Blanco, José Núñez, José Vilchis, Joseph Cassano, Joseph Chasan, Joseph Sepia, Joseph Shao Chong Tan, Joseph West, Joséphine, Josh Morris, Joshua Dolgin, Joshua Heath, Joshua Milligan, Josiane Morel, Josiane Roger, Josiane Valverde, Josselin Authelet, Joumana Al Zonji, Juan Antonio Gálvez, Juan Antonio Sáinz de la Maza, Juan Antonio Soler, Juan Carlos Lozano, Juan Esteban Diaz, Juan José Duarte, Juan Navarro, Juan Pablo Vieyra, Juan Rojo, Juan Rueda, Judit Tur Cladera, Judith Flanders, Judith Grubber-Stitzer, Jules Gagnon, Julia Kaufmann, Julia Melvin, Julia Stöpel, Julian Casey, Julian Richings, Julián Rodríguez, Julian Teofilov, Julie Cavanna, Julie Nuckle, Julie Paulin-Tardif, Julien Mayeux, Julien Beilles, Julien Carron, Julien Chatelet, Julien Chevallier, Julien Debono, Julien Desaulniers, Julien Galloudec, Julien Guérif, Julien Huguenin, Julien Hummer, Julien Jourdain, Julien Karaouni, Julien Kauffmann, Julien Lemaire, Julien Mauger-Dumais, Julien Petruio, Julien Prissette, Julien Renoux, Julien Ronnaux, Julien Sibre, Julieta Rivera, Juliette Degenne, Julio Chaves, Julio Monjardim, Julius Jellinek, Jun Jie Wang, June Tian, Justin Arden Farren, Justin Boily, Justin Buzzell, Justin Cerilli,

THE ESSENTIALS
WALKTHROUGH
SIDE QUESTS
COLLECTIBLES
REFERENCE & ANALYSIS
INDEX
SKILLS
PERKS
GANG UPGRADES
CRAFTING
EQUIPMENT
ALLIES & ENEMIES
ACHIEVEMENTS
MISSION PROGRESSION

[Credits — list of contributor names spanning the lower portion of the page.]

ASSASSIN'S CREED SYNDICATE

COLLECTOR'S EDITION STRATEGY GUIDE

Written by Tim Bogenn and Will Murray

© 2015 DK/Prima Games, a division of Penguin Random House LLC. Prima Games® is a registered trademark of Penguin Random House LLC. All rights reserved, including the right of reproduction in whole or in part in any form.

The Prima Games logo and Primagames.com are registered trademarks of Penguin Random House LLC, registered in the United States. Prima Games is an imprint of DK, a division of Penguin Random House LLC, New York.

DK/Prima Games, a division of Penguin Random House LLC
6081 East 82nd Street, Suite #400
Indianapolis, IN 46250

©2015 Ubisoft Entertainment. All Rights Reserved. Assassin's Creed, Ubisoft, and the Ubisoft logo are trademarks of Ubisoft Entertainment in the US and/or other countries.

Please be advised that the ESRB ratings icons, "EC", "E", "E10+", "T", "M", "AO", and "RP" are trademarks owned by the Entertainment Software Association, and may only be used with their permission and authority. For information regarding whether a product has been rated by the ESRB, please visit www.esrb.org. For permission to use the ratings icons, please contact the ESA at esrblicenseinfo@theesa.com.

ISBN: 978-0-7440-1638-3

Printing Code: The rightmost double-digit number is the year of the book's printing; the rightmost single-digit number is the number of the book's printing. For example, 15-1 shows that the first printing of the book occurred in 2015.

18 17 16 15   4 3 2 1

Printed in the Italy.

CREDITS

Senior Development Editor
Jennifer Sims

Book Designer
Dan Caparo

PRIMA GAMES STAFF

VP & Publisher
Mike Degler

Editorial Manager
Tim Fitzpatrick

Design and Layout Manager
Tracy Wehmeyer

Licensing
Christian Sumner
Paul Giacomotto

Production Designer
Areva

Production
Angela Graef

Marketing
Katie Hemlock

Digital Publishing
Julie Asbury
Tim Cox
Shaida Boroumand

Operations Manager
Stacey Beheler

ACKNOWLEDGMENTS

Prima Games would like to thank Trey Williamson, Marie Cauchon, Antoine Ceszynski, and the rest of the amazing team at Ubisoft for their help and support in creating this guide.